BATTLE FOR WARSAW
1939–1944

MICHAEL ALFRED PESZKE

EAST EUROPEAN MONOGRAPHS, BOULDER
DISTRIBUTED BY COLUMBIA UNIVERSITY PRESS, NEW YORK
1995

EAST EUROPEAN MONOGRAPHS, NO. CDXXVII

Publication of this book was facilitated by a grant from Joseph B. Slotkowski Publication Fund of the Kosciuszko Foundation.

ISBN 0-88033-324-3
Library of Congress Catalog Card Number 95-61204

Printed in the United States of America

Contents

Preface

Personal Introduction

The reader of this monograph may well ask how a study of the Polish Military during World War II is written by a psychiatrist. The answer is very simple. I lived throughout this period and was acutely and very much personally aware of most of the events that influenced my life and shaped my psyche. My postwar research was to confirm and to clarify the facts that I remembered.

For me, the war started late in the evening of August 31, 1939, just short of my seventh birthday when I bade my father good-bye. He was leaving the peacetime garrison, of the then Polish city of Lwow, mobilized by secret orders to move his light bomber wing to a secret base. I was always very much aware that his combat unit left for war before the first bombs fell, and was not destroyed on the ground as I was to read so often in scholarly publications.

By late autumn of 1941 I was enrolled in a Scottish prep school in the small border town of Dumfries. In between I had journeyed through Romania, lived in France and then Vichy France, and for a short time in Lisbon. I traveled to the United Kingdom in July 1941, in the middle of the Battle of the Atlantic. That experience of spending about ten days aboard a large transport, SS *Scythia*, in the middle of a convoy of many ships, including the H.M.S. *Furious*, is my most memorable of all from the war. It was then that I was to see a Polish destroyer, O.R.P. *Piorun*, join the convoy, and it was then that more than anything I wanted to be a Polish Naval Officer. Many years later I began my research ventures by looking in the British Public Record for the logs of the Royal Navy carrier *Furious*, and in the Polish Institute for the logs of the *Piorun*. This was a great introduction into the joys and frustrations of archival research. I learned for one that not all materials are still in existence or available. I could not locate the logs of the *Scythia* yet I knew she existed and I did sail on her.

I arrived in Scotland in September 1941, and though not yet even in my teens, I was very much aware of the momentous events that were being played out on the world stage. Yet in a very strange way I lived the life of a typical schoolboy: playing games, loving the long summer vacations (called holidays in the United Kingdom), and hating the drudgery of the long day in the schoolroom and the heavy load of homework. But even in this relatively peaceful corner of the British Isles, it was a schoolboy's life in a Britain very much at war. We all carried gas masks, were experts at maintaining a "black-out," and vied with each other in being able to tell the silhouette of a Spitfire from that of a Hurricane. Even in that small south Scottish border town, famous only for the mausoleum of Scotland's famous poet, Robert Burns, and the wild beauty of its glens, we had our share of German Luftwaffe air raids.

For nearly four years we were constantly exposed to the ubiquitous presence of the military preparing for war.

Dumfries was a major R.A.F. training base and there were airmen always to be seen on the streets of the town. These were primarily British, but with a fair sprinkling of Canadians and Poles. The noise of plane engines was ever present. We all became experts in prognosticating bad weather when the engine noises subsided.

There were also some land forces, in addition to the now legendary Home Guard, these were predominantly British (the Coldstream Guards—"second to none"—and the King's Own Scottish Borderers, who were recruited locally), but also there were Poles of the Armored Division and Parachute Brigade and Free Norwegians. We were not innocent of the fact of death and how close it stalked our friends and families, and yet it was a relatively peaceful life, most of my friends and certainly I were more terrified of a critical master than of the German Luftwaffe.

But though my life was typical of the other Scottish boys, I was not quite the typical Scottish schoolboy; there was another side to my life, my Polish side. I mourned with my mother the news of the death of her brother at Katyn; glowed with pride when the Poles placed their amaranth and white flag over Monte Cassino; anguished over the Warsaw Uprising; and stood with a peculiar wonderment of disbelief when attending the burial of Polish crews killed in so-called milk run training operations, so often officers whom I had recently met and saw at my parents' Sunday dinner table. This small Catholic cemetery, in a small provincial town, had close to twenty Polish graves. There are hundreds of such small cemeteries scattered throughout Europe and even in North Africa and the Middle East. Polish soldiers were buried where they fell, and they fell in many places. We visited this cemetery every year, on All Saint's Eve, as is the Polish custom, but it was many years before I really comprehended my father's remark—they were the lucky ones.

> They shall grow not old, as we that are left, grow old: Age shall not weary them, nor the years condemn.
>
> —Lawrence Binyon

In 1943, when I was eleven, my father, who had been Polish Liaison Officer to a Royal Air Force Training Command Group, based at Cardogan House, was transferred to London to take up the post of head of the planning division of the Polish Air Force Staff Section of the Polish General Staff, which was at the Rubens Hotel in Buckingham Palace road. (This hotel is still in business and has a small bronze plaque commemorating the fact that it was General Sikorski's headquarters.)

During our too infrequent contacts we would discourse on the war. My father loved to talk about military history whether it had to do with Napoleon, Frederick the Great, the Polish Hetmans, or his own experiences in the Polish-Soviet war of 1919–1920. I, in turn, loved to listen. We would talk and discuss the September 1939 Campaign and the valiant efforts of Poland's Military Aviation, later renamed Polish Air Force by General Sikorski. We discussed then and for many years the combat activities of the light bomber-reconnaissance wing commanded by my father. After his death in 1966 I edited his notes and published his work on the Polish Bomber Brigade in the *Polish Review*. We had frequent guests, predominantly Polish Air Force officers who were either being trained in the local R.A.F. base or, after having completed their obligatory tour of thirty combat missions, were enjoying the relative rest of flying trainees.

During that period of time I met Lt. Col. Jan Bialy, an old friend of my father, and also a wing commander in the September 1939 Campaign. His visit to us took place just prior to his being dropped in Poland, though I didn't know that at the time. He honored me with his friendship and we corresponded until his death. I met Col. Michael Bokalski when he visited Cardogan House in his role as Polish Liaison Officer, R.A.F. Training Command. He had been the executive officer of the Polish Bomber Brigade in September 1939 and for a time the Commandant of the Polish Higher Air Force Academy that had been recreated in the United Kingdom. In 1943 Col. Bokalski assumed the post of the Head of the Air Force Section of the Polish General Staff. When those officers visited our house, I was always present though I strictly adhered to the English rule for children, "to be seen but not heard."

From such contacts I was more than aware of the many so-called secrets and issues aiding and confounding the Allied military, such as radar, the work on the atom bomb, jet engines, and navigational aids for the bomber offensive. There was one secret that I never heard of at that time—the work of the Polish cryptographers on the German code and *Enigma* machine.

I was, as the Americans would say, an air force brat. I was born in Deblin, the cradle of Polish Military Aviation (*Lotnictwo Wojskowe*) as the Polish air force was then called, and subsequently lived in close proximity to the Lawica base of the III Aviation Regiment in Poznan, and then Sknilow, the VI Aviation Regiment in Lwow.

The end of the war frustrated my ambitions of becoming a Polish naval officer. Its final and symbolic end came when I accompanied my father, still in uniform, to the unveiling of the Polish Air Force Memorial near Northolt, west of London. This was the Royal Air Force's final good-bye and they did it in a way that only the British know how to do. I have been there many times and once I was happy to have my son with me for the annual celebrations of wreath laying and tribute to the dead.

With war's end I was forced to a pragmatic choice. I matriculated to and graduated from Trinity College, Dublin, with a medical degree. I would like here to acknowledge my great debt to the faculty and student body of Trinity College and to the people of Dublin where I was welcomed. During those years of 1950–1956, TCD, as we all called it, was indeed a great liberal institution.

My love, interest (and my family would say obsession) with the history of the Polish endeavors in the Second World War continued. If I owe my love of history to my father, then I have to openly acknowledge that my motivation for writing about it is due to my two children, Michele Halina and Michael Alexander. My early works in this area were primarily based on Polish language secondary sources and were addressed at answering the many canards relating to Poland's preparation for the war and the frequently repeated snide remarks about the destruction of the Polish air units on the ground and the fantasy of the tank charges by cavalry.

This monograph is the fruit of my long labors spent in my free time outside of professional academic activity as a psychiatrist.

I would like to express my love and appreciation to my wife, Alice Margaret Sherman, who put up with my absences and proof-read my drafts. I would also like to express my esteem and appreciation to the late Komandor Bohdan Wronski, for many years the Director of the Polish Institute in London, who was always available with advice, and to Mgr. Andrzej Suchcitz and Mgr. Andrzej Gorczycki who facilitated my work in the archives of the Polish Institute, where most of the research was done. I was also always treated courteously at the British Public Record Office in Kew Gardens, where the second half of my research was accomplished on my vacations in London. The S.O.E. records, which are not part of the Public Record Office and are kept at the Foreign Office Section in the old Admiralty Building, Whitehall, are not yet available for individual research. Who knows what, if anything, they hide?

This monograph is relatively short. It cannot cover all the accomplishments of the Polish Military in Exile. The official history of the Polish Military in Exile published by the Polish Institute is already two full volumes. But I believe this monograph does give an overview, and it does offer a unique and comprehensive account of the efforts by the Polish staffs to aid the Polish Underground.

Since the capital city of Warsaw was the symbol of Polish resistance, since that city was the center as well as the heart, soul, and mind of the Polish Underground, I have titled this piece as *Battle for Warsaw, 1939–1944*. During these long five years of German occupation and German terror, the city remained defiant and never lost its spirit. While physically captured it was never conquered by the Germans.

For many, the essence of military history are accounts of bloody battles fought by fearless warriors. But just as for a surgeon, the actual operation, however glamorous and important for the patient, merely represents many years of training and preceptorship and team building, so the fundamental keystone of military history is the preparation and the planning. The battlefield is merely where it all comes together. I have therefore given much attention to the staff background of the conflicts.

For the reader who is not absolutely familiar with either Polish or World War II history, I have prepared a chronological list of significant events. I would urge that the reader once in a while glance at the list to put the narrative in perspective. Finally I have appended the relevant texts of Polish-Allied military agreements that governed the policies of the Polish Government and the formation of the Polish Armed Forces.

Publication of this book was facilitated by a grant from the Joseph B. Slotkowski Publication Fund of the Kosciuszko Foundation. Material from Winston Churchill's *The Second World War* is reprinted by permission of Houghton Mifflin Company, which owns the copyright. Transcripts of Crown records in the Public Record Office appear by permission of the Controller of Her Majesty's Stationery Office. Last but not least, I wish to thank Dr. Stephen Fischer-Galati, editor of the East European Monographs, for his support and advice, and Ms. Beth Rosenfeld for the outstanding job in typesetting and final editing of the text.

Sources and Citing Conventions

The two major archival sources on which this monograph is based are the holdings of the Polish Institute in London and of the British Public Record Office in Kew Gardens, London. The archives of the Polish Institute are the repository of all the Polish Government and military archives from the period of the Second World War. For the sake of brevity the Polish Institute holdings will be cited as PIL, and the British, as PRO. British archives pertaining to the S.O.E. (Special Operations Executive) are located in the Foreign and Commonwealth Office, and the material pertaining to Poland is still closed as of the date of writing.

In addition to the archival sources there a number of published works based on the holdings of the Polish Institute and these form a major background to the monograph. The *Polskie Sily Zbrojne w Drugiej Wojnie Swiatowej* was initiated by the Historical Commission of the Polish Staff in London after the war and the task is being carried on by the Polish Institute. Currently it has reached eight volumes, five being dedicated to the September Campaign, two to the Polish Forces in Exile, and one to the Polish Home Army. This will be cited *PSZ-1939; PSZ na ob. (obczyznie)* and *PSZ-AK (Armia Krajowa)*. The section of the Polish Institute dealing with the Polish Underground Army, Polish Underground Army Trust, has also published five volumes of material related to the Polish Underground Army (*Armia Krajowa*, or *AK*). Halina Czarnocka, ed., *Armia*

Krajowa w Dokumentach, 1939–1945, was published over the period of 1970–1981 in London and is cited as *AK Docs.* The Polish Institute, in addition, has edited and published an excellent two-volume study in English, *Documents on Polish-Soviet Relations 1939–1945* (in two volumes: Vol. I, 1939–1943; and Vol. II, 1943–1945), London, 1961 and 1967 respectively; cited as *Docs. Vol. I* or *Vol. II.*

The Jozef Pilsudski Institute of America, editor Waclaw Jedrzejewicz, published an excellent and seminal study in three volumes, *Poland in the British Parliament,* in 1946, 1959, 1962, respectively; cited as *Poland in the Brit. Parliament.* This is a superb account of the history of the war from a Polish vantage with a detailed account of the Polish debates of the House of Commons based on *Hansard.*

I have attempted to limit my background references to English language studies. This is comparatively easy in the area of history, since general Polish history has seen a considerable number of outstanding publications. This is not the case for the military side, where there is a real paucity of English language books.

I have also cited a number of short, propaganda-style books published in England and in English during the war. These do not represent any value as history, but are a very compelling documentary on the social and political climate of the times. I have marked these citations by an asterisk (*) at the end of the full citation.

For general studies of the Second World War, I can only fall back on the six-volume treatise by Winston Churchill, *The Second World War.* The American edition by Houghton Mifflin Co., New York, is the source used, though the British edition by Cassell differs in certain areas; cited as Churchill, followed by the name of the volume. The value of this monograph is not only its quality of writing, which was recognized by a Nobel Prize for literature, but that its scope is without parallel. In some ways, what Churchill does not write is as telling as what he writes. For an author to devote time to his accounts of the o. de b. of the R.A.F. Regiment, but to omit any mention of the Sikorski accident is at the very least an eyebrow raiser. The American edition is cited unless otherwise stated. Gerhard L. Weinberg's *A World at Arms. A Global History of World War II,* Cambridge U. Press, 1994, is also a major reference for any student of that conflict.

1

Historical Background

The war of 1939–1945 was one more bloody episode in the two centuries of Poland's struggles to preserve a national identity and its western inspired but indigenous culture, language, and political system. Polish independence had been compromised in the late seventeenth and eighteenth centuries by a self-serving parliament of privilege and corruption with weak executive and administrative leadership. This inexorably led to political and particularly economic weakness, which when confronted by the relative and growing power of its three autocratic neighbors resulted in the partitions of 1773, 1793, and the final demise of the Polish Kingdom in 1795.[1]

Yet during these same years of the late eighteenth century, there were prominent men who strove in the civic and political arena to undo the privatism of the *Sejm* and to place the country on the right social and political track. In the final years of the Polish Kingdom many progressive steps had been taken, such as the reforms of the four-year *Sejm*, 1788–1792, which recodified the laws, provided for the first ministry of education, and legislated a better system of financing a standing army. It also reorganized the traditionally separate armies of the Kingdom of Poland and the Grand Duchy of Lithuania by an integration that was to reach an establishment of 100,000. An officer's school was also created, Kosciuszko being one of its early alumni. The reawakening of the country and the mobilization of all its citizens would have made the Polish-Lithuanian Kingdom a modern and much stronger state, hence no longer a country that could easily be influenced by the powerful neighbor to the east. The period culminated in that greatly cherished Polish document the *3rd of May Constitution*, which was a Bill of Rights for the Polish people and has been celebrated as a national holiday ever since. The implied strengthening of the country led to concerns in Petrograd and the ensuing invasion by a Russian Army, determined to stamp out Polish aspiration and to bring the Poles to heel, while in the west, the Prussians did their part to aid and abet the Russians, taking their share of the territorial booty and creating a precedence that continued to shape not only Russian and German policies into the twentieth century but also Polish atavistic fears of their predatory neighbors. In 1793 the Russians ostensibly came at the invitation of a small group of reactionary aristocrats to protect the rights of the establishment, in the twentieth century the Russian armies came at the ostensible invitation of the peasant and worker.

King Stanislaw Poniatowski and his still relatively small army succumbed and the second partition of 1793 followed. Many Poles in later years felt strongly that the King had failed to fight strenuously for Poland's independence and that he gave in too quickly to undoubtedly superior forces. This seeming acquiescence in the loss of liberty was seen as shameful and humiliating and the lesson to be learned was that it would never be again repeated. A year later Kosciuszko proclaimed his manifesto of universal freedom in the market square of Krakow (1793), raised an army, and at Raclawice won a victory that was to inspire the nation. A year later his defeat and capture at Maciejowice seemed to be *finis Polonia* (1794). Kosciuszko's forces were again opposed by the combined armies of Russia and Prussia. The memory of independence and the ingrained cultural strength of the Polish people sustained the next hundred and twenty years of political and armed struggles. The first military effort after the failed Kosciuszko uprising was the formation of legions, which fought at the side of Napoleonic Armies. It was from this time that Poland's national anthem derives, with words written by Wysocki to a traditional Polish tune, the mazurka, often called Dabrowski's mazurka after the General Officer commanding the Polish Legion in Italy—"Poland is not dead as long as we still live." Polish efforts were initially successful and resulted in the relatively short-lived but autonomous Duchy of Warsaw, with its truly heroic military contribution to Napoleon in the war against Austria and subsequently Russia. But the Duchy suffered the fate of Napoleon in 1814, and the country was again divided between Russia, Prussia, and the Austrian Empire, with a symbolic free city of Krakow and a satellite Congressional Kingdom centered on Warsaw with the Tsar as the King of Poland.[2]

Uprisings in 1830 and 1863 were bloodily put down, its leaders executed, exiled, or sent to Siberia, a prologue for the events of this monograph. However, all these endeavors attested to the striving for sovereignty and succeeded in keeping alive the idea of a free Poland from one generation to its successor, even though at a terrible price in life, wealth, and cultural heritage. Plundered, despoiled, and partitioned Poland may have been, but it continued to exist in the hearts and minds of its people and in the uneasy memory of its new rulers who kept emphasizing, to all concerned, that Poland was extinct.

In all these historical memories and nationalistic remembrances the Polish Army took center stage. Its presence and success was tantamount to a free Poland; its absence with slavery.[3] One of the greatest Polish novels, and probably its all time Polish best seller— *Trylogia*—by Henryk Sienkiewicz romanticized the Polish warrior.[4] Furthermore, the Polish soldier enjoyed an enviable reputation among the world's professional soldiers.

It was the promise of a Polish Army and the traditional reputation of the Pole as a soldier that allowed Pilsudski to recruit for his legions in the Austrian part of partitioned Poland. It was the well-known soldiering skills of the Pole which led to the two other partitioning powers to vie for a semiautonomous Poland so that they could tap into this potential pool of excellent warriors. For the partitioning powers the Pole may have been cannon fodder, for the Polish people a Pole in a Polish uniform was a step closer to freedom. The recovery of independence in 1918 was endorsed enthusiastically by the Polish people and the fledgling Polish Army, whose core was Pilsudski's Legions, attracted volunteers. But other political and regional groups also played their part and demonstrated Polish patriotism. Pilsudski's group was strongest in the region that had been under Russian and Austrian rule. The uprisings in Poznan and in Silesia were generated by the same spirit of Polish nationalism but at times marched to a different political drummer. In France, a Polish Army sponsored by Pilsudski's political adversary, Roman Dmowski, was created and became known as the Haller, or Blue Army, from the color of its French blue uniforms. It came to Poland well after the armistice but took a gallant part in the Polish-Russian war as did the army of the Province of Poznan after the Germans had been driven out.

Bitter frontier wars followed. Some were little better than boundary squabbles, but in the uprisings of Silesia and Poznan the Poles demonstrated that after a century they were still Poles. The

Polish-Russian war of 1919–1920 was a major conflict, won by the Polish armies, which inflicted two major defeats on the Russians, the first one at Warsaw in August 1920, hailed as the Eighteenth Most Decisive Battle of War History,[5] the second and decisive in September 1920, in the region of the river Niemen.

In the ever so short period of independence from November 1918 to September 1939, Poland was confronted by many problems. Restive or hostile national minorities, a ruined infrastructure, unemployment, lack of investment capital, the loss of natural marketplaces due to the customs war with Weimar Germany all contributed to a stagnant economy, which was further aggravated by the worldwide depression.

The most prominent of these minorities were the Ukrainians, Jews, Germans, and Lithuanians. These minorities were at best lukewarm to Polish aspirations while many were inimical to Polish interests yet used Polish parliamentary procedures to advance their cause. The short period of French-style parliamentary democracy in Poland was short-lived and not a great tribute to the integrity of the many political parties (that had sprung and which represented very factional interests) or for that matter to the political sophistication of the exploited electorate. Poland, in addition to internal economic and ethnic problems, was also faced by a revanchist Weimar Republic actively collaborating with the Soviet Union. The Rapallo Treaty of 1922, followed by the Treaty of Berlin in 1926, was the ghost of the traditional anti-Polish alliance between Germany and the Soviet Union. The Locarno Treaty (1925) was a major Polish diplomatic disaster. It diminished the strength of French guarantees. As a result Poland sought refuge in a strong, authoritarian rule of Pilsudski.[6]

In all of this Poland only had one asset, The Polish Army (*Wojsko Polskie*), proven in 1920. France paid attention to Poland because the Poles had won in 1920, and the Polish guarantee to keep a thirty-division army on Germany's eastern flank was important if not crucial to France. Romania entered into an alliance with Poland because of the Polish Army. Hitler's Germany attempted to entice Poland to its side as a bulwark to the Soviet Union because of the Polish Army. It was the Polish Army that was the major reason for the British to break with their long-standing tradition of staying uninvolved in eastern Europe. The British guarantee of March 1939 was an attempt to restrain Hitler and keep Poland from throwing its destiny with Germany. That Poland is unlikely to have done that, is not the issue here, but the point is the British concern.[7]

The pre-1939 Polish Forces were forged by a variety of historical influences. The tradition of the Polish Army from its early days and the successes in the 1920 war were inspirations and ideals; the serious economic situation, the main restraint. The convoluted boundaries accentuated the difficulties of linear defense. But many of the factors that formed the Polish military psyche were due to the vicissitudes of Polish history, the continued enmity of two of Poland's neighbors, Germany and the Soviet Union. These two large giants did not accept the loss of territories that had been conquered from Poland in the preceding hundred years. The Soviet Union had in the Treaty of Riga accepted the Polish-Soviet boundary, but the Weimar Republic never conceded the Polish-German boundaries even though they had been determined by a plebiscite under international supervision.

Because the command structure and, most importantly, the mold and culture of the Polish Armed Forces in the west was identical to the pre-1939 system, its historical roots need to be known. The senior officers who led Polish units in the West and worked in Polish staffs had earned their spurs in the Polish clandestine military organizations in 1914–1918 and had fought in the Polish-Soviet War and in the many Polish uprisings against the Germans in Silesia. The younger officers had been educated and indoctrinated in the spirit of intense Polish patriotism and nationalism.

In the period of the Polish Parliamentary rule (from 1919 to 1926) the Polish Military (*Wojsko Polskie*) was responsible to the President of the Republic and to the Government through the Minister of Military Affairs (*Ministerstwo Spraw Wojskowych*). The General Staff was appointed by the Minister of Military Affairs. The Constitution also provided that in the event of war and during the period of hostilities, the President with the advice and consent of the Government would appoint the Commander-in-Chief, or *Naczelny Wodz*.

In 1926 Pilsudski staged his coup d'état. Pilsudski's supporters were small in number but passionate and energetic; his opponents more numerous but less committed and less well organized. But the majority of the citizens and even of the military (as for example General Sikorski and even Sosnkowski, who were both to enter front stage in exile during the war), stayed neutral in the internecine conflict and waited out the short, yet quite bloody, civil war, which was physically localized to Warsaw. There were some strange bedfellows in this revolt. The small communist party, still legal, supported Pilsudski as did the socialists, while the National Democrats, the party of Dmowski, were opposed. Those who believed in a parliamentary system were strongly against the Marshal. The deciding factor in Pilsudki's success was the socialist control of the railroads, which ensured that Pilsudksi's relatively few but very ardent supporters were able to concentrate at Warsaw, while his quite numerous, but primarily western Poland–based, opposition were delayed in transport.

Marshal Pilsudski wasted no time in changing the military command of the Military. Pilsudski was concerned about the influence of the political system on the command structure of the Military. He wanted to separate the political parties and their elected officials from a direct role in the running of the military; and also wanted to develop a peacetime administrative track of command separate from the potential combat command situation. He wished to ensure that the future war army commanders would be able to devote their full energies to the formulation of plans for war unencumbered by the peacetime issues of budgets, the construction of barracks, the provisioning of the garrisons, the training of the cadres.

The administrative structure was delegated to the Minister of Military Affairs, and the country divided into ten military districts (Corps) under the command of Corps Commanders and given Latin numerals from I to X. These Corps were headquartered at Warsaw, Grodno, Lodz, Krakow, Lwow, Poznan, Torun, Brzesc, Przemysl. Since the peacetime army had thirty infantry divisions and eleven cavalry brigades, it worked out that each administrative Corps had an average of three infantry divisions and one cavalry brigade.[8] The Inspector General, who would automatically become the Commander-in-Chief in event of war, was responsible for the quality of the Armed Forces and carried out his peacetime duties through a number of senior generals, who bore the titles of Inspectors.

The new constitution written in 1935 reflected the actual realities of the postcoup era and mandated that the position of *Naczelny Wodz* was only accountable to the Presidency. Thus the Polish Constitution, which was in effect throughout the war, placed the post of the Commander-in-Chief of *Naczelny Wodz* outside of the control of the Prime Minister. It is an interesting paradox of the Polish historical scene that during the monarchical period, the Polish King was elected by the body politic of the Polish Kingdom, the *szlachta*, which made the King merely *primus inter pares,* while in the Republican Poland of the late 1930s the elective Presidency had near royal powers.[9]

From 1926 until his death in 1935, Marshal Pilsudski held both the positions of Inspector General and Minister of Military Affairs. The day to day work of the Ministry was delegated to a deputy minister. After the September Campaign, in exile, General Sikorski also occupied the positions of Commander-in-Chief and Minister of Military Affairs, as did Winston Churchill in the British Government delegating many of his daily responsibilities to "Pug" Ismay.[10]

The Minister of Military Affairs (until his death this was held by Marshall Pilsudski) was a member of the cabinet and had the responsibility for implementing recommendations emanating from the Inspectors and from the General Staff. This duality of command, a peacetime administrative and a potential combat command has given rise to much criticism. The Polish situation was not that unusual, as many countries separated the territorial commands from the potential war command.

The duality of command only began at a command level higher than that of a division. The G.O.C. of a division in peacetime would also be the G.O.C. of his unit after mobilization and would expect to command his division in combat. But his immediate peacetime superior, the Army Corps Commander, would in wartime continue to be responsible for the orderly continued logistical support of the units mobilized by his district and have responsibility for his district. After mobilization and being placed on a war footing, the division under the same command, depending on its assignment, could be moved to a different geographical region, say from eastern to western Poland, and placed under the command of a designated senior general, who in peacetime would have held the post of Inspector. These senior generals, unencumbered with peacetime administrative routine, worked closely with the Inspector General in preparing for operations in a specific area, the region of the concentration of the future army. They and their staff would have or were expected to have an intimate knowledge of the terrain, logistical supplies, rail depots, and the overall mission of that particular army.

Following Marshal Pilsudski's death in 1935, Edward Smigly-Rydz became the Inspector General of the Polish Armed Forces. He

quickly embarked on a major program of rearmament and modernization of the Polish Forces.[11] This seemed in such a dramatic
and stark contrast to Pilsudski's posture of relative neglect of the
military.[12] The Polish Armed Forces had no chance of fighting
against the Germans, whether fully modernized or not, and therefore the only policy was to play the diplomatic strategy on which he
embarked. A modern Polish Army was as much an inducement as a
poorly equipped one, and this was the point completely missed by
Beck in April 1939. The signature of the Polish-British treaty should
have been absolutely conditioned on a major credit for Polish rearmament.

Poland's interwar foreign policy and hence military strategy and
planning was based on the French Alliance negotiated in 1921.[13]
There were obviously other factors and other foreign policy initiatives, such as the Romanian Treaty of 1921 and the Nonaggression
Treaty with the Soviet Union of 1932. The most controversial was
the Nonaggression Declaration with Nazi Germany of 1934. But
though it was alleged to have secret clauses, it was clearly signed
with the explicit understanding that the obligation of Poland to
France was not affected by the Polish-German declaration.[14] The
French Alliance also had periods of stress, and the French participation in the Locarno Treaty of 1925 led to significant soul search-
ing in Poland. Pilsudski's last will and testament to his Foreign
Minister, Jozef Beck, urged that the Polish foreign policy had to in-
volve the United Kingdom in addition to France.[15] It was in this
context that the Polish Armed Forces planned their doctrine, and
with this putative alliance they went to war in 1939.

But until the formal signing of the Polish-British Alliance on
August 26, 1939, Britain avoided formal and specific territorial obligations attempting to act as a catalyst for a Polish-German dialog
and always taking a stance that a correction of the Versailles Treaty
was justified and indicated. When the signing of the German-Soviet
nonaggression treaty on August 23 changed the balance in Eastern
Europe, Britain upped its diplomatic ante in a calculated way and
gave Poland specific territorial guarantees. While decisions are
made by humans and are a result of various imponderables, there is
a good rule that a logical and parsimonious explanation is inevitably the most plausible.

The only parsimonious explanation of British foreign policy
characterized by its unwillingness to advance a loan, with no plans
to come to Poland's military aid or even to implement its promises

of aerial attacks, is in fact that the British wished to ensure that the Polish Armed Forces would not be at the side of the Germans, not that they cared for Polish independence. Later in the war the British in a very calculated and brutal manner sunk the French fleet off Mers el Kebir to prevent it from falling into German hands and control, even though in retrospect there was no evidence that the Vichy French admirals had any plans to make their warships available to the Germans. It was the Polish Armed Forces that after Poland's defeat and partition in 1939 gave the Polish Government international status and at least a modicum of negotiating strength.

The focus of this study is the unrivaled administrative effort of the Polish Government recreated outside of Poland in creating an Armed Force that would play a credible Part in the conduct of war. It is the history of a government physically removed from its country and national territory, which was occupied by hostile powers, which recruited, husbanded and trained a military force that had to be reckoned with, and which gave the otherwise exiled government in London a role in attempting to secure Polish interests. It is also the history of a People who never capitulated, who never compromised, and who fought on every European front of the Second World War.

It has often been said that history is the story of great men. There is undoubtedly considerable truth to that generalization. Much history, good and bad, has been made by great or at least unique men, such as Napoleon, Stalin, Hitler, DeGaulle, Pilsudski, Churchill. Poland was well served in its reconstruction by the presence of two great Poles—Pilsudski and Dmowski. During the immediate prewar years and during the conflict, Poland's leadership was at best mediocre and history was made by the men and women of the Polish Armed Forces. It was that group of dedicated and brave citizens in uniform, many career military (but as the war progressed, mostly volunteer soldiers), who not only represented Poland to the world at large by wearing the Polish uniform on all fronts of the European war, but who did it in a dignified and courageous manner.

The Polish Government's goals for its Armed Forces in exile were to demonstrate—by active military participation at the side of the British—that while occupied, Poland was very much in the war. As important was to create a nucleus of a modern and technologically advanced Armed Force that at the conclusion of hostilities would establish de jure and de facto control over liberated Polish territories. For the Poles, the September Campaign was the first campaign of the grand coalition.

The Polish Government's and, in particular, the Polish General Staff's five-year effort, initiated in late 1939 and continued to late 1944, to integrate the Polish Underground Army into the strategic plans of the western Allies are the focus of this study. In the Polish Forces, which fought at the side of the western Allies—France and the United Kingdom directly and the United States and Canada indirectly—all executive frontline and staff officer positions were held by Polish prewar trained officers. This was true in the army down to battalion level, in the air force at the squadron command, while for the navy all officer and noncommissioned officer positions were in the hands of men trained in pre-1939 Polish service academies. All were deeply imbued with Polish patriotic spirit and conscious of the thousand-year history of Polish martial tradition of which they were proud heirs. All were true to the Pilsudski dictum—"To be victorious and rest on laurels is defeat, to be defeated but unconquered is victory." It was an effort which was condemned to oblivion by the many hostile or at best indifferent elements both in the west and in postwar Soviet-occupied Poland.

Ultimately all armies have one function: to fight and to win. The function of the Polish Armed Forces in Exile was indeed to fight, to prevail, and whenever possible to win, but always to survive and by its very presence to attest to the continued existence of the Polish State. It was thus a political statement, well characterized by the words of one of many Polish wartime propaganda slogans: "We do not beg for freedom; we fight for freedom." But since the Polish Armed Forces were a political and psychological weapon of the Polish State, it was inevitable that the forces opposed to Polish interest sought also to discredit the Polish Military, then and later, whether by propagating myths or by silence.

The Polish Republic fought not only the obvious enemy— Germany; it also had to contend with more subtle enemies, political opinions inimical to Polish interests, and having their ultimate roots in the popularity of left wing, pro-Soviet ideology, which it is very difficult in this day and age to grasp. Those views have in some way left more lasting scars than the destruction of the war.

2

The First Campaign: 1921–September 1939

The State of the Polish Armed Forces Prior to 1939

Following the Polish victory over the Soviets in 1920, considered by many as the one of the decisive battles of world history, the Polish Army entered a period comparative stagnation. Immediately after the war it was generously supplied by the French out of their war surplus. This generous injection of material coupled with the French military alliance and augmented by commercial loans made the Polish Army a credible deterrent to the hostility of the Weimar Republic. But the military related industrial infrastructure of the country was limited to a small (Mauser) factory granted to Poland as part of the postwar spoils. Due to the experience in the Polish-Soviet war, when military equipment was delayed in transit by British dockworkers at the point of embarkation, by the German stevedores in Danzig at the point of unloading, and by Czechs in transit, who professed both pro-Soviet sympathies, stressed their neutrality and occupied Cieszyn, the Poles strove to become self-sufficient in arms production.

The plans were great, the aspirations even greater, but the reality was pitiful due to inadequate capital and the backwardness of the country. The goal was to develop an industrial base that would serve the civilian and also the military needs of the country. While the energy and the vision came from the Polish leadership, most of the investment capital came from France. All of this took place while Poland was experiencing an economic war with Weimar Germany. To obviate Poland's dependence on Danzig, where Polish rights were legalistic and symbolic, Gdynia was planned and within ten years surpassed Danzig as Poland's premier port. In this

effort, many major firms were nationalized and new state enter-
prises initiated, as for example the *Polskie Zaklady Lotnicze*, better
known as the *P.Z.L.*, which very shortly began to be a viable com-
petitor in the international aviation industry.[1] In those instances
where the Poles lacked the engineers or factories to construct new
product, licenses were sought from western industrial corporations
to produce sophisticated military and military-related products in
Poland. As a result of this policy guns were built by license from
Bofors, aircraft engines by license from the British company Bristol,
and the French Gnome-Rhone, tanks from Vickers of Britain, and
automobiles from General Motors and Fiat.

Strategic Doctrine

Polish military doctrine was primarily a product of the Polish
experience in the 1919–1920 Polish-Russian war. It was then leav-
ened by the French military advisors and lecturers in the Polish
Wyzsza Szkola Wojskowa (Military Staff Academy), which was created as early as 1919.[2] The Polish-Russian war was one of fluid tactics, fought over a huge terrain in which there were no trenches but
where the capture of rail junctions or bridges was of the utmost importance. Success was not measured in advance of miles, as on the
Western Front in France, but sometimes of a hundred miles. One of
the very first examples of a blitzkrieg operation was the 1920 Polish
thrust of a small motorized unit that operated independently over a
hundred miles and captured the rail junction of Kowel and numerous war booty and prisoners.[3]

This system of defense in depth and of an offense based on the
grand maneuver failed in 1939 since the Polish Army was to fight
not in the undeveloped eastern territories but in the highly indus-
trialized regions of western Poland, the very cradle of the Polish
Nation. In 1920 the Poles could advance a hundred miles, capture
Kiev, and just as easily give it up. In the war of 1920, the loss of
Kiev had political repercussions to the Poles but no economic significance. This fluidity of operations and emotional uninvolvement
with the land over which the Poles fought was in fact analogous to
the campaigns of Northern Africa in the years of 1940 to 1943. The
loss of Wilno or Lwow was a symbolic catastrophe, while the loss of
Poznan or of the Silesian region was an economic disaster. In 1919–
1920 the Poles had better communications, better intelligence gathering, and broke the Russian code. In 1939 the Poles faced an en-

emy not merely superior in numbers but with better communications, enjoying higher mobility, superior fire power, and air superiority. The most overwhelming advantage that the Germans possessed was their ability to enjoy the initiative of the offense, picking both the time and place for their offensive.

The military doctrine was taught at the Staff Academy. The presence of Colonel Faury (a Frenchman) gave its readers a certain perspective, which was quickly changed by Pilsudski as incompatible with the Polish reality. The French army enjoyed a logistical support that was not available to the Poles. After Pilsudski's coup and the relaxation of the very close economic ties—some would even argue, bordering on colonial exploitation—the French General Faury was replaced by General Tadeusz Kutrzeba. It was at the Staff Academy that major maneuvers were planned and analyzed and a whole generation of Polish staff officers trained. This was of paramount importance since the Polish army in its embryonic days had officers from many different armies (Russian, Austrian, and even Prussian) in addition to Pilsudski's Legions. At the lower level each military branch had its own career and reserve *Podchororzowka*, or Officer Cadet School. Thus infantry had its cadet school at Rembertow, the cavalry at Grudziadz, and the aviation service at Deblin (the famous school of eagles). It can be truthfully said that there were no officers in the Polish Forces in Exile below the rank of lieutenant who had not graduated from one of these service academies. On the other hand, the majority of generals had done their early service, either in the legions or in the armies of one of the partitioning powers.

One of the theoretical exercises was the question of feasibility of an offensive and a defensive war against Germany with and without French military intervention in the west. The conclusion was a most realistic assessment, that Germany would not have the strength to fight both France and Poland until 1940, but that at the time of the analysis (1936) Poland had already not only lost any chance of a successful offensive war, but that without French intervention Poland would succumb in six weeks.[4] This estimate proved very accurate and confronts the patronizing comments that the Poles were unrealistic and talked about watering their horses in the Oder. Apparently even now people fail to differentiate public opinion and propaganda from military reality.

The successor to Pilsudski as Inspector General, Edward Smigly-Rydz, had been very close to Pilsudski and was the Head of the

Polish clandestine organization the *Polska Organizacia Wojskowa*.[5] In 1920 Smigly-Rydz had been the victorious commander at the final and deciding battle of the Polish-Russian war, The Battle of Niemen. The events of 1939 were not kind to Smigly-Rydz. His critics have portrayed him as being promoted beyond his abilities. The argument for this opinion is the tragedy of the September Campaign. However, the new Inspector General knew only too well the limitations of his command. He was forced to dispose his armies in the far west, for political reasons, as the Poles did not trust their western Allies.[6]

One of the senior Polish staff officers describes Smigly-Rydz's reaction to a map exercise in 1938 when it became apparent that an army strength counteroffensive would in a twenty-four-hour period consume a whole month's production of ammunition. After analyzing the situation Smigly-Rydz stated: "Whatever happens, with or without ammunition, fight we must and fight we shall." The commentator wrote later in the United Kingdom, "these words made a deep impact on the audience. This was an expression of the real Polish Military Doctrine—the Doctrine of poverty."[7]

There are very frequent allegations that Poland's army was a cavalry army. These myths have been perpetrated by even intelligent historians[8] and can be easily refuted by the most perfunctory analysis of the size of the various branches of the Polish Army.

Table 1 illustrates the allocation of officers in the various branches of the Polish Army and the growth of certain services in the last two crucial years.

These figures show that the cavalry corps was relatively static compared to infantry, engineers, and aviation. But it is important to

TABLE 1 **Allocation of Officers in the Various Branches of the Polish Army**

Service	January 1937	June 1939
Infantry	5,438	7,161
Artillery	2,230	2,589
Cavalry	1,401	1,556
Aviation	970	1,237
Engineers	562	1,114
Armored Forces	408	490

Source: Kozlowski, op. cit., pages 352 and addendum #7.

bear in mind that Poland's obligation to the French Alliance was an undertaking to have a standing army of at least thirty infantry divisions and eleven cavalry brigades. This was a bottom line position around which all other modernization plans were made. Many critics have condemned Pilsudski for his apathy in facing up the need for a modernized army. It is the contention of the author that Pilsudski was more than aware of the inadequacies of the Polish Forces to face up the Germans but accepted that if the French Alliance was to work, then what little Poland had, would be adequate; and if the alliance did not work, then Poland by itself could do absolutely nothing. This is the only rational and convincing explanation for his seeming inactivity in the area of modernizing the Forces which he so loved and with which he was so intimately involved.

In 1936 the German entry into the demilitarized zone west of the Rhine contrary to the provisions of the Versailles Treaty forced not just the Poles but also the French and even the British to face the reality of the German threat.

The French invited the successor of Marshal Pilsudski, Edward Smigly-Rydz, to France and a new loan was negotiated at Rambouillet in September 1936.[9] This was a significant infusion of credit to Poland, and its sum of two billion francs over a four-year period was allocated in the following manner: the lion's share to purchase military goods in France, and the rest divided equally between investment in military-related industry and the purchase of equipment from these new Polish factories. Now the Polish Government embarked on a huge capital investment of military-related industries in the central region of Poland, between the Pilica as the westernmost boundary and the Vistula as its eastern limit. This was planned to locate and centralize Polish industry in as protected a region as possible, as far as possible from both neighbors—the potential adversaries. The region was called *Centralny Okreg Przemyslowy*, or *COP* (Central Industrial Region). A hologram for the construction of primary and secondary factories was developed with the finalization of this most ambitious project for 1942–1945. This was to make Poland self-sufficient in the production of all defense-related equipment.[10]

The cavalry brigades were in the process of constant reappraisal. Skibinski, who was the first Chief of Staff of the first motorized brigade (the 10th motorized cavalry brigade), comments in his memoirs that the brigade in reality functioned as an ongoing and continuing experiment in respect to its organic composition and actual function. The questions that were analyzed were: was it to be a highly mobile antitank force, and should it have its own artillery and tanks to be capable of a attack were the unresolved questions by 1939.[11]

The Budget and Modernization

The demands on the Polish Treasury were immense and in retrospect were irreconcilable. On achieving independence Poland did not have a uniform health, judicial, or educational system. Most cities that had been under Russian rule lacked sewage and electricity while the railroad system had been built to facilitate the transportation and strategic needs of the partitioning powers while to compound the problem the Russian system had a different gauge. The road system was inadequate at best, many roads were cobbled, while in eastern Poland were completely absent. All these social needs competed with the military, none could be postponed. The major thrust of the modernization program was the motorization of the army, improvement in communications, and great emphasis on the strengthened capability of engineering forces, antitank and antiaircraft defenses. The eleven cavalry brigades were to be enhanced by motorized infantry and reconnaissance units, while the thirty infantry divisions were to gain organic motor transport with all medium and heavy artillery motorized. Furthermore, four completely motorized brigades were to be formed, two of which were in fact on establishment in September 1939. These expenditures were beyond the annual recurring budget allotted to the Ministry of Military Affairs. This allocation remained essentially unchanged for most of the interwar period and averaged 760 million zloty annually between 1936 and 1939. To allow for the modernization of the Forces special monies had to be allocated and they came from: (a) French loans, (b) the sale of war bonds, and (c) revenues generated by the export of Polish military equipment.

The export of military products was vital to the Polish military (as it has been to many countries like France, the United Kingdom, and Israel in the seventies and eighties of this century), because it not merely generated funds, but by increasing production it reduced the unit cost.

In 1936 a special Committee—*Komitet do Spraw Uzbrojenia i Sprzetu*, or *KSUS* for short—was reactivated under the chairmanship of General Kazimierz Sosnkowski, (who in 1943 in exile became the constitutional *Naczelny Wodz*, or Commander-in-Chief) to make the specific decisions regarding how the extra budget would be allocated. It was the role of the *KSUS* to ensure that the monies allocated for the modernization of the forces were spent in a planned and rational manner. The long-term plan for this incremental budget position posited the expenditure for the following: (a) the creation of an industrial base making Poland self-sufficient in its arms procurements, (b) for a logistical strategic reserve, (c) the construction of static fortifications, (d) the modernization and technical upgrading of civilian–public sector-industries (e.g., railroads), which would be crucial in event of hostilities (see Table 2).

It needs to be commented that 2 billion zloty (70 percent of all capital investment) between 1936 and 1939 was channeled into military industry.[12] In industrially developed countries private industry competed for military orders by developing various prototypes according to defense specifications. For example, the famous Battle of Britain fighters, the Hawker *Hurricane* and the Supermarine *Spitfire*, were both private ventures that found acceptance with the Air Ministry. In the case of Poland, the Ministry had to educate the engineers, train technicians, plan and construct factories as well as the infrastructure. Finally, housing for the workers had to be constructed as well as schools for their children and health faculties for workers and their families.

By 1939 Poland had managed to create the foundation of a military industrial base and had succeeded in developing a number of unique weapons, such as the Bofors 37mm antitank and the 40mm antiaircraft gun. Tanks originating from Vickers designs were modified for Polish needs with diesel engines and more powerful

TABLE 2 Budget Allocations, in Millions of Polish Zloty

Fiscal Year	Total State Budget	Military Budget		Total
		Recurring	Reserve	
1936/1937	2,213	768	170	938
1937/1938	2,335	768	270	1,038
1938/1939	2,475	800	440	1,240
1939/1940 proposed	2,526	800	540	1,340

Note: In 1939 the exchange rate was 8.9 zloty to the American dollar.
Source: Polskie Sily Zbrojne, op. cit. p. 205.

guns.[13] Original Polish designs for light and heavy machine guns, most notably the 20mm gun, were just entering service in 1939 as well as the superb 75mm antiaircraft gun. A heavy long-range gun was in the final stages of development.

The most notable achievement of the Polish prewar military engineers and factories was in the area of the aviation development. The vicissitudes of the Polish Military Aviation in its procurement plans and the history of the Polish aviation industry are an excellent paradigm for all of Poland's pre-1939 modernization efforts. Poland, thanks to its great effort and the dedication of its engineers, developed an industry that placed Poland comfortably in a major position of the second tier of countries with aviation industries.

In 1918 Poland's aeronautical industry was at the most primitive stage of development. There were a few small factories producing one-engined planes. The runs were small and the planes bereft of any sophisticated equipment. General Ludomil Rayski, who became Commanding Officer of the Polish Military Aviation in 1926, single-mindedly pursued the development of a Polish indigenous aircraft industry to ensure self-sufficiency in every respect. Rayski also endorsed if not promoted the nationalization of most war-related industry, so that by 1935 all Polish aircraft industry was state owned, the major factory being the *Panstwowe Zaklady Lotnicze* (*P.Z.L.*). Polish fighter squadrons were the first to be equipped with an all metal monoplane that was designed and built in Poland. However, the engine plants for all of these Polish planes, while built in Poland, were produced by contractual licensing agreements with the British.

Poland and its aviation leadership also went through the phase of hoping to develop a strategic bomber force that would be able to interdict any German forces and offensive east of the Odra river.[14] Table 3 illustrates the importance with which the Poles viewed their aviation and antiaircraft defenses. This is the breakdown of the *KSUS* rearmament budget.

Prologue to War

In March of 1939 the Germans occupied Prague. As a result of German aggression, Poland mobilized a number of its western garrisons. At the same time the Polish General Staff ratcheted up its preparations for a war with Germany.

One of the most significant changes was the perception that the

TABLE 3 Rearmament Budget, in Millions of Zloty (total is 4,759 million)

Function or Service	Amount Spent	Percentage of Total
Military Aviation	860	18.0
Anti-Aircraft	668	14.0
Armored Forces	278	6.0
Fortifications	185	4.0
Military Industry	424	10.0
Engineers	147	5.0
Communication	99	2.0
Infantry	20	0.5
Cavalry	14	0.2

Source: E. Kozlowski, op. cit., p. 35.

impending war would not be waged and won by the bomber forces. This realization came to the British in late 1938 and it also came to the Polish Staff.

In late 1938 General Jozef Zajac, Inspector of Poland's antiaircraft defenses, came to an opposite opinion regarding the priorities in Poland's Military Aviation from Rayski. He opined that Poland's primary weakness in aviation was in its inadequate system of communications, radio navigation and the outdated equipment of its fighter squadrons. The first two identified problems precluded a successful bomber offensive.[15]

Zajac, concerned that the new fighter planes would only become available in 1940 at the earliest, placed his whole authority on redressing the fighter equipment crisis and advised massive purchases of suitable fighters in the west, a major turn away from the past decade of stressing independence in plane production. Zajac went a step further, and emphasized fighter production even at the price of reduction of bomber production. This led to the curtailment in the production run of the excellent two-engined bomber P.Z.L.-37 Los, a decision much decried by many and derided by the ignorant without any understanding of the issues. Zajac's views of the importance of fighter planes had prevailed but the Lotnictwo Wojskowe was now caught in the proverbial "changing horses in mid stream." At the same time orders for the new fighter Jastrzab were put on hold due to its unsatisfactory performance.[16] The reality was that Poland did not have enough resources to build up both fighter and bomber forces, and in hindsight the strategic doctrine of

Poland having a bomber force of strategic significance was a fantasy.

Zajac's search for foreign planes was bogged down by either lack of hard currency (for acquisition of planes in the United States) or the reality that Poland's Allies (France and the United Kingdom) were also in the middle of rearming. The British were not prepared to sell their modern fighters while France procrastinated with the sale of the *Morane-Saulniers*.[17] Finally in late summer a contract for 140 French fighters was signed with deliveries to begin in early fall. Poles only took possession of these planes in France in 1940.

After the British Prime Minister guaranteed Polish integrity on March 31, 1939, Hitler responded to the British challenge and in turn threw his own gauntlet in the face of Poland and the United Kingdom by revoking the Polish-German declaration of nonaggression, as well as the British-German naval limitation treaty April 28. But it was not till May 10 that instructions for *Fall Weiss were issued by Hitler to his now cowed general staff.* During the long hot and, for Polish war needs, regrettably very dry summer, the Polish staffs worked intensively to implement the plans for resisting German aggression. This plan, referred to as plan *Zachod*, had been initiated in the summer of 1938 and constantly updated in the light of the constantly changing circumstances stemming from the progressive German aggression in Czecho-Slovakia and the resulting deterioration of Poland's strategic position.

Prior to the German occupation of Prague the Poles had assumed that the main German attack would come from the Pomeranian region, but in the summer of 1939 it was posited that it would develop from the southwest. The Polish grand design was summarized as follows: in view of the overwhelming superiority enjoyed by the enemy, the plan had to be defensive and the goal was to inflict the highest casualties on the enemy while withdrawing in an organized cohesive fashion. The short-term tactics were to force the enemy to commit and deploy all his resources at every Polish major defensive position while the ultimate strategy was for the Poles to preserve the ability to counterattack when the French offensive was initiated and thus to pass from a defensive to an offensive posture.

During the summer a number of meetings were held by the Polish staffs with their British and French counterparts. This was the first step in the long and at times glorious and also too frequently bitter and frustrating collaboration between the Polish military and its western Allies. The first of these occurred in Paris on May 16,

1939, in which the Poles were represented by the Minister of Military Affairs, General Kasprzycki, while the French side was led by Generals Gamelin and Georges. The French representatives expressed some concern that the primary attack of a new war could be an invasion of France by combined German and Italian forces. But in event of a German attack on Poland, Gamelin assured the Poles that the French Army would develop an offensive by the fifteenth day of the war. However, air operations by the French were to be initiated immediately. This meeting was followed by a special subcommittee on air matters. The Poles were represented by Colonel Karpinski and the French by General Vuillemin, chief of staff of the French Air Force.[18] The French agreed in principle to move five bomber squadrons to Polish bases for shuttle bombing of German targets. In fact very preliminary steps in this direction were implemented.[19] The joint commission agreed to undertake immediate negotiations on all the essentials involved with such plans, such as radio communications, logistical support, preparation of bases on Polish territory and their maintenance.

Following these talks, the Polish Staff dispatched General Kossakowski to Paris. He was accompanied by experts in the area of ground, air, and naval matters. The task of this group was to promote the acquisition of war material vital to Polish war needs. In Warsaw on May 24, the British naval and air force representatives met with their Polish colleagues. The discussions were merely informative, and the British refused to consider the move of any British surface ships to the Baltic. The Poles specifically requested the transfer of the British heavy gunned monitors and the Royal Navy representative, Commodore Rawlings, promised to support the concept in London. It was in these talks that the idea of moving the major Polish surface ships to the United Kingdom was first bruited.

During these summer months the Polish staff, representedby General Stachiewicz, Polish Chief of Staff, also had talks with the British military representative, General Clayton. On July 19, the British Chief of the General Staff, General Ironsides, arrived in Warsaw and held a number of meetings in which he was forthcoming in promise of aid and restrained in any commitment of British military actions except for the immediate imposition of a blockade by the Royal Navy and operations by the Royal Air Force. In view of these joint talks at the highest levels of the military the argument advanced by the Poles throughout the war, that in fact it was a coalition effort, can be validated.

The army had already been on a partial mobilization since March 1939, but during the summer months the intensity of preparations heightened. The field armies were assigned their sectors, staffs were mobilized, field fortifications were expeditiously constructed, particularly in the densely populated region of Silesia.

But the Poles were still very concerned that a limited ingerence by the Germans into Polish territory, as for example the occupation of the Free City of Danzig or of Polish Silesia, would be countenanced by the western Allies. The Polish Foreign Ministry was sensitive to the fact that many in the United Kingdom were sympathetic to German revisionist claims, particularly the conservative elements who feared Soviet communism and saw in Germany a strong shield against Soviet Marxist encroachment. These conservative groups were of the opinion that the Germans should be allowed their rightful place in the concert of the European nations and allowed to exercise a controlling influence in central and eastern Europe. It was often argued that such a sympathetic pro-German stance would defang Hitler, possibly even lead to his overthrow, and bring about a highly desired stability, albeit very much at Poland's expense.

The date at which the Polish Government and General Staff accepted that Hitler was not bluffing and that war, though possibly still limited to specific territorial regions, was inevitable, has to be dated to July when the Poles shared their *Enigma* breakthrough with their Western Allies.[20]

The German attack on Poland was not a surprise akin to the American experience at Pearl Harbor. Polish military intelligence correctly predicted the main German attack and also identified the German units.[21] It is also probably true that the Germans made little effort to hide their potential strength since the intimidation factor was also part of their policy. It is assumed by most historians that right up the final moment, some in the German power structure hoped that war would be avoided and Poland forced into a satellite role analogous to Hungary, Romania, Bulgaria, and Slovakia. The archival evidence that proves that the Polish General Staff predicted the date of the German attack are the mobilization orders for Poland's aviation. On August 26, mobilization orders for ground components of combat units were issued, and these were moved to secret bases. On August 31, the majority of the combat units were flown out to secret bases. Thus no aviation units were destroyed on the ground as has often been written. The continued prevarications on this subject are bizarre.[22] On August 30 Poland declared general mobilization, but the British and French ambassadors protested that such a move on Poland's part would be perceived as a provocative act and might make it harder for the western parliaments to honor their treaty obligation. The general mobilization was rescinded. It is a sad commentary on the way that history is written that some western politicians condemned Poland for failure to order a timely mobilization.

During the summer of 1939 all shipping offices were moved from Gdynia to Warsaw. In August all merchant marine and fishing fleets were placed on a state of alert, and Polish transports were diverted from Polish ports, delayed in their sailing for Poland, or, if in Polish waters, expedited in departure. On August 28 all Polish flag carriers were ordered to stay out of the Baltic and to obey only coded orders from Warsaw.

Thus on the eve of the war the only Polish merchant ships in Polish waters were those that had been mobilized by the naval service.

On August 30 the following orders were received by the C.O. of the Polish destroyer O.R.P. *Blyskawica,* which was the flagship of the destroyer division and was at anchor off Oksywie, the naval port of Gdynia—*Execute Peking.* The sealed envelope was opened and read as follows: "Destroyer Division, consisting of *Blyskawica, Grom* and *Burza* to sail for Britain, reaching position between Bornholm and Christians by sunset, passing Malmo at midnight. Departure immediate and arrival Britain during daylight."

The three destroyers weighed anchor on August 30 at 14.15 hours and sailed west, increasing their speed to 25 knots. Bornholm was passed at 21.40 and the Sund entered at 00.10 of August 31. It was sunrise when the warships entered the Kattegat. At 15.30 while on a course for the Firth of Forth, a German plane was observed tracking the Polish destroyers. The course was changed to 315° and after sunset back to 256°. At 09.25 of September 1, radio message was received that the Germans had attacked Poland. Crews were placed on an alert. At 12.58 approximately thirty miles west off the Isle of May two Royal Navy destroyers of the *Wallace* class met and escorted the Polish warships into Leith.[23]

The Polish destroyers joined two other Polish naval ships in the west, namely two training warships with officer cadets and other trainees. These five Polish warships were the core of the Polish Forces in exile. The serendipity of this allowed the Polish Naval

Service to have its own crop of professionally trained young officers throughout the war.

The Polish naval forces were complemented by the majority of the Polish mercantile marine, which amounted to about 120,000 tons and included a number modern liners that were to serve with distinction in the Allied war effort as troop transports. A number of ships were purposely left in Swedish ports because there was a hope that a sea communication would be continued between Swedish and Finnish ports on one hand and the ports of the neutral Baltic countries with their rail connections to Poland.

September 1939

The German attack was carried out on September 1. On September 3, 1939, the British and French Governments after having issued a joint ultimatum to Germany to cease offensive operations against Poland, which was ignored, declared war. For Hitler the actual declaration was an unpleasant surprise since the prior pacifist tendencies of the western democracies impeached their credibility. In the final judgment the United Kingdom had a majority of honorable men in its Parliament, who believed that their pledge should be their bond.[24]

During the next seven days the Germans broke the back of Polish resistance west of the Vistula. Armia *Pomorze* was rolled back and badly mauled. The Silesian salient was enveloped and Armia *Krakow* forced to retreat out of its projected eastward trajectory into a northeast track.

But what decided the outcome was the inability of Armia *Prusy* to achieve a combat effectiveness and the bloody defeat of Armia *Lodz*, which opened up the road to Warsaw.

While the Polish Armies were reeling back and the Fighter Brigade, that had put up a gallant though unequal struggle over the skies of Warsaw, was being deployed well east of the Vistula, the Polish Destroyer Division sailed on its first patrol out of British waters.

On September 6 the Polish warships sailed from a British port on the North Sea. Thus a bare six days after the German attack on Poland, Polish naval forces began operations alongside the Royal Navy with a depth charge attack against a German submarine. The Polish destroyer squadron sailed into the Atlantic and on September 8 west of Wales a second depth charge attack was carried out.

On September 9 *Blyskawica* was detached to escort a British freighter bound for Constance with military cargo for Poland.

By September 9 the Polish Government had to look at the worst case scenario, the possibility that the Polish Armed Forces would be overwhelmed and the Polish Government forced to abandon the country to take up residence in France. There was a precedent for this from the First World War in which the governments of Siberia and Belgium continued their legitimate authority while exiled.

On September 15 the French Government placed a military compound in Coetquidan at the disposal of the Polish military authorities in France to base and train the Polish infantry division, whose formation was agreed to in prewar negotiations. There were already about fifteen thousand volunteers from the Polish diaspora in France for such service. The first of the ground forces in the west was being formed, shortly to be transformed into the forces in exile.

This is not a history of the September Campaign.[25] It is a historical sketch of the thirty days that brought down the Second Republic. It is a truism that the Poles lost the war before it was started. The long-exposed boundaries devoid of any natural barriers, and the exposed bulge of the Poznan salient with the absolutely indefensible Pomeranian corridor surrounded on both sides by German territory guaranteed a German advantage. Even the Silesian region, which until the German annexation of the remnants of the Czech state was protected by the Carpathians mountains in the south, was now also a vulnerable exposed region. For the German command the problem was as to how far east to carry out the classic pincer with troops moving from the East Prussian region and those from Czech provinces. It would appear that the Germans actually planned a very conservative operation, expecting to eliminate the Polish Army west of the Vistula.

The constraint for the Germans was not their military imagination but concern that a two-war front was a possibility and that their armies needed to get the job done quickly, without becoming too entrapped in the far eastern reaches of Poland, and be available as soon as possible to face the French.

For the Poles the strategy was exactly the reciprocal. For the Poles victory could only come as part of a coalition effort. This demanded the sacrifice of many Polish lives, the drawing in of the German forces into Poland, the tying in of as many German divisions as possible so that there would be as few as possible facing the French. The Poles strove to make the Germans develop their

primary attack right on the Polish boundary, then to fall back force
the Germans to regroup for a move and to fight once again. It was
hope that when the French attacked on the seventeenth day of the
war as called for by the military convention, the Poles would
counterattack with their reserve army group—Army *Prusy.*

It is this part of the Polish strategy that is so completely unap-
preciated in the West. Since the western Allies had no intention of
coming to Poland's help, it has been conveniently ignored that the
prewar military task called for a joint effort on land and in the air.
The general attitude in the West to Polish plans and efforts is based
on the final outcome, and since the outcome was not only tragic but
until the French debacle of 1940 nearly humiliating and devastating, then the majority opinion is that clearly the Polish dispositions
had to be inherently flawed. This strategy of a defensive retreat,
always strong enough to force the opponent to deploy, always fluid
to escape the encirclement was Smigly-Rydz's plan. The Silesian
fortifications were to anchor the south, the Poznan salient and the
corridor were to be given up but only after the evacuation of all
military assets. The Germans were to be inveigled and then tied up
in a final fight around the region of Lodz, Kielce, and Piotrkow.

But the German Army was better equipped for a war of movement. The Polish Armies were outflanked, outmaneuvered, and the
opposite happened to what had been planned. The whole tempo of
campaign was dictated by the Germans. Polish reserves were
paralyzed by the German air attacks. Polish frontline troops forced
to retreat without fighting. Polish communications disrupted and
the whole chain of command destroyed.

The night marches sapped the strength and the will. Brief and
frequently successful day stands were followed by the inexplicable
night retreats. Most tragic were the refugees and the burning towns
and villages. The sight of bombed-out towns, the pitiful sights of
the homeless and the wounded were the constant companions of
the Polish soldier. The tragic refugees disrupted the military traffic.
These desperate people, intent on escaping the hated Germans,
trudged on the sandy roads of Poland, pushing their wordly be-
longings in small carts, pulling their cows, all heading east.
Whether the Germans intended to strafe these people or, as they
claimed, mistook them for military is not an issue. The Polish soldier witnessed this tragic plight.

British and American troops also suffered defeats and were
forced to surrender and to retreat. But this did not occur on their

own land. They did not have to abandon their own towns, villages and endure the despair in the faces of their compatriots as was the lot of the Polish soldiers in September. The British or American soldier did not hear the curses for the apparent betrayal of defeat and retreat from their own people. The nearest experience to that of the Poles in September 1939 that affected the Americans was the widely viewed—thanks to the technology of television—evacuation of the American embassy in Saigon when the Americans were pulling out. That sad plight of chaos, of desperate hurry to get out leaving many begging to be taken was multiplied a thousand times in September 1939. But here in Poland in September the civilians were Poles. The Poles marched through their own burning cities,. which had been restored and built with love and piety, and blew up their own bridges that had taken so much effort and pride to construct. They abandoned their families, not as in the case of the Americans in Saigon, foreigners.

Only the best trained, steel willed, and motivated slogged on, marching ever further east always with the hope and expectation that a stand would be made, on the Vistula, on the Bug, and finally on the Romanian beachhead. That was the final hope of the C-in-C, since the Romanians had treaty obligations to Poland for transit of military goods and material from the west through the port of Constance. Even that hope was crushed as the Soviets invaded Poland on September 17, implementing the Molotov-Ribentropp Pact.

But even in this dismal scene the Polish strategy had some success. The Germans were forced to deploy their full strength in a number of boundary battles. The stand by the Wolynska Cavalry Brigade (C.O. Col. J. Filipowicz) on September 1, at Mokra, near Czestochowa, is a tribute to the fighting efficiency of the Polish soldier. This three-cavalry regiment brigade, strengthened by a detached battalion of the 18 Infantry Division and a horse artillery field regiment with reconnaissance armor faced up to the whole of the German 4th Panzer Division and held it up for over twenty-four hours as ordered.

The counteroffensive by the *Poznan* Army (G.O.C. Lt. General Tadeusz Kutrzeba) threw German plans into further disarray, as their divisions had to regroup and again wasted valuable time and committed resources in Poland thus making them unavailable for action in the West.

Paradoxically it was the cavalry, the horsed cavalry, that best kept their cohesion and survived the retreat in good style and remained fit fighting units. The tanks and trucks run out of gasoline or diesel fuel and had to be abandoned. The artillery could not ford the rivers since only too frequently bridges were blown up before all Polish units cleared the area. The night marches took great toll of the infantry. But the horsed cavalry could obtain fodder easily, the horses could ford muddy-bottom rivers, and the trooper could cat-nap in the saddle, getting some rest.

But there were also some outstanding infantry divisions. The First Legionnaire, the old guard of Pilsudski, as well as the divisions of the *Poznan* Army, which kept the best and enviable tradition of their Poznan forebears, have to be noted. It was the *Poznan* Army, reinforced by the remnants of the *Pomorze* Army, badly mauled as a result of less than inspired dispositions and command in the Pomeranian Corridor, that fought at Kutno, in the Battle of the Bzura. In this battle three Polish generals died in the front line and many regiments lost successive commanders.

Worthy of mention were also the pilots and ground crew of the Fighter Brigade. Their performance was well characterized by the English writers:

> In individual spirit and determination the excellently trained Polish aircrews were second to none in the world; but more than courage was needed when a thousand enemy aircraft invaded air space defended by a hundred fifty . . . when liaison and ground facilities broke down under the hammer blows of the Wehrmacht, these isolated groups could only make shift as best as they could, and die—superbly.[26]

As the German offensive unfolded and Polish forces were pressed ever further back east a decision was made to make a final stand with the back to the Romanian border—the Romanian beach-head. Romania had agreements guaranteeing transit of war materials from the port of Constance to Poland. Ships with supplies were already sailing for Constance. In the early hours of September 17 the Soviets invaded Poland, breaking their Nonaggression Treaty, which they had only recently reiterated as binding. In the late hours of that fateful day, the Polish Government crossed the boundary into Romania, and Smigly-Rydz gave up on his last-ditch attempt to form a defensive perimeter on the Romanian boundary. The Soviet invaders faced only skeleton units of the *Korpus Ochrony Pogranicza*, and had no problem sweeping through what was in most situations symbolic resistance, except for the determined resistance of the Wilno garrison. The situation was confused by the fact that Smigly-Rydz gave orders for Polish troops not to fight the Soviets unless attacked. Some of the Soviet units also insisted that they were coming to Poland to fight the Germans.[27]

Polish units crossed into Romania, Hungary, and Lithuania. While the numbers of land units were relatively small, the majority of the Polish Military Aviation personnel were safely moved to Romania. A number of combat planes were also flown out since the bases were already under direct threat of occupation by Soviet land units.

As the Polish forces evacuated to Romania and Hungary, the tragic battle and the bloody defense of Warsaw ensued. Warsaw was repeatedly battered by German heavy artillery, and bombed by German planes in what later became known as carpet bombing. Incendiaries were also dropped and many historic buildings burned down. This included the Royal Castle.

The Germans have always been convinced that it was their air and ground bombardment that led to the surrender of Warsaw. In time it probably would have been the cause, but the cause for the capitulation has to be sought in a more heroic deed.

On September 26 a Polish plane, interned by the Romanians, was surreptitiously taken over by Stanislaw Riess, a test pilot for the *P.Z.L. (Polskie Zaklady Lotnicze)*. On the pretense of flying within Romania, he flew a passenger, Major Galinat, the personal emissary of the Marshal, to the G.O.C. of Warsaw. Riess flew the hazardous mission to Warsaw, landing in Mokotow, which was a piece of no-man's land between Polish and German positions. The emissary was disembarked and after three and half hours when an artillery cannonade masked the noise of the engine, Riess took off and landed in neutral Lithuania. Major Galinat carried two orders from Smigly-Rydz, one for the city to capitulate to save further loss of life and property and one for the eyes only of the senior officer with a legionnaire background to form a Polish clandestine military organization. This most senior officer was Lt-General Michael Karasiewicz-Tokarzewski, who thus became the first G.O.C. of Poland's Underground Movement. Riess made it to the United Kingdom. This was Smigly-Rydz's last executive order, and also his final attempt to ensure that the torch of Polish leadership was carried on by the officers of the Pilsudski tradition.[28]

One day after Warsaw capitulated, the fortress of Modlin also surrendered. The Polish peninsula of Hel, which also contained the naval port of Hel, fought till October 1. On October 4, General Kleeberg and his decimated divisions fought the last symbolic battle at Kock.

The surrender of Lwow by the garrison commander to the Soviets without firing a shot, after a very successful and protracted siege against the Germans, is one of the few shameful and inexplicable decisions. Many military decisions were unwise, a number that should have been undertaken were not, as for example the failure of the Warsaw garrison to march out aggressively to aid the combined Poznan/Pomorze Armies in their break through into Warsaw. Regardless of the orders that General Rommel (Warsaw G.O.C.) had or assumed he had, no general can ever be faulted for marching to the sound of the guns. And the guns of the Poles in Kampinos forests were audible in Warsaw!

But the capitulation of Lwow was a political and psychological disaster. It was Lwow where the Polish defenders should have established for all posterity that the city—*Semper Fidelis*—was a Polish bulwark! The G.O.C., who will be nameless, for the promise of lenient treatment, shortly reneged on by the Soviets, surrendered the city and its large garrison and by his act weakened future Polish Government negotiations to preserve Lwow for Poland.

The Soviets were to be as malignant and perfidious an enemy as the Germans, and in the final outcome it was to the Soviets that Poland lost the war and her sovereignty. Many hundreds of thousands of Polish citizens were arrested and transported to the Soviet Gulags and many thousands of Polish officers were murdered or died of privation in that horrible captivity. But the presence of the many hundreds of thousands of Polish citizens in the Soviet Union was a force which inexorably pressured the Polish Government to accommodate to Soviets with risk to its own policy. The September Campaign is still a topic that excites passion or relative disinterest if not disdain. One of the more patronizing praises uttered has been that the Poles went to war with an army that was good by First World War standards. In fact the Poles went to war with a fine army, as good as most in September 1939. They were up against an army that was better than all the other armies put together. In September 1939 the Germans actually defeated the Poles within four weeks, but the campaign would have undoubtedly lasted longer without the Soviet invasion in the East. In May/June 1940 the Germans defeated the combined armies of France, Belgium, Holland,

and a sizeable and very well-equipped British Expeditionary Corps in less than six weeks. While against Poland they enjoyed the surprise of new tactics, that should not have been the case in France. But the most vital difference is that against the Poles the German had a thousand kilometer boundary devoid of natural barriers; the French had the Maginot Line and the German broke through the Ardennes on a very narrow front. Against the Poles in September the Germans sustained approximately fifteen thousand casualties, whilst in 1940, about twenty-seven thousand. The German successes against the Soviets in the first months of their offensive in 1941 were spectacular. As the old British soldier said, "You haven't been to war until you've fought the Germans."

In view of the many frequently repeated canards about the Polish Military Aviation it is also interesting to see what a German historian, Cajus Bekker, wrote about the Polish effort in the air and on the ground.

> Despite all assertions to the contrary, the Polish Air Force was not destroyed on the ground in the first two days of fighting. The Bomber Brigade in particular continued to make determined attacks on the German forces up to September 16. [Author's note: the Soviets crossed the Polish border early on September 17.]

> The lightning campaign against Poland was no easy undertaking. The Poles put up a stubborn resistance, and although the campaign lasted only four weeks in all the Luftwaffe lost during this time no less than 743 men and 285 aircraft.[29]

Also the Polish Military Aviation was credited after the war for having been the main source of military intelligence for the Polish High Command.[30]

As the bloody final battles were being fought, and the Germans were disentangling from their Polish enemies and drawing back to their assigned demarcation line with the Soviets, which lay west of what their armies had reached, the Poles were already escaping through Romania, Hungary and Lithuania to the west and the Polish Navy had already began its first combat patrols and convoying at the side of the Royal Navy. But there was still one final, symbolic act being played out, one final hopeless struggle, which at the time captured the imagination of the world—the Polish submarine *Orzel* was still in operations in the Baltic. As the final shots of the Campaign were being fired in Poland, and as the first patrols of the Polish Navy were under way out of British ports a saga at sea unfolded and captured the imagination of all seafaring people.

The Polish submarine O.R.P. *Orzel* patrolled in the shallow and constricted waters of the Bay of Gdansk. The initial days at sea were identical to those of the other submarines. Depth-charged, tracked by German air and surface assets, *Orzel* changed its venue of patrol. The news from the home front was discouraging. Westerplatte capitulated on September 7, and then the C.O. became sick and made a very controversial decision to enter a neutral port to seek medical care. *Orzel* entered Tallin harbor and the captain was disembarked and taken to hospital. The executive officer, Kapitan J. Grudzinski, took over command but the submarine was interned after a series of Estonian prevarications. Estonian armed guards boarded the submarine, posted guards, and began to disarm the submarine. All charts and navigating equipment were removed as well as the gun and some torpedoes. Grudzinski escaped and without charts patrolled the Baltic for ten more days before making his way to the United Kingdom.[31] Winston Churchill, who was already in the Cabinet as the First Lord of the Admiralty, wrote, "the young Polish Navy had distinguished itself," and that the "escape of the *Orzel* was an epic."[32]

Less than ten days later, the Polish destroyer division was in full combat operations, patrolling the western shores of Ireland. The resurgence of IRA activity in the British Isles led to some speculation, possibly based on intelligence data, that the German submarines were about to use the small bays and inlets of the wild western shore for refueling and provisioning the U-Boats. The Poles were used for this task since a transgression of Irish neutrality by the Polish naval units was less likely to have serious political repercussions in the United States, with its strong Irish lobby, endemically anti-British in its stance.[33]

Symbolic it may have been, but this continuity of military effort inspired the Polish Nation and the Polish Military. For the Poles, there was no phony war, or *sitz-krieg*. Combat operations were pursued with as much force and vigor as the Polish Nation could command. In fact, the Poles did more to aid their Allies in the month of September than the Allies did for the Poles. The continuity of naval operations between the warships based in the Baltic and the Polish warships operating out of the United Kingdom may have had little military significance, but it was highly symbolic of the continued Polish effort in spite of the loss of the First Campaign, but even this small increment of three destroyers has to be confronted with the fact that Churchill expressed his concern at the beginning of the war, that only nine new destroyers were due to be commissioned by the end of 1940 for the Royal Navy! Later in the war the British appealed to the Americans for the transfer of fifty vintage and decrepit four-stack destroyers. In September 1939, the Royal Navy was strengthened by three modern and fully crewed warships

Polish Merchant Marine

The British ally was also strengthened by the infusion of about thirty merchant ships. Some were small freighters, but a number such as the *Pilsudski, Batory Sobieski, Chrobry* were brand new liners, which made a great contribution in transporting Allied soldiers.

The majority of the Polish Merchant marine was saved in September, primarily by the central Government decision to keep all shipping out of the Baltic with some planned exceptions. A number of the small fishing trawlers that had been mobilized were lost with the naval units, but even those ships that were kept in the Baltic to facilitate a supply route from Swedish or Finnish ports to the Baltic countries for transit by rail to Poland were saved as their masters stealthily moved their ships out to the United Kingdom.

Being civilian ships they could not be interned by the neutrals but were subject to German capture or sinking. Over a period of weeks, once it was obvious that the would-be transit route was merely a historical dream, their masters congregated them in Goteborg. These ships also carried all the cadets of the Polish Mercantile Marine who were aboard the Polish training ship *Dar Pomorza*, which was too slow to risk escaping from the Baltic and stayed in Sweden throughout the war in a strange legal limbo, since it was also a noncombatant and could not be interned. The *Dar Pomorza* returned to Poland after the war and took part in many Sail Operations until the mid-eighties. The young cadets joined the Polish Detachment of the College of Navigation of Southampton University.

Thus thanks to some good fortune both the Naval training ship *Iskra* and the Mercantile Marine ship were able to get their young trainees to the West and thus to provide the Polish Naval and Mercantile Marine Service with a rich crop of young officers throughout the war years.

From Goteborg it was a night's sail to Bergen, and then the Royal Navy provided the escort for the ships to get to the United Kingdom.

Three other ships that had been deep in the Baltic took longer but also eventually made it to the United Kingdom in October.

All Polish merchantmen became integrated into the Allied Merchant Navy pool and sailed with Allied and Polish troops and Allied cargoes all over the world.

Some carried Poles from the Balkans to the Levant. Polish merchantmen took part in the run to Murmansk, sailed back and forth between the Americas and the United Kingdom, participated in the North African landings, the Salerno landings, and the invasion of Normandy and the subsequent invasion of South France. Two Polish liners actually carried the troops of the 2 Polish Corps to Italy in late 1943.

Eleven ships were lost due to enemy action, the major losses being the three liners *Pilsudski, Chrobry,* and *Warszawa.*

3

The Second Campaign: In France, October 1939–June 1940

The Constitution is Preserved

The option of transferring the Polish Government to France, an Allied country, had been considered as early as September 9 when the French ambassador, Noel, urged the Polish Government to consider moving its residence to France in event of a breakdown of Polish defenses. Two days later the Polish Foreign Minister, Beck, formally asked the French Government through its ambassador, Noel, whether the French would agree to give the Poles a *droit de residence*, on the same precedent as given the Belgians in 1914.

The invasion by the Soviets in the early hours of September 17 found the Polish Government in Kuty, near the Romanian border. Romania's treaty obligations to give military support to Poland was limited to a response in event of an unprovoked attack by the Soviets on Poland. The Soviet attack on Poland, itself in defiance of the existing treaties of nonaggression between Poland and the Soviets, appeared to trigger the automatic implementation of the Romanian-Polish Treaty of Mutual Aid. But in this tragic situation the Polish Government formally released the Romanians from their treaty obligation but requested a *droit de passage* for the Polish Government, the Polish High Command, and the Polish military through Romania to France. The Romanian reply was instantaneous and gave the Polish Government and the Polish President the right of passage in an unofficial capacity but expressed reservations about the military. At this juncture the French ambassador formally and affirmatively replied to the Polish request assuring the Polish Government and the Polish High Command of French hospitality and unswerving loyalty.

In the evening hours as the Soviet troops approached Kuty near the Romanian border where the Polish Government was located, a decision was reached that all Polish institutions and all military formations were to cross to Romania with the intent of continuing the war at the side of the French ally. It was at midnight that the Poles carried out their plans and were hospitably received by the Romanians. All military units and all Polish aviation units were ordered to cross the Romanian, Hungarian, or in the north, the Lithuanian boundaries. This point is of extreme importance, since the units, many of them still very well armed and cohesive, crossed the boundary and were forced to give up their military equipment. Unkind words were said after the event, even by Poles, that they had "escaped." This was particularly hurtful to the crews of the many Polish planes who obeyed orders flew to Romania and then were faced with sarcastic comments that while Warsaw was still fighting and bleeding, they were fleeing.

The first rude shock was that the Romanians politely requested that the members of the Polish Government, including the President, resign their office and travel through Romania as private citizens. The reason given was the Romanian wish to preserve their neutrality. At this point, the Romanians separated the President and the various members of the Polish Government from each other and housed them in various different, but extremely isolated, places. The President of Poland, the Polish Government, and of course the Polish High Command and the Polish military were interned.[1]

The most plausible explanation for this tragic situation is that the Romanians, caught between the rock and hard place of their position between the Soviet Union, with its territorial claims for Moldavia, and the Germans, advancing the merits of the Hungarian claim to Transylvania, bent to external pressure and reneged on their agreements. But there is a conspiracy theory which implicates the French and even General Wladyslaw Sikorski a member of the opposition *front-morges*. Sikorski, a brilliant general in the Polish-Russian war and a statesman of distinction in the early years of Polish Parliamentary democracy, crossed the Romanian boundary and after meeting with the French ambassador to Poland, Noel, departed with him by train for Paris September 22.[2] This was while Smigly-Rydz remained in Romanian internment.[3]

President Moscicki was also interned and isolated in the royal hunting lodge at Bicaz and, unable to exercise his prerogatives, resigned, but following the provisions of the Polish Constitution appointed a successor.[4] The Polish ambassador in Paris (Juliusz Lukasiewicz) played the role of regent and liaison between the Polish Government interned in Romania and the French Government with great skill.[5] President Moscicki ardently wished to appoint General Kazimierz Sosnkowski, a distinguished legionnaire general to the post but Sosnkowski was still fighting with the last divisions in Poland and there was no guaranty that he would be able to accept this position. This effort to place General Sosnkowski in the line of succession was a thread that continued throughout the war years. Moscicki then picked Wladyslaw Raczkiewicz from a list that also included the Polish primate—Cardinal Hlond, Ignacy Paderewski, and August Zaleski. The final choice fell on Wladyslaw Raczkiewicz, who became President on September 30, and for the next six years served his country with great dignity, wisdom, and endured many trials and tribulations. As President, Raczkiewicz was also the constitutional Head of the Polish Armed Forces.

Prior to that event, on September 25, General Sikorski, by the nature of his seniority, was appointed G.O.C. of the Polish Forces in France by the Polish Ambassador in Paris. President Raczkiewicz called for a coalition government and asked Sikorski to be the Prime Minister.

Before Sikorski agreed to form a coalition government, he made the following condition, that the president formally relinquish the 1935 constitutional prerogatives of power and agree to consult the government in all matters. This became known in Polish constitutional law as the *Paris Declaration*. In his speech to the nation on November 30, the President formally acknowledged that he would exercise his presidential authority strictly with the counsel of the Government. Raczkiewicz at the same time formally appointed General Kazimierz Sosnkowski as his designated successor, who had now appeared in France, hailed as a hero for fighting a last ditch-action in southeast Poland. The prewar Polish *Sanacja* was weakened but still held many important positions, namely the Presidency, the post of foreign ministry (Zaleski), and the loyalty of many of the rank and file officer corps.

The ensuing formation of the Polish Government was accomplished speedily. It was a coalition government, with a number of individuals whose only provenance was their opposition to the prewar *Sanacjia*. But it did include the Polish Peasant Party, the Polish Socialists, the Labor Party, and some elements of the National Democrats. The majority of the National Democrats stayed aloof of the coalition government, strongly supporting the President, deploring the appointment of Sikorski to the position of Prime Minister, and vehemently condemning a number of the cabinet appointments that Sikorski made. This last party was the only one that had been right of center and its ideological roots were in the Dmowski past, and it was representative of the educated petite bourgeois and was strong in western Poland.

Sikorski, in addition to being the Prime Minister, also took over the duties of Minister of Military Affairs and also, on November 7, the constitutional post of Commander-in-Chief (*Naczelny Wodz*). Lieutenant General Marian Kukiel was appointed to the position of first deputy and Major General Izydor Modelski became second deputy to the Minister of Military Affairs. On November 7, 1939, the Polish General Staff was formed and its first chief was Colonel Alexander Kedzior. The Naval structure of command was essentially identical to the prewar, with Rear Admiral Jerzy Swirski, in command. The Military Aviation, shortly renamed the Polish Air Force (*Polskie Sily Lotnicze*), continued for a while to be commanded by General Jozef Zajac. Except for the position of the Commander-in-Chief and the two deputy Ministers for Military Affairs, the other posts were retained by prewar senior officers. The Poles once again went about forming a military organization in exile. But the circumstances were in many ways more propitious this time. Polish since the administrative authority was centralized and recognized by most foreign governments, while two of the most powerful democracies of Europe were declared Allies and committed to continuing the war. The exiles, regardless of their own political biases, were overwhelmingly loyal to the Polish Government formed in Paris. The only exception to this was the small number of adherents of the communist party, who followed the Soviet-dictated policy.

As an ally, the Polish Government was extended many considerations, yet in the area of the military the enthusiasm was muted. Neither the French nor the British were aggressive in rearming the Poles and certainly very passive in their conduct of the war, which quickly became known as the *sitz-krieg*, or phony war. The only anti-German strategy that was articulated was the naval blockade. There were small limited ground patrols, while bombing raids were confined to some German off shore naval installations, such as Heligoland. The Royal Air Force flew over Germany and dropped leaflets assuring the Germans that they were thoroughly naughty.

The Polish Underground Movement Is Formed

The first battle of Warsaw thus came to an end on September 27. But the fight for Warsaw, a city that centered all that was the most heroic, noble, and free in Poland, continued. It was a fight to preserve the cultural artifacts from the Germans, to promote an underground Polish press, to continue Polish university-level seminars in a clandestine setting, since all Polish schools of higher education had been closed. It was a fight to ensure that at the most propitious moment, the legitimate representatives of the Polish Government would assume de jure and de facto authority of the city and thus symbolically of the country. It was a five-year fight against two explicit foes and against a third hidden, malevolent enemy—the left wing elements in the United Kingdom and the United States. It was a fight which led to the creation of one of the most vibrant and successful clandestine organizations, civil and military—the Polish Underground State.

It needs to be remembered that in the first stages of the German occupation, many clandestine military groups were formed, which attempted to both take an ideological and military character. A number of political parties, such as the National Democrats and the Peasant Party, which entered in full or in part the Polish coalition government in Paris, protected the existence of their, at times quite large, partisan groups. But the first clandestine group of any significance was, in fact, the child of the *Sanacjia*, created by the orders of Marshal Smigly-Rydz and commanded by one of the most prominent of the legionnaires—Lt. General Michael Karasiewicz-Tokarzewski. This group, called *Sluzba Zwyciestwu Polski*, or SZP (Service for Poland's Victory), combined political and military aims, and its provenance did not sit well with Sikorski, who quickly defused any opposition by separating the political from the military leadership. Sikorski quickly made changes as much to make his own stamp on the clandestine groups as to follow the reasonable logic of separating the military from the political. On the civil side Sikorski formed a subcommittee of the Cabinet for Home Affairs, *Komitet Ministrow dla Spraw Kraju* (The Minister's Committee for

Home Affairs) and also created the post of a Government delegate (*Delegat Rzadu*) in Poland with the formal rank of Vice-Prime Minister. The first person appointed to this post was Ratajski, a prominent member of the Polish Peasant Party. But even this gesture towards the Peasant Party, which certainly experienced unreasonable harrassment in the prewar days at the hands of the *Sanacjia*, failed to prevent the party from continuing to recruit to its own clandestine military units outside of the command structure of the official Polish Army. While at times there was some degree of collaboration, as during the Warsaw Uprising, the two groups distrusted each other. The A.K. saw the *bataliony chlopskie* as too radical and too close to the communists; while the peasants in turn talked disparagingly of the A.K. units as the *"panskie wojsko"* (the gentlemen's army). The Peasant units were particularly strong east of the Vistula in the poverty-stricken regions of Lublin.

The other political party, which was only marginally represented in the coalition, was the National Democrats, who also recruited their own clandestine forces and were particularly strong among the young, upwardly mobile small-town inhabitants of west and central Poland. Very identified with Polish nationalism, the Catholic Church; at their worst they were xenophobic while at best they had some of the most brilliant politicians in Poland, in the true tradition of Dmowski. They were articulate adherents of the theory of two enemies and did not wish to aid either against the other.

Sikorski, to ensure his control of the underground, appointed General Kazimierz Sosnkowski, resident in Paris, to the post of G.O.C. of the *Zwiazek Walki Zbrojnej*, the new name of the secret army, and then broke up the local commands in Poland by seconding Tokarzewski to the Soviet zone of occupation and appointing General Stefan Rowecki to command the undergrond in the German zone of occupation. This appointment of a true Pilsudski protégé and of a man who had fought with gallantry if not success in the final days of the September Campaign could not be ignored by Tokarzewski, who immediately placed himself under his orders and traveled in disguise to Lwow. Tokarzewski was shortly arrested by the Soviets who failed to break his disguise. The Soviets did not need much probable cause for arresting Poles in those days. Unlike many, Tokarzewski survived and lived to fight another day.

During the first two years of the war, the Soviets were actual allies of the Germans and the communists deplored the war, not that the Polish communist party had much of an indigenous following.

But outside of the official Polish Home Army (A.K.), which owed its allegiance to the Polish Government in the West, none of the other groupings were aided by supplies from the West.[6]

The Polish Forces Are Created in the West

Negotiations for Polish Armed Forces in France in event of war with Germany had been bruited during the Sikorski visit to Paris as early as 1925. This topic was again discussed and agreement reached in the Polish-French military talks in May 1939, in Paris. The Poles and the French were aware that there were many hundreds of thousands of Polish immigrant industrial workers in France and Belgium. Most of these remained Polish citizens. Recruitment began on September 3, with the French placing the camp at Coetquidan in Brittany at Polish disposal.

On September 29, Sikorski made it clear that the formation of a Polish Army at the side of the French ally was his highest priority, and this was repeated in his formal speech to the Polish Government and the National Council (*Rada Narodowa*) on January 23, 1940. "The recreation of the Polish Army in its greatest size is the most important and essential goal of the Government," and also on March 5, 1940, "this main goal should be the main effort of all our diplomatic missions and of our propaganda. We have to reach every Polish community in exile, move it and inspire it to fight for a free Poland."[7]

There were large groups of Polish migrants in France who were still Polish citizens and thus subject to Polish law regarding compulsory conscription, or call-up from the automatic reserve status, which followed the obligatory military service. The French agreed in principle that the Polish authorities had the right to enforce their law but apart from allowing voluntary service, placed a number of civilian occupations in a protected, exempt status. This was true for coal miners and agricultural workers, two areas in which the majority of the Polish migrants were employed. Even with these caveats from the French, the Polish Government reformed in Paris estimated that there would be a pool of about 120,000 men, all Polish citizens, who would be eligible for service in the Polish Armed Forces.

But there were other countries where there were Polish immigrants and hope that their governments would either allow Poles to proceed with compulsory service or at the very least facilitate voluntary recruitment. In the first group was the United Kingdom

(3,000 citizens) and Canada (estimated at 170,000), and in the second the countries of South America, United States (thought to be about 4,500,000 Polish immigrants of whom 10 percent were thought to be still Polish citizens), finally Belgium (40,000). The number of volunteers from Belgium and the United States was small, and Canada, though a Commonwealth country and at war with Germany, refused to allow its executive branch to implement Polish conscription orders.

The immigrants to the United States were reluctant to repeat the historical deed of their forbears from 1917, and many Poles in France were also quite adroit at failing to answer the summons. The volunteers were clearly enthusiastic and patriotic individuals; but many of the conscripts came from ideological and social groups that had been alienated from prewar Polish values. They were from economically deprived segments of the industrial and peasant population that had been forced to leave Poland for economic reasons and had become radicalized in a French society with its strong communist and socialist climate.

By June 1940, fewer than 70,000 Polish citizens in France had been inducted or had volunteered. Furthermore, the majority of these men were untrained. But there was a pool of trained and experienced men, interned in a number of countries neighboring Poland; these were the airmen and soldiers of the units that had crossed the neutral borders on the night of September 17 and had been interned. Hungary had the greatest number—forty thousand, including the nearly intact 10th Motorized Cavalry Brigade that had fought a superb retreating action under the command of Colonel Stanislaw Maczek. Romania hosted nearly thirty thousand, but of this number nearly nine thousand were combat aviation personnel. This represented more than two-thirds of the fully mobilized establishment of the Polish Aviation Service on September 1.

There were fifteen thousand in Lithuania and about thirteen hundred in Latvia. The task for Polish authorities in France and their embassies in Hungary and Romania was how to expedite the clandestine evacuation of these men without too obvious an implication of the host countries. The two governments of Hungary and Romania were under considerable pressure from both the Soviet Union and Germany to adhere to international conventions, which were clear: military men or civilians of an age group and physical condition consistent with military service from a belligerent country were to be interned.

The evacuation from Lithuania was difficult and was through Estonia to Finland, but the outbreak of the Soviet-Finnish put an end to that escape route and it had to be redirected to Sweden, either by plane or by ship. The Baltic was patrolled by German warships, who often boarded traffic between Lithuania and Latvia and the Swedish ports and on two occasions arrested Polish citizens.

The brutal and duplicitous incorporation of the Baltic states into the Soviet Union in 1940 placed the Polish internees in Soviet hands.

The British and French Governments assisted the Poles in their evacuation plans, which were carried out by all means and routes. The most successful evacuation was from Romania and Hungary and most took place directly by train through Jugoslavia and Italy to France. Some went south, to Greece and then by ship to Lebanon and then to France, while others were shipped directly from Romanian ports to various French or British controlled ports of destination such as the Levantine region.

Forty percent of the 43,000 were evacuated by the land route through Jugoslavia and the still neutral Italy, and sixty percent by sea from the Romanian port of Constance or the Greek port of Piraeus directly to France. Among the chartered ships utilized in the evacuation were Polish liners that had been kept out of the Baltic prior to the first of September, and which continued to operate under the Polish flag throughout the war. The old Polish liner SS *Warszawa*, relegated prior to the war to the Levantine route, played a major part in expediting Polish evacuation.

First Steps in Aiding the Underground

The Polish Government in Exile was initially based in France (Paris and subsequently Angers), and after the French capitulation in June 1940, transferred its base to its only remaining European ally—the United Kingdom. Right from the beginning the issue was of supporting the Polish clandestine organization in German- as well as Soviet-occupied Polish territories. The Polish Prime Minister and Commander-in-Chief, General Sikorski, omitted no opportunity to emphasize the integral nature of Polish endeavors in the West with those of the Polish secret forces.

General Sosnkowski, Minister for Polish Affairs and in overall command of the military struggle in Poland, directed his first efforts at implementing a courier route from France to Poland and the assessment of the best way to provide the embryonic underground military groups in Poland with appropriate equipment and support. The problem of radio communication was also high on the list of priorities, and this was solved expeditiously. In addition to this position, the President of Poland also appointed General K. Sosnkowski as his designated successor.

Thus was created one of the most vibrant and efficient underground, clandestine military organizations, which Merrick described in the following words: "Poland had a fully operative underground network in place before the Germans had finished shooting."[8]

As early as December 1939 Polish authorities (while still in France) contacted the British regarding technical assistance in flying couriers to Poland.[9] The Polish State Airlines (Lot) had managed to evacuate a number of their civilian planes (Lockheed Super-Electras) to the West, and it was planned to modify them for use as courier planes to Poland. Other smaller planes able to actually land in Poland were also considered, such as Percival Gull. After a prolonged exchange of ideas the realistic view prevailed that it was easier to have Polish couriers travel through neutral Italy and the Balkans and then to cross the boundary over the Carpathian Mountains, than to have a plane fly that long distance from France, let alone Britain. During this first phase of contacts between Polish authorities in France and the occupied Homeland, this route gave good results. After France's capitulation, in June 1940, and when Italy became a belligerent by attacking France and declaring war on Britain, the situation became very difficult though not impossible. The reality of Germany extending its direct hegemony over the Balkans further compounded the problems and that overland route became ever more time-consuming and dangerous. But it continued to be the primary route for agents going from Poland to the West.

Sikorski's War Strategy

From the very beginning, Sikorski looked to the Balkan strategy for the eventual victory over Germany. He hoped for a grand alliance of the various Balkan countries, based on the old traditional alliance of Poland and Romania, complemented by Turkish interests in that region. He also began his rapprochement with the Czech exiled leader, Benes, that eventually was to come to its apogee in

1941, in London. This led to very advanced negotiations for the Polish-Czechoslovak federation.[10] It is also worth keeping in mind that until June 1940, that is throughout the period of the "phony war," Italy continued to be a neutral and nonbelligerent power and continued to have friendly and diplomatic relations with the Polish Government in France. Historically, Poland and Italy had very warm relations until 1939, and the Polish Minister of Foreign Affairs, Jozef Beck, looked to the Polish-Italian alliance as anchoring the extreme ends of a Middle European alliance which would act as a counter to German and Soviet expansion. The British in 1940 still courted the Italians and attempted to keep them in a neutral and thus pro-Allied situation. On the other hand, the French were cool to an Italian alliance, arguing, with some degree of merit, that it was always better to have Italy as an enemy than an ally. Mussolini certainly did not look with favor on the successes of Germany in 1938, the annexation of Austria in particular. Following the occupation of Warsaw by the Germans in September 1939, the Italian embassy in that city continued to function though under a different name; and the Italian diplomats as well as the Italian royal family and the Vatican were able to alleviate some of the most cruel excesses of the German occupation in the early part of the war, including the release of imprisoned professors of Cracow University.[11]

It was with that in mind that, early in April 1940, Sikorski began to divert some Polish evacuees from the Balkans to Syria and appointed Colonel Stanislaw Kopanski take command of this unit.[12]

Sikorski, as always full of optimism and enthusiasm, projected a mixed mechanized infantry and armored corps but the final size of the unit was a five-thousand-man mountain (independent) infantry brigade. When Sikorski was developing and implementing these ideas, he was also struggling to get a Polish representative into the Allied War Council.[13] The French meanwhile showed no eagerness for a military offensive, which was probably beyond their ability and their imagination. The British at least hoped to starve Germany into submission by their maritime blockade.[14] The reluctance of the French to encourage a serious growth and centralization of the Polish Armed Forces in France may in fact be partially understood in this context of the French hope that negotiations would terminate the unfortunate and unhappy martial interlude. The presence of centralized and well-equipped Polish units committed to regaining

full sovereignty and territorial integrity may not have been com-
patible with French plans for negotiated peace and a compromise at
clearly Polish expense.

Recreation of the Polish Forces

The Poles experienced considerable difficulty due to the conduct
of French liaison officers whose constant interference was incompatible with Polish interests. It was a constant struggle between the
Polish perception that they were an Allied army that had suffered a
serious but only temporary setback, and a French patronizing attitude. With time and probably as a result of the understanding
gleaned by intelligence from German sources that armistice and
compromise were not acceptable to Germany, French attitudes
mellowed. Polish units of division size began to be formed.
Whether Sikorski's plan for a Polish Army would have come about
is a matter of pure speculation. In reality the first two Polish infantry divisions to achieve operational status were moved and assigned to different French armies for combat purposes. However,
not everybody in the French military was anti-Polish. There were a
number of extremely sympathetic officials and generals who bent
backwards to accommodate Polish interests and to show their pro-
Polish sympathy and to convey Allied cordiality.

The Polish staff assumed that the pool of available manpower
would be approximately 180,000 men and laid plans accordingly.
The Poles planned on the formation of two army corps each of two
infantry divisions and of one armored division. It was planned that
in Canada one infantry division would be formed and trained,
while the military aviation would consist of between fifteen and
twenty squadrons, distributed between the United Kingdom and
France.

The First Corps was to be ready for action in April 1940. The
Second was to reach ready status in August 1940. The French made
it clear that there was absolutely no chance of the armored division
being equipped prior to late 1941. The military agreement signed
by the Polish and French authorities in theory confirmed Polish aspirations. The existing agreements between Poland and France
were no longer sufficient to cover all the potential needs of the Polish forces and a new agreement was signed between the two countries on January 4, 1940.[15]

There was one other country that had millions of Poles, including many thousands of Polish career and reserve officers and men—the Soviet Union. In early spring Sikorski requested his staff to give him a set of options about the possibility of a German-Soviet war and the implications for the recruitment of Poles to the Polish Forces.[16]

The initial negotiations between the Poles and the British regarding the transfer of the Polish aviation personnel to the United Kingdom were started in late October 1939, and were both protracted and highly unsatisfactory for the Poles.

As the Polish personnel arrived through a variety of clandestine ways from Romania, they were processed and waited for the formation of Polish units. Partly because of this, the Polish Air Force Inspectorate in Paris argued for a British partnership. The familiarity of prewar Polish personnel with British equipment, which had been manufactured in Poland under license agreements with British firms, was given as the main reason. What probably was left unsaid and was more persuasive was the fame of the Royal Air Force and its obvious technical and administrative superiority over the French L'Armee de l'Air. By January 1940, the Poles also were clearly disappointed and frustrated at the slow progress in the formation of Polish air units in France. While Polish naval units were already functioning effectively out of British harbors and participating in Allied maritime operations in the North Sea and in the English Channel, Polish air personnel in France were still waiting for equipment. While the Polish Naval units, small in number, were already engaged in combat operations, the excellent aviation personnel were not merely underutilized but were in fact merely garrisoned and with a resulting lowering of morale. The major Polish air base was in Bron, Lyons, using the old Olympic grounds. But the British Air Ministry insisted on conditions that challenged the very heart of the Allied relationship. The agreement specifically omitted any reference to the Polish Air Force Command, thus all Polish Air Force personnel by a strict interpretation of the treaty became relegated to the status of paid mercenaries. The most contentious and humiliating points required all Polish personnel to be enrolled in the Royal Air Force Volunteer Reserve and to take an oath of allegiance to the King of England. The wearing of British uniforms and cap badges was required. All Polish officers, regardless of rank, were to begin at the rank of Pilot Officer, and British officers were to double all Polish command positions. King's regulations governed all military matters. The Allied commission that would review volunteers for service in Britain would have as its chairman an officer of the Royal Air Force, casting the final vote.

In fact, the Polish Government gave up all authority over a group of officers and men who were dispatched to England in the early part of 1940. The majority of Polish officers who volunteered to go to Britain were not informed of the conditions of the agreement. The oath of allegiance, in particular, was troubling, as was the change of uniform. Only high morale and a great sense of discipline persuaded the majority to go along with this situation, but there were a few instances where Polish officers felt unable to take the second oath of allegiance, seeing it as incompatible with their honor and loyalty to Poland.

The British for their part undertook to facilitate the formation of two bomber squadrons with a 200 percent reserve. When the rest of the Polish Air Force personnel arrived in the United Kingdom in June 1940, after the capitulation of France, the agreement was modified. The oath of allegiance to the King was discontinued and Polish military discipline, law, and custom were officially reintroduced, except that British King's regulations took precedence if the two were in conflict. The Polish staff was permitted to form a Polish Air Force Inspectorate with the right of inspection of Polish air units, but no right to command.[17]

But this should be confronted with the positive outcome of negotiations between Polish and British Naval representatives signed November 19, 1939.[18]

The contrast between the two agreements is like night and day. The Naval treaty accepted as its keystone the absolute sovereignty of Polish ships and of Polish personnel. Polish ships sailed under the Polish flag, were commanded by Polish officers, and were responsible to the Polish Ministry of Military Affairs through the Naval Headquarters. To facilitate communications, the British assigned their own signals officers for the coding and uncoding of messages. There were no provisions that Polish commanding officers or appointments had to be cleared with the British Admiralty. The British Admiralty undertook to provide for the financial support of the Polish fleet and personnel until the end of hostilities and to provide facilities in London for the Polish Naval Headquarters. This move was effected in June 1940. There has to be a question of why the Polish Navy was able to negotiate such a perfectly reasonable and equitable agreement while Sikorski and Zajac in Paris failed to preserve even a scintilla of Polish autonomy in the case of the aviation agreement. Were the Admiralty officials and Churchill, who was already First Lord of the Admiralty, so much more accommodating to Polish aspirations, or was the performance of the Polish warships in those early days of the war sufficiently impressive to allay the British insularity? Was the negotiating skill of the British educated and highly anglicized Polish ambassador to the Court of Saint James Count Edward Raczynski so much better than that of Sikorski and Zajac? Were the British Air Ministry representatives so patronizing and disinterested in the Polish contribution to their air effort? Regardless, the aviation agreement was more than a blot on the Polish posture of being an independent and Allied armed force, it was an augury for the future and a sign that Sikorski would be influenced by short-term pragmatic reasons.

War at Sea and the Polish Naval Forces

The period of October 1939 through April 1940 is invariably described as the "phony war," or *sitz-krieg*. While undoubtedly true for the ground forces, it was anything but true for the naval units, which were deployed in a grand game of hide and seek over the oceans of the world. The strategy was simple. The British and French attempted to institute a futile blockade of Germany. It was futile since shipping went to Germany from Sweden and through the Soviet Union. The Germans attempted by using their long-range oceangoing submarines and surface raiders to choke the British trade. This was a potential threat and in 1941 and early 1942 became a real crisis, but in the early years of the war so puny as to be nearly negligible. The Germans had many U-Boats operating in British waters, and the British suffered one very embarrassing loss, when their battleship *Royal Oak* was sunk in protected waters of the main base of the home Fleet, Scapa Flow. The Germans shortly achieved another spectacular success with the sinking of the aircraft carrier *Courageous*.

On October 29, 1939, the British must have decided that the Poles had passed their test of seamanship, since the three Poles were seconded to the Royal Navy's First Destroyer Flotilla in Harwich, arguably the most difficult area of naval operations in late 1939 and early 1940. The Polish Division operated as a Polish group carrying out intensive patrols and mine laying operations in the North Sea. Constant air attacks and the danger of negotiating waters often strewn by enemy mines made this dangerous and tiring work.

Furthermore the North Sea was a navigational challenge with strong tidal currents, scattered shoals, prone to fog and violent storms. During this time the Germans also began to deploy their new magnetic mines. On October 26, 1939, Poland's pride, the liner SS *Pilsudski*, was in fact sunk by one of these still secret and very lethal weapons. In a short time the British developed the system of degaussing their ships and the magnetic mine became history.

The task of the Destroyer Flotilla was to carry out patrols off the shores of Belgium and Holland, both countries pitifully holding on to their proclaimed neutrality, and thus trading with Germany. The task of the Flotilla was to implement the next to useless blockade by inspecting merchant men heading in the direction of Germany and also by laying mines in German waters. The crews were at a constant alert, with four-hour notice at best for departure.

The area of particular attention now began to shift to Norwegian waters. The Germans were using Norwegian territorial waters for moving their ships in from the Atlantic to say nothing of the heavy trade in Swedish iron that was shipped via Norwegian ports. The proof that the Norwegians had lost all control of their waters, or had decided to look the other way, occurred on February 16, 1940, when a British destroyer (*Cossack*) under the command of the soon to be famous Captain Vian boarded a German transport, *Altmark*, in Norwegian waters, needless to say against all international conventions, and found aboard hundreds of British seamen taken prisoner by the German surface raiders, such as the *Graf Spee*, in the south Atlantic. It was obvious that the Norwegians should never have allowed German ships to carry prisoners into Norwegian waters, and their failure to exercise jurisdiction over their territory certainly justified the British action. London was jubilant, Churchill triumphant. The Navy is here was the rallying cry of the country. Both sides were now eyeing Norway as the locus for control of the blockade or a window onto the Atlantic waters.

Two Polish submarines had broken out of the Baltic. *Orzel* was a modern boat, but minus the breech for its gun and thus not completely up to snuff. *Wilk* was a relatively old boat, also its performance was nowhere near what had been hoped from the French yards who built it in the late twenties. But both had full complement of crews, which had achieved more than most other Allied submarines at that time, and after major refits both were assigned to the Royal Navy's Second Submarine Flotilla based in Rosyth, Scotland. By the end of the year *Wilk* had accomplished two combat patrols but was plagued by frequent breakdowns, and was finally placed in dry dock for a major refit, which was not completed until June 1940.

Orzel, on the other hand, sailed out on her first patrol on December 29. Four patrols were accomplished in a very uneventful fashion. They averaged fourteen days and were the classic mixture of reconnaissance and enemy shipping interdiction. The region patrolled was usually south of Norway and the island of Heligoland.

Eve of the Norwegian Campaign

In France the dynamics of the Polish initiatives, the increase in the numbers of men, began to have its effect. In the United Kingdom the Poles had centralized all their naval personnel: 1,347 officers and sailors as well as 2,315 officers and other rank of their Air Force. French Syria had 4,038 officers and men in the soon to be famous Carpathian Brigade. There were by June 7,235 officers and airmen in France while the Polish land combat units consisted of 41,992 officers and men. There were also another 25,301 officers and men in various training centers. Coetquidan was the main infantry officers' training school; as well as infantry noncommissioned officers' school, plus artillery and communication training centers for a total of 7,429 officers and men.

Angers was the Polish engineers training center and had a total of 1,463 officers and men. Cerizay had 1,303 officers waiting for assignment and was the first place where the concept of the officer legions was created. Versailles had a total of 806 officers and men in training, while Avignon was the center for the Polish armored forces and had 5,305 officers and men.

Of these numbers, 44,700 were volunteers or conscripts from France, 38,900 were evacuated from Poland via neutral countries, and a disappointing 900 were Polish volunteers from residents in the United Kingdom.

It was in the crisis of impotence, in the middle of the "phony war," that the Podhalanska Brigade was born. The Soviet Union attacked Finland in the latter part of 1939. The League of Nations urged help for Finland. The Polish Government in France, de facto at war with the Soviet Union, was only too happy to attempt to respond and to prepare a brigade for war to assist the Finns. Norway presented a very attractive prize both to the Allies and to the Germans. The prize was the ice-free port of Narvik at the end of a rail-

road from Gallivare in Sweden, which has the biggest iron ore de-
posits in Europe. In April 1940, the Germans caught the Allies by
surprise by occupying Denmark and invading Norway. The Podhalanska Brigade did not see war against the Soviets in Finland but
became part of the Allied expeditionary force sent to assist the
Norwegians.

The Norwegian Campaign

The Germans wanted to protect this route, to enlarge their
opening into the Atlantic, to minimize the British maritime blockade, and to surround Sweden. The British wished to prevent German access to the iron and if possible to benefit from it themselves.
The Norwegians hoped to remain neutral. The Poles desperately
wanted to fight, Germans or Soviets.

But in April 1940 the pace accelerated dramatically as the Germans, sensing that the British might place their troops in Norway,
implemented very successful combined ground, air, and naval operations. The first step was simple beyond expectation. A German
squad arrived hidden in a barge, as if a Trojan Horse, and the
troops disembarked while the foreign office was given the ultimatum of either destruction of Copenhagen or the country being
placed under German protection. The second alternative was accepted by the Danes, who had been beaten by the Germans earlier
in the century and who were being offered a continued independent existence with their own Government, armed forces, legislature,
and the continuation of their monarchy.

The invasion of Norway was more bloody for all sides. The
Germans were aided by a small group of pro-German senior officers and politicians led by Quisling, whose name was to become the
synonym for treacherous collaboration. Some Norwegian units
fought hard, some were given confusing instructions, and some
were pro-German and anti-British. The Germans moved their
troops into Norway by ship and by air transport. But the British
and French also reacted quickly to move their forces to confront the
Germans. One of the first harbingers of this invasion occurred on
April 8, 1940, when *Orzel* (Kapitan Marynarki Jan Grudzinski) was
on her fifth patrol near the south shore of Norway. On April 8,
1940, at 0945 hours *Orzel* observed a ship at the entrance to
Oslofjord. The captain ordered an intercept course while sub-
merged, and at 1100 hours logged that the ship was not showing a

flag. A few minutes later the name of the ship was read as *Rio de Janeiro* out of Hamburg, according to the Deutscher Lloyd registered as a 9,800 ton passenger vessel.

At 1103 hours, *Orzel*, still obeying the prewar London agreements, surfaced approximately 1,200 meters from the suspect vessel and ordered it to stop and for the captain of *Rio de Janeiro* to come aboard *Orzel* with papers. The ship stopped, but no ship's boat was launched. At 1112, *Orzel* gave a burst of machine gun fire at the ship. At this point a boat was launched, but simulated rowing made no headway. At 1120 hours, Captain Grudzinski gave the order for the suspect vessel to be abandoned within fifteen minutes and at 1145, torpedoes were launched after one more warning. Many hours later the captain observed numerous floating bodies in the uniform of the German Army. The sunken ship was one of the armada of German vessels that sailed into Norwegian ports without declaration of war.[19]

Before the Podhalanska Brigade landed in Norway, Polish warships participated in naval operations. The Destroyer Squadron, O.R.P. *Burza* (Storm), O.R.P. *Blyskawica* (Lightning), and O.R.P. *Grom* (Thunder), battled in the icy waters of the Norwegian fiords at the side of the Royal Navy. The Polish destroyers were engaged in operations between Narvik and Lofoten Islands, at times actually transporting Allied units, providing them with escort and antiaircraft fire protection. On May 3, *Burza* landed French Alpine troops in Graatangend Fjord. From May 4 she was Naval Officer in charge of Skaaland. In addition, the Allied warships engaged enemy ground positions with their own artillery giving support to the ground troops. Also on May 3, *Grom* fired 500 shells against German positions while *Blyskawica* also engaged the enemy with all its armament, and her artillery officer, Kapitan Marynarki B. Wronski, received the Virtuti Militari for his splendid work and self-sacrifice.

The German Navy suffered a series of crippling defeats at the hands of the Allies, but the German Air Force maintained significant air superiority and O.R.P. *Grom* was hit by bombs and sunk. On April 14, 1940, an Allied expeditionary force disembarked in Norway with the goal of capturing the strategic port of Narvik, already in German hands. This force consisted of three battalions of the British 24th Guards Brigade, five battalions of French troops (three Alpine *Chasseurs* and two Foreign Legion), and four battalions of the Polish Podhalanska Brigade.[20] In ground troops the Poles numbered one-third of the Narvik Allied Expeditionary

Force, and the proportion of the Polish contribution increased as the British Brigade was withdrawn and moved to Bodo.[21]

The fighting was a series of isolated assaults on well-entrenched positions, with Allied forces well assisted by Allied warships which functioned as the main artillery support.

Before the final and successful attack on Narvik, the Allied Expeditionary Command was informed that because of the serious situation in France all troops would be withdrawn, and the capture of the port was to be expedited merely to destroy its harbor facilities. It was unfortunately characteristic that neither the Polish nor the Norwegian commanders were informed of this development in the plans.

The port and city of Narvik were captured on the night of May 28. Preparations were immediately made for intensive demolition of the harbor and simultaneous evacuation of Allied units. It is still unclear why this Allied decision was made in view of the long-range strategic value of Norway to the Allies and to the Germans. Possession of the north Norwegian ports gave the Germans an opening onto the Atlantic, which they lacked up to that time and which they successfully exploited in the future.

The phony war came to an abrupt end on May 10, 1940, when the Germans, taking no heed of the proclamations of neutrality by Holland and Belgium, invaded these countries in a modified von Schlieffen maneuver and went on to defeat the combined Dutch, Belgian, French, and British Armies in less than six weeks.

During the period when Allied units had been fighting in Norway, the following events had already occurred on the continent of Europe. The Belgians had capitulated, Holland had been overrun, the British had evacuated from the beaches of Dunkirk on June 3.

The German Navy, on the other hand, had suffered a series of crippling defeats at the hands of the Allies, experiencing a number of bloody losses which did not predispose them to take on the Royal Navy in the future without a clear air superiority. This series of battles, one of them entering history as massacre of the German Destroyers from the guns of the battleship *Warspite,* undoubtedly led to the postponement of the invasion in late 1940 when the Luftwaffe failed to wrest control of the air during the Battle of Britain. The decision to abandon Norway was tragic and led to the overthrow of the Chamberlain Government and the formation of the British Coalition Government, chaired at the strong pressure of the

British Labour Party by Winston Churchill, while in France Daladier was replaced Reynaud.

It is still unclear why this Allied decision was made in view of the long-range strategic value of Norway to the Allies and to the Germans. Possession of the north Norwegian ports gave the Germans an opening onto the Atlantic, which they lacked up to that time, and locked Sweden into an embrace that also guaranteed Germany its steel products.

The Allied fleets were withdrawn, the remaining two Polish destroyers sailed for Scapa Flow, and by May 14 had reached Harwich to begin the long naval operations that culminated with the final evacuation of all British and remnants of Polish forces from the continent.

The French Campaign

On May 21, *Burza* sailed to Calaise and shelled German troop concentrations. Later that same day, attacked by at least a *geshwader* of Junkers-87's, *Burza* was hit, while her companions HMS *Wessex* sunk and HMS *Vimiera* badly damaged and dead in the water. *Burza* was able to make it back to Dover under her own steam and then was towed to Plymouth for repairs. *Blyskawica's* experiences were similar. Patrols out of Harwich, enemy air attacks, and the constant pervasive danger of mines. On May 29, she towed the disabled Royal Navy destroyer, *Greyhound*, to Dover. *Blyskawica*, under the command of Komandor pod-porucznik S. Nahorski, endured six days of this for which a number of crew received the *Krzyz Walecznych*. A commentator wrote that it would be difficult to imagine more difficult situations. There were the very strong tidal currents, for which the Channel is famous; the shoals, smoke from burning towns, exploding ships, enemy air attacks, and even German E-Boat attacks. On June 7, *Blyskawica* finally departed for Portsmouth for a refit.

The months of May and June were the nadir of Polish naval fortunes. The Polish submarine *Orzel* carried out its sixth and uneventful patrol between April 28 and May 11, 1940. She left on her seventh, and what turned out to be her final patrol on May 23, 1940, being reported missing on June 8, 1940.

The other submarine, *Wilk*, continued to carry out combat patrols from the ports of Rosyth or Dundee all in the direction of Skagerrak. The boat continued to be plagued by mechanical problems and finally it was decided towards the end of the year to place her in the training squadron and give the Poles a new submarine. During the period of her last six patrols, *Wilk* was commanded either by her old skipper, B. Krawczyk, now promoted to Komandor pod-porucznik, or by Kapitan Marynarki B. Karnicki, who achieved fame later commanding the famous *Sokol* in the Mediterranean.

The reason for Karnicki doubling for Krawczyk was the situation of the three Polish submarines interned in Sweden. Having Norway occupied and France successfully forced to a humbling capitulation, it was speculated that Sweden would be next. The Poles, in very discreet talks with the Swedes, ascertained the feasibility of the three Polish submarines being allowed to sail for Britain in such an event. Krawczyk's missions were to plan this breakout and to keep the Polish crews alerted. However, in one of the very few sound diplomatic decisions, the Germans realized that a neutral Sweden was more profitable for them than an occupied country. Polish plans became moot.

But at the same time as the Podhalanska Brigade was being prepared for Finland, a small group of Polish fighter pilots were seconded to the French training base in Montpellier. The history of the *Groupe de Chasse Polonaise de Varsovie* 1/145 shows that when it served French interests their bureaucracy could move efficiently and speedily. As part of the Western intent to help Finland in its fight against the Soviets, the Poles were invited to provide an air unit. In a very short time, between January 22 and March 12, a group of Polish volunteers was recruited and, consisting of 35 pilots and about 130 ground crew, were ready for shipping to Finland. On March 12, 1940, the Finns signed an armistice with the Soviets and the ready unit was again placed in the French limbo of future planning.

In addition to the four planned fighter squadrons, the Poles were in the process of forming two reconnaissance squadrons and one bomber squadron. In addition to the eight thousand Polish airmen in France, there were also nearly fifteen hundred Polish air personnel in northern Africa.[22]

The French Campaign may historically be divided into two parts: the first part begins on May 10, with the German breakthrough out of the Ardennes and terminates with the evacuation of the British and French troops hemmed into the perimeter around the English Channel ports of Dunkirk, Boulogne, and Calais. Polish ground troops did not participate in this phase of the Battle of France. The second phase began on June 5, with the German attack on French positions at the Somme and Aisne, and concluded with the French asking for an armistice as the Germans reached the River Gironde on June 22.[23]

The First Grenadier Division was assigned to the French Second Army Corps on May 18, and its first loss came at the hand of the French Allies who, on May 26, detached all of the antitank companies and a battalion of engineers to a French division. Thus this Polish division, prior to becoming engaged in combat, was already significantly crippled. It was also sent into combat by itself, not as part of a Polish Corps as the Polish-French agreements called for. As a result the Chief of Staff, Col. Alexander Kedzior, resigned his position in protest. The Grenadiers, minus their antitank artillery, began a delaying action June 12. In spite of heavy fighting and serious losses, with their flanking French units also beginning to disintegrate as a result of the French debacle and rumors of armistice, the Poles held their ground and fought a successful retreat. On June 19, the Polish G.O.C. General Duch became aware of Sikorski's message from London for all Polish units to evacuate to Atlantic or Mediterranean ports to embark for England. General Duch requested his French superior for permission to execute the orders of his Polish Commander-in-Chief. This was categorically refused. As all around them retreated in demoralized fashion, the Polish Grenadiers held their ground until June 22 (the signing of the armistice), when surrounded by German forces the division disbanded with orders for individuals to make their way to French ports and neutral countries. In six days of fighting the division lost six thousand officers and men.

The fate of the Second Infantry Division was more fortuitous. A part of the French VIII Army, this Polish division became operational June 10. Also fighting a retreat action, it was forced back to the Swiss border which it crossed June 20 to become interned as a cohesive unit. It had a very interesting existence since the Swiss, concerned lest their own neutrality be infringed as had been the experience of Holland, Belgium, Denmark, and Norway, not only made preparations to repel the Germans but secretly agreed that in such circumstances the Poles would fight as a Polish division. In later stages of the war, when such an exigency was no longer considered likely, many Poles were allowed to attend Swiss universities and technical schools.[24]

The French, conservative, unhurried, chiding the Poles for their impetuosity, arguing that all had to be learned from basics, suddenly became galvanized into activity by the events of May and June. While for months the Poles had been urged to establish basics of training on the French model, which the Poles with their bitter experience of 1939 saw as outdated, in turn the French now begged and cajoled the Poles to commit into combat units that had not reached combat status, without requisite training, to the front. A good example of this was the Polish Armored Force Training Center, which was to be the nucleus of a Polish Armored Division by 1941, as promised by the French. Equipment that had not been available suddenly materialized, and the Poles were asked and entreated to commit units to the front without any familiarity with their tanks, and without having had any exercises even at a battalion level. It was a desperate call from Weygand that led to a small detached unit of 102 officers and 1,607 soldiers being seconded to the French Army group 4 (G.O.C. General Huntziger) for combat operations. This was led by General Maczek personally. The rest of the armored training center was saved. The rest of the brigade was to undergo high-priority training and to achieve operational status as soon as possible. However, in the next few days, without Maczek's restraining presence, a second tank battalion was detached for covering the French retreat. The French order, which sent Polish officer and noncommissioned officer training schools as frontline infantry to plug French defensive positions, was truly tragic.[25]

The only major cohesive aviation unit was the *Groupe de Chasse Polonaise de Varsovie* 1/145. None of the other planned aviation units were ready by May, but well over 100 Polish fighter pilots fought in the skies of France, flying a motley collection of various French planes. Many of these pilots were organized in small three-plane flights, called the chimney flights, formed and stationed to provide defense for French industrial regions. The Polish fighters achieved over fifty documented victories, at times flying obsolescent aircraft such as the Morane-Saulnier and Caudron. Numerous Polish aviation personnel were also seconded to French combat units.[26]

The impending military and political French debacle came as a shock to Poles, who admired French culture and in the French Army, honed in the bloody battles of World War One, saw the acme of élan and military doctrine. It was particularly stunning for that Francophile, Sikorski. He not only continued to express the strongest words of support for the French and for their new Commander-in-Chief, General Weygand who replaced Gamelin, but categorically castigated as a defeatist any one who wanted to make plans based on the worst-case scenario. For that lack of reality he has been strongly criticized, and even Kukiel, one of his closest friends, admitted that Sikorski's convictions of the final French victory were obstinately held.[27]

The importance of the events of this two-week period is the fact that it had impact on future Polish internal and even international affairs. Thus the events that unfolded precipitously and dramatically need to be chronicled.

On May 11, Churchill replaced Chamberlain as the Prime Minister of the British Coalition Government; at this juncture also Raynaud replaced Daladier as Prime Minister of the French Government and Weygand, the frail and hopelessly apathetic Gamelin. On June 13 Weygand appealed to Sikorski for all Polish troops to be thrown into the battle. On June 13 Paris, an open city, was occupied by the Germans and on June 16 Petain replaced Raynaud with the explicit understanding that France would seek an armistice.

The day-to-day events were outside Sikorski's knowledge, primarily because the French did not share them with their Polish ally, but to a secondary and significant extent, because Sikorski was away from the seat of the Polish Government in Angers. On June 11, Sikorski left Paris and the Polish Headquarters, heading east, hoping to get a firsthand idea of the situation and, it has even been suggested, hoping to get personal command over the right flank of the French Army that was expected to counterattack the extended German drive on Paris. Had it been executed and had it been successful, it would have been the repeat of the French miracle of the Marne in 1914. But on June 11, Weygand had advised his Government that the situation was catastrophic and that armistice talks should be initiated.

Sikorski left the Polish Military Headquarters in Paris and did not find Weygand and also lost touch with his own goverment and his own military headquarters. The French liaison officer to the Polish Government, General Denain, was not believed and his assessment of the situation discounted, since it was assumed that he was pessimistic and depressed due to the loss of his two sons in the French air force. Sikorski spent the next six days driving around, completely out of touch with everybody. The Polish Foreign Minister, Zaleski, was advised on June 13 that the French Government were evacuating Paris and was advised of the advisability of leaving Angers and heading south to Libourne, near Bordeaux. Zaleski immediately requested the British ambassador to Poland, Kennard, to assist in the evacuation of the Polish Government and Polish military to the United Kingdom and received an immediate positive response. But the other Polish Deputy Minister of Military Affairs, General Izydor Modelski, refused to allow the embarkation of Polish military units or personnel without Sikorski's specific authorization. Writing these words in the 1990s, one has to be reminded that in France of 1940 the system of communications was no more advanced than had been the case in Poland in September 1939, since long-range radios were rare and the telephone cables easily sabotaged or damaged in bombing.

Sikorski, having failed in his mission, arrived in Vichy on June 16 and, disappointed at not finding Weygand was so exhausted that he spent the night resting. It was there that he received the first communication from General Zygmunt Szyszko-Bohusz, the G.O.C. of the Podhalanska Brigade, that after its fine performance in Narvik, the Poles were now being disembarked in Brittany at the same time that the British were pulling out, since on June 15, General Brooke, the British Commander in France had advised Churchill that British troops had to be evacuated from Brittany. The Polish general requested orders, since presumably he was well cognizant of the general situation having spent time with British officers aboard British ships. In answer, Sikorski gave the exhortation: preserve the soldier's honor, carry out the orders of your superiors and preserve the Brigade.

The Polish Government, having reached Libourne, was still unable to contact Sikorski until he arrived in Libourne on June 17. As the Polish Government was preparing a text of an appeal to Churchill, the latter coincidentally invited Sikorski for consultations. It was quickly agreed that the Polish President and certain members of the Government board the British cruiser H.M.S. *Arethuse*. Sikorski on June 18 was picked up by a R.A.F. plane and flown to London to contact Churchill. General Sosnowski was now left in charge of the military.

On June 17 the French initiated talks with the Germans through their embassy in Spain. Petain had now replaced Raynaud as Prime Minister and the overtures to Germany were contrary to the Polish-French Agreement, which precluded either signatory from initiating political talks with the enemy without prior initial consultation.

Churchill met with Sikorski in Downing Street and, the witness to this meeting, Raczynski, describes the meeting as full of melodramatics. Sikorski posed one question to Churchill, did Britain intend to fight. Allegedly with tears in eyes, Churchill responded, to the death or to victory. Sikorski then asked for British help in evacuating the Poles from France. On June 19, Sikorski made his famous B.B.C. speech to all Poles in France, and urged Poland to continue the fight in the Underground and in exile. After making his speech Sikorski flew back to France and arrived June 20 in Libourne. But it was of also of great political import that while in London he allowed himself to be drawn into the Litauer Memorandum issue. Raczynski writes that it was with some difficulty that he extricated the Polish Prime Minister from a potentially dangerous diplomatic debacle.[28] Back in Libourne the Polish radio station used for communication with Poland had now arrived and played a key role in communicating with the many scattered Polish units.

Sikorski flew back to London, taking Sosnkowski with him and a small number of staff officers. Prior to flying off to the United Kingdom, Sosnkowski sent a message to Poland, giving General Rowecki sole and total command of the whole Polish clandestine military organization. The final evacuation was left to generals Kukiel, Modelski, and Burkhardt. The Polish Government and military staffs in Libourne, unable to obtain French help in facilitating the evacuation, were delighted to be informed that British shipping, so far reluctant to embark Polish units, would be available for the transport of all Polish military and civilian personnel from France to the United Kingdom.

The Evacuation from France

Sikorski's successful trip to London did little to undo the chaos of the situation facing the Polish units, training centers, and aviation units scattered all over France. The French for their part were perplexed at the idea of the Poles evacuating to the United Kingdom since it was their conviction that the British would also capitulate in a short time. At the local level Polish forces were frequently confronted with hostile French civilian administrations, and at times encouraged by the most pro-Polish and heartwarming expression of sympathy. The majority of the Poles were just not aware of the extent of the catastrophe suffered by their French ally; others not aware of the order from Sikorski. For Major General Bronislaw

Duch, the G.O.C. of the Grenadier Division, which was deeply embroiled in heavy fighting, Sikorski's orders posed a dilemma since they contradicted his loyalty to his French Army superior. Thus the Grenadier Division continued to hold the front line and to fight until after the armistice went into effect. By then it was too late to disentangle the division, which was surrounded by German forces. The Grenadier Division shared the fate of many French divisions and its officers and men taken prisoner of war.

Those Polish units that were in the rear or in early stages of formation, and thus not committed piecemeal to battle, as well as some training centers were evacuated as long as they had access to radio communication with Polish headquarters and organic transport.

The majority of the Polish ground forces were lost. This included the Grenadier Division and the Second Infantry Division. The Podhalanska Brigade, saved from its fruitless victory at Narvik, was sacrificed by Polish idealism and Allied stupidity bordering on duplicity. It was disembarked in Brittany to reinforce the nonexistent stronghold. Most of the Brigade was lost as was the Fourth Infantry Division, which in early stages of formation was also moved north to reinforce the nonexistent front.

The last Polish unit to embark was the Second Battalion of the Armored Brigade, which, detached for rear guard action from its main training center, was able to break away and reached St. Jean de Luz on June 24, two days after the armistice had gone into effect. As the Poles were embarking, the last units set up a defensive perimeter, as much from the Germans, only a few miles away, as from the hostile French administration, which, not unreasonably, saw the Polish action as incompatible with the terms of the armistice.

Forty thousand Poles had fought in the Battle of France and all were lost. Only 19,000 officers and men of the Polish Armed Forces were evacuated to the United Kingdom from France in June 1940. Of this number, 5,600 were transported on Polish merchant ships. This number of evacuees to Britain represented only 23 percent of the Polish forces in France in the summer of 1940.

The following Polish ships participated in the evacuation: the liners *Batory* and *Sobieski*, m/s *Lechistan*, s/s *Chorzow*, s/s *Kmicic*, s/s *Wilno*, and two Polish fishing trawlers, *Korab* and *Delfin*. These Polish ships transported 5,600 men to the United Kingdom.[29]

The Polish Brigade in French Syria was, however, saved. The commanding officer of the Carpathian Brigade, General Kopanski, had clear orders to move to British Palestine if the French commander obeyed the French Government call for an armistice. His unit, well centralized and cohesive, was on a full alert. The attitudes of two French officers in Syria with whom the Poles had to deal well-exemplified the myriad of attitudes of the French to the Poles. The French Chief of Staff cooperated with the Poles in planning the rail move to British Palestine. The French Corps commander insisted that if the Poles were to leave, then they would have to leave behind all the military equipment that the French had provided. Kopanski refused and was threatened with arrest. In turn Kopanski made it clear that all officers had clear orders to evacuate the Brigade, with or without his presence. Finally, as the argument between the former allies became more acerbic, Kopanski emphasized that if forced the Brigade would fight the French, though with the greatest regret.[30] The Brigade was allowed to proceed to British Palestine unhindered. There its arrival caused surprise, since the local British commanders did not expect the arrival of a four-thousand-man unit fully equipped and nearly combat ready.

The crisis of the evacuation from France also had political overtones for the Poles. The British provided a warship, H.M.S. *Arethuse*, to transport the Polish President, Raczkiewicz, and members of the Polish Government to England. After boarding, and thus being dependent on the wireless facilities of the British, the cruiser stayed anchored in the estuary for three days. This was when Sikorski was in England meeting with Churchill. This historical fact still awaits a detailed study.[31]

There were positive aspects to the French debacle. The Poles had suffered an absolute military catastrophe in 1939 and developed an inferiority complex that was aided and abetted by the French and encouraged by the prewar politicians who had suffered real and imaginary persecutions at the hands of Poland's ruling *Sanacjia*. In 1940, the defeat of a much larger and better prepared French Army and the precipitate evacuation of the British Expeditionary Corps put the situation in a different perspective. The 1939 Campaign was now seen in a perspective that improved the morale of the personnel of the Polish Armed Forces. Also, the evacuation to Britain was arranged by Polish officers; the men traveled as organized units in uniform under Polish command and in many instances on Polish ships.

4

The Beginnings of the Third and Final Campaign, June 1940–June 1941

In the United Kingdom

When the Polish Government and the remnants of its forces, saved from the French debacle, arrived in the United Kingdom, they had been preceded by the small Polish Navy and its Naval Headquarters, and by a small group of Polish Air Force personnel who were based in Eastchurch. The arrival of the nearly twenty thousand additional Polish military presented the British with a constitutional dilemma. The realities of the possibility of an imminent German invasion led remarkably quickly to the signing of a Polish-British military agreement and enabled legislature in the House of Commons. Special military conventions signed between the Polish Government and the host (the Government of the United Kingdom) regulated the administrative and disciplinary aspects of the garrisoning of the Polish Armed Forces.[1]

The Poles were now after their second lost campaign, but third time lucky was the universal optimistic feeling. The Polish Government was located in London, as were the governments of many German-occupied countries. It was accorded full diplomatic recognition by all governments, allied and neutral. It maintained embassies in most countries, the most important being London, Washington, Lisbon, Madrid, Stockholm, Ottawa, Ankara, Tokyo and, for a period of time, Moscow.

The Polish Military Headquarters were also in London, at the Rubens Hotel on Buckingham Palace Road. In addition to the London Headquarters, Sikorski, who always dreamed of taking a field command and leading his troops personally, had a field H.Q. in Gask, Scotland.

During this time General Wladyslaw Sikorski held the positions of Prime Minister, Commander-in-Chief, and Minister for Military Affairs.

The Polish Government saw its Armed Forces as playing a crucial part in the formulation and implementation of its policy. The Armed Forces were officially divided into the Home (Underground) Army in Poland and the Forces in Exile at the side of the British ally. The ultimate purpose of the Underground Army—the name of Home Army (*Armia Krajowa*) was only given in 1942—was to guarantee that in the most expeditious moment an armed rising would take place that would establish de facto and not just de jure control of Polish territory in the name of the Polish Government. But the most immediate goal was to gather intelligence and to promote the morale of the Polish nation, suffering from brutal German repression. This was done in many ways, by the publication of underground papers, selective sabotage, and by the trial and highly publicized execution of selected oppressors who were most guilty of inhuman treatment of the Polish citizens.

The task of the Polish Military in Exile was in some ways both simpler and more difficult. It was to be a support base for the Polish Underground by training cadres for those elements of the Armed Forces that could not be developed or trained in German-occupied Poland—such as the Air Force, the Navy, and certain specialized components of the land forces as armored units, engineers, etc. It was to be a highly visible force whose performance and bravery at the side of the Western Allies would address the basic motif of the Polish forces and Government in Exile—*We do not beg for freedom, we fight for freedom.* Finally, at the most appropriate moment the forces were to be moved to Poland to reinforce the Home Army. It was on the active participation of the Armed Forces that the Polish Government based its foreign policy. It was simply to be an entry fee for the Poles to take part in Allied planning of the war and the postwar European settlement. Until the time that both the Soviets and the USA came into the war, it was nearly successful.

General W. Sikorski, the Polish Prime Minister and Commander-in-Chief, was of the opinion that the only strategy that would ensure the liberation of Poland by the Western Allies, and hopefully with the participation of Polish troops, was the Balkan route. The Balkan strategy was also espoused by Churchill. His concept of the "soft under-belly" of Europe was firmly held and strongly argued until just before the invasion of Normandy in 1944.

The events of the summer of 1940 were momentous indeed. The major Polish continental ally had capitulated. The Poles were now hanging on with their island hosts facing a strangulating naval submarine blockade after having survived the air battle. The military problems facing the British, enhanced by the capitulation of France and the entry of Italy on the side of the Axis powers, made manpower a most pressing issue. Churchill, as the new British Prime Minister, also exerted all his efforts to inveigle both the Soviet Union and the United States into the grand coalition against Germany. From the very first contact between Sikorski and Churchill these two issues were broached and efforts made to get the Poles to accommodate with the Soviets so as to get the Soviets to at least release the many hundred thousands of Polish prisoners who could then be available to fight in the Polish Forces in Exile. The three momentous days in June 1940 were both the harbinger of future events as well as the first cue that Polish manpower was vital to the British, and the constitutional issues of the Polish government only important so far as they guaranteed the participation of Polish Armed Forces on the British side.[2]

Polish Wartime Goals

Firmly ensconced in Britain in July 1940, after evacuating his Government and some of the Polish Units from the French debacle, the Polish Prime Minister and C-in-C General Sikorski continued to implement his plans to tie the Home Army firmly with the Poles in the West and the Western Allies. There were five specific, albeit complementary, aspects of the Polish endeavors:

1. the creation of a Polish-controlled system of radio communications with Poland, utilizing its own secret cipher codes;

2. the development of a Polish-controlled system of dropping couriers;

3. the recruitment and training of such couriers in parachute techniques;

4. the development of Polish Land and Air Forces for concentration in Poland to strengthen the Polish Underground Army; and finally,

5. tying in the Polish Underground Army to the Western strategic and military goals.

On June 29, 1940 Sikorski formed a new section in the Polish General Staff (Section VI) to liaison with the Polish underground now commanded exclusively by Major General Stefan Rowecki.[3]

Polish Internal Disputes

After the evacuation from France was completed and the Poles had settled in Britain, the Polish National Council passed a motion of "no confidence" in regard to Sikorski. There were many hidden agendas behind that motion, such as Sikorski's authoritarian personality and demarche in regard to the Soviet Union, and his uncritical condemnation of the pre-1939 leadership without ever publicly chastising the French for their failure to abide by the military convention and to aid Poland in 1939.

The overt reason was the loss of nearly three-quarters of the Polish troops and of all the Polish gold bullion that had been saved in 1939.[4]

On July 18, Raczkiewicz dismissed Sikorski as Prime Minister. But the next day representatives of the Polish Military Staff (handpicked by Kukiel) arrived in Zaleski's office (the new Prime Minister) and made it clear that Sikorski had the unquestioning allegiance of Fighting Poland, the Military Staff, and that attempts to oust him would have the most serious repercussions for the continuity of the Polish Government. Whether Sikorski indeed enjoyed that overwhelming popularity among the military is not merely debatable but highly unlikely. That Sikorski had the full support of the British is beyond argument. General Sosnkowski, the elder statesman, counseled the President to retract the letter in view of the serious consequences of a split between a Sikorski (British supported) governing committee and the constitutional government. The possible consequences of a split, both in the Underground Army loyalties and the Forces in Exile, could not be contemplated. The letter relieving Sikorski of his Prime Ministership (his constitutional position as Commander-in-Chief was never affected) was withdrawn. Kukiel, as punishment for his behavior, was sent to Scotland as G.O.C. of the Polish First Corps. He held that position until 1942 when he returned as Minister of Defense, the old Ministry of Military Affairs.

Sikorski's political base was now the illusory friendship with Churchill. But the real political and diplomatic strength of the Polish Government in Exile was indeed the Armed Forces. As long as the British needed Polish Forces, the Polish Government would be heard; when the forces became irrelevant, as after May 1945, the Polish Government was regarded merely as a collection of unwanted civilians, war's debris, cast on the shores of the British islands. The British quickly accommodated Sikorski's penchant for pettiness by providing a holiday resort, Rothesay in Scotland, where Sikorski banished his political opponents.

There are interesting comparisons between Sikorski, who came out of the French debacle wounded politically but still very much in charge, and the tragic Smigly-Rydz. When on September 17, 1939, the Commander-in-Chief of the Polish Armed Forces, Marshal Edward Smigly-Rydz, crossed the Romanian boundary while his capital was fighting and while many of his decimated divisions were still in the field and fighting, he became reviled by his countrymen. Many expressed strong opinions that the old tradition of Zolkiewski, who died with his defeated army, should have been followed. One of the most severe critics of Smigly-Rydz was Sikorski. But if one compares the behavior of the two men there are similarities. Both in their own way were committed to preserving the leadership of the Polish Forces at the side of the ally. But whilst Sikorski found in Churchill a man who threw him the lifeline, the tragic Smigly-Rydz was interned and abandoned by all.[5] Smigly-Rydz lost the September Campaign. It was not his fault exclusively. Sikorski lost most of the Polish Army in the French debacle. It was clearly not his fault, but who else allowed the dispositions of the two Polish infantry divisions or authorized the landing of the Polish Podhalanska Brigade in Brittany? Given the fact that Sikorski countenanced, if not in fact promoted, a witch hunt for the men responsible for the September defeat, then it is not surprising that after June 1940 many turned against him. While much of the criticism directed against Sikorski was undoubtedly unfair, given the events that confronted the French and the British, it should also be commented with some justice that the yardstick of equity and mercy by which Sikorski was measured and found wanting was the same that he had used against the Polish authorities and his political opponents following September 1939.

But the war went on. The Polish Armed Forces were now after their second lost campaign. The Poles from the very first were absolutely committed to being full participants in the struggle against

Germany. The Polish Navy had been operating out of British ports since 1939; the Polish Fighter Squadrons became an active partner in the defense of the British Isles; the Polish Bomber Squadrons were also entering combat operations in attacks on German ports and invasion barge concentrations. From Sikorski down to the last soldier, the Poles were determined to be counted on to fulfill their Allied obligation and to be taken seriously by allies, neutrals, and the enemy. There was an initial period of despondency, accentuated by the dismal Scottish climate, the quality of life in unheated tents and barracks, lack of money, different food, and worry about loved ones back in Poland. This led to some isolated and short-lived discipline problems in the ground forces. But the Poles quickly adjusted and began to pride themselves on their appellation, *Sikorski's Tourists*.

Polish Naval Operations

Polish destroyers had operated intensively during the evacuation of British and French troops from Dunkirk, supporting the defense of Calais with artillery fire as well as assisting in the embarkation of Allied personnel. In the Mediterranean the newly commissioned destroyer *Garland* served out of the British-controlled port of Alexandria and in the month of August, escorted a Polish ship with further Polish evacuees from the Balkans. In the second part of 1940, the Polish warships, after major refits, became part of the Atlantic Western Approaches and participated in intensive convoy work. Constant patrols were carried out in waters where air and surface control were being challenged by the Germans. In October 1940, two Polish destroyers were ordered to base in Greenock (near Glasgow on the Clyde) to assist in convoy work. Also in October 1940, the Polish Navy was reinforced by a new British-built destroyer, ORP *Piorun* (Thunderbolt). In late spring 1941, this destroyer participated in a very successful naval operation against the *Bismarck*.[6] In early 1941, the Poles also took over a brand new British-built U-class submarine which was named ORP *Sokol* (Falcon). In such a short period of time this very small number of ships had participated intensively in surface and underwater operations in the North Sea, North Atlantic, Western Approaches, and the Bay of Biscayne, the English Channel, and the Mediterranean.[7]

But there was another fundamental fact associated with the Polish Naval units. They were in fact sovereign Poland. And later in the war the Polish Government, with the approval of the British authorities, issued postage stamps, which were legal throughout the world. These stamps became much sought after by collectors, and their design highlighted Polish war efforts.

Battle of Britain

The evacuation from France was shortly followed by the aerial battle known as the Battle of Britain. The German U-Boat offensive had not yet reached its acme, but the German preparations for invasion in occupied France were obvious, and the preliminary step was going to be an air offensive to establish air superiority over the English Channel. The German Navy had taken such a beating at the hands of the Royal Navy in the Norwegian waters, in spite of German air superiority in that campaign, that the Head of the Kriegsmarine, Admiral Raeder, made it clear that he could not guarantee a successful invasion and the safety of the German land troops.

In this situation, the British now realized the value of the Polish fighter pilots, though there was considerable concern about the language skills, since all R.A.F. units were directed by ground control.

In the air struggle over southern England and London two Polish fighter squadrons took part: the 302 *Poznanski* and 303 *Kosciuszko*. But there were also many Polish pilots in R.A.F. squadrons. [The R.A.F. ratio of successes to its own losses was 1:3. Polish pilots in R.A.F. squadrons reached a ratio of 1:4, but the completely Polish squadrons were unsurpassed with 1:9—i.e., for every Polish pilot killed, the Germans lost nine planes).[8]

The success of the Poles in the Battle of Britain bore fruit in 1941. The British, formally upholding the initial agreement, bent over backwards in practice to accommodate Polish interests. The Royal Air Force Fighter Command set up a mini-Polish fighter command staff as part of its own headquarters. This was a development not at all provided for or entertained in the agreement. Polish officers were also assigned to ground control and technical operations in various R.A.F. Commands. During 1941, Polish liaison officers were appointed to various R.A.F. Commands and to all bases where Poles were stationed. The R.A.F., initially standoffish, was accepting the Poles as Allies.

Less glamorous, but more onerous and much bloodier, was the bomber offensive that began to develop in the late 1940s and accentuated in intensity during 1941. In this, the four Polish squadrons, initially equipped with the outdated, single-engined Fairey Battle, were full participants. During 1941, the four Polish bomber squadrons converted to the two-engined Wellington.

Beginning of Liaison with the Occupied Homeland

But the Poles brought much more than the small number of superb fighter pilots and twenty thousand fighting men. Their major dowry to the British was again in the field of intelligence, just as in the summer it had been the Enigma Machine. The Poles had a superb intelligence network based in France and Switzerland.[9] They placed it at the disposal of the British but as a quid pro quo requested and obtained (at that time without any reservations) the right to use their own ciphers without British oversight, which they had developed in France. The Poles were the only Allied country that was given this unique status, though as the war progressed it was resented and eventually challenged by the British.[10] Foot writes that the Poles working in Letchworth were outdistancing SIS transmitters designs and quotes Lorain that "the advanced technology of their devices pushed all other existing devices to the status of museum pieces."[11]

Polish Units in Scotland and Recruitment Efforts

While the Polish General Staff laid long-term plans, the host country faced a direct peril, the possibility of a German invasion, which could come by sea and air. The impressive success of the German paratroopers in Crete was still to come (Spring 1941), but the Germans had already demonstrated their proficiency in the capture of the Belgian forts considered impregnable from ground attack. Hence the task that the Poles in the United Kingdom faced was not only to bring order to their units, to retrain the men with British equipment, but also to achieve prompt combat readiness.

The Poles were stationed in Scotland, and while nobody considered that this would be the main invasion point, the possibility of small diversionary and troubling paratroop attacks had to be borne in mind. As early as July a battalion of the Polish First Infantry Brigade Group began its anti-invasion duties near Glasgow. By August 1940, within two months of the evacuation of the Polish

Forces from France, the Polish ground units were going through an intense process of retraining, reorganization, and redeployment. While the numbers were small, they still represented a force sufficiently combat trained, and in most instances combat experienced, to be given responsibility for a defensive perimeter north of Edinburgh. The eighteen thousand officers and men who made up the corps were fewer than would have been needed to form one division with reasonable reserves. In the unique situation faced by the Poles and by their British hosts, still in expectation of a German assault, the organizational idiosyncracies were of secondary importance. At first, all infantry units were organized into infantry brigades, each composed of three battalions. A tank regiment was organized and was the combat arm of the Armored Forces Training Center. This eventually evolved into the 16 Tank Brigade (much later renamed the 16 Armored Brigade). Each of the infantry brigades was also supported by organic artillery and engineers. The corps in addition had its own organic units such as artillery, engineers, heavy machine gun battalion, and even its own air cooperation squadron flying the outdated *Lysander*.

The corps may not have been capable of resisting a full-scale German offensive, but it was clearly well able to defend against even a major German airborne landing and had the mobility to respond to situations of an emergency nature. The grandiose title of a corps was self evident; but it was a praetorian guard compared to the British Home Guard, which was still armed with shotguns and walking sticks. To obviate some confusion the Polish Corps in Scotland was always called by the spelled out number, i.e., First Polish Corps. Later in the war as the Polish troops in the Middle East were formed the convention was accepted of a number, i.e., 2 Polish Army Corps.

The situation in Scotland in 1940 resulted in a potential embarrassment to the Polish High Command, since there were excessive numbers of officers. Very senior officers were easily retired to special camps set up to house them. But there were hundreds of young, physically active, dedicated, and well-trained young men who were career or reserve officers who had already committed themselves to serving the cause of Poland. These young and able officers were unable to have appropriate roles to play and faced a potentially demoralizing situation. The Polish High Command came up with a number of imaginative plans that were successfully implemented. Many hundreds of young Polish officers were offered contractual service with the British African Colonial Troops.[12] Also, in view of the concern about the impending nature of sea as well as airborne landings by the Germans in Britain, the Poles were requested to man a number of British railroad armored trains, which could be easily routed towards any eventual emergency. A number of these trains were run exclusively by Polish officers.[13]

Even with these two options, a number of junior officers were left without appropriate assignment. To take care of this problem, the Poles created the Cadre Brigades in Scotland and the Officers Legion in Palestine. The Cadre Brigade structure was essentially based on the premise that physically fit junior officers would serve as ordinary privates in combat. Senior officers (of captain rank and above) were given the function of platoon leaders, usually a position held by senior noncommissioned officers or very junior officers. On official duty all officers wore the uniform commensurate with their functional position. However, off duty they were entitled to wear their officer's uniform with commensurate and appropriate insignia of rank and continued to be paid salary appropriate to status.

This third solution was premised on the imperative need that every single gun-bearing man, whatever his rank, had to be available to repel the potential invader. It was also hoped that as recruitment of volunteers from Polish migrants in Canada, the United States, and South America developed, the Cadre Brigades would lose this unique character, and indeed could be fleshed out to become regular brigade-sized units of the Polish Army. There were some pragmatic and immediate results of this plan. The First Polish Army Corps was strengthened with a number of mobile, independent company-sized units of skilled and highly motivated and experienced troops. Putting the officers in such cadre battalions enabled the Polish High Command to undertake immediate and aggressive steps to retrain the officers as well as to give them very concrete and practical tasks that took their minds off their obvious concern about the future of the war, the fate of their country, and of their families left behind in Poland. The excess of officers to other ranks in 1940 and 1941 dramatically became a shortage of officers in 1941 when, after the German invasion of the Soviet Union and as a result of the Sikorski-Maiski talks, the Soviets granted "amnesty" to Polish prisoners in the Soviet Union. This step released many thousands of Poles for potential service in the Polish Armed Forces. However, the disappearance of many thousands of Polish career and reserve officers led to the need for transfer of Polish officers to the Soviet Union to the newly created units of the Polish ground forces. Thus the Cadre Brigades of the Polish Armed Forces in the United Kingdom were actually a very short-lived but quite unique phenomenon.

General Stanislaw Maczek arrived in Scotland towards the end of 1940, having had to travel in disguise via French North Africa. Just as in France, Maczek became the articulated leader in working towards the formation of a Polish Armored Division and, as in France, was strongly supported by Sikorski. Unlike France, however, the British were much more forthcoming and supportive even though very short of tanks for their own divisions and fighting a war in the North African region.

Traditional military prerogatives and customs quickly began to be reasserted. The Second Infantry Brigade was renamed the 10th Motorized Cavalry and Maczek became its G.O.C. An exchange of battalions between the two brigades grouped the old units together again and historic regimental names reappeared. One of the infantry battalions in the First Brigade was renamed the Podhalanski Battalion in memory of the gallant brigade that had ceased to exist in French Brittany.

The Polish authorities were at this time still not quite clear how many more Poles would manage to escape to Britain from Vichy France. It is, in retrospect, obvious that hopes for large numbers of volunteers from the Polish immigrants living in Canada and the U.S.A. were unfounded. The Poles were desperate for additional manpower and hoped that they would be able to recruit among the Polish immigrants in Canada and the United States.[14] It was surmised that while the immigrants in Canada and the United States would fulfil their patriotic duties, the pool would be short of officers. The Polish staff decided that it would be the 4th Cadre Rifle Brigade (Commanding Officer, Colonel Stanislaw Sosabowski) that would be shipped to Canada to provide senior noncommissioned and junior officer material. But even as these plans were being made, the Cadre Brigade embarked on anti-invasion training in collaboration with territorial units of the British Home Guard. The hopes and expectations that large numbers of Polish migrants living in Canada and the United States would flock to the Polish colors to express their patriotic zeal, as did their forbears in 1917, failed to materialize. It was a different era and a different generation from 1917. The Canadian and American Polonia gave generously of its money and in later years attempted to lobby on behalf of the Polish cause, but was reluctant to send its young men to be slaughtered in a foreign continent on behalf of values that it no longer completely endorsed or shared, and fewer than five hundred volunteered.[15] The Canadian mission of the 4th Cadre Brigade was canceled.

The recruitment to the Polish Armed Forces came to a practical stop in the autumn of 1940. About 2,000 air men were evacuated from France via North Africa in July 1940. Also another 3,288 officers and men were transported from Romania and Hungary to Palestine. Poles in France continued to attempt to escape to Britain but many thousands were caught by the Spanish police and were interned in horrible and deplorable conditions by the Spaniards. The infamous Spanish camp of *Miranda* is in tragic contrast to the hospitality and humaneness shown the Poles by the Romanians and Hungarians.

There were to be no major increments to the Polish Armed Forces in Exile until the release of thousands of Poles by the Soviets in late 1941 following the German invasion of the Soviet Union.

Polish Troops in the Middle East

The Carpathian Brigade, stationed in the French-mandated territory of Syria, consisted of over 4,000 soldiers, of whom approximately 2,800 were in the front line by the middle of 1940. The Brigade was far from ready for combat operations, but was being trained in mountain warfare and outfitted with suitable mountain warfare equipment and artillery. The decision of the French government to capitulate led to orders from London that the Brigade should either stay with the French if they were willing to continue to fight at the side of the Allies, or cross over to British-controlled territories of Palestine. After a few days of vacillations, the French commander of the central Mediterranean region, General Mittelhauser, decided to obey the orders of the French Vichy Government and expressed surprise at the decision of the Poles to continue fighting in conjunction with the British. A number of the French officers in the staff were very sympathetic to the Polish decision, and after a number of interventions Mittelhauser agreed that the Poles could evacuate.

Initially the Poles were in an ambiguous position in that the only combat activities in that area of the world were conducted by British and British Commonwealth forces against the Italians and where British Forces, slim and heavily dependent on Common-wealth and Colonial troops, had achieved spectacular military suc-cesses. The Poles were not at war with Italy, with whom they had very good political and cultural relations. However, Sikorski came to the pragmatic conclusion that as Allies of Britain, the Polish forces were de facto at war with the Italians, and that while aggres-sive use of the Polish Brigade against Italian territories was not to be encouraged, the Poles could be used to man defensive positions to facilitate the operations of the British ally.[16]

As a result the Polish Brigade was moved from Palestine to Egypt and took up positions of a defensive nature around the im-portant naval harbor of Alexandria. At this point, the Brigade be-gan to retrain as a mobile unit for potential use in desert operations. The Poles were also involved in guarding the nearly sixty-five thousand Italian prisoners captured by the British. Then there were a number of dramatic events that hark back to Napoleon's famous, though possibly apocryphal, statement: that he only wanted lucky generals to command his armies. The Carpathian Brigade and its commanding officer were indeed lucky. In April 1941 the Brigade was destined for Greece, and the first units of the Poles were actu-ally boarded, only to have the orders reversed as a result of the dramatic gains made by the German Afrika Korps.

The Brigade was retained for the defense of Alexandria. In June 1941 the British, concerned by the collaboration of Vichy authorities in Syria with the Germans, decided to occupy the old French man-date. The Poles were asked for the Brigade but this time Sikorski refused and in his message stated that the Poles would not fight the French. On August 17, 1941, the Brigade was moved to Tobruk by ship and entered history as part of the legendary "Rats of Tobruk." It held its perimeter in Tobruk from August till December 12, 1942, longer than any other Allied unit, and then took part in the success-ful battle of El Gazala. The final laurel leaf of the Brigade was that it came out of its campaign victorious, but also that it was the first Polish army unit to enter combat after the French Campaign.

In addition to combat units, all based in the United Kingdom ex-cept for the Carpathian Brigade, which was in North Africa, there were a number of training centers, including the Staff College, military hospitals, and civilian educational and cultural centers, to which military personnel were at times seconded. The most promi-nent was the Polish Medical School at Edinburgh University.[17] There were also a School of Law at Oxford, of Architecture at Liverpool, and a Polish University College, which was an external college of the University of London.

First Plans on Behalf of the Homeland

On October 10, 1940, the Polish Prime Minister and Commander-in-Chief, General Wladyslaw Sikorski, issued a highly secret order to his closest military advisors—the Officer in Charge for liaison with the Polish Home Army (General Kazimierz Sosnkowski) as well as the Chief of Staff and Inspector General of the Polish Air Force. This document spelled out political, diplomatic, and military goals. The goal for the Polish Armed Forces in Exile was to mobilize the greatest number of troops for an airlift to Poland in order to buttress and strengthen a Polish Uprising. This was to include both air units as well as ground forces. In December 1940 Sikorski, in his correspondence with Sir Archibald Sinclair, requested British assistance in the formation of a Polish Parachute Brigade. In his memorandum that dealt primarily with various aspects of the Polish Air Force in the United Kingdom, such as training, technical and administrative branches, Sikorski went on to write:

> Finally, I should like to call another and no less important matter to your attention, i.e., the preparation of Polish parachute units. These units will be destined to land on a Polish territory in order to take command of the general rising anticipated for the final phase of the war.[18]

The Polish Government in Exile embarked on a very ambitious diplomacy whose long-term goals were to enhance Poland's strategic situation in East-Central Europe.[19] In the pursuit of this policy, the Polish Government placed major effort and all its resources, both material and moral, on a policy of developing an armed force in exile at the side of the Allies, as well as organizing an underground political and military structure in occupied Poland. The two specific goals for the military effort in the West were to create a favorable political climate that would facilitate Polish diplomatic overtures, and the control of a military force that would be capable of assuming control over liberated Polish territories. The Parachute Brigade was specifically created for that purpose, though obviously. all the military were to be ultimately destined for Poland. For the Poles the war was in Poland, and it was in that direction that their efforts were directed. Sosabowski had gathered a group of highly motivated and patriotic officers in his Cadre Brigade. He inspired them to aspire to be the elite unit of the Polish Army, and they rose to his challenge. But it would be misleading to assume that the Polish Parachute Brigade was merely the product of his own initiative, though his part in its formation is a matter of history and now even of legend. The historical facts show that the Polish High Command even in France entertained plans for such a unit to establish courier duties with the Homeland.[20]

First Staff Work on Behalf of the A.K.

Within weeks of the cancellation of the Canadian plans, the Chief of Staff to General Sikorski, Col. Tadeusz Klimecki, alerted Sosabowski to the fact that the British were interested in training Poles in diversionary activities and were prepared to make their training centers available to Polish volunteers. It is unclear whether Klimecki picked Sosabowski's unit because it consisted of young, intelligent, and dedicated yet uncommitted officers or whether Sosabowski persuaded Klimecki that the 4th Cadre Brigade was the unit for the job.

Polish plans for intelligence gathering and for sabotage were enthusiastically endorsed by the British, who had in the months just after the Dunkirk evacuation initiated their policy of "setting Europe ablaze."[21] Though as Foot writes, for about eighteen months after the creation of S.O.E. (Special Operations Executive) "the twigs of early resistance were still too damp outside of Poland, which the SOE could hardly reach, to do more than smolder."[22]

Consistent with his own goals of tying the Polish Underground Army, now known as the *Armia Krajowa* (A.K.), or Home Army, to the West, Sikorski staff ordered that two battalions of the Polish First Army Corps be trained in parachute technique, while the 4th Cadre Rifle Brigade was to be the center for training for diversionary activity.

The parachute training was done at Ringway where the Poles had established a strong presence with two prewar Polish officers and instructors from the Bydgoszcz parachute center—Captains Gorski and Kalenkiewicz and Gebolys.[23] These Polish officers were very important in the creation of Polish parachute units. Colonel Sosabowski's memoirs are anything but replete with compliments, but have only words of praise for these officers and for the British commanding officer at Ringway, Group Captain Newham. At Inverlochy Castle the Poles also had their own small group headed by Major J. Hartman. All Polish volunteers as well as the officers of the 4th Cadre (Parachute) Brigade went to Ringway and to Inverlochy Castle. At the Brigade headquarters in Largo House, Polish engineers constructed a parachute training tower for free falls.

Thus was the Parachute Brigade conceived. Colonel Sosabowski's efforts in the direction of a Polish Parachute Unit were brought to fruition on September 23, 1941, when the Polish Commander-in-Chief and Prime Minister, General Sikorski, visited the cadre unit and observed maneuvers. The exercise involved capturing a hypothetical landing strip in Poland and providing cover for the landing of other ground forces and of Polish combat fighter squadrons. On that same day, General Sikorski renamed the Fourth Cadre Brigade the The First Parachute Brigade (*Pierwsza Brygada Spadochronowa*) and took it out of the o. de b. (order of battle) of the First Polish Army Corps and placed it directly under the command of the Polish staff in London.

But landing a Polish parachute brigade was merely a prelude to transferring elements of the Polish Air Force from the United Kingdom to Poland. The Polish Air Force Inspectorate and the Polish General Staff began to work on this project. This was to be fourth leg of the project.

While the Polish-British collaboration in the area of parachute training was smooth and satisfactory from the Polish viewpoint, difficulties arose when it came to the establishment of a Polish-controlled system of dropping couriers and supplies to Poland, though this was more of a jurisdictional dispute between the Ministry of Economic Warfare and the Air Ministry than between the Poles and the British.

It is often forgotten how short of suitable planes and experienced crews the R.A.F. was in the early years of the war. The shortage of crews and planes was such that even the King's Flight was converted into a special duties squadron. Even by the end of the war, the R.A.F. only had two squadrons of four-engined special duties aircraft based in the United Kingdom.[24] The Air Ministry endorsed their staff's views that all effort should be on the bomber offensive against German targets. The life expectancy of multi-engined crews was about one-in-four survival. The gallows humor in bomber units, British and the four Polish bomber squadrons, was that they were "dead men on leave." The performance of planes even in late 1941 was limited. The R.A.F. did not even have any four-engined bomber units until late 1941. The range of Wellingtons was limited; Berlin was as far as the British could bomb. Supplies to France could be flown by the one-engined *Lysander*, Norway could be reached by the famous "Shetland Express" of Norwegian and Scottish fishing trawlers. But Poland was beyond the ready reach of any planes until the four-engined Halifax became available. Efforts were made to fly the Whitley, but its slow speed and horrible flying characteristics were anathema to crews. Furthermore, bearing in mind the northern latitudes of Britain, the nights in summer were too short for the planes to fly to and back under the cover of darkness. It was impossible for the planes to fly the direct route, they had to be detoured over Denmark and the Baltic, and after a few missions even as far as southern Sweden, which added considerable distance and, of course, time.

These were the background facts when early in February 1941 the Polish Prime Minister, General W. Sikorski, requested that the British Air Ministry second experienced Polish crews from the Polish Bomber Squadrons of the R.A.F. Bomber Command to train in special duties for flights to Poland. The request was only granted towards the end of that year, and on November 7, 1941, the first successful flight to Poland occurred. The route was over the North Sea, Denmark, and crossing the Polish Baltic shore between Gdansk and Kolobrzeg. The distance was approximately 1,600 kilometers each way.[25]

In December 1941, Oddzial VI of the Commander-in-Chief' Staff, initiated the discussion for preliminary planning to give the Polish Underground Army air support. This comprehensive outline of strategic and tactical goals included the first articulated plan for moving Polish combat squadrons to Poland: *Plan Uzycia i Organizcji Lotnictwa oraz Wojsk Desantowych na Korzysc Kraju*[26] (Plan for the Use and Organization of Air and Airborne Forces on behalf of the Homeland).

The plan's main points concerned practical as well as doctrinal issues. The plan stated a major principle: that the role of air power, as the only service capable of bringing needed supplies and manpower to Poland as well as giving needed air cover to the projected uprising, was so vital that any decision regarding the timing of the future insurrection should be conditioned on its active participation. The staff asked a question (rhetorical?) whether an uprising should even be started without securing air support.

The memorandum proposed the following targets vital to

achieve the strategic goals. The capture of a number of major airfields by A.K. units, which would need to be supported by airdrops
from the west. Following such local success, Polish fighter squadrons from the west were to fly to Poland and begin close air support
operations from bases controlled by insurgents.[27] To accomplish
this ambitious and imaginative plan, the staff stated that 450 four-
engined planes would need to be dedicated to this task, so that 150
craft could operate daily for the first five crucial days of operations.
The plan also went into details of communication needs and asked
for study of suitable areas where local control could be wrested
from the Germans. This plan was written after the German attack
on the Soviets and all Polish territory was now exclusively under
German control. By the end of 1941, the Polish Forces had also created a training cadre of a parachute unit but lacked even a vestige
of air transport capability, which even the Royal Air Force did not
posses in required numbers. One point dealt with the criticism of
the Air Treaty signed by the Poles and the British in 1940, which
was referred to euphemistically as "unfortunate," and stated that it
had to be modified so that the Polish Air Staffs would be created
and have the potential for autonomous functioning.[28] The internal
memorandum urged that the Polish Air Force be allocated more
manpower, so that it could become autonomous by developing its
own supporting services.

The plan was forwarded to the Polish Air Force Inspectorate for
detailed implementation and what elicited the most outrage from
the Air Staff was the plan's suggestion for the decentralization of
Polish fighter squadrons once they had arrived in Poland. This was
contrary to all R.A.F. doctrine, and the Polish Air Staff were
strongly influenced by the prestige of the Service, which had won
the Battle of Britain due to its centralized control system. The senior
Polish Air Force officers who reviewed the memorandum were
uninhibited in their opposition, and the scrawled "*Nie, Nie, Nie,
Nie*" on the margins of the drafts are a matter of historical record.
But again it needs to be commented that the Battle of Britain was
won by a centrally commanded force, directed to a narrow and
highly predictable area of operations, where radar played a crucial
role. At this time there were no field and movable radar facilities
and right to the end of the war, therefore, the suggestion for decentralization was not that outrageous given the circumstances of a
projected operation from primitive air fields.

The plan also emphasized the crucial aspect of the growth of

Polish Air Staff and the goal of twelve fighter and four dive-bomber squadrons, which could be achieved by dissolving two bomber squadrons. The memorandum addressed the reality that the Poles would depend on their British Allies for air transport, but would need to be independent in the provision of actual local support. The conclusion was still rather optimistic since it gave 1942 as the year in which the Polish Air Force could be capable of independent operations. But also acknowledges that the lack of British air transport made any such operations unlikely before the end of 1943 at best. The memorandum discussed a number of options and accepted that without the airborne forces it would require six transport planes to give logistical support to each fighter squadron. Mechanics and other ground support personnel were to come from specialized units of the A.K. supports for each squadron. This would still have required a total of seventy-two planes, which the Poles neither possessed nor had the trained crews and mechanics to support. The memorandum had a number of sketch maps illustrating the distances to Poland from such regions as United Kingdom (920 miles), Middle East (1,366 miles), Caucasus (1,040 miles), northern France (790 miles), very intriguing for 1941, south Norway (710 miles), and northern Turkey (1,070 miles). The staffs were of the opinion that the United Kingdom bases gave the best promise for anchoring the operation.

The political underpinning of the proposed plan is obvious since it stated that while in the then current political configuration Germany remained Poland's number one enemy, the uprising had to be timed so the Poles by their efforts, and not the Allies by their negotiations, would establish Polish sovereignty and boundaries. This is an open-ended statement that, given the projected distances, suggests that the Polish Staff were considering all possible contingencies, such as a British invasion of Norway, the Turks coming in on the side of the Allies, an eventuality strongly worked for by Churchill, as well as the possibility of Soviet military exhaustion and capitulation under German pressure.

The memorandum described the areas to be captured by the A.K. as complexes of air bases that would become centers of resistance and would contain at least one base suitable to handle big transports.

The staff stated that in certain unexpected situations the fighter squadrons may have to fly to Poland and would have had to be equipped with long-range drop tanks. The staff opined that Polish mechanics would be capable and required to make these modifications.

This was the first and in fact most comprehensive and even imaginative plan for addressing a number of contingencies that could develop on Polish territory.

It needs to be remembered that late 1941 was undoubtedly the acme of Polish fortunes during the war. Sikorski's Government in Exile enjoyed considerable prestige in London, and his first trip to the United States was a public relations success. In late 1941 he visited Moscow and reaped the fruits of his agreement, signed in London on August 30, 1941, with Maiski, which led to the release of (at least of some) imprisoned Poles and the formation of a Polish Army in the USSR. On his long and dangerous flight to Moscow, Sikorski stopped to visit and inspect the Polish brigade in Tobruk. All these Polish contributions to Allied military endeavors, whether on land in the siege of Tobruk, in the air over Britain, or even in the Battle of the Atlantic had generated a feeling of confidence among the Poles and sympathy towards them among the British. There was a can-do attitude, which permeated future plans. Polish negotiations with Benes of the Czecho-Slovak Government in Exile for a postwar confederation of the two neighbors, concluded in January 1942, also heightened Sikorski's prestige in the United Kingdom. Finally in November of 1941 the first airdrop to Poland from Britain took place, establishing a sense of optimism.

The first year on British soil was in every respect a Polish success story. Thanks to the efforts of its aircrew, sailors, and the small Carpathian Brigade, the Poles had paid their dues to the British and Allied side. Polish political fortunes were also blooming, and Sikorski enjoyed wide acclaim in British circles. Dalton, in his *Diaries*, writes on January 15, 1941, meeting with Eden: "I speak of the Belgian Government and Pierlots' refusal to broaden it, of the Poles and Sikorski's predominance over all the rest. . . ."[29] These were not isolated statements at that time. Perhaps the most persuasive is Churchill's address to the Polish Nation to celebrate the Polish National Day of May 3rd.

> To-night I am speaking to the Polish people all over the world. This is the hundred-and-fiftieth anniversary of the adoption by your Parliament of the Constitution. You are right to keep this days as a national holiday, because your Constitution of 1791 was a pattern, when it was framed, of enlightened political thought. Your neighbours in those bygone days saw in the adoption of this system the

beginning of the partition of your country before the Polish nation could consolidate its position.

The same tragedy, the same crime was repeated in 1939. The Germans became alarmed at the success achieved by the Polish nation in setting its house in order. They saw that strong, independent Polish State. At the time of the brutal German attack in September, 1939, your country had in the face of tremendous difficulties achieved notable progress during the twenty years of its revived national existence. To complete this work of national reconstruction, you needed, and you hoped for, a similar period of peaceful development. When the call came, Poland did not hesitate. She did not hesitate to risk all the national progress she had made rather than compromise her national honour; and she showed in the spontaneous response of her sons and daughters that spirit of national unity and of self-sacrifice which has maintained her among the great nations of Europe through all her many trials and tribulations.

I know from talks I have had with Poles now in this country how magnificently the mass of the Polish nation answered the appeal to duty in the hour of need. I have been deeply moved by what I have heard of the inhabitants of Warsaw during the three weeks of the siege, and their continued strenuous resistance to the alien oppressor who now occupies their city. We in this country who are conscious that our strength is built on the broad masses of the British nation appreciate and admire the Polish nation for its noble attitude since the outbreak of the war. Mainly for geographical reasons, personal contacts between our two peoples have been restricted in the past; and fighting as we are at two ends of Europe against our common foe, this war has not yet provided an opportunity for personal contacts on any large scale between you and my own countrymen. The fortunes of war have, however, brought to these shores your President, your Government and many thousands of brave Polish soldiers, airmen, sailors and merchant seamen. Their bearing has won them universal admiration in this country and cast further lustre, if that were possible, upon the proud, heroic traditions of Poland. It has been my privilege to come to know your Prime Minister and Commander-in-Chief, General Sikorski, whose leadership, energy, and unfaltering confidence are a source of great encouragement to all who meet him. I have visited your soldiers in Scotland while they were waiting to repel the invader, and while they were longing in their hearts above all to carry back the flag of freedom to their fellow countrymen at home. I have seen your pilots, who have by their prowess played a glorious part in the repulse of the German air hordes. Meanwhile, your sailors have been earning the respect and high regard of their comrades in the Royal Navy and Merchant Marine, with whom they are sharing the task of maintaining those contacts with America and with the outside world through which will come the liberation of your country. The presence here of your Government and armed forces has enabled us to get to know each other better, and to build a foundation for Anglo-Polish relations after our common victory and the restoration of your freedom.

Our thoughts go out to-night not only to those valiant exiled Poles whom we have learned to like and respect in the British islands and who stand armed in the ranks of the armies of liberation, but even more to those who are gripped at home in the merciless oppression of the Hun.

All over Europe, races and States whose culture and history made them a part of the general life of Christendom in centuries when the Prussians were no better than a barbarous tribe, and the German Empire no more than an agglomeration of pumpernickel principalities, are now prostrate under the dark, cruel yoke of Hitler and his Nazi gang. Every week his firing parties are busy in a dozen lands. Monday he shoots Dutchmen; Tuesday Norwegians; Wednesday, French or Belgians stand against the wall; Thursday it is the Czechs who must suffer. And now there are the Serbs and the Greeks to fill his repulsive bill of executions. But always, all the days, there are the Poles. The atrocities committed by Hitler upon the Poles, the ravaging of their country, the scattering of their man-power, exceed in severity and in scale the villainies perpetrated by Hitler in any other conquered land.

It is to you Poles, in Poland, who bear the full brunt of the Nazi oppression—at once pitiless and venal—that the hearts of the British and American Democracies go out in a full and generous tide. We send you our message of hope and encouragement to-night, knowing that the Poles will never despair, and that the soul of Poland will remain unconquerable.

This war against the mechanised barbarians, who, slave-hearted themselves, are fitted only to carry their curse to others—this war will be long and hard. But the end is suffering in those who faithful serve the cause of European and world freedom. A day will dawn, perhaps sooner than we now have a right to hope, when the insane attempt to found a Prussian domination on racial hatred, on the armoured vehicle, on the secret police, on the alien overseer, and on the still more filthy Quislings, will pass like a monstrous dream. And in that morning of hope and freedom, not only the embattled and at last well-armed Democracies, but all that is noble and fearless in the New World as well as in the Old, will salute the rise of Poland to be a nation once again.[30]

5

Attempt to Implement Strategic Goals, June 1941–Late 1943

Germany Invades the Soviet Union and the International Equation Is Changed

The German invasion of the Soviet Union (June 22, 1941) changed the whole political and strategic situation in the world. Overnight one of the partitioning powers of Poland became an ally of the West. Communists and their sympathizers who had been lying low, or had in many instances espoused the Stalinist position of condemning the capitalist war, were now vociferous patriots and advocates of the anti-Nazi war. The background was best stated by Churchill, who wrote after the war:

> Up to the moment when the Soviet Government was set upon by Hitler they seemed to care for nobody but themselves. Afterwards this mood naturally became more marked. Hitherto they had watched with stony composure the destruction of the front in France in 1940, and our vain efforts in 1941 to create a front in the Balkans. They had given important economic aid to Nazi Germany and had helped them in more minor ways. Now, having been deceived and taken by surprise, they were themselves under the flaming German sword. Their first impulse and lasting policy was to demand all possible succor from Great Britain and her Empire, the possible partition of which between Stalin and Hitler had for the last eight months beguiled Soviet minds from the progress of German concentrations in the East. They did not hesitate to appeal in urgent and strident terms to harassed and struggling Britain to send them the munitions on which we were counting, above all, even in the sum-

mer of 1941 they clamored for British landings in Europe, regardless of risk and cost, to establish a second front. The British communists, who had hitherto done their worst which was not much, in our factories, and had denounced the "capitalist and imperialist war" turned about again overnight and began to scrawl the slogan, "Second Front Now", upon the walls and hoardings.[1]

This citation gives the perspective to the events as they were but regrettably Churchill only wrote and articulated these views well after the war, and after the so-called iron curtain had fallen over Europe. In these wartime years, few dared to make such comments.

But it has to be clear that the purpose of the Polish strategy was not just fighting the Germans, but as Sikorski wrote Anders before his accident, the development of sufficient military force to preserve Polish Government authority in a Poland free of the Germans. While the Poles did not shirk spilling their blood on fighting the Germans, the strategic goal was to ensure that the questions of Poland and its boundaries and political system would be in the hands of the Polish Government in London, its duly appointed representatives in occupied Poland, or within the jurisdiction of the Western democratic Allies, which until December 1941 was exclusively Britain. With each passing year, the inevitability of having to confront or to accommodate the Soviets became a political dilemma.

For that purpose the Poles planned to move their air squadrons to Poland and to strengthen the fighting capacity of their Home Army. To ensure both, more supplies and trained staff had to be parachuted to Poland. To effect the transfer a Polish special duties squadron, under Polish control, was imperative. Therefore the Poles continued to use all their accumulated goodwill and their persistence to press the need for more aircraft for Poland and specifically more and more suitable aircraft assigned to the Polish flight, which also entailed more Polish crews being removed from bomber operations. But in much of this long-range planning the Poles were confronted by the acute shortage of men, of suitable long-range planes, and stymied by the political dilemmas of the new Soviet ally and their mass media adulation.

The Poles who had been Allied heroes now became progressively portrayed in the liberal press as romantic visionaries lacking political realism, feudal and reactionary landlords who failed to appreciate the benevolence and generosity of the Soviets.

The most immediate bone of contention was the question of the Polish prisoners in the Soviet Union, both military who were captured in 1939 and the many hundreds of thousands of civilians who were arrested and in horrible circumstances transported as of old Tsarist days to hard labor in the many Soviet gulags. But a close second problem was the question of the legitimacy of the Polish-Soviet boundary that had been settled in the Riga Treaty. Churchill wrote:

> The British Government were in a dilemma from the beginning. We had gone to war with Germany as the direct result of our guarantee to Poland. We had a strong obligation to support the interest of our first ally. At this stage in the struggle we could not admit the legality of the Russian occupation of Polish territory in 1939. In the summer of 1941, less than two weeks after the appearance of Russia on our side in the struggle against Germany, we could not force our new and sorely threatened ally to abandon, even on paper, regions on her frontiers which she had regarded for generations as vital to her security. There was no way out.[2]

In Poland the Zionists set up a Jewish fighting organization. As Kurzman writes, "this call for resistance was echoed (now) by the Polish communist party."[3] This now led to the formation of a third separate clandestine guerrilla group, one which not only did not collaborate with the official underground agencies, but which with time became a Trojan Horse for the new enemy.

As a result of the discussion held in London between General Sikorski and the Soviet Ambassador to Britain, Mr. Maiski, a political agreement was signed on July 30, 1941, which stipulated that all previous Soviet-German agreements concerning the partition of Poland had lost their validity and were null and void; that the Polish Government and the Soviet Union would reestablish diplomatic relations; and finally that a Polish Army would be formed on Soviet territory. The recruits for this army would come from the many hundreds of thousands of Poles who had been arrested in Poland by the occupying Soviet authorities and who had been exiled to Soviet concentration labor camps. After some negotiating the Soviets accepted the categorical position of the Polish Prime Minister that such an army would be responsible only to the Polish Government in London and would be officered by personnel appointed by the Polish authorities. The analogy was to the status of the Polish forces in the United Kingdom and as had been the case for the Polish Army in France in 1939–1940. The Polish Government also agreed that Polish units once formed would be placed under Soviet operational command, again as was the case for the Polish forces in the United Kingdom.

There were a number of points that were contentious and were not settled, particularly issues of boundary and of the citizenship of Poles. The Soviets took the position that since there were elections in Poland (under Soviet control), and since the results of the vote were the usual and exemplary Soviet 99.9% majority to accede to the Soviet Union, then only Polish nationals and only by a special dispensation of the Soviet Presidium would be allowed to join the Polish Army. To add insult to injury the Soviets offered to give Polish nationals an "amnesty" prior to their release but only after the Soviet authorities were satisfied of their Polish nationality! This determination was to be made by Soviet bureaucrats whose attitude to Poles varied from benign indifference to outright hostility.

Sikorski found himself isolated in the Polish Government. Driven by his vision that the Polish forces had to be strengthened, pragmatic enough to see that his negotiating options were not unlimited, and saddened by the plight of the Poles in the Soviet Union, he sought British help in guaranteeing the Polish rights vis-à-vis the Soviet Union. The British at best did not appreciate the Polish problem and many in British circles were distressed by what was seen as Polish obstruction to an Allied and anti-Hitler coalition. Also it has to be remembered that unfortunate and unjust as was the British attitude to Polish territorial questions, the British had always resisted any guarantee of the Polish-Soviet boundary and in fact had supported an ethnographic resolution to the Polish question. What the British failed to appreciate, or perhaps more fairly what did not concern them, was that their policy placed millions of non-Russians, such as Ukrainians, Poles, and Belorussians, in the Soviet Union.

Finally, after strong pressure from the British, Sikorski signed the agreement that became known as the Sikorski-Maiski Pact.[4] To assure himself of British support Sikorski requested a statement from the British Foreign Secretary on the boundary issue. Sir Anthony Eden in a House of Commons statement disavowed British approval of any changes in boundaries made after September 1, 1939. The positive impact of this position statement was immediately undercut by a clarification in a Parliamentary debate in which Sir Anthony Eden stated that Britain had never guaranteed any specific Polish boundary.[5] Three members of the Polish Government resigned as a protest against an agreement that they viewed as flawed and as damaging to Polish interests and the President of Poland refused to countersign the agreement. Thus from a purely Polish Constitutional aspect it was simply an agreement between two individuals.

It is ironic that once again Sikorski, who had always stood in opposition to prewar Polish authorities on the principle of the legitimacy of a democratic participatory and parliamentary rule, followed a course that took him away for whatever good and noble purpose from the established and constitutional principles of government. The three members of the Polish Government who resigned, Zaleski (the Minister for Foreign Affairs), General Sosnkowski (the President's nominated successor and Minister for Home Affairs), and Seyda (Justice Minister), were undoubtedly influenced by the historic perception and the argument of Poland's neighbors that the partitions of Poland in the eighteenth century were accepted by the last King of Poland and the Polish Sejm, thus the revisionist theory held that the partitions of Poland were not a heinous crime but a legitimate and Polish-sanctioned act of self-dismemberment. Such arguments ignored the reality of intimidation and coercion, a fact that impeaches any contract. Similar arguments would now be made for the so-called elections in Soviet-occupied Poland.

These three men and the President who refused to sign the agreement were determined that there would be no future interpretation of history to suggest that a legitimate Polish Government had yielded and agreed to a situation that seemed to be inevitably leading to the loss of territory and of the rights of Polish citizens.

The signing of the agreement allowed Sikorski to dispatch a military mission headed by General Zygmunt Szyszko-Bohusz to Moscow in August 1941.[6] The Polish representative proposed a draft of a military agreement based on the Polish-French military accords. One particular point was to bedevil future Polish-Soviet relations. It stated that Polish units "will operate in groups not smaller than division." It is important to add that a Soviet division was a much smaller unit than a division in the French or British Armies. As soon as Sikorski read the draft he urgently cabled a correction that nothing less than a Polish Army with full supporting services would enter combat operations. General Szyszko-Bohusz indeed made a written demarche to that effect and received a verbal statement from the Soviet representative that there was no discrepancy between the Polish position and the Soviet interpretation of the agreement, and that no written changes were necessary in the written accord.[7] Unfortunately, the Polish side did not insist on a written correction to the protocol and the possibility of a differing interpretation and the ambiguity was allowed to remain in place. In 1942 the Soviets requested that one of the Polish infantry divisions be shipped out to the front. The Poles refused, arguing that they would enter combat operations only as a complete and autonomous field army. The Soviets did not persist in their request, but in later times emphasized that the Poles had refused to aid their Soviet Allies and had refused to fight the Germans. Even responsible historians have bought into this self-serving Soviet interpretation.

General W. Sikorski nominated General W. Anders as the Polish Commanding Officer in the Soviet Union. Sikorski's choice of Anders also speaks volumes of Sikorski's continued obsession with the politics of the Polish past. General Anders had been the commanding officer of the Government forces that opposed Pilsudski in 1926. That was enough to make Sikorski choose Anders over men like Tokarzewski (liberated and amnestied) or Boruta-Spiechowicz. In retrospect this decision was unfortunate since Anders was one of the Soviet prisoners who had been badly treated by his Soviet captors. This experience could not have been without its consequences to Anders' attitude toward the Soviets. As a result, a very logical one, Anders distrusted all things Soviet and was in open opposition to Sikorski's plans for a collaborative relationship with them, since he just could not trust that the Soviets would ever honor their part of any agreement.[8]

The actual history of the formation, disposition, provisioning, and the final evacuation of the Polish Army in the Soviet Union is the keystone to the history of the Polish endeavor in World War II. It is a history of Polish aspirations, of Allied exploitation, of Soviet duplicity and, finally, of Polish tragedy. This review can only touch the surface of the significant facts, but the hypothesis is that to understand the seemingly contradictory issues that followed on each other in a relatively short period of time, the following facts were important. That the policies of the Polish Government and its representatives (General Anders) in the Soviet Union were not always identical and in fact at times were nearly contradictory. That the policy of the Soviet Union as symbolized by Stalin underwent a change between 1941 and 1942, after the Soviets successfully survived the winter of 1941/42. That the British had their own agenda for the use of Polish troops.

Soviet policy towards the Poles was not monolithic or rigid but undoubtedly Machiavellian and skillfully pragmatic. It was influenced by their long-range policies for Eastern Europe and tuned by their perception of their own military strength and their importance to the Western Allies. Their policies were aided by skillful propaganda and its success on the fertile ground of admiration for Soviet military heroism at a time when the Western Allies had only failures. The liberal left and those who looked to the Marxist philosophy as an answer to the problems of the world were enchanted.[9] As a result of this, the Soviet attitude toward the Polish Government became progressively more calculating and demanding. As Stalin realized that his behavior did not elicit any rebukes or negative consequences, but that it was the Poles who, opposing his policies, were condemned, Soviet policy became aggressive and brutally disdainful.

The Polish estimates were that between September 1939 and the invasion of the Soviet Union by the Germans in June 1941 over 1,000,000 Polish citizens had been deported to the Soviet Union. It was estimated that over 100,000 were prewar Polish reservists or active duty personnel, while 150,000 Polish citizens were thought to have been inducted into the Armed Forces of the Soviet Union. It was expected that nearly a 250,000 men might be available for service in the Polish Army. The British were only a trifle less optimistic; on November 9, 1941, the Chief of Imperial Staff noted: "It is believed that the total number of Poles who might eventually become available in Russia is 120,000–150,000." A memo dated November 19, 1941, goes on record as already planning the use of Polish troops in the Middle East.[10]

The reality was different. The Soviets initially claimed that there were only a mere 30,000 Polish citizens in the Soviet Union. They asserted that they had no knowledge of the whereabouts of the many thousands of Polish officers who had been captured in Eastern Poland in 1939, and whose existence in Soviet camps was documented by correspondence with their families through 1940. But that was not the only point to cause confusion, and the Soviets were not the only cause.

The attitude of the Poles released from Soviet camps was inimical to the Soviets. They had been arrested in their own country by an occupying force and transported in horrible conditions to an alien land where they had been forced to work in the most primitive conditions. They had seen their loved ones die of physical exhaustion and epidemic illness and were now being given an amnesty by their oppressors. There was a feeling of rage, resentment, and hostility to all things Soviet and understandable but injudicious hopes were often expressed that the Germans would overrun the Soviets and treat the Russians in the way that the Poles had been treated. The authors of *Destiny Can Wait* write as follows:

> Those Polish soldiers and airmen who were captured by the Russians during their invasion of Poland and later were in by far the worst plight. Escape was almsot impossible, and they were treated with such gross inhumanity that relatively few survived. The Polish internees in Romania, Hungary, Latvia, and Estonia were treated as soldiers. With some outstanding exceptions the Polish prisoners of war in the German oflags and stalags were dealt with according to the international conventions. But the Poles captured by the Russians were in the great majority of cases treated as political offenders— guilty of Polish patriotism, of holding Western ideas, of not being Communists, and so on. Most of them were sent to penal servitude in the Arctic tundra or in the sub-Arctic wastes of Siberia, where they laboured under such frightful treatment that the death rate was appalling.[11]

The Polish recruitment camps were just northeast of Stalingrad. The Soviets accepted the idea that two infantry divisions would be formed and Soviet equipped. By November 1941 there were about 40,000 men in those camps and it was noted that 60 percent of them did not have boots, while the food rations had been reduced to the original Soviet limit of 30,000 men. In addition to the Polish soldiers, numerous Polish women (wives, widows, and single) had gathered around these Polish oases in the land of communism. There were also hundreds of children. The Poles faced a winter of starvation, cold, and sickness since there was inadequate clothing and food and no medicines. In the background was the continued specter of the missing 10,000 Polish officers.

At this point General W. Sikorski made his decision to travel to the Soviet Union to inspect the Polish troops and meet with Stalin. On his way General Sikorski visited Tobruk, besieged by combined German and Italian forces, and visited the Polish Carpathian Brigade, which was part of the defensive garrison. This episode well illustrates the bravery and complete abnegation of personal concern and ability to tolerate considerable discomfort on the part of General Sikorski, who always thrived on contacts with the fighting man.

On December 3, 1941, Sikorski and Stalin met to discuss the overall political situation and the specifics of the Polish camps in the Soviet Union. Stalin made overtures to Sikorski to discuss the territorial dispute between Poland and the Soviets. Sikorski categorically refused to negotiate, holding firm to the idea that the Sikorski-Maiski agreement had declared all Soviet-German pacts as null and void and further discussions moot. On the other hand Sikorski demanded to know what had happened to his many officers missing in the Soviet Union and received the ingenuous reply that all Poles had been released and that the officers must have all escaped. Sikorski riposted, "to where?" The reply was, "to Mongolia." But the Polish Prime Minister and Commander-in-Chief was able to get a satisfactory outcome to the question of the top limit of the Polish Forces in the Soviet Union, which was now set at 96,000 officers and men (six infantry divisions). Sikorski also obtained Stalin's agreement to the evacuation of all Air Force personnel and those numbers necessary to bring the Polish Land Forces in the United Kingdom to strength (25,000 were agreed as the number to be evacuated), and to have Stalin relocate the Polish camps in the Asian provinces of the Uzbek Soviet Socialist Republic.[12]

This became known as the first evacuation but in reality the movement of men was a nearly continuous process and those who were designated to be transported in the first evacuation left with those who were being moved in the second or even third, the final evacuation.

Throughout this period continued acrimony persisted over a number of issues seen as having fundamental substance by the Poles but perceived as minor by the Western Allies. The Soviets refused to budge from their position that the plebiscite in Poland during their occupation had binding force and that all non-Polish nationals were Soviet citizens, and in fact that the Poles had been given a special and preferential treatment! Increasingly and with more persistence it was argued that the territories of Poland which had been their share of the partitions were legally Soviet. As Soviet military triumphs increased and were favorably compared to the paucity of military successes of the British, so did Soviet propaganda have increasing results, always at the cost of Polish interests.[13]

Yet, the visit had its positive aspects. The food portions were increased, camps were relocated, and there was an agreement that the number of Poles recruited would increase to 96,000. But the psychological gap could not be bridged. Poles despised all things communist; they hated the Russians and expressed their feelings openly. The overwhelming majority desperately wished to leave the Soviet Union and could not imagine any policy short of such complete evacuation. On the other hand, the Soviets were amazed by the behavior of the Poles, which contradicted their own ideological teaching and beliefs. Polish soldiers and officers had a trusting relationship. They attended Mass together, prayed in unison and exchanged military courtesies. Polish embassy officials traveled throughout the Soviet Union seeking out Polish families and attempting to give aid, moral as well as material, and were warmly received. In that brief period of time, 800 relief agencies were set up, 105 Polish schools, and 58 old people's homes. This was considerably different from the way the Soviet Government treated its citizens and contrary to what a capitalist society was supposed to do with the exploited worker. The Soviets must have begun to realize that there was no way this mass of people could be influenced to their way of life. Their very presence was a source of potential embarrassment to the Soviets.[14]

The history of the creation of the Polish Army in the Soviet Union and its eventual evacuation to the Middle East is beguiled by conflicting political and ideological interpretations and corrupted by the most base prevarication. It deserves a major treatment since the history of this short period mirrors and illustrates the conflicting hopes and realities of Polish relationships with the Soviet Union and also the British ally. The existence of a large pool of Polish manpower opened the possibilities of assuaging the desperate manpower shortages plaguing the Polish Forces in the United Kingdom. The new development created by the German invasion hinted at the possibility of a genuine rapprochement between Poland and the Soviet Union. It was also seen by the British as a reserve of potential manpower at a time when their resources were strained to the limit, particularly after the Japanese attack and ensuing loss of Singapore.

The history of the Polish Army in the Soviet Union is furthermore a reflection of Soviet views on the benefits of a Polish alliance and of the conflicting views of the members of the Polish Cabinet on the honesty of Soviet policies vis-à-vis Poland.[15] There were also very strong concerns among the Poles that the Soviet Union might be overrun by the Germans and that if Polish troops remained in the Soviet Union they would be lost as were the Polish divisions in France in 1940.

The War in the West Continued

But while the Poles were attempting to salvage their countrymen from the Soviet hell and also working to reconstruct an army and a viable foreign policy, the war in the west did not ameliorate. The British were now involved in two major struggles, against U-Boats and the disguised long-range armed raiders, which preyed on Allied ships, and the inherently flawed bomber offensive against German industrial targets. The U-Boat menace threatened the very existence of the British Isles, and Churchill wrote, "The only thing that ever really frightened me during the war was the U-Boat peril."[16] In both bloody and protracted struggles, the Poles took part.

The Battle of the Atlantic went on for the whole war but its crisis point was the summer of 1941 to the spring of 1943. In this pivotal struggle, the small Polish Navy took full part. The small destroyers, gallantly carried on the convoying, brutally treated by the weather, which in the winter was merciless. Sailors were washed overboard by mountainous Atlantic swells while structures were damaged. The gales, fogs, rain, cold and, in the northern reaches, the ice that formed on all deck fixtures and guns stressed the men to the breaking point. And then there were the German submarines and even long-range raiders and patrol planes. This was a battle where there was no glamour, no obvious victories but constant losses of men, ships, and of the priceless food and supplies. In early 1941 the Polish Navy was strengthened by two small escort destroyers of the British Hunt Class, named *Krakowiak* and the *Kujawiak*.

The Bomber offensive was also being carried on with all-out intensity. But the results were disappointing and even Churchill noted that "air photographs show how little damage was being done. It also appeared that the crews knew this and were discouraged by the poor results of so much hazard."[17] Sikorski had became aware of this bloodletting early in 1941 and was painfully conscious of the lack of reserves in the Polish Air Force. On February 1941 he initiated efforts to second experienced Polish crews for duty in supplying Poland. This was a difficult time to plan a new strategy given the realities of crew shortages in the Royal Air Force. The four Polish bomber squadrons were vital to the British effort. Sikorski wrote to Sir Charles Portal in the British Air Ministry, on July 22, 1941,

My Dear Sir Charles,

The Polish Air Force have of late been taking a considerable part in action and are the object of my particular concern. I would be very grateful if you shared my observations with regard to the Polish Bomber Squadrons. The Bomber Squadrons have as yet not attained their full strength. The average strength of a squadron is not more than 12 crews which is considerably below the establishment. During their long period of operational activity they suffered considerable losses and in spite of a great effort the 18th OTU is incapable of training a number of crews sufficient to replace the current losses and complete establishments. Numerically, the question appears as follows. Up to July 10th, the Polish Bomber Squadrons have performed 133 operation flights engaging 727 aircraft. The losses including killed, missing and wounded were 139 men. During the same period only 120 flying personnel were trained. In view of the difficulties and time required for training of bomber crews, I would suggest that the operational activity of the bomber squadrons should be diminished until their full establishments are completed. I will be very grateful to you for giving the matter your kind consideration.

Yours Very Sincerely, Sikorski[18]

Sir Charles Portal must have communicated with the Bomber Command Chief, Air Marshal Sir Richard Peirse, because on July 30, 1941, the later confirms the inadequate number of aircraft in the O.T.U but finishes with this point.

With regard to Sikorski's last point. I am very much averse to taking the Polish Squadrons off operations or attempting to reduce their present effort. Apart from the fact that we all want the operational effort we can get just now, it would have a depressing effect on the very keen Polish crews and in any case their new crews have to graduate through shorter and more simple operations.

There were at that time four operational Polish bomber squadrons, flying the two-engined Wellington bomber. The 18th O.T.U at Bramcote was a nearly all Polish operation. But it is touching to see the concern of the Royal Air Force Marshal about the possible depressing effect on the Polish crews were they not to be allowed to fly and lose their lives on the clearly flawed operations.

Sikorski acknowledged the letter but expressed his continued concern, stating: "I am aware of their keen fighting spirit which will never allow them to admit that they are worn out, especially at a moment when air operations are so important to the final issue of the war."

The British archives document a continued exchange of letters between Portal and Peirse, and the projection that by October 12, 1941, there will be another forty Polish crews available and Peirse's disagreement about the state of the Polish crews while admitting that "the casualties together with the failure of the Squadrons to raise their strength—they have in facted wasted—is having a depressing effect." Portal cuts through this semantic nonsense and writes that whatever is the correct name for the situation, "We all remember from the last war the enormous importance attached to the full breakfast table, and I really cannot wonder at general Sikorski becoming uneasy."

On August 31, 1941, the British Air Ministry communicated to Sikorski that pending further output of trained crews the Polish bomber effort will be reduced. The important part of this poorly known historical fact, one which both the Poles and the British have not publicized, is not merely the great effort of the Polish bomber crews, who spoke of themselves as "dead men on leave," but that it was in this context of the all-out bomber offensive that the Poles were trying to create their special duties flight for missions to Poland.[19]

The first Polish overture in the direction of developing a Polish-controlled capacity to airdrop supplies to Poland came in 1940, but the situation was complicated not merely by shortage of aircraft but by lack of suitable aircraft and by the fact that the G.O.C. Bomber Command had little sympathy with clandestine activities of any sort and was short of experienced crews for his bomber offensive.

The British never did develop a major air component for liaison with underground movements until the latest stages of the war. The air link with France was carried out by the old single-engined *Lysander*, which only required one pilot. This plane was being phased out of service with the reconstituted Army Air Cooperation Command. But with great perseverance, the Poles were able to second some veteran crews to the Royal Air Force Special Duties Squadron. Their experience is best described by the Polish Aide-Memoire to the Air Ministry in February 1942.

> The best men have been appointed and the best available aircraft, the Halifax, have been supplied for their job. These men, picked from Polish Bomber squadrons, have been attached to 138 Squadron where they have found themselves among strangers who are not in a position to appreciate their value.

The memoir bluntly stated that the British ground personnel were not responsive, that automatic pilots malfunctioned causing severe and unnecessary stress on flights, which often took over twelve hours. It stated that routine maintenance performed by British ground crews was inferior to that of Polish mechanics who served with exclusively Polish squadrons. It requested that three Halifax aircraft be exclusively at Polish disposal and that Polish mechanics be transferred to service the aircraft. It also expressed the hope that as soon as possible American Liberators would be made available. Finally it urged that a Polish flight be formed under Polish Command.[20]

The British had a different view of the problem and a memo to the Chief of Air Staff, dated February 2, 1942, identified the following causes for the difficulties:

> No. 138 Squadron comprises British, Polish, and Czech air crews. This arrangement adversely affects the general operational flexibility since the Squadron Commander is unable to make the maximum effort where it is most needed at any time. The Squadron, Station, Group and I myself consider that a much greater output would be possible if British crews only were employed. This mixture of nationalities has been felt none the less by the Poles themselves, but in view of their strong desire to have a separate unit the Polish Inspectorate have encouraged Polish crews in No. 138 Squadron to pay direct allegiance to and make direct contact with their own Headquarters rather than to consider themselves normal squadron crews. British crews in No. 138 Squadron have successfully completed operations on behalf of the Czechs, French, Norwegians, Dutch, Belgians and in Denmark. Although the Czeck crews have been in the Squadron, all successful Czech operations have been completed by British pilots. The same could readily be done for Poland if the Poles were willing. This would entail posting all foreign crews away from No. 138 Squadron to vacancies in normal Bomber Squadrons.
>
> The alternative of raising a Polish flight would be most uneconomical for the following reasons: (1) Flights to Poland are limited to the long hours of darkness i.e. about 5½ months of the year. (2) Owing to the rare occasions when flights to are possible in the winter months, there is a large wastage of man-power and aircraft potential if the crews and aircraft cannot be used for special operations in other European Countries.

The problem was that the Poles seconded to the R.A.F. 138 squadron complained that they were asked to fly long missions to

Norway and Austria but that flights to Poland were canceled. The R.A.F. officer who wrote this report also rebutted some Polish criticism. He pointed out that automatic pilots were a luxury not a necessity and that the flight to Poland of a Halifax without an automatic pilot took place at the most pressing insistence of the Polish H.Q. The memorandum also commented with some depreciation that "the Poles, unlike all other nationals whose operations are coordinated by SOE, retain under their control, certain detailed information of their operations until the actual day of the flight." This last-minute Polish briefing, in the words of the R.A.F. officer, "causes last minute lack of composure." However, it was left unsaid who was losing composure and Polish sources hint strongly that the British resented the last-minute briefing of Polish staff officers given to Polish crews. The report confirmed that the Halifax plane had a range limited to west of the Vistula.[21]

There must have been a fair amount of correspondence on this subject between the various British Ministries and undoubtedly demarche on the part of Sikorski with Dalton if not even with Portal and Churchill. The Poles did a find an ally in the Minister of Economic Warfare (Dalton), who on February 12, 1942, wrote to Sir Archibald Sinclair, Minister for Air:

I have for some time been on the point of taking up with you again the question of flights to Poland, but, as the whole problem of aircraft facilities for S.O.E. has been under active discussion between your officers and mine, I have not done so. Now, however, General Sikorski tells me that he has once again approached you directly on the Polish aspect of the questions. I, therefore, send my views on this subject, as my officers have, as you know, been very intimately concerned in these arrangements and have kept me constantly informed of their progress. I can appreciate quite clearly the Polish standpoint. Their case is that they were promised, early last year, that the winter of 1941/42 would see the establishment of regular flights from here to Poland in order to transport the staff officers, money and material so badly needed by their secret army at home to enable them to continue their struggle, which is paying a handsome dividend at present, against the Germans. Actually, this promise has only been fulfilled to the extent of three flights (all of which have been successful) in place of the minimum twelve which, after negotiations with your Ministry, they had been led, with reason, to expect. Equally I can understand the point of view of your officers, as explained to me by my own staff and by your A.C.A.S. (I). I realise the shortage of aircraft and I realise also that, not unreasonably your staff is unwilling to hand over, the entire conduct of such flights to the Poles, or to accept Polish interference in the operational arrangements of 138 Squadron (in which the Halifaxes used by the Polish flights are now incorporated), since they consider this a purely Air Force responsibility.

Dalton's recommendation and conclusion:

I feel the only solution of this most complex problem is to allow the Poles, within the limits imposed by you and by me, in our respective spheres to run their own show for a trial period, to see whether they can make a success of it. I cannot help feeling that, if we do not do this, both you and I will be badgered by the Poles, who will blame us for the ineffectiveness of our support, and, on the other, by your 138 Squadron, who will complain of the continual trouble that the Poles are creating within the squadron.

A solution which suggests itself to me is that, of the Halifaxes now on the strength of 138 Squadron since its recent increase, two or three should be set aside for the primary use of Poles and Czechs, and attached to a Halifax station. Reluctant as I am to place any limitation on the employment of the Halifaxes, I consider the relative value of the secret organization in Poland and Czechoslovakia is sufficiently great, compared with activities in other parts of Europe, to justify this allotment, the more so as I am assured by both governments that, if for any reason flights to Poland or Czechoslovakia are impossible, these aircraft and their allied crews would be made available for such long range flights to other countries as I may require.[22]

The Halifax was clearly not up to the job, and the Poles now pressed for taking delivery of the heavy four-engined Liberator from the United States.

Evacuations from the Soviet Union

In the Soviet Union during the spring of 1942, the situation was deteriorating. Malaria, hepatitis, and vitamin-deficiency diseases were so prevalent and the physical health of the men so poor that between April and August of 1942 over four thousand Polish soldiers died of debilitating disease. Thus 38.9 percent of all soldiers were unable to perform their duties because of sickness, and of that 38.9 percent a staggering 17.5 percent died. This was 10 percent of the total establishment, a loss which would not be even approximated by the most bloody battles, such as the storming of Monte Cassino and at Falaise. In addition to the hardships, the troops were concerned about the situation of their families, often also deported to the Soviet Union and still not reunited. Equipment was short of establishment since the three infantry divisions (Soviet style) only had 8,651 rifles and 16 artillery pieces for the 44,000 men.

It was in such circumstances that the Soviets made a request for the 5th Infantry Division to be sent to the front line. The request was refused on two grounds: (1) that the Polish-Soviet military convention precluded the use of Polish forces in an organization of less than an army strength; (2) that there was inadequate equipment and training to justify the Polish troops being sent into combat. The Soviets acquiesced but later used the Polish refusal as evidence of Polish unwillingness to fight.

By March 1942 the strength of the Polish Army in the Soviet Union reached about 67,500 officers and men. In addition to the military personnel there were thousands of Polish civilians living in the periphery of the Polish camps and existing on the food portions of the military. Thus when the Soviets cut the food portions to 26,000, starvation faced the Poles. At this time General Sikorski was on his second visit to the United States. General Anders protested the cut in food and requested and was granted a visit with Stalin. This was also the time of Churchill's first visit to Moscow. In addition to the talks between Stalin and Churchill and between Anders and Stalin, the Polish C.O. also met with Churchill and senior British generals.[23] Anders's meeting with Stalin resulted in a number of agreements that had far-reaching consequences. Polish minutes of this meeting comment on the courtesy shown Anders by Stalin, who excused the situation as being outside of his control since the Japanese were now at war with the United States, and American shipping could not sail to the Soviet ports in the Pacific, while Soviet tonnage was limited.[24] Stalin did agree to raise the number of Polish food rations to 44,000 and gave Anders permission to evacuate the balance to the Middle East. But the other side of the coin was that the strength of the Polish Army was now fixed at 44,000 and all new recruitment was stopped after Churchill was safely on his way. The Soviet position was that Anders was at full strength. While the decision was greeted with joy by many Poles still in the Soviet Union, the stark reality was that Stalin made an administrative decision regarding Polish forces without consulting the Polish Government, but presumably after obtaining Churchill's approval. This led to what became known as the second evacuation.

Churchill, who must have been involved in the outcome of the discussions, cabled Sikorski in the United States that the balance of the Poles should be evacuated to Palestine. Churchill thus solicited Sikorski's agreement and consent to the proposition that all Polish troops remain in the Middle East and only small numbers of indispensable replacement be transported to the United Kingdom. Sikorski replied that a minimum of 14,000 were needed to address the needs of the Armored Division, the Parachute Brigade and the Air and Naval Forces.[25]

Planning Conference, London, April 1942

In April 1942 General Sikorski called a meeting of the senior Polish military advisors in London to discuss the future structure and disposition of the Polish Armed Forces. The most important senior officers were Lt. General Wladyslaw Anders, who flew in from the Soviet Union; Lt. General Jozef Zajac (G.O.C. Polish Forces, Middle East); Lt. General Marian Kukiel (G.O.C. First Polish Army Corps in Scotland); Major General Tadeusz Klimecki (Chief of Staff); Major General Stanislaw Ujejski (Inspector General of the Air Force); and Admiral Jerzy Swirski (Commandant of the Polish Navy). In addition a number of other senior generals also attended, including Major General Stanislaw Sosabowski (G.O.C. Polish Parachute Brigade) and Major General Stanislaw Kopanski (G.O.C. Polish Carpathian Division, which had been moved from Libya to Palestine and was being fleshed out to a division size by increments from the Soviet Union).

The agenda was the future growth and distribution of the Polish Armed Forces. The actual conference took two days and was punctuated by a meeting of Sikorski with Churchill and his advisors. General Kukiel and the Polish Chief of Staff both argued that as much as possible all Polish troops should be concentrated in the United Kingdom. General Ujejski strongly argued the need for more replacements for his bloodied squadrons and concurred that the United Kingdom offered the best location for such training. General Anders urged, and was supported by Zajac, that all Poles should be concentrated in the Middle East, including the Air Force, since it was the Balkan route that offered the Poles the best and quickest route to their homeland. This option also allowed the easiest return to the Soviet Union if the political developments became propitious. Sikorski dismissed the second option and offered his own option, which was probably a compromise between his political and diplomatic hopes for continued cooperation with the Soviets and the reality of the recent Churchillian message about shortage of transportation. He supported the transfer of about 14,000 men to the United Kingdom, and expressed his hope to have a Polish Army in the Soviet Union, as well as a corps in the Middle East. General Kukiel argued (in fact, predicted) that it would be from the United Kingdom that the invasion of Europe would be undertaken and that it behooved the Poles to be at the focus of military operations and not at the side line. Anders countered the argument by stating that to move Polish troops to the United Kingdom would guarantee that the Soviets would stop all further recruitment to the Polish Forces. (The Soviets stopped all such recruitment anyway and Anders was aware of that by the time of the London meeting.) After meeting with Churchill and other British leaders, Sikorski reworked his proposal and now requested only 8,000 men for transfer to the United Kingdom. The proposed allocation of 5,500 to the First Army Corps in Scotland, 1,500 to the Air Force and 1,000 to the Navy was pitifully small and quite inadequate. Admiral Swirski stated that such a small increment would not allow him to commission two new fleet destroyers that the British had offered. General Ujejski argued that a minimum of 4,000 men of good health and education were required just to support the current needs of the Polish Air Force, to say nothing of future growth. He further advised that for the Polish Air Force to develop into an autonomous and independent air arm would require 30,000 men.

Further discussion became concrete, namely the o. de b. of the First Polish Army Corps and of the Polish Parachute Brigade.

Two options were offered: (1) a Corps of one armored division (consisting of a brigade of tanks and one of infantry) plus supporting services; (2) an armored division plus a brigade of infantry. Both options included the development of the Parachute Brigade. The increment of 5,500 met neither option, but the second option was even less practical. The final recommendation was that the increment would be added to the existing major units of the First Polish Army Corps: The First Infantry Brigade, the 10th Motorized Cavalry Brigade, and the 6th Armored (renamed from Tank Brigade).

After further debate a decision was also made that the Parachute Brigade would be fleshed out to become an autonomous fighting unit, though an argument had been made to keep it as a cadre training unit for specialized liaison with Poland. The conference also recommended that the Carpathian Division in the Middle East be enlarged to three brigades with extra supporting services so that it would become the nucleus of a corps.

Most Polish plans were thwarted by both the continued lack of manpower and British unwillingness or inability to provide shipping. The reality was that in the spring of 1942 the British were desperately short of transport ships and of manpower but were able to find the means to ship Australians back to Australia. It is also a fact that the two Polish transports working with the British (M.S. *Batory* and M.S. *Sobieski*) had the potential to transport about five thousand men between them on each mission. The Poles could have made an argument that Polish ships were aiding the Allied cause and hence should be available for missions that enhanced Polish policies. In fact, a year later the Polish 2 Army Corps was partially moved from Egypt to Italy on Polish ships. The fundamental fact that dictated the ultimate Polish dispositions was British shortage of personnel in the Middle East, and their reluctance to move divisions based in the United Kingdom that were intended for the eventual invasion of the continent.

When the future of the Parachute Brigade was brought up for discussion, General Gustaw Paszkiewicz, G.O.C. Third Infantry Brigade Group in Scotland, uttered the prophetic words that if the Brigade were brought up to full strength, the British would use it for their own purposes. He furthermore suggested that it was better to leave it a strength of about 400 officers and 300 other rank to serve as a cadre unit for courier and clandestine operations in Poland. In turn, Major General Stanislaw Sosabowski replied that a cadre unit did not represent a combat-efficient unit and added that were men to be found, the English would undoubtedly provide the equipment. Again, ironically prophetic, the final decision reached by Sikorski was to develop the unit to full strength by transfer of men from the Middle East out of the Soviet Union.[26]

On May 1, 1942, Sikorski thus articulated Polish military goals in his instructions to Lt. General Wladyslaw Anders, the Polish G.O.C. in the Soviet Union.

> There are three factors on the Allied side which will be decisive for the final outcome of the war. They are:
> 1. Soviet Armed Forces.

2. Allied Armed Forces (in particular those of Great Britain and the United States, and at their side, a portion of the Polish Armed Forces).

3. The subjugated countries of Europe.

Sikorski outlined a rather optimistic view of the Polish case in the eyes of the Western Powers, but did articulate his policy quite well:

> Our war effort, carried on unceasingly and with increased intensity, has but one aim: Poland, Poland only, a Poland which might be sounder, safer and stronger that the Poland which so resolutely started to fight against the barbarian aggression of our secular enemy.

Sikorski then allowed himself some petty remarks directed at the pre-1939 Polish leadership and went on to:

> Our present position is infinitely better. However, let us not forget at what cost it has been achieved, by Polish blood, suffering and labour. Which is the shortest way to Poland? From Russia, the Middle East or Great Britain? Nobody can answer this now. However, what matters most is that at least a portion of the Polish Armed Forces, staying outside Poland, should reinforce the Home Army with modern weapons, in order that the latter may become a center of order and authority and enable us, in the most efficient way, to take hold of East Prussia, Gdansk and the German part of Upper Silesia, removing the Germans from those provinces. In this decisive historical moment only accomplished facts will count.
>
> The Polish Armed Forces must be posted on the existing and future war fronts in such a way that they would be able to, in any case, to reach Poland within the shortest possible time. We do not refuse to allow participation of Polish Armed Forces in the war.
>
> On the contrary. Heretofore, the Polish soldiers have fought on all the war fronts. However, I have neither the right nor the intention to risk a concentration of the whole or a major part of the Polish Armed Forces on one theater of war, where a possible misfortune could bring about their excessive, if not complete, destruction.[27]

Sikorski was undoubtedly still cognizant of the attempt to dismiss him from his premiership after the fiasco of the French Campaign, in which his emotional, but hardly realistic or statesmanlike faith in the French ally led to the loss of the majority of the Polish

combat divisions. In his very long instructions to Anders, the Polish
C-in-C and Premier touched on many general, specific, political,
and organizational matters. The theme was one of entreaty to Anders and his men to hang tough in the very difficult and cruel envi-
ronment of the Soviet Union. While Sikorski was attempting to
formulate Polish goals, Churchill and his military advisors were
hard at work in springing the Poles from a very accommodating
obliging Stalin. The British shortage, bordering on desperate in the
Middle East, is evident from the communication of June 22, 1942,
between Major General Regulski to the Polish Chief of Staff, Major
Klimecki in London:

> The War Office has inquired of me several times what has hap-
> pened about the further evacuation of our troops from the USSR to
> Palestine; it appears, beyond any doubt, from these enquiries, that
> the English are greatly interested in the further stage of this evacua-
> tion and that they are anxious for it being speeded up.[28]

What deserves emphasis from the instructions to Anders is that
Sikorski clearly looks ahead to the struggle in Poland where the
Polish Forces will become a "a center of order and authority." Sikorski in his discourse states that in the United Kingdom certain
combat units will be formed including, "one Parachute Brigade as
an advance guard to Poland." There is a very old Polish proverb,
"man proposes but God disposes," and in this instance the British
were the ultimate disposers of Polish fortunes. Sikorski plans for a
Polish Army to be left in the Soviet Union were thwarted by the
bitterness of the Poles in the Soviet Union and British guile in engineering the evacuation from a very obliging and accommodating
Stalin. Politically the Polish Government was still committed to a
policy of having a Polish Army in the Soviet Union, and even as
late as May 1942 Sikorski cabled General Anders instructions and
the Polish Government's express wishes. The following quotes are
particularly relevant:

> I strongly desire that you should grasp my intentions regarding
> the Polish Armed Forces, and because of that I am briefly summing
> up my views in writing, to enable you to see my opinions on the
> general military situation and the plans for the organization, dispo-
> sition and use of the Polish Armed Forces arising from it.
> I have full understanding of the feelings of the soliders in Russia
> under your command, General, especially after the last evacuation. I

appeal, nevertheless, to their patriotism and their trained will, which has so well stood the test. They should remain in absolute discipline in a post so important for Poland.

General Sikorski enclosed an official message from the Polish Government which stated:

> The Polish Cabinet reaffirms that it would be in accordance with Polish interests and with the policy that found expression in the Agreement concluded with the Soviet Government of 30 July 1941 to leave on Soviet territory part of the Polish Armed Forces which would subsequently fight on the Eastern front side by side with the Soviet Army.[29]

That was the official position of the Polish Government, of the Polish C-in-C, but it was undermined by the British and eroded by the feelings of the Poles in the Soviet Union. They just wanted out of the Soviet Union and grasped at any excuse to get out, and were aided and abetted by the Soviets, who also wanted the Poles out.

However, the British were short of troops and were faced with tremendous problems in the Middle East. The final decision about the evacuation was made by Churchill and Stalin, which completely bypassed the Polish Constitutional Government in London. On July 17, 1942, Churchill wrote to Stalin about the difficulties in the North Atlantic and Arctic Sea convoys and the need to beat Rommell in North Africa. He then referred to the Polish forces still in the Soviet Union:

> I am sure it would be in our common interest, Premier Stalin, to have the three divisions of Poles you so kindly offered join their compatriots in Palestine, where we can arm them fully. These would play a most important part in future fighting, as well as keeping the Turks in good heart by the sense of growing numbers to the southward. Hope this project of yours, which we greatly value, will not fall to the ground on account of the Poles wanting to bring with the troops a considerable mass of their women and children, who are largely dependent on the rations of the Polish soldiers. The feeding of these dependents will be a considerable burden to us. We think it well worthwhile bearing that burden for the sake of forming this Polish army, which will be used faithfully for our common advantage. We are very hard up for food ourselves in the Levant area but there is enough in India if we can bring it from there. If we do not get the Poles, we should have to fill their places by drawing on the

preparations now going forward on a vast scale for the Anglo-American mass invasion of the continent.[30]

This offer was most likely made by Molotov to Churchill while the Russian Commissar was in London in July 1942. It is very obvious that Stalin was happy to do Mr. Churchill this favor. The need of the British for troops in that region can be better understood if it is kept in mind that on February 15, 1942, the Japanese captured Singapore, which Churchill described as "the worst disaster and capitulation in British history." The British victory at El Alamein only took place in October 1942. The final evacuation of all Polish forces from the Soviet Union occurred in August 1942. It highlighted the fact that Churchill and Stalin disposed of Polish troops with some possibly ingenuous complicity on the part of General Anders. It did, however, build a legend of Anders as a man who saved 112,000 men, women, and children from Soviet extermination and made Anders more than just a senior general, but a man who led an exodus.[31]

The Soviets, in their message to General Anders authorizing the evacuation and offering their assistance in the transport of Poles (arranged in the most expeditious manner), stated that they were granting the Polish Commander's request to evacuate from the Soviet Union. The Soviet position has insisted that the Poles wished to leave because of their unwillingness to fight the Germans.

The British were still faced with the possibility of a German breakthrough into the north Iraq oil producing region, either from Turkey or from the Soviet Caucasus; and General Wilson, the British Commander of PAIFORC, was delighted to place the Polish forces in a region where they could add military muscle to his defense as well as to begin the retraining with British equipment. Churchill wrote,

> The Levant-Caspian front is almost bare. If General Auchinleck wins the Battle of Egypt we could no doubt build up a force of perhaps eight divisions which with the four Polish divisions when trained, would play a strong part in delaying a German southward advance.[32]

Many commentators have criticized General Anders for being a political figure. The situation and the circumstances place him in that role. Photographs of General Anders show him with Premier Stalin, King George VI, Prime Minister Churchill, Mr. Eden, and

General Patton. This is not the kind of attention that is normally lavished on a corps commander, however brave and distinguished, which General Anders undoubtedly was.[33]

New problems arose after arrival in the Middle East between Polish plans for an army and the more realistic British assessment of Polish potential. The British proposal was that out of the numerous forces being evacuated and already in place in Palestine a corps of two infantry divisions and a brigade of tanks be created. (This in reality was what eventually materialized in December 1943.) General Sikorski strongly opposed this plan and wished to have a far more ambitious development of two infantry corps (each consisting of two divisions) plus a brigade of tanks. Each of the corps was to have a heavy artillery regiment, antitank regiments and aircraft artillery, a reconnaissance regiment, a battalion of heavy machine guns, communications, military police, and engineers for a total of 55,000 officers and men. The reality was that the Poles had a lot of men who were just not fit for military service since their hardships caused chronic health problems and since the Soviets had selectively released only the elderly from their work battalions. That available manpower eroded to barely 45,000 officers and men. General Sikorski's hopes were thwarted.

General Klimecki, the Polish Chief of Staff, in August 1942 traveled to Cairo to meet with General Alexander and General Nathan Wilson. It would be tiresome to elaborate all the various proposals and counter-proposals that were made and studied and dismissed either by the British or the Polish side. The British staffs, for logistical reasons, wanted the Poles to be modeled exactly on the British establishment, while the Poles wanted to project as large a force as possible.

The British argued that the Poles lacked not only the requisite manpower but even the numbers of skilled men for such an ambitious undertaking. Churchill minuted the following memorandum to General Ismay and broke through the impasse.

> I regard the equipment of the Polish Corps as of first importance and urgency in view of the cannibalisation of British divisions and the withdarawal of the Australians and South Africans from the Eighth Army. Let a scheme be prepared showing dates by which the various divisions can be equipped with rifles, 25-pounders, anti-tank and anti-aircraft mortars and machine guns, and Bren gun carriers; also tanks. It is not necessary to adhere to exactly British standards. These can be attained later. Let me have the earliest dates when

these fine troops will have the minimum equipment to acquire substantial fighting value. Let me have forecasts for January 31, February 28, March 21.[34]

Generally, however, equipment and food were available, and health improved; and in spite of the at times rigorous nature of the country in which the Poles were based and to which they were not acclimatized, training proceeded well. In 1943, when General Patton visited the Polish troops, he described them as "the best looking troops, including the British and American, that I have ever seen."[35]

Parachute Brigade and Its Ultimate Goal

The Poles treasured their Parachute Brigade and placed hopes on its future role, way beyond its potential let alone actual capabilities. The also continued to press the British for an ultimate commitment to facilitating air transport to Poland. The Parachute Brigade was to be the vanguard for Poland. At the same time, the Polish Commander-in-Chief hoped to have the First Polish Army Corps in Scotland used as a major Polish contribution in the foreseen operations in Northwest Europe. The British were more realistic and did not see how the shortage of personnel could be undone to allow the Poles to play their part.

In August 21, 1942, the British accepted the cadre unit as a full-fledged parachute brigade and placed it under Lieutenant-General Frederick Browning, the commanding general of the British Airborne Corps. In September 1942 the first contingent of 300 Poles arrived from the Soviet Union. Further increments followed, including some of the men from the Third Infantry Brigade Group who had already received parachute training.

The Polish High Command was adamant about the ultimate mission of the unit. In a letter to General Sir Bernard Paget, Sikorski wrote:

> With reference to our correspondence of August 21, 1942, concerning the organization of the Polish Army in Great Britain, I would like to inform you that having thoroughly considered on the spot both our needs and our potentials, I believe that a number of alterations should be introduced into the plan of organization of our Army Corps. At the outset I wish to confirm the main and accepted points: 1) Employment of the Polish units in offensive actions in the Conti-

nent. 2) Stipulate that the Parachute Brigade only be used for liaison with Poland and for support of an armed movement in Poland.[36]

In their quarterly progress reports on Allied Forces in the United Kingdom, the British followed the progress of this unit. Their comments were very laudatory.

> September 30, 1941. The Poles have for some time been working at preliminary instruction and exercises for the parachute unit which they hope to train. They have their own training ground and are competent to make a very show of it.
>
> June 30, 1942. Parachutists were dropped from Whitley Bombers on the rear of a system of beach defenses which were holding up an imaginary sea landing. A wind of 30–40 mph was blowing at the time, and the fact that there were no casualties among the men dropped, testifies to the excellence of their preliminary training.
>
> September 30, 1943. The Polish Parachute Brigade organized in four battalions with supporting arms has been reinforced and is now composed of the best material and is about 2,500 men strong. It is reserved in the hands of the Polish Commander-in-Chief for operations in Poland.[37]

By and large all Allied Quarterly reports on Polish units—air, naval, or land—were positive, though the comments on the Para chute Brigade are particularly glowing. Such was not the case for all of the other Allied countries' armed forces. These were not mass media–release tidbits but critical staff assessments of the functioning of the units.

While the British praised the accomplishments of the Polish Parachute Brigade and acknowledged its ultimate goal, "reserved for operations in Poland," there is evidence that as early as May 1942 they considered this to be impossible. There is a draft of a memo to have been sent to General Sikorski, but no evidence in the British or Polish archives that it was delivered.

> We have been reluctantly forced to the conclusion that the physical problem of transporting materials for secret armies in Eastern Europe is insuperable. I hope, however, that in September [1942] it will be possible to resume on an increasing scale, the dropping of a limited number of personnel (Staff officers for the secret Army and Air Force) and stores for diversionary activities. The Chiefs of Staff

are fully alive to your desire that preparation should be made for a Polish airborne force to be despatched to Poland when a general rising takes place. This question has been fully considered and the conclusion has been reached, with regret, that the despatch of such a force is not a practical possibility in the foreseeable future, bearing in mind, amongst other factors, the long distance involved and the severe shortage of suitable aircraft and gliders.[38]

In August 1942 General Sikorski, still eager to have at least a Polish Armored Division in the forthcoming operations in northwest Europe, sent the following message to Sir Bernard Paget, the British Commander Home Forces, from his field quarters in Gask, Scotland:

> Having examined on the spot both our needs and our possibilities, I believe that a number of alterations should be introduced into the plan of organization of our Army Corps. At the outset I wish to confirm the main and accepted points: employment of Polish units in offensive action on the continent; stipulation to use the Parachute Brigade only for liaison with Poland and for supporting an armed movement in the continent from reserves of personnel existing over there—as shown in the letter to Lord Selvorne, No. 4685/XIV/2/42, dated 25.8.42. Consequently, in fulfillment of these principles it is my intention to bring into battle on the continent the whole of the Polish Corps as an operational formation under its own command.[39]

Sikorski developed this point further, spelling out in detail the current numbers of military personnel being transported to the United Kingdom and addressed various details. It is obvious that the British had not absolutely agreed to the inclusion of the Polish First Army Corps in operations on the continent. But that possibility was also not excluded as later correspondence suggests. They certainly accepted the existence of the First Army Corps as an administrative entity. Sikorski also spelled out that the personnel on the continent would come from the Poles still living in France and that De Gaulle had agreed to the Poles recruiting in France. There were also many thousands of Poles interned in Switzerland since the whole of the Second Infantry Division had crossed the Swiss boundary in June 1940 from France after the French armistice. Finally Sikorski again argued that the Parachute Brigade would guarantee the support of an insurrection in Poland. This point was accepted by the British though the question of how the Parachute Brigade would be transported to Poland was never clarified.

Silent and Unseen

It was from the ranks of the 4th Cadre Brigade that many of the first "Silent and Unseen" (*Cichociemni*) officers were recruited for parachuting to Poland. But in addition many other junior and even very senior officers (including generals) were recruited from many different branches of the Polish Armed Forces. They were hand picked with the primary purpose of enhancing the administrative, technical, and staff work of the Polish Secret Army, the Home Army, and in a number of isolated instances to actually lead combat units of the Home Army. In this later group were officers seconded to the operation called *Wachlarz*, which was an attempt to demonstrate to the British ally that the Poles were capable of organizing active sabotage behind the German front lines on behalf of the Soviet Union. This was a high-visibility political demonstration.

The kernel of *Wachlarz* occurred on September 29, 1941, when Sikorski requested two sections of his General Staff, the III and VI, to begin preparing extensive plans for active intervention on behalf of the Soviet Union. In October 1941 the Soviet General, Zukow, representing the Soviet General Staff, arrived in London for talks with the British but also met with Polish Staff around issues of Polish anti-German sabotage on behalf of the Soviets. To actualize such a major diversionary activity Polish Headquarters in London decided that officers from the UK, cognizant and sympathetic to the policy aims of the Polish Government, needed to be placed in command. Approximately half of the officers in command of this operation, which extended over thousands of square miles in the hinterlands of pre-1939 Poland and extended east into Belorussian, Lithuanian, and Ukrainian territories, came from the ranks of *cichociemni*. There were no Polish indigenous populations to act as a base of material or moral support for these units.

Wachlarz operated throughout 1942 and early 1943 with somewhat disappointing results. Some of it was the lack of sufficient war material, which was partially due to the necessity of moving all supplies from central Poland through German occupied and controlled territory. Also, the initial blush of Soviet collaboration in this effort quickly evaporated because it became more important to the Soviets to emphasize the Soviet nature of the marchlands. The G.O.C. A.K. telegraphed the Polish London Headquarters on February 11, 1943 (that is after the German defeat at Stalingrad), that his organization would be able to carry out massive sabotage of

German rail and communication links in areas behind the German front lines. This was in part a response to Sikorski's requests that the Poles demonstrate their capability for such active sabotage. The offer was coupled with certain *desiderata,* such as increased drops of military equipment and the necessity of increasing the range of air operations to drops east of Wilno. This last was an impossible request due to the limitations of the planes available at the time. However, some of these proposals were based on the possibility that such airdrops could originate in the Soviet Union. On February 26, 1943, the Polish ambassador to Moscow, Mr. Tadeusz Romer, was called to see Stalin and in the all-night conference offered the Soviets a reactivation of the Polish diversionary activity behind German lines. It is not clear whether this was in any way coupled with a request to use Soviet air bases for the supply of necessary military supplies. The ideal situation would have been shuttle runs, with a small number of Polish planes dropping specialized equipment from British bases, landing in the Soviet Union, and on the way back dropping captured German equipment, which was in fact in standard use by the A.K. Stalin rejected the Polish proposal as placing the local population at too high a risk. In reality by this time the Soviets had caught their second breath and were developing their own clandestine activities in western Russia and even in the old pre-1939 Polish territories.[40]

By the end of the war a total of 2,412 officers and senior non-commissioned officers had volunteered for such service in Poland, and 579 were actually dropped.[41] Thus by planning or perhaps by pure chance the brigade became the only and sole parachute training unit for the Polish Army. But there were other skills that the *cichociemni* needed to learn. Sabotage and explosive training was provided at Inverlochy Castle; physical training at Garramowr; counterintelligence at Glasgow; communications at Dundee and Auchtertool and later Polmont. In later years, when the Polish Special Duty Flight moved to Italy, the training was done completely near Brindisi. This became known as Base 11 and its C.O. was Lt. Col. Ryszard Hancza.[42]

The life of a soldier in the Polish Underground was indeed a test of character. The Polish airman, soldier, or sailor, even in the heat of battle and of suffering, was surrounded by his comrades. He was commanded, he was fed, and if wounded he would be treated; if killed, he would be given a soldier's burial; if captured by and large he was treated correctly according to the Geneve conventions. The soldier of the A.K. was always on his own. He or she used a pseudonym, and even loved ones were kept in ignorance, though often suspected with pride the activities of their sons and daughters, husbands, wives, and parents. The organization was based on small concentric circles so that an arrest and a breach could be quickly localized. But treachery was always feared. The Polish underground counterintelligence services had relatively little problem identifying the so called volksdeutch, who after the German occupation of Poland claimed German ethnicity. But the highest titre of suspicion was attached to individual who were suspected of left-wing leanings. Foot wrote of the collaborators: "all over Europe they were the bane of honest men and women. Even in Norway there were some; even in Poland they were not abolutely unknown, though rare; in France they pullulated; in Holland there were more than enough."[43]

For the captured soldier of the A.K. a quick death was a blessing, an arrest and torture was dreaded by all for all. I list three short actual histories of the face of war under occupation. A senior officer in the A.K. was captured by the Germans and after a number of days was released. He then committed suicide. The inference is obvious. A young officer was suspected by the Polish counterintelligence agency and arrested by the Poles on the charge of collaborating with the Germans. He admitted that the Germans had broken his pseudonym, and were blackmailing him with threats against his aged mother. The terrible tragedy finished with an execution by the Poles of a young distraught man who had lost his bearing in the terrible war. The third story, not untypical, is that of an officer who was arrested by the Germans and resisted the tortures throughout the first day. On the second day, the Poles were able to smuggle in a bar of soap which had a cyanide pill and the order of Virtuti Militari.

By and large the Poles trusted each other, but few were able to resist the tortures and not spill out all they knew. Thus, the iron rule was never to say more to anyone than was necessary. Life was a jungle in which the individual walked on his own. To be wounded might mean to be abandoned, to be captured was worse than death. To be killed meant to be buried in a nameless grave with nobody even knowing of the fact, since all the soldiers used false names. The Germans reacted to the Polish clandestine groups with their typical efficiency. But in spite of all the street arrests, the torture and the intimidation the underground grew. The men who in the West volunteered for such service were indeed heroes.

Staff Work on Moving Polish Air Units to Poland

At the same time as the events were unfolding between Sikorski and Churchill, and between Sikorski and Anders and, more importantly for the Polish future, between Churchill and Stalin, the everyday of staffs went on. The main effort was directed at determining the manner in which the Poles could be moved to Poland and the manner in which the Polish Home Army could be assisted and also tied into the strategy of the Western Powers. The formal reply to the 1941 memorandum initiated by the C-in-C staff from the Polish Air Force Inspectorate was written by Lt. Col. Bohuszewicz on June 20, 1942. "Uwagi do Planu Wsparcia Powstania Przez Lotnictwo" (Comments to the Plan for Air Support of the Uprising).[44] Where the Staff of the C-in-C were basing their future options on the configuration of the most optimistic events, the Air Force Inspectorate was coldly realistic. Its report was short, and to the point. Firstly it pointed out that the Polish Air Force in the United Kingdom was in a diametrically different circumstances from the Polish Land Forces since it lacked its own autonomous administrative staffs and its logistical and quartermaster support services. It pointed out that the Agreement of 1940 was not merely unfortunate, it was disastrous for the long-term growth of the Polish Service since it placed it under R.A.F. operational control and that many prewar senior Polish air officers were in active combat service and could not be seconded to Polish staffs or to the re-created Polish Staff College without British permission, which in the circumstances the British were loath to grant given the exigencies of the bomber offensive. It was argued that the first step had to be a revision of the Agreement so that the Polish Air Force could develop its own staffs. It also stated that the Polish Government had to ask the United Kingdom for air transport assistance and, failing that, the Poles needed to resign from any plans to support the A.K. by air from the United Kingdom.

The Inspectorate also commented that the then current equipment of the Polish Squadrons did not lend itself for operations in Poland, since the Spitfire needed a long start and the light bombers required asphalt or concrete landing fields. The staff officer, with

great civil courage, concluded that the major problem that precluded realistic progress in most of these areas was the failure of
the Polish C-in-C to implement the directive of February 1942, for
securing an agreement of the British Air Ministry to support the
Polish Underground by the Polish Air Force. The memorandum
referred to the need to replenish the personnel of the bloodied Polish bomber squadrons, the imperative to form support units, and
concluded with a detailed analysis of the communication needs in
case Polish squadrons were moved to Poland. The problem of
communication was vital, and while the radio communication between "Polish" London and the Homeland was solved thanks to
some excellent work by Polish specialists, the problem of radio
communication between arriving planes and the ground (in Poland), and subsequently how to control combat squadrons within
Poland, was never completely solved. Failing the support of the
British ally to implement all Polish postulates, the Polish Home
Army Commander should be advised that there was no hope for
direct air assistance.

By the winter of 1942/43 regular flights to Poland were being
flown, but the Halifax was clearly not up to the job. The range was
limited and the engines tended to either overheat or in the winter
weather the plane experienced the nightmare of all crews—icing.
The Poles now embarked on a concerted effort to obtain American-
built long-range Liberators. In this venture, they were supported by
the British, albeit with the stipulation that any consignment of these
planes to the Poles should not come out of the British assignment.
Sikorski was looking for a total of twelve such long-range planes,
and the British stated that they would endorse the acquisition of six
such planes directly from the United States. There is an internal
memo dated June 23, 1942, which clarifies the British position. "We
should support the Poles in the acquisition of the six Liberators in
addition to our own allocation and that we should instruct our representative to emphasize to those American authorities the importance we attach to those Polish operations."[45]

At the same time the internal memorandum made it clear that
the Poles could not expect to get six Liberators and still keep their
six Halifaxes. On December 9, 1942, the British Chiefs of Staff were
alerted that the Poles had approached the Americans directly for
supply of Liberators. This was very much what had been proposed
by the British but the United States Chiefs of Staff turned down the
request for the following reasons:

cannot take action on this request without jeopardizing basic
agreements in which the U.S. and Great Britain have accepted definite responsibilities for the provision of aircraft within the various
theatres of operations. In accordance with these agreements Poland
is within a British theatre of operations and responsibility. In view of
the unfulfilled demands in its own theatres and areas of responsibility the U.S. has no Liberators available for additional commitments.
Your request therefore has been referred to the British COS for consideration in connection with possible allocation from British
sources.[46]

During that period of time there was a number of exchanges
between the British Air Ministry in London and their representatives in Washington at CCS (RAFDEL), as well as between the Poles
and the British. When the British realized that there would be no
planes for the Poles from the United States outside of their own allocation, then they urged that the matter be dropped. But on January 8, 1943, Roosevelt, after his talks with Sikorski, wrote directly to
Churchill and endorsed the Polish plan and suggested that the
planes be made available from the British allotment. His final paragraph is worth quoting:

> I feel, however, that his proposal [Sikorski] has a great deal of
> merit, and I told him, therefore, that I would refer the matter to you,
> with the request that you give it all possible consideration. It was my
> thought (which I did not, however, convey to him) that you might
> perhpas be able to spare him six out of the total of 398 B-24's allo-
> cated from U.S. production under the recent Arnold-Evill-McCain-
> Patterson agreement.[47]

This contact between Sikorski and Roosevelt took place during
the Polish leader's third and final visit to the United States in December 1942. In general, Sikorski's visit to the United States was an
abject failure, since little of substance was accomplished.

In the new Minister of Economic Warfare, Lord Selborne, the
Poles continued to find support for their strategic plans. Lord Selborne wrote a long memorandum to Sir Archibald Sinclair, Minister
for Air, first of all outlining the Polish Government's irritation and
then stating his position in a very sympathetic manner. This was
dated August 17, 1942.

> I should be very grateful if you could lend your personal help to
> clear up serious difficulties that have arisen between the Air Minis-

try and our Polish Allies. The cause of this friction is, I understand, twofold:

(1) The Air Ministry refuse to allow officers from Polish headquarters to accompany their operational parties to Tempsford aerodrome.
(2) The Air Ministry has refused to provide the Poles with three Polish crews to form a reserve for the three Halifax aircraft already manned by Polish personnel.

Lord Selborne continued:

The matter is really important, and very serious, because these very difficult dropping operations in Poland (which are playing a vital part in the attack on German communications) cannot be successfully accomplished unless there is complete mutual confidence between the R.A.F., S.O.E., and the Poles. I attach the greatest importance to this Polish work. During the last operational season the Polish crews were conspicuously successful and on one occasion only (which was partly our fault) failed to find the reception area. As communications between the reception committee and Polish G.H.Q. may go on until the last moment, we think the presence of a responsible Polish Staff officer at the time of emplaning is an operational necessity. Apart from this, the exclusion of these officers is a humiliation which the Poles can hardly be expected to accept in view of their contribution of fourteen squadrons now fighting with the R.A.F.

General Sikorski feels so strongly on the point that he has instructed his Chief of Staff to tell me that he cannot go on under present conditions.

In regard to the 100% reserve crews requested by the Poles, this also is supported by S.O.E. If we do lose a Polish crew on a trip, it would take a very long time to obtain and train another on in four-engined bomber work. If we were to lose two crews, we should be in a very bad way indeed.[48]

In spite of British official reluctance to become too involved in Polish clandestine affairs outside of intelligence gathering, in spite of the real difficulties associated with the long distances and shortages of suitable planes, flights were carried out, supplies, couriers as well as military personnel flown in.

Selborne refers in his aide de memoire of August 1942 to the fourteen Polish Squadrons. Four of these were fully committed to the bomber offensive. The acme of Polish Bomber operations occurred in 1942 and was commented on by the British Air Minister, Sir Archibald Sinclair, in his message to General Sikorski:

Polish crews to the number 101 took part in the large scale operations in Cologne and Ruhr. The Royal Air Force has learned to admire the valor, tenacity and efficiency of their Polish Allies. In these operations again they here show how admirable is their contribution in support of our common cause to the destruction of the war power of the enemy. We are grateful to you and to Poland for these redoubtable squadrons.[49]

Shortly after that all-out effort, a number of major changes took place. The 301 Squadron was disbanded and existed merely as a symbolic presence since the appellation was unofficially given to the Polish Special Duties Flight. The 304 Squadron was assigned in May 1942 to the Royal Air Coastal Command and began operations aimed at destroying German U-Boats. Finally, Squadron 305 was re-equipped with the two-engined Mosquito and assigned to the 2nd Tactical Command. This fantastic wood-built plane was an incremental advance in every respect, speed, endurance and bomb carrying capacity. It served the Royal Air Force as a bomber, pathfinder, reconnaissance, and even fighter plane. It fulfilled all roles without rivals. Even now when seen in the Royal Air Force Museum at Hendon, it looks as sleek as any modern jet.

The other Polish squadrons, with the exception of 307 (two-engined night fighter), were all single-engined day fighter units. The Poles had distinguished themselves in the Battle of Britain, but fought either as individual squadrons or in small twelve-plane squadrons. The Allied probe directed at testing German coastal defences in Dieppe gave the Polish Fighter units their next laurels. Five Polish Squadrons, 302 (*Poznanski*), 303 (*Kosziuszko*), 306 (*Torunski*), 308 (*Krakowski*), and, 317 (*Wilenski*) fought as one Polish commanded (Major Stefan Janus) operational wing. The commanding officers of 303, Zumbach, and 317, Skalski, together worked out a trap for the Germans. The 317 (*Wilenski*) squadron played the part of inexperienced pilots who had difficulty in keeping formation and were generally unaware. This proved a tempting bait for the Germans who descended on the Poles, to be in turn attacked by Zumbach and the *Kosciuszko* fliers from above. The Poles flew 224 missions, shot down 16 German planes, which was 18 percent of all enemy craft destroyed, for the loss of two Polish pilots. A spectacular victory.[50]

Major Janus was awarded the British Distinguished Service Cross and four Distinguished Flying Crosses went to two other pilots, while Zumbach and Skalski received bars to their previous awards. Within weeks, the R.A.F. Station Northolt became a Polish command, and the first Polish base commander was the 1939 Poznan Wing leader, Col. Mieczyslaw Mumler.

First Staff Officers Parachuted to Poland

In January 1943 the first cadre of Air Force officers was parachuted into Poland. The Commanding Officer was Colonel Rutkowski, who had completed a full tour of thirty bomber combat missions and had also flown the first airdrop missions to Poland.[51] The orders for the cadre were to acquaint the Polish Underground Staff with the capabilities of the Polish Air Force and its limitations. The message to Polish Home Army was that *Polish plans had not been approved by the British* and their full realization could only take place after acceptance and approval by the British. Rutkowski and his colleagues were also given instructions to develop plans to utilize all captured German equipment, including planes, for immediate use by arriving Polish squadrons. Finally the cadre was to function as a Polish Air Force staff in the A.K. to augment the small group of prewar aviation officers, the most notable being Colonel Adam Kurowski. What needs to be emphasized is that the instructions to the air force officers made it clear that the transfer of Polish units from the West would occur only after complete German military collapse or surrender.

On March 15, 1943, the C-in-C expedited his own courier to Poland. The officer (Captain Jan Gorski) chosen for this task was a very distinguished officer of the Polish Air Force who had been working primarily with the embryonic Polish Parachute Brigade at the British training center—Ringway. He carried a short and succinct order:

> Captain Jan Gorski is to be seconded to the Air Force section of the Home Army Staff and is to advise the Home Army Commander regarding the extent of the changes which have occurred in the Polish Air Force in the United Kingdom; and to acquaint the Home Staff with the new proposed plans for Air Force support of the Uprising. Because of his personal background he is to develop plans locally for the parachuting of the Polish Para Brigade to capture a base or complex of air bases.[52]

It would appear in hindsight that the Air Force cadre parachuted to Poland had the task of being realistic while the task assigned to

Captain Gorski by his orders was much more optimistic and verging on the improbable. To address the problem of communication and air force personnel shortages, the Poles embarked on a pragmatic solution to this need. In June 1943, the Polish staff organized a course for 50 army officers and 120 noncommissioned officers of the land army at the Polish Center of Communications in Scotland. After training they were to be parachuted to Poland to work on behalf of the communication needs of the Polish Air Force.[53] But the main route for the couriers coming back was still the long way through the neutral countries, and then through Vichy France. It was a long and dangerous route, and the only reason it more often succeeded than not, was the fact that Germany at this point of the war was full of foreign workers (French, Belgian, Poles, Czechs, etc.) who had been either arrested or in some instances even volunteered for economic reasons to work in Germany. The couriers traveled in all kinds of disguises and used all kinds of false papers. It was people like Karski and Nowak who not only kept the Polish Government in touch with what was going on in Poland, but also brought the first news of the terrible genocide of the Jews, a planned mass murder that has become known as the Holocaust.[54]

Battle of the Atlantic

While the Polish Staff were dealing with issues of long-range policy, strategy, and personnel shortages, the Polish Navy fought without pause.

In the summer of 1942 the Battle of the Atlantic reached its climax. The Germans had now developed their wolf pack tactics, and had at long last also initiated successful long-range air patrols from the French occupied territory of Brittany. This allowed the German submarines to take up waiting, ambush positions and, being in large numbers, they formed a picket which could not be avoided. Even the advance warnings of the Ultra decrypting from Bletchley could not prevent the Allied convoys from having to fight through the numerous and silent enemy. The losses mounted as the Atlantic was in flames. It would be dreary to enumerate all the operations, but the Polish destroyers sailed and returned. The crews went on leave as the ships were refitted and modernized with better killing equipment. The crews were then trained in the new equipment, such as the squid, hedgehog, asdic, new radar, headache for surveillance of enemy radio and, after an obligatory work-up period, resumed their patrols.

Between July 1941 and early 1942, *Burza* was part of the Irish Sea Escort Force and convoyed ships between Plymouth and Iceland. During that same period *Blyskawica* underwent a major overhaul with dual purpose 102 mm guns and antisubmarine mortars and new sonar. But all the work was in convoying, essential but dull as well as dangerous.

In April 1942 the following was written in the report on Allied contingents serving with the British.

> It has been said by a British officer who has had Polish and other allied ships under his command: "They share our sorrows and rejoice in our victories in a manner which makes them seem closest of all our allies. They have the gift of being sympathetic rather than critical and enthusiastic instead of envious."
>
> The Destroyers have been working with zeal and efficiency on escort and it is suggested that some should be employed where there is greater opportunity for action.[55]

In late 1942 the British began to implement that suggestion. *Piorun*, in May 1942, was assigned to the Third Destroyer Flotilla based at Scapa Flow to protect the Home Fleet, including the new Royal Navy battleship *Anson*, whose task in turn was to protect the Murmansk-bound convoys from the major German warships based in Northern Norway. *Garland* in turn took part in the convoys in Northern Waters. On May 27, 1942, the Polish warship began its journey through hell when it left Seydifiord in Iceland as escort for the Royal Navy cruisers *Kent*, *Norfolk*, *Liverpool*, and the flagship *Nigeria*. On May 25 the Allies met Convoy PQ-16, consisting of thirty-five transports bound for the Soviet Union.

At 08.00 hours of May 25, in a position east of Jan Mayen Land, the battle was joined when the German air patrols from Norway spotted the convoy. At that latitude and that time of the year there is no night and the convoy sailed on undergoing three major air attacks. On may 26 the Germans carried out three more air attacks with dive and torpedo bombers. On May 27, just south of Bear Island the Allied convoy was at the closest proximity to the German air bases in Norway, a mere forty minutes flying time, and thirteen air attacks were carried out. On that day German submarines also joined the battle.

The crews had been on action stations for forty-eight hours and the smaller warships were running short of ammunition. At 13.55 hours of May 27 the *Garland* was attacked by seven JU-88s, with major damage to the Polish destroyer and loss of life. The central artillery control was put out of commission and a number of fires started. One of the heroes of this operation was the ship's surgeon, Lt. W. Zabron, who worked for thirty hours without respite. Eight more attacks were sustained but at 23.00 hours when the last German plane left, the Polish skipper, Commander Henryk Eibel, requested permission to sail for Murmansk to save the wounded. At 24.00 the British destroyer *Achates* loaned her ship's surgeon, Lt. Surgeon Lloyd Armstrong, but even two surgeons could not cope with the amputations and casualities. *Garland* was then given permission to sail for Murmansk, which she reached on May 29. The Captain, Eibel, the artillery officer, Bartosik, and the surgeon, Zabron, were all decorated with the Virtuti Militari.

The two small destroyers *Krakowiak* and *Kujawiak* escorted and fought off enemy aircraft and ships in the English Channel. The *Kujawiak* was lost while escorting a crucial convoy to Malta. The Poles received another small but improved *Hunt* Class destroyer and named it *Slazak.*

During that time *Blyskawica* participated in the North Africa landings, Operation Torch off Bougie, and stayed in the Mediterranean throughout most of 1943, taking part in the Sicily landings.

Burza sailed on the North Atlantic convoys and in February 21, 1943, while off New Foundland, detected a German U-Boat by asdic. *Burza* carried out a depth charge attack that brought the enemy to surface. The United States Coast Guard Cutter *Campbell* administered the coup de grace by ramming the German submarine. Unfortunately the German submarine's hydroplanes, which stick out like wings, tore the side of the American ships and the crew of the *Campbell* had to be transferred to the Polish warship. The Coast Guard Cutter with her captain, Lt. Cdr. Hirshfield, aboard, was protected by the *Burza* and successfully towed to safety.

The small Polish Navy took possession of two major ships around that time. On November 18, 1942, the Poles ran up their standard on a brand new *Milne* Class fleet destroyer and christened it O.R.P. *Orkan.* On January 15, 1943, the Poles took over an old English medium cruiser, H.M.S. *Dragon.* Polish efforts to name it the O.R.P. *Lwow* were seen as provocative and the final decision in face of an absolute British refusal to go along with this was to keep the old English name. The ships was commissioned as the O.R.P. *Dragon*.

In the Mediterranean the two Polish submarines, the O.R.P. *Sokol* (C.O. Kapitan J. Koziolowski) and O.R.P. *Dzik* (C.O. Kapitan Romanowski) operated out of Valleta as part of the Tenth Submarine Flotilla. Later both were transferred to Beirut to the First Submarine Flotilla. During this stage of naval operations the area of patrolling was the Dodecanese. *Sokol* carried out a total of thirty-one patrols and sank 23,460 tons of enemy shipping, *Dzik* carried out a mere twelve patrols and sank 45,080 tons.

In late 1943 both returned to the United Kingdom and were refitted. They became part of the Ninth Submarine Flotilla based in Dundee, but their glory days were finished.

At least one sentence needs to be given the small Polish Motor-Torpedo and Motor-Torpedo-Gunboats that served in the close confines of the English Channel for all of the war. Also Polish Naval Personnel were placed on Polish merchantmen as gunners.[56]

And then there were the freighters, slow-sailing ships, without which the war could not have been won. Their crews were always aware of the danger, and the losses until mid-1943 were staggering. In this Allied fleet the Polish merchant ships played their role, absorbing losses and regenerating so that in actual numbers the small fleet was about the same at the end of the war.[57]

6

Strategic Plans Go Awry, Early 1943–Late 1943

Polish International Situation Deteriorates

On January 16, 1943, the Soviets communicated to the Polish ambassador in Moscow, Adam Romer, who had just replaced Kot, that the Agreement of December 1, 1941, governing the right to claim Polish citizenship of individuals who had lived in the Polish prewar territories that had been incorporated into the Soviet Republics, was rescinded. It was under the proviso of this agreement that the Poles were able to muster their land forces and that a small number of their families were allowed to leave the Soviet Union in 1942. This agreement was very specific and pertained only to those prewar Polish citizens who could verify their Polish nationality to the satisfaction of the Soviet functionaries. Prewar Polish citizens of non-Polish ethnicity, such as Jews, were precluded from this agreement. Now, even Poles who had the misfortune to have been residents of these territories were, in the eyes of the Soviets, forever Soviet citizens. This immediately closed any possibility of the Poles recruiting any further men for their evacuated forces, a hope expressed by Churchill.

The Soviets had by January 1943 survived a second major German offensive and were now slowly grinding down the trapped German Armies at Stalingrad. The whole world was in awe of the splendid courage of the Soviet soldier, and of the willpower to endure the greatest privations. The Soviets had also become quite reassured that their callous and intimidating behavior towards the Poles only elicited remarks of criticism at the Polish reaction or, at best, pleas for maintaining Allied solidarity.

This political and planned act was followed by a discovery that nobody wanted and that was totally unplanned. On April 12, 1943, the German radio announced that a mass grave of Polish officers had been discovered near Smolensk in Soviet territories now under German occupation. The very first announcement identified some of the names of the officers who had been missing since 1940 and about whom Sikorski and other Polish diplomats had made repeated interventions.

Katyn!

That word, which has entered the Polish lexicon describing the old atavistic horrors of calculated, brutal murder of men whose hands are tied behind their backs and whose skulls have bullet holes in their backs. Katyn. The word that for many decades could not be uttered in Poland, or if spoken, was tantamount to a base lie and deceit. Katyn. The place alluded to by the Pope in his first pontifical visit to Poland, when he spoke in his homily that Polish soldiers are buried all over the world and in places only known to *Him*. Katyn, where the bodies of five thousand Poles were indeed found, with another close to ten thousand still remaining interred in places only known to *Him*. Katyn, where the description of the bodies brings tears to every eye, and breaks the heart; of officers whose tattered uniforms still contained identity cards, and postcards from their loved ones in Poland, all last dated in the late spring of 1940. Katyn, which led to the isolation of the Polish Government in London, which led to the break-off in diplomatic relations between the Soviet Government and the Poles because the Polish Government dared and had the temerity to ask for an impartial investigation by the International Red Cross. The Poles were guilty of breaching a covenant that Allied solidarity was paramount and Soviets' pleasure to be cultivated and displeasure to be avoided.

Stalin professed to be so insulted by the Polish request for an impartial International Red Cross investigation that he broke diplomatic relations with the Polish Government. The Western Powers were also very offended at the politically incorrect step of the Poles in asking for an investigation of the cause of death of thousands of Polish officers. That was in itself an indictment of the Soviets, since if the liberal West really believed that this atrocity was one of the many perpetrated by the Germans, then why all the umbrage? Poles were now castigated openly, and not just by the communists.

During Sikorski's visit to Moscow in late 1941, and to his insistent question as to the whereabouts of his officers, he received a reply from Stalin that all had been released and the missing ones must have escaped. There was no hint then that the camps might have been taken by the German offensive. Then two years later the bodies came out to haunt not only the Poles but their oppressors.

Churchill clearly did not buy the Stalin version but argued with Sikorski that if dead there was nothing that anybody could do about it. After the war, Churchill wrote:

> Eventually in September, 1943, the region of Katyn was occupied by the Russians. After the recapture of Smolensk a committee composed exclusively of Russians was appointed to inquire about the fate of the Poles of Katyn. Their report, issued in January, 1944, claims that the three camps were not evacuated in time, owing to the rapidity of German advance, and that the Polish prisoners fell into German hands and were later slaughtered by them. This version to be believed involves acceptance of the fact that nearly 15,000 Polish officers and men, of whom there was no record since the spring of 1940, passed into German hands in July, 1941, and were later destroyed by the Germans without one single person escaping and reporting, either to the Russian authorities or to the Polish Consul in Russia or to the underground Movement in Poland. When we remember the confusion caused by the German advance, that the guards of the camps must have fled as the invaders came nearer, and all the contacts afterwards during this period of Russo-Polish cooperation, the belief seems an act of faith.[1]

Sikorski's plans of a foreign policy based on a good neighbor relationship with the Soviet Union were destroyed. The British supported the Polish hopes to rebuild the ties but the conditions now made by the Soviets were the complete dismantling of the Polish Government and their creation of the puppet Committee. This predicted the future course.[2]

The hint of the British policy towards the Poles came in a personal communication from Churchill to Stalin appealing the Soviet decision to break ties with the Polish Government and defending Sikorski from charges that he was pro-German. Churchill wrote that if Sikorski was replaced, worse might happen. The litmus test for the British was now the willingness of the Polish leadership to play the passive role of acquiescence if not actual appeasement towards Soviet claims on Polish territory.

The Polish troops in the Middle East were restive. They had al-

ways deep down been convinced that their officers had been murdered, because of their own experiences of the brutal life in the Soviet concentration camps.[3] Many had left some members of their
family behind. The overwhelming majority hailed from the Eastern
Polish provinces, the Kresy, Lwow, and the disputed regions of
Polish Lithuania, the old Duchy of Lithuania. They were painfully
aware that the Soviets were claiming their lands and that their allies, the British, were at best disinterested, at worst, in favor of Soviet claims. Anders himself kept an iron grip on his troops and had
their overwhelming loyalty. The unasked question that haunted the
Polish staff in London and must have perturbed the British, albeit
there is nothing in the British archives to confirm it, is where goes
Anders and his troops?

Sikorski's Trip to the Middle East and Accident

It was with this purpose that Sikorski flew off to the Middle East
to visit the Polish Army. This was his fifth major trip of the war. He
did not return.

The accident occurred in the late hours of July 4, 1943, as the
American-built B-24 (Liberator—#AL523), assigned to a R.A.F. unit
(squadron 511) for ferrying VIPs and piloted by a Czech (Edward
Prchal) in R.A.F. service, crashed within minutes of taking off from
the Gibraltar field. It plunged at full speed into the sea, in full sight
of many spectators.

All aboard, with the exception of the pilot, were killed. General
Wladyslaw Sikorski's body was found and his uniform is still ex-
hibited at the Polish Institute in London, in the museum section
named after him—the Sikorski Museum. Major General Tadeusz
Klimecki, the Polish Chief of Staff, and Colonel Andrzej Marecki,
Chief of Operations of the Polish Army, were also killed, as was
General Sikorski's only daughter, Mrs. Zofia Lesniowska, the Gen-
eral's personal secretary, and Lt. Jozef Ponikiewski, his adjutant.

General Sikorski had also been accompanied by an Englishman,
one of those men whose integrity gave the world the concept that
an Englishman's word is his bond. Major Victor Cazalet, Member of
Parliament, was the British Government's liaison with Sikorski.[4]
Known for his strong Polish sympathies, he was also becoming a
well-known, albeit restrained, critic of Churchill's pro-Soviet policies. Madam Lesniowska's body was never recovered. In addition
the plane carried Brigadier J.P. Whiteley and two British civilians,

Mr. Walter H. Lock and Mr. Pinder, both reputedly members of the British intelligence services. In addition to the pilot, the crew was complemented by five R.A.F. officers and other rank. The members of the British party whose bodies were recovered are buried in Gibraltar, North Front cemetery. All the Poles, including the Commander-in-Chief, were eventually buried at the Polish military cemetery in Newark, England.[5]

The Polish destroyer O.R.P. *Orkan* was ordered to Gibraltar to pick up Sikorski's body for transport to the United Kingdom, and the funeral took place at the Roman Catholic Cathedral of Westminster in London. The Polish Armed Forces provided the guard of honor, with Polish units being brought down from Scotland for the funeral. The British provided the Coldstream Guards for ceremonial duties.

Churchill and Eden attended the funeral as did the Polish President and the whole Polish Government. Churchill, as usual, rose to the occasion and wrote a magnificent obituary.

> At the invitation of the President and Government of Poland, who are our guests in London, I speak these words to Poles all over the world; to the Armed Forces of Poland in Britain and the Middle East; to Poles in exile in many countries; to Poles in German prisons camps and Poles forced to labour for the enemy; and in particular to the inhabitants of Poland itself, who are enduring with unlimited fortitude the worst that any enemy of unexampled brutality can do to them.
>
> I mourn with you the tragic loss of your Prime Minister and Commander-in-Chief, General Sikorski. I knew him well. He was a true statesman, a true soldier, a true comrade, a true ally, and above all a true Pole.
>
> He is gone; but if he were here at my side I think he would wish me to say this and I say it from my heart. Soldiers must die, but by their death they nourish the nation that gave them birth. Sikorski is dead, but it is in this sense that you must think of your dead Prime Minister and Commander-in-Chief. Remember that he strove for the unity of all Poles, the unity of in a single aim the defeat and punishment of the German despoilers of Poland, he strove too, unceasingly, for that larger unity of all the European peoples, for the closest collaboration in the common struggle with Poland's Allies in the West and in the East. He knew that in such partnership lies the surest hope of Poland's speedy liberation and greatness. His efforts and your sacrifices shall not be in vain. Be worthy of his example.
>
> Prepare yourselves to die for Poland—for many of you to whom I

speak must die, as many of us must die, and as he died, for his country, and the common cause. In the farewell to your dear leader let us mingle renewed loyalties. We shall not forget him. I shall not forget you. My own thoughts are with you and will be with you always.[6]

This eloquent and moving speech heartened the Poles who had been reeling under the barrage of anti-Polish editorials, and questions in Parliament.[7]

The Royal Air Force, as is policy, convened a Court of Inquiry, on July 7, 1943, by the order of Air Marshal Sir John C. Slessor KCB DSO MC. The president was Group Captain J.G. Elton DFC. It included Wing Commander A W Kay and Squadron Leader DM Wellings DFC. A Polish Air Force officer, Major S. Dudzinski, was invited to be present as an observer.[8] Shortly, the Polish Ambassador in London received a cover letter from the Air Ministry: "I have the honour to submit to your excellency the draft of Air Ministry Press Communiqué which the Air Ministry is anxious to issue immediately on the approval of the Polish authority."

The actual, proposed, press communiqué that was enclosed read as follows:

> The report of the Court of Inquiry which has been investigating the cause of the Liberator accident on July 4, 1943, in which General Sikorski lost his life, has now been received. The findings of the Court and the observations of the officers whose duty is to review the and comment on these findings have been considered, and it is apparent that the accident was due to jamming of elevator controls shortly after take off with the result that the aircraft became uncontrollable.
>
> After most careful examination of all available evidence, including that of the pilot, it has not been possible to determine how the jamming occurred but it has been established that there was no sabotage.
>
> It is also clear that the captain of the aircraft, who is a pilot of great experience and exceptional ability, was in no way to blame.
>
> An officer of the Polish Air Force attended throughout the proceedings.

The statement that the cause was not determined, but that sabotage was ruled out, was inherently illogical. The Polish Government refused to endorse the communiqué, stating its objections. The communiqué was released anyway. That was the first and final word of the British. The Poles were in a bind and caught up in the dilemma of either acceding to what was most obviously a whitewash or appearing to challenge their British hosts and impute their integrity. Given the recent experience with the news of the Katyn massacre, this was a sensitive problem. But the Polish Government, through the Ministry of the Interior, delegated a Polish engineer to investigate the report. Mr. T. Ullman questioned the conclusion of the Court of Inquiry. Independently the Polish Air Force also appointed a commission to look at the evidence and the report and came to the following conclusion: that the pilot's testimony (that the cause of the accident was due to the blocking of the rudder control) cannot be verified, because not all parts of the plane have been recovered. The materials and testimony available do not permit a conclusion that the accident occurred as a result of sabotage. With the available materials and testimony, it is impossible to establish the cause of the accident, a frequent finding on the investigation of plane crashes.

Following this seeming impasse the Polish Minister of Justice impaneled a three-man commission, which was chaired by the State Procurator, Dr. Tadeusz Cyprian. The commission came up with the following points.

- The available materials and testimony did not answer the questions of the cause of the accident.
- Since it was impossible to establish that sabotage occurred, the cause had to remain as due to due unknown factors.
- All parts of the plane would need to be recovered and examined by experts to establish the cause of blocking of the rudder.
- The three-man commission concluded that they shared the opinion of the Polish Air Force Inspectors's Commission regarding the Royal Air Force Court conclusion as too categorical on the basis of available material.[9]

But why were the British so cavalier and so untypically illogical? One of the conspiracy theories has the British responsible for the accident. The fact that it occurred on their field, and that their court came to such an illogical and very hasty conclusion, certainly supports that speculation. If in fact the British thought Sikorski was a strong leader who would command the loyalty of the exiled Poles, then in the troublesome future that was apparent to all, Sikorski would also be most inconvenient.

There is another concern the British might have had, namely that he would emulate Benes and go over to the Soviet side.[10] Could the British have considered this as a serious threat to their long-term concept of a balance of power in postwar Europe. The British were bent on accommodating the Soviets as far as the Polish eastern boundaries were concerned, but it became clear in 1944 that they also wished to protect a small but independent Poland from Soviet hegemony. We know that by the time of Yalta they had abjectly capitulated, but it needs to be emphasized that by the first months of 1945, the British were so dependent on the Americans that their foreign policy was completely dictated by Washington.

Having written all of that it also needs need to be stated that most Poles were and continue to be convinced that the accident was sabotage, and that the perpetrators were the Soviets and their agent Philby, the British secret service officer in Gibraltar. The explanation for the British whitewash may have been that the British Secret Services were able to exercise a gag rule on the deliberations or that they were aware of the suspect role of Philby and wished him to continue as a conduit to Moscow.

There was another Polish tragedy in this same period. The G.O.C of the A.K., Major General Stefan Rowecki, was captured by the Germans in late June 1943. He was replaced by Major General Tadeusz Komorowski, who used the pseudonym of Bor.

Churchill, shortly after the accident and death of General Sikorski wrote:

> The time has come to bring the Polish troops from Persia into the Mediterranean theatre. Politically, this is highly desirable, as the men wish to fight, and once engaged will worry less about their own affairs which are tragic. The whole corps should be moved from Persia to Port Said and Alexandria. The intention is to use them immediately.[11]

Once moved from the Iraq and Iran (Persia) regions to Palestine the Poles suffered further attrition, this time due to the desertion of thousands of Polish Jews.

When the Polish Army began to recruit in the Soviet Union in late 1941, there was little interest among the Jews of Polish descent or background to volunteer for such service. Furthermore, the Soviets as part of their agreement with the Poles insisted that all Jews who had lived in prewar Polish territory were now citizens of the Soviet Union. They made difficulties for the Jews to join and the fact that the number of places in the Polish military was limited by the number of food portions did not exactly help the situation. When it became obvious that the Poles would be transferred to the Middle East, many Jews attempted to volunteer and many were enrolled. One of the most prominent being Menachem Begin. There was also latent suspicion of the Jews because of their pro-Soviet attitudes, and the Poles feared that they would be Soviet agents. But many did volunteer and, after reaching the Middle East, well over two thousand deserted. The Polish military authorities made no effort to track them down even though this was unacceptable to the British authorities of Palestine, who were engaged in a bitter war with the Jewish underground, Stern Gang. Silver quotes Marek Kahan, "there was sympathy among Polish officers for the Irgun." In fact most of the Poles who in their war odyssey sojourned or traveled through Palestine have the warmest memories of the Polish-Jewish population and of their receptions and cordiality.[12]

The Poles were again urged and in fact requested by British military authorities to pare their dispositions even further, this time to one (three brigade) division of infantry and a brigade of tanks. It was the new Commander-in-Chief, General Sosnkowski, who now became involved in the discussions. His counterproposal was to have a corps of one (two brigade) infantry division and one armored division. The British categorically rejected this proposal. The Poles then suggested that the increment to the brigade of tanks (to bring it up to a full armored division establishment) would come from the First Armored in Scotland. But the British at this point needed infantry more than they needed armor in the Italian Campaign for which the Polish Corps was destined. Obviously they also needed the Polish Armored Division in northwest Europe more than they admitted in their later negotiations. The final arbitrator of the Polish fortune was again Churchill. The authors of *P.S.Z.* quote his message, July 13, 1943, to Sir Alan Brooke. The cable addressed the urgency of reinforcements for Italy and the need to bring the Polish Corps into operations. It further commented that a lot of time and energy had been spent on the Poles who for two years had done nothing. Churchill again categorically stated that this was not the time for new organizational changes and that the risk of sending them without reserves was worthwhile; and should their strength be depleted they could still call themselves a Polish Corps. Finally Churchill finished by saying, "We will need to look for their reinforcement elsewhere."[13] It is unclear what Churchill meant, possibly he speculated on the idea of moving the Polish First Corps from Scotland to the Middle East; possibly he thought of being able to persuade Stalin to allow the many thousands of Poles, still trapped in the Soviet Union, freedom to leave. But what happened was that many thousands of young Poles forcibly conscripted into the German Army from western Poland after being taken prisoner of war by the Allies, declared themselves to be Polish and were given a choice of joining the Polish Armed Forces. These were young men, from regions that had fought the most successful anti-German uprisings a mere twenty years back, namely Poznan and Silesia. The Germans having incorporated these provinces into Germany naturally drafted them. This was contrary to international conventions and had also been done by the Soviets after their plebiscite in Eastern Poland. By war's end a total of forty thousand such young men were now wearing the Polish uniform, and there is not one case of double treachery. It is not known how many such young people did not opt for such an option and preferred to stay safe in a British or American prisoner of war camp.

Eventually, and partially as the result of the Prime Minister's support and partially because of the exigencies of the situation, the 2 Army Corps, consisting of two depleted infantry divisions and an armored brigade, but very strong in artillery and supporting services, was moved to Italy in December 1943.[14]

In Washington with the CCS

But the war continued and the work of the staffs also proceeded. The continued efforts were to make coherent plans of the organizational standards of the Polish First (Scotland) and 2 Army Corps (Middle East) and to integrate the Polish A.K. into the strategy of the Western Allied Powers. The Polish representative was Colonel L. Mitkiewicz, ably aided by the elegant and British-educated Count Captain Stefan Zamoyski.

On June 30, 1943, the Poles presented a brief to the Allies, which began as follows:

The Military Forces of Poland, today, consist of the Polish Armed Forces in the United Kingdom, an army in the Middle East and a secret military organization in Poland.

The Secret Military Organization is the principle component of the Polish Military Forces at the disposal of the Polish Commander-in-Chief.

The memorandum further outlined the actual composition of the Polish Armed Forces in the UK and the Middle East but specifically underscored the importance of the Polish Home Army to Allied Strategy.

Immediately after the occupation of Poland a Secret Army had been formed in the country which was centered in the Warsaw, Cracow, Lodz and Lublin area. This army was in contact with the Polish Government in London and under the command of General Sikorski. Liaison was maintained by radio and by a Polish flight of a British Squadron. Men, particularly officers, small arms, signal equipment and demolition material had been flown in to them. General Sikorski considered this Secret Army as the main force of Poland since it was situated in the country and supported by the People. The intention was to coordinate action by this secret army with that of the Polish Forces now abroad and with Allied plans.

It was important that the closest liaison should be maintained with this army since its tie with the Polish General Staff must by strengthened, and the interests of the Allies in its well being and operations demonstrated. Unless the ties were close there was danger of an ill timed movement started without direct coordination with Allied Command. The geographical situation of this army was immensely valuable. It separated the main German Forces on the Eastern front from their bases in the Reich and was in a position to cut their lines of communication should Germany wish to draw forces from the East for action in the West.

General Sikorski's conception was to seize control of central Poland with the secret Army, then to reinforce them by the transfer of Polish Air Forces and the Polish Parachute Brigade from the U.K. later, if possible, Polish Land Forces would be added. All these plans required the use of considerable air transport, and further, it was essential that they should be coordinated with and form part of the Allied offensive in Europe.

In addition to severing German concentrations between the Eastern front and the Reich, the Secret Army would engage considerable German forces and a very important area in Europe would be under Allied control.[15]

This is a very clear and not at all subtle enunciation of the Polish strategy. The Poles wish to be part of the Western Allied effort, and offer their underground (secret) army to support an Allied enclave in East-Central Europe and will prevent as much as possible the transfer of German troops from the East to the West. It is also a very strong hint that the Poles, if supported, would be a strong bastion of Western interests in the region of East-Central Europe.

It was around that very time that the British Chiefs developed their Directive regarding Polish Forces. It would seem that Sikorski either never saw it or had no opportunity to respond to it. This directive, dated July 14, 1943, affirmed most points that had been previously urged by the Poles. It agreed that the Polish First Armored Division would participate in the Northwest Europe operations, and that the "ultimate aim will be to concentrate the Polish Forces in Poland. The time when this object can be achieved will depend in particular upon the establishment of communications and opening of supply routes." The directive also acknowledged that "The Polish Parachute Brigade will be reserved for direct action in Poland, but the moment and method of this employment must be governed by the availability of aircraft." This is important in that as late as July 1943 the British still acknowledged the primary mission and role of the Polish Parachute Brigade. This was to change in the summer of 1944, as we will see later.

This should have been a sufficient warning to the Polish command and perhaps it may have been still been timely for the Polish Staff to keep the Parachute Brigade at a cadre level for sabotage activity in Poland and for the training of officers for drops to Poland.

If that language was not enough, the statement regarding the arming of the Polish Underground Army should have been the final warning and should have led to a major revision of the 1942 Polish strategic plans formulated at the London Conference of the Polish generals. In alluding to the arming of the Polish Secret Army the directive used the term *desirability* instead of *necessity*.

> The desirability of preparing the Secret Army in Poland for action co-ordinated with the military operations of the Allies is recognized and the very effective sabotage carried out by that Army fully appreciated. It is therefore of great importance that this Army should be supplied with largest possible quantity of equipment before large scale operations on the continent begin. The quantity that will be delivered will only be limited by the availability from time to time of suitable aircraft. SOE will continue to act as coordinating authority and agent to whom the Polish General Staff should refer all matters

in connection with sabotage and organization of resistance and secret armies. In order to assist in planning the future operations of
these Polish Forces SOE will produce as soon as possible an estimate
of the amount of equipment which it is hoped to set aside over a period for transport to Poland as opportunity offers.[16]

This was a terrible defeat of the Polish strategy. First of all the
statement is clear that supplies will be flown in as opportunity allows. War is not carried out by logistics as opportunity allows. Second, and perhaps even more telling, was the defeat of the Polish
principle that Polish Underground activity was not an S.O.E. activity, but a Polish autonomous operation. The Poles had always gone
on record that their Underground Secret Army was "the principal
component at the disposal of the Polish Commander-in-Chief";
while the British essentially saw it as part of the overall sabotage
work being carried out by the S.O.E. The seeds of failure and defeat
were sown. It was very obvious that in spite of polite platitudes, the
Allied CCS and the British viewed the Polish activities as best confined to sabotage and intelligence gathering. The proverbial bottom
line was that the Poles could either accommodate their underground work to the dictates of the S.O.E.; or, as a British Air Marshall would say a bare year later: "stew in their own juice."

But the Poles still had great hopes that this very disappointing
turn of events would be redressed. On September 17, 1943, at the
119th meeting of the CCS, the Polish representative, Colonel L.
Mitkiewicz, presented the following memorandum to the Allied
Staff.

> The Polish General Staff deem the recognition by the Combined
> Chiefs of Staff of the plan for the immediate preparation of the Secret
> Army in Poland as vitally important to the overall war effort.
> Poland occupies a central position in the region defined in the
> West by Germany proper, in the North by the Baltic Sea, in the East
> by the German EAST-WALL and the Black Sea, and in the South by
> the Mediterranean. In consequence of the development of Allied op-
> erations in Southern Eruope the whole of the above determined area
> has acquired preeminent strategic significance.
> While these territories are held by the enemy, there remains a
> strong potential resistance which requires only means and direction
> for timely activation. The countries of this German hegemony are to
> a greater or lesser degree preparing for open military revolt. With
> adequate assistance they could undoubtedly precipitate the fall of
> the German European defenses. These forces would at the same time

provide for Allied military secruity against chaos and organized movements, either from within the Reich or from elements of the Wehrmacht dispersed throughout Europe. In this area Poland has retained an advanced military organization operating under the orders of the Polish General Staff in London.

Recent military progress both in Eastern Europe and in the Mediterranean area, brings forward a demand for determining strategic responsibility with regard to the territory of Poland.

In active operations the Polish Armed Forces in the United Kingdom will probably be employed under a joint Anglo-American Command. The purpose and employment of the Secret Army in Poland are of primary strategic interest to the Allies, engaged in military operations against Germany.

In accordance with the requirements of coordinated leadership, the Polish General Staff, therefore, consider it essential that the entire Polish Armed Forces should be placed under a common Allied Command, and the area of Poland should be considered one of joint strategic responsibility. Equipment is flown from the United Kingdom for the maintenance of subversive activities, sabotage, and intelligence conducted by the Secret Army.

It has now become essential to intensify considerably the scale of these activities. Moreover, it is necessary to transfer to Poland a sufficient quantity of arms for the seizure, at the given signal, of certain points of subsequent reception for the bulk of combat equipment.

The performance of this task requires 500 operations flights to Poland before April 1944. The execution of 300 flights has been agreed upon by the British Joint Staff. In order to cover the remaining 200 flights and for reasons of increasing liaison requirements, the Polish General Staff recommend the establishment of a Special Squadron of 18–20 B-24 bombers.

The success of the general rising of the Secret Army will be conditioned upon the supply of sufficient combat equipment to the points previously captured and secured by the initial insurgent groups. The development of the operation will mainly depend upon the extent of equipment and reinforcement supplied from abroad.

The insurrection should occur when the bulk of the German forces are fully engaged, and when the rears are demoralized by facing an apparently hopeless struggle. The German High Command will then be incapable of directing and coordinating action against an organized rising on its own rear and on hostile soil.

The determination of a propitious opportunity for the rising by the Secret Army will be difficult. It will, however, become inevitable in order to prevent the rising from being occasioned by an uncontrollable flow of events. Nor should this decision under any circumstance delay the preparation or influence the execution of the plan.

Timely preparation and assistance will assure the direction of the military effort of Poland in conformance with Allied intentions.[17]

The concern of the Polish staff that events in Poland with the impending progress of Soviet troops into the country came to pass in August 1944 when the City of Warsaw took up arms. But the quick answer given Mitkiewicz on September 23, 1943, may have been realistic but buried all Polish hopes for Western participation in Poland's future. The only road was of abject capitulation to the Soviet demands, or of desperation. Generals Redman and Deane, on behalf of the Combined Secretariat, wrote:

The Combined Chiefs of Staff have given careful consideration to the paper which you submitted to them at their meeting on 2nd July, 1943, and we have been directed to foreward you their comments.

The Combined Chiefs of Staff appreciate the great importance that is attached by the Polish Commander-in-Chief to the role envisaged by him for the Polish Secret Army. The operation requirements of active theaters, however, are heavy; the Secret Army could not openly take an active part against the Axis until direct land or sea communications were immediately in prospect; there is also a lack of suitable aircraft for the delivery of large quantities of supplies to Poland.

For these reasons the Combined Chiefs of Staff are unable at the present time to see their way to the allocation of the equipment required for the Polish Secret Army.

The supplies requested from U.S. and British sources for sabotage and intelligence activities in Poland have been approved, and the appropriate authorities have been so informed.

The shortage of heavy bomber aircraft continues and the Combined Chiefs of Staff regret therefore that at present it is not possible to allocate such aircraft to the Polish Government for delivery to Poland of supplies for sabotage and subversive activities. At the same time they are most anxious to render what help may be possible. With this in view one squadron and eventually two squadrons of U.S. heavy bombers, which are not operational for full daylight combat will be organized to operate from the UK under Commanding General of the Eighth Air Force for the support of sabotage and intelligence activities by Polish and other underground groups in Europe. Instructions have been issued to the Commanding General, European Theater of Operations, to this effect. These aircraft will be in addition to those aircraft sorties now being found under British arrangements.

signed H. Redman and JR Deane for the Combined Secretariat.[18]

In a personal contact General Wedemeyer allegedly told Mitkiewicz that the problem had to do with the unresolved dispute
between the Soviets and the Poles.[19]

The Polish Underground Articulates Its Plans

But there was a third partner on the Polish side, and on September 10, 1943, the G.O.C. of the A.K. sent his historic telegram to
London. This telegram was philosophical in its context and not in
the typical military language. It undoubtedly reflected the circumstances of the Polish clandestine army in a terror-stricken country.
The message can be summarized as follows. While it is impossible
to predict the exact circumstances and the nature in which the Polish Air Force may have to operate in Poland during the Uprising,
one thing is certain, that the nature of operations will be different
from that in which the squadrons operate in the United Kingdom,
where they are based on secure and logistically well-provided
bases. The G.O.C of the A.K. saw the participation of the Air Force
as carrying a great risk, but commented that the whole nature of the
projected Uprising was a serious risk if it were to accomplish its
goals. The telegram made the exhortation that all effort in the West
should be concentrated on the Air Force since it was the only way
that the forces in exile would be able to play any part in the first
and thus the most crucial phase of the Uprising. The telegram concluded that neither time nor place could be guaranteed since both
would be conditioned on the nature of the unfolding military
events outside of Polish control. The date of 1943 was mentioned as
a possibility and the G.O.C. urged that the Polish Air Force be
ready immediately. The main postulate of the proposed plan was
"the Uprising Cannot Fail."[20]

The telegram then listed forty priority bombing targets and described the current situation in regard to communications between
Poland and the United Kingdom. It was an excellent and thoughtful
analysis of the situation from the vantage point of a dedicated and
gallant officer whose every day under German occupation was a
high-risk gamble. There was one flaw, the Polish Air Force in the
West was not able to undertake such an independent action.

What has been a continuing and even bitter debate among many
Polish military historians is whether this expectation was due to the
overly optimistic cables emanating from Sikorski and then Sosn-

kowski, or the A.K. commander's own conception of the ultimate final gamble on which the future of a free Poland depended.

A New Commander-in-Chief
Takes Over Planning

Sosnkowski, having succeeded Sikorski in July 1943 as the Polish Commander-in-Chief, wrote to Sir Alan Brooke on September 20, 1943, after the first Directive was promulgated. The letter addressed many issues, including the importance of "avoiding dispersion" of Polish Forces and the principle that as much as possible the Polish Corps in the Middle East be used as one major formation under Polish Command, while the First Polish Corps in the United Kingdom be fleshed out in the near future and also used as a single major Polish formation.

But the most serious point raised by Sosnkowski was the specific wording of the original directive regarding the Polish Underground Army.

Sosnkowski wrote:

> I would like to give my support to the opinion already expressed by the Polish Command concerning the necessity of leaving at the beginning of para 5. the sentence "it is considered necessary" and not only "desirable" that the Polish Secret Army be prepared for operations coordinated with those of the Allies, as the adequate equipment of this Army in war materials is one of the fundamental conditions for starting the rising. I trust that the execution of this plan will be a practical proposition in the nearest future, considering the present Allied possibilities in the air.
>
> As a result of conferences between representatives of the British and the Polish General Staffs/ on 27th March 1943, between Colonel Marecki and General Ismay and on 7th April, 1943 between Colonel Marecki and General Kennedy/ the principle was established that all matters concerning diversive activities and intelligence work in Poland, as well as questions of supply for the Secret Army operations will be dealt with in direct talks between the British and the Polish staffs.
>
> It seems to me that this just principle ought to find its expression in a modification of the second part of par. 5. of the "Directive" in the following manner:
>
> The SOE shall continue to act a coordinating authority and as a body, whom the Polish General Staff should consult in all matters

connected with the current diversive action and with the supplying of the Secret Army with armaments and equipment necessary to start the rising. Operational matters coordination of the rising with Allied Operations will subjected to mutual consultation between the Polish General Staff and the Imperial General Staff.

I should therefore be grateful for kindly expressing your opinion about these suggestions

General Sosnkowski[21]

An internal British memo (September 28, 1943) comments that two recommendations have been arrived at in Washington by the CCS 267/3 on 17th September, 1943: (1) that an increased measure of support for the Polish Underground is desirable, and that (2) it is not proposed to go so far as to equip the Secret Army for military purposes. The memo continues that since the Poles in London do not seem aware of point (1) then they should be informed as soon as possible, preferably in Washington through CCS, so that "they can concentrate their energies on sabotage, para-military and intelligence work."[22]

On October 3, 1943, another internal War Office memo addressed the disputed point forthrightly:

> With regard to General Sosnkowski's letter to the C.I.G.S. and the draft reply, I think this covers completely all the points which we would wish to raise and I have no comments upon it.
>
> With regard to the more general point raised, both in General Sosnkowski's letter and in J.S.M. 1198, I feel that the time is fast approaching when we must tell the Poles firmly and without ambiguity, what the fate of their main plan for the support of the Secret Army is to be.
>
> As I understand it, as a result of CCS 267/3 dated 17th September, the Combined Chiefs have already turned down the plan as it stands. If this is so, then the quicker the Poles are told so, the better. I have written to Hollis to this effect and attach a copy of my letter to him. I should obviously have sent you a copy and apologise for not doing so before.
>
> I think it is clear that the plan, as at present proposed, is impracticable. We have held long discussions with Polish H.Q. on the subject, pointing out, among others things, that the conception of maintaining by air an Air Force inside Poland seems quite impossible.
>
> In their reply to our comments, the Poles made the following points:—
>
> There were two hypotheses upon which the Secret Army might be ordered to rise:—

(i) In the event of a general German crack-up.

In this case it seems to me that we should have won the war already, and there would therefore be no military necessity to support a Secret Army.

(ii) In the event of Allied penetration into Central Europe.

It seems highly unlikely since the Poles made it clear that by "Allied" they meant British and/or American Forces, not Russian.

They still consider the maintenance of an Air Force inside Poland to be essential.

In order to try and tie the situation up finally, I was proposing to put forward to the J.P.S. a paper, asking for strategical direction regarding the action required from resistance groups in Czecho-Slovakia, Poland and Hungary. The root of the trouble seems to be that we have never really decided how we wish to use these people in the final phases, and moreover, these three countries do not fall within any of the operational theaters, and therefore there is no one below the Chiefs of Staffs to whom we can look for detailed directives.

signed Barry

ps. Since dictating the above, I have spoken with Price of the Chiefs of Staff Secretariat. He does not feel that they could take action on my letter attached, and suggests that I raise the whole problem in the paper for the J.P.S. to which I have referred above.[23]

The p.s. is paradoxical. But some speculation is in order. It would appear that the honest opinion of a British staffer, who is unaware or pretends to be unaware that the Poles are planning to preserve their sovereignty from the Russians and not just planning on fighting the Germans, is tabled. The Polish Forces in the West were fighting the Germans, and the A.K. was to preserve Poland's sovereignty. Perhaps the motives are that the political future is still too misty, or that one should not discourage the Poles from participating in those operations where their contribution is useful, important, or perhaps even essential.

The letter from Sir Alan Brooke, (polite to the extreme and forthright as behooved that gentleman who along with Lord Ismay and Field Marshal Alexander lived up to the image of the English man of honour) stipulated to prior agreements about the advantage of using the Polish Corps (i.e., the First Motorized Corps, in 1943, consisting of only one armored division and some training elements), as one major tactical unit once it was brought up to full establishment; and then addressed Sosnkowski's concerns about the word "desirability" versus "necessity."

At the time that the Chiefs of Staff Committee approved the "Directive Governing the Future Employment of the Polish Land Forces," the question of using the word "necessity" in place of "desirability" with reference to preparing the Polish Secret Army, was fully examined. I should like to make it plain that in using the word "desirability," as was finally decided by the Committee, they did not in any way minimize the importance that would have been implied by the use of the alternative word. You will, however, have learned from my letter dated October 7th, how it is at present unavoidable that the scale of effort which can be applied to the equipping of the Secret Army must remain limited. I am not therefore in favor of altering the terms of the Directive, which might imply an overriding priority for this work, unco-ordinated with the successive developments of the war.[24]

Brooke then went on to re-emphasize the role of S.O.E. in the organization and coordination of the activities of the underground Forces of the German occupied countries, concluding with this: "I and my staff are, of course, always at your disposal for such consultations as are necessary, but I should be very reluctant to interfere with the responsibilities which have been laid upon SOE in this respect, which they are undoubtedly best fitted to discharge."

In retrospect we now know that the Polish plans for tying in the Polish Underground to Allied military planning came to naught. But as can be seen from the above correspondence, the situation was sufficiently fluid that the Polish General Staff continued to make the best-case option plans. In this endeavor, the Poles were supported by the Minister of Economic Warfare, Lord Selborne, who thus took up the Polish cause, writing on the following memorandum on October 21, 1943.

The season during which the night is long enough to infiltrate men and equipment to Poland by air from the U.K. extends from September to April. In August last General Sosnkowski pressed us for acceptance of a programme of 600 successful sorties during the coming season, i.e., 75 a month. We said this was impossible, but that we hoped to achieve 300 successful operations, i.e., 35–40 a month. General Sosnkowski now says that he never accepted this figure. In effect we were only able to achieve 16 operations in September and so far only 7 in October. The reason for this failure is the increase in the German night fighter force in N.W. Germany. During September we lost 6 aircraft in 22 sorties and in October, 1 out of 8. These losses compelled the Air Ministry to route S.O.E. aircraft on a more northerly course. The effect of this is so to increase the mileage that the aircraft can only reach the N.W. corner of Poland, whereas General Sosnkowski wants his equipment delivered all over Poland, and has a large number of men standing by to receive them.

Lord Selborne then suggests that the Polish flight be moved to Italy, that these planes be earmarked for use to Poland and not be part of a pool of planes for use in the Balkans, since both Secretary of State for Air and CIGS have stated that they are "primarily at their disposal."

Selborne concludes:

> In the circumstances, I do not propose to ask for an increased allotment of aircraft for S.O.E. work now but I shall feel bound to ask shortly for more aircraft for 1944 and the claims of Poland will occupy a prominent place in my case.
>
> I confess to great sympathy with the Polish standpoint. They braved Hitler in 1939 on Britain's guaranteed support. They have been crucified. They have not winced. Alone among our occupied Allies they have no Quisling. They have incurred considerable casualties in very successfully attacking German organized army of 250,000 in Poland which only needs equipment. To be told that Britain cannot afford them more than 6 aircraft is a bit hard.
>
> The case for increased assistance to Poland rests less on strategy than on Polish morale, to which I attach great importance. I also think that the very difficult role we may later have to play with them in regard to their Eastern frontier may perhaps be facilitated if we succeed in making some response to the appeal which General Sosnkowski has addressed to me. To the Poles the war is in Poland and this is their last chance of fighting there.[25]

This is an interesting comment from a man, who as his predecessor, Dalton, was very sympathetic to the Polish cause. But what is the issue of the Polish morale? Is it concern that the Polish forces in the West may lose heart, or that Polish policies vis-à-vis the Soviet Union may undertake a change, as occurred in the case of Benes?

As part of the S.O.E.-endorsed effort, it was agreed that the R.A.F. Bomber Command would use its crews between bombing missions to carry out aid to the Poles. This was a result of the intercession made by Sosnkowski in October 1943, that the number of missions was below that had been promised. The promise made was that until the Poles got well established in Italy there would be nine sorties a month from the United Kingdom. Selborne further commented that in expectation of the nine sorties, twenty-four Polish couriers had been gathered and reception committees in Poland prepared. Suddenly the C-in-C Bomber Command placed a veto on all such flights.

> I feel, and I am sure you will agree, that we have a very heavy responsibility towards the Poles concerning the Reception Committees. The Polish heroes composing them have to tramp or bicycle long miles from their homes to the rendezvous and there exist in hiding amid the rigors of a Polish winter. This is bad enough when they are buoyed up by the hope of a successful operation but, as night succeeds night and disappointment continues, the strongest may be forgiven if their will to continue resistance becomes impaired. The plan on which these Committees work cannot be switched or cancelled at a moment's notice in the way that orders to an air force with full base facilities at tis disposal can be varied.
>
> In the circumstances, is it really fair for C.-in-C. Bomber Command to force us to tell the Poles that the route from the United Kingdom is so dangerous that it cannot be contemplated by Bomber Command? If we add to such a statement an excuse that we are not satisfied with the integrity of their organisation in Poland until an enquiry into the matter has been concluded, in spite of all the evidence that exists of the splendid work the Resistance Groups in Poland are doing, then I feel we shall indeed have placed ourselves in a most humiliating and unenviable position and one which we shall really have no answer whatever to the resulting Polish outburst.[26]

Selborne again interceded on behalf of the Polish effort but really to little avail. Bomber Command had its own priorities and to be objective their crews had little chance to find very difficult targets in Poland. Bomber Command's whole strategy depended on the small group of superbly trained and experienced crews of the pathfinders. These gallant crews marked out the bombing zones with multicolored incendiary bombs and then estimated the actual target in relation to the position of the multicolored fires. As the waves of bombers flew over, the head navigator from the pathfinders would give instructions as whether bombs were to be dropped north, south, or whatever of the actual fires. The navigational skills of the average Bomber Command crew were very primitive. Polish crews were hardly better in astral navigation but knew the Polish countryside and topography and could follow the contours of rivers, lakes, etc., so that the small hamlets or woods sheltering the reception committees were found. For an Allied crew a Polish wood was one of many, but to a Polish crew a wood, copse, hamlet was a place well-known, loved, and familiar.

On October 16, 1943, General Mateusz Izycki, who had succeeded Ujejski, as the new Inspector of the Polish Air Force, requested the authorization of the Polish C-in-C (which was given) to reply to the telegram of the A.K. Izycki's reply consisted of four bullet statements: that due to the lack of presence of Allies on the continent, support of the Uprising by air units from the United Kingdom was impossible; that a select group of air force officers would be dispatched to Poland to clarify the situation; that instructions regarding German equipment would be transmitted to Poland; and finally, a request for more details about a number of other airfields located on Polish territory.[27] If one stipulates that the British were willing to give the Poles the resources requested, and the Polish squadrons flown to operate out of ill-prepared and possibly poorly defended bases, then it seems certain that the Luftwaffe would still have had the superiority to destroy the Poles, unless the whole German military strength was so demoralized as to be incapable of fighting. Therefore the plan was based on the supposition of a complete German military collapse, and the imperative to establish Polish constitutional Government control over Polish central territories. It was in fact as much anti-Soviet as anti-German. Given the climate of pro-Soviet policies in the West, it was in retrospect a nonstarter, but in mid-1943 hope was all that the Poles had.

By October 20, 1943, the Polish Air Force Inspectorate had fleshed out its short cable and there is no more controversial item in this situation than the final editing of the cable by General of the Army K. Sosnkowski, successor to Sikorski as C-in-C.[28]

The Polish Air Force Inspectorate again recapitulated many of the same points that had been made in the prior cables, such as the lack of autonomy and insufficient staffs above wing level. The cable again reiterated that the Poles were completely dependent on British support services, such as radar, meteorological reports, reconnaissance, supplies, logistics. Only in the area of medical support was there relative Polish autonomy since the Poles had their own hospitals, doctors, dentists, and in Edinburgh even their own Medical School. The report also repeated that Polish tactical groups did not have their own staffs and certainly no independent communication system.[29] The report again commented that the drastic personnel shortages not only prevented the expansion of the Polish Air Force, but that the bloody losses in the Bomber Offensive had forced the dissolution of one of the four bomber squadrons. The report concluded that the British were also struggling with personnel shortages and were unlikely to be in a situation to give any concrete assistance. The Air Force Inspector advised the Homeland that he was working on the creation of a Polish Independent Tactical Air Group, comprising eight fighter squadrons, four ground support squadrons, and all serviced by Polish personnel and commanded by a Polish tactical staff. It was presumed that such an independent air group would be in a position to undertake independent air operations. But as always the Polish Air Inspector cautioned that all such endeavors would require not only British permission for the growth of the Polish Air Force but the authorization of the Polish C-in-C to move the necessary numbers of personnel from the ground forces to the Air Force; acquisition of suitable equipment and the retraining of crews in new roles. Finally, it would require the Air Ministry to guarantee the availability of sufficient number of transport planes to move the quartermaster services and supplies to Poland. The points relating to the necessity of Allied permission and internal transfer of Polish personnel were crossed out, allegedly by Sosnkowski.

It is vital to note that the Polish Air Force Inspector concluded that air support for the Polish Uprising could only occur with the full concurrence and support of the Allies, which to date has not been received. This last point was also crossed out.

In December 1943 the three major leaders of the anti-Nazi coalition, two democrats and one who was until recently allied with Hitler's Germany, met at Tehran. The news of the debate, which began to leak out shortly, was a near mortal blow to the Poles. The major powers had met and then decided their future boundaries.[30]

On December 13, 1943, Major General Stanislaw Kopanski, the Polish Armed Forces Chief of Staff[31] and hero of Tobruk, issued instructions to the Air For Staff for further work on the feasibility of aiding the Polish Underground—*"Plan Wsparcia Powstania. Prace przygotowawcze"*[32] (Initial plans for the support of the Uprising. Preparatory Plan). This order, in itself a comprehensive document, to the Air Force Staff led to the most comprehensive and elaborate plan for air support of the Uprising. In his memorandum General Kopanski wrote that the A.K. Command still counted on the arrival of the Polish Air Force to support their Uprising. This conviction was allegedly based on prior telegrams and the monthly communiqués from which it was unclear that lack of personnel reserves precluded the ability of the Polish Air Force to achieve autonomous combat operations. This memorandum inevitably led to the to the conclusion that the A.K. Command had to be advised that the Polish Air Force could not be expected to move its operations to the territory of Poland or give any meaningful support for the Home Army.

Col. Michael Bokalski personally wrote in the margin of the Kopanski memorandum, *"Nie bujac Kraju"* (Don't fool the Homeland).[33] But orders are orders and the Section of Operations of the Polish Air wrote a brief rejoinder on February 1944, under the very unmilitary title of *"Nie Ludzic Kraju!"* (Don't Mislead the Homeland)[34] and recapitulated all the staff work back to 1942, and again emphasized the crucial importance of the basic condition for such a move and engagement in combat operations: the creation of a Polish Independent Tactical Group; the transfer of more human resources from the land forces to the Air Force; and the approval for such action by the British Air Ministry, which was equal to a political acquiescence in such Polish plans. This was a very terse and, one might even add an editorial comment, an inpatient memorandum. It concluded that it was vital to send air officers to Poland to clarify the situation.

The officer in charge of this air group that was parachuted into Poland was Colonel Jan Bialy. His written instructions came from Major General Izycki and in his postwar debriefing on his mission, Bialy recapitulated all of the above issues.[35] Bialy stated that after his successful drop on April 28, near Lublin, he contacted the Commanding Officer of the Air Section of the A.K., Colonel Adamecki and then again repeated the same basic facts to the Chief of Air Operations of the A.K., Colonel Adam Kurowski. The message conveyed was that the A.K. could not count on the help of the Polish or Allied Air Forces in event of an uprising. Colonel Bialy also wrote that he was not received by the Command of the A.K. but that in the clandestine organization and secrecy which prevailed in Poland this was neither unexpected nor surprising.

The only remaining question is whether the Home Army Command had other more optimistic and less realistic messages conveyed by other couriers or by radio messages from London. Szoldraska[36] describes many details of the functioning of the different subsections of the A.K. section of the Air Force but has no comment or any information or discussion on the bleak possibility of moving any Polish air units to Poland. One has to come to the conclusion that the realities of the Allied Air Force and in particular of the Polish Squadrons was never completely understood by the Home Army Commanders. The fact is that even if the British, in a moment of complete Allied harmony, designated all their two-engined Dakotas for transport duties to Poland, the final proverbial bottom line would have been negligible. The British never had sufficient transport planes or crews and as late as 1944 depended on Americans for flying in their Airborne forces in the Arnhem operation. Furthermore the slow Dakotas would have been annihilated on their flight to Poland.

In this series of frustrations, the Poles came closest to the creation of an independent Polish Tactical Group. This was a result of some serendipity when in the summer of 1943 the Royal Air Force, which was preparing for the invasion of the continent, formed the Second Tactical Air Force.[37] This was quickly exploited by the Poles who sought and received British Air Ministry approval for a major Polish Tactical Group conditioned on a transfer of a further 10,000 men for ground support duties.[38]

The British were in fact sympathetic to Polish aspirations for enhanced autonomy. Their staffs in the summer of 1943 minuted:

> In view of the fact that it is the Air Ministry policy to extend to the Polish Air Force every facility, in order that a well balanced nucleus of an Air Force capable of standing on its feet when it returned to Poland, should be available, it is considered that the representations as set out in the attached letter from the P.L.S.O. (Polish Liaison Senior Officer), should be borne in mind when forming this Polish Airfield.[39]

This had to do with the comprehensive staffing of support services for a Polish tactical wing. But following the signing of the new Air Force, which came into effect on April 6, 1944, there is further evidence that the Air Ministry wished to be helpful and accommodate Polish needs. There is no evidence that the British ever failed to live up the spirit or the letter of this collaboration and agreement.

But the Poles never had enough personnel to be able to develop such a major air component.

No such transfer occurred since the Polish High Command did not have any human reserves. This would have meant cannibalizing some Polish ground forces and it is unclear whether the British would have allowed that given the fact of their own desperate manpower shortages.[40]

The Poles had not been able to get a Tactical Group but were able to field the Polish 18th Fighter Group, which consisted of three wings; the First Wing: 302, 308, and 317 Polish Squadrons; the Second Wing: 306 and 317 Polish and 129 R.A.F.; and the Third Wing: 222 R.A.F., 349 Belgian, and 485 New Zealand. Air Officer Commanding was Colonel Gabszewicz. This only lasted a short time, since the German flying bomb offensive required the redeployment of many fighter squadrons back to R.A.F. Home Command.

The creation of a women's air service was an attempt to address the personnel deficiencies. The women were assigned to duties in communication, as drivers, military police, meteorologists, mechanics, medical personnel, etc.[41]

Marshal Edward Smigly-Rydz, the Inspector General of the Polish Armed Forces and Polish Commander-in-Chief in September 1939; accompanied by General Wladyslaw Bortnowski, inspecting a Polish Armored battalion in 1939. Equipped with Polish-built 7TP. These tanks were diesel powered and armed with a 37 mm Polish-built Bofors cannon. (Courtesy of George Bradford and Steven Zaloga, original copyright belonged to Planet News Ltd., London.)

A battery of Polish-designed and -built 75 mm antiaircraft guns.
(Courtesy of the Pilsudski Institute of North America).

Crews of the First Aviation Regiment, Warsaw, stand in front of their two-engined medium bombers, the P.Z.L. 37b. (Courtesy of the Pilsudski Institute of North America).

The President of Poland, Wladyslaw Raczkiewicz, being greeted by King George VI in London, June 1940. (Peszke collection.)

Their Royal Highnesses, King George VI and Queen Elizabeth, visiting the Polish First Corps in Scotland in early 1941. Their host was the Polish Prime Minister and Commander-in-Chief, General Wladyslaw Sikorski. (Courtesy of the Polish Institute and Sikorski Museum, London.)

Winston Spencer Churchill accompanied by Mrs. C. Churchill on a visit to the Polish First Army Corps in Scotland. Striding manfully is their host General Sikorski. The Polish ambassador to the Court of Saint James, Count Raczynski, is the civilian immediately behind Churchill. (Courtesy of the Polish Institute and Sikorski Museum, London.)

Polish Commandos. (Courtesy of the Polish Library, London.)

A number of accredited Polish Institutions of Higher Learning were created in the United Kingdom by the Polish Government during the Second World War. This photo shows faculty and students, mostly military, of the Polish Medical School in Edinburgh. (Courtesy of the Polish Library, London.)

General W. Sikorski decorating Polish airmen. (Courtesy of the Polish Library, London.)

The Honor Guard of the Parachute Brigade, after receiving their Standard, embroidered by the women of Warsaw. (Courtesy of the Polish Institute and Sikorski Museum, London.)

General W. Sikorski, accompanied by Marshal of the Royal Air Force, Sir Charles Portal, Chief of the British Air Staff, presents a Standard, embroidered by the Polish women of Wilno, to the Polish Air Force. The symbolic recipient is the Inspector General of the Polish Air Force, General Stanislaw Ujejski. (Courtesy of the Polish Air Force Association, London.)

Tanks of the Polish First Armored Division, Scotland. (Courtesy of the Polish Library, London.)

A Spitfire of the Polish City of Gdansk (318) Squadron, which was based in Italy. It flew air support missions, as well as artillery ranging for the Allied British Eight Army in general and the Polish 2 Army Corps in particular. (Courtesy of John Grodzinski.)

The beneficiaries of the unpopular Sikorski-Maiski Agreement. These young boys, many orphans, were released from the Soviet Gulags in 1941 and found a home and haven in the Polish Armed Forces. (Courtesy of the Polish Library, London.)

An American four-engined B-24, Liberator, used by the Polish special duties flight to air-drop supplies and couriers from Italy to German-occupied Poland. (Courtesy of the Polish Institute and Sikorski Museum, London.)

General Kazimierz Sosnkowski, who succeeded Sikorski as the
Polish Commander-in-Chief, inspecting the pack artillery of the
Polish Parachute Brigade. (Courtesy of the Polish Library, London.)

7

Only Hope Remained Now, Early 1944–August 1944

International and Political Background to Events of Early 1944

The news of the Tehran Conference were devastating. The majority of the Poles were undoubtedly depressed, embittered, and shell shocked, but remained committed to their policies of holding fast and planning for the best eventuality.

There was a feeling that at worst, the Poles would lose their historic and cherished lands in the east, the *Kresy*, which had played a long and noble role in Polish history. The possible loss of the city of Lwow was particularly feared and grieved. But many attempted to be optimistic and to see potential gains in the territories to be acquired at the expense of Germany. There was an expectation that at the very least the other city so tied in to Polish history, Gdansk, which was denied the Poles by the Western Powers in the postwar First World War era, would now, with the rest of Silesia and East Prussia, return to Poland. Some saw in this a satisfactory compensation.

On April 4, 1944, Jozef Retinger, Churchill's personal fact finder, was parachuted into Poland and was brought back on July 25 by one of the three *mosty* air pickups from Italy. There is every reason to infer from the mission and its secrecy that Churchill was hoping to be able to negotiate on behalf of Mikolajczyk or, even without his approval, as support for a different Polish Government. Clearly, what was found in Poland was a strong determination to preserve both the legitimacy of the Polish Governmm ent in London and the integrity of Polish boundaries.[1] Churchill could not manage to split the two groups. Retinger's report seemed to buttress Churchill's resolve that the Polish cause should be pursued, but also that the predominant political elements would be in the rural regions and represented by the Polish Peasant Party. At this point it appears that Churchill was still determined to champion the Polish cause, to support Mikolajczyk as the leader of the Peasant Party, who was also conveniently the Prime Minister, but appeared to turn his back on the Polish Government. His own dealings and of his ministers became perfunctory (they were to cease completely after Mikolajczyk's resignation in late 1944) and only the reality that the Polish Forces supported the Government maintained its presence. Had it not been for the Polish Forces, there can be no question that major compromises would have been implemented by Churchill as was to happen after the Yalta Conference.

The Peasant Party was indeed numerous and reflected the views of Poland's largest demographic group, the rural population, which before the war composed close to 70 percent of the country. But the National Democrats were as large in terms of numbers and also had a long tradition of patriotic activity going back to the times of Dmowski. The Peasant Party was part of the coalition government and held the prime ministership, yet it maintained its own clandestine military formations—the *battaliony chlopskie*—which refused all invitations to join the A.K. The National Democrats had split as to their participation in the coalition government and also continued to have their own force in Poland—the *Narodowe Sily Zbrojne*—but finally were pressed to integrate and the majority joined the A.K. The small group remained aloof and became a maverick fringe, fighting their own political and ideological war and, however well-intentioned, caused never ending embarrassment to the cause of Poland. Many of their acts were indiscriminately attributed to the Polish A.K.

But the climate for the Poles in the United Kingdom had changed. There were still many gestures of real friendship, but the majority of the British press had now completely gone to the side of the Soviets, and not just in the ongoing territorial dispute. This was the time that Burgess, one of the famous Cambridge alumni, was director of the B.B.C.

In the House of Commons debate on the Tehran Conference, the British acquiescence to the so-called Curzon Line elicited little disagreement, albeit there was much real sympathy for the Polish side. But the majority of the British press accepted this with complacency.[2]

This debate was shortly followed by an attack on the Poles and their institutions, but particularly directed at the Polish military forces in Scotland. The victim had to be found contemptible so there would not be any more sympathy. The issue was anti-Semitism. The world was beginning to learn about the Holocaust and much of this came from the Polish couriers. The Soviets omitted no opportunity to castigate all Polish leaders and senior officers as Nazis. Of course the problem of anti-Semitism was the most obvious symptom of such pernicious ideology, *ergo* prove the anti-Semitism and *quod erad demonstrandum*, the Poles are Nazis and not to be respected. Not that the Poles were immune to that prejudice, which was also found in many other societies.[3] But for a Government that had gone to war against the Poles in Alliance with Hitler to raise such a charge, and for the majority of the Western press not to dismiss it derisively was symptomatic of the influence of the Soviet protagonists in the United Kingdom and the United States.

The Poles were to be charged, found guilty, and condemned to expulsion from the Allied side. The charge and the proof was as follows.

On January 15, 1944, a group of 68 Polish Jews deserted from the Polish Armored Division in Scotland. This group was led by private R., a member of the New Zionist (Revisionist) Organization, and stayed at the Ohel Hotel, being visited by a representative of the New Zionist Organization.

The second group of nearly two hundred deserters who all came together were financed by a man called P., one of the deserters in the first group. In both instances the Polish authorities refused to arrest them, a right which was granted under the Polish-British Military Agreements. The British feared for the combat effectiveness of the Polish Armored Division destined for the Normandy landings and made it clear that they would not take any more transfers from the Poles. The Allied Quarterly Report stated:

> During the last few months parties of Polish Jewish soldiers from the Armd Div have deserted and come to London. The total number amounts to some 200. Unrest amongst the Jews is organised and supported by British and Polish Jewish organisations and has the sympathy of some Jewish Members of the House of Commons. The deserters were induced to return to Scotland with a view to transfer to the British Pioneer Corps. No further transfers will be permitted and disciplinary action had been taken against the most recent Jewish deserters which it is hoped will prevent further trouble. The Polish unit cannot afford to lose trained and fit men.[4]

But the witches' brew was not yet ready. A third group, close to a hundred, arrived by train in London at the behest of a number of Jewish Parliamentarians and managed to make a major news event. The following people were identified in this anti-Polish demarche: Lord Strabolgi, Mr. Shinwell, Mr. Driberg, Mr. Pritt. This now had the whole of London in an uproar.

Frank Savery of the British Foreign Office noted that visiting cards of the Soviet Embassy were found in the effects of the deserters. Savery commented that he was of the opinion that the efforts behind this were as much Soviet inspired as Revisionist-Zionist influenced in an attempt to create a Jewish Army. The argument had merit, since there were also desertions of Jews from the Czech Brigade at a time when relations between Benes and the Soviets were excellent. But the mass media did not attack the Czechs, only the Poles. Savery of the British Foreign Office minuted: "Lord Strabolgi's second point is probably the fundamental one, namely he is anxious that these men should be transferred not to the British Pioneer Corps, but to some specifically Jewish units."[5]

The files of the British F.O. makes it clear that the whole situation was calculated to be an embarrassment to the Poles and that the British Army wished no part of the deserters who are also described as "shirkers and of little military use anyway" and that "there is not the slightest chance of our being able to persuade the War Office to agree to this," namely a transfer to a Jewish unit. The conclusion of this long report is important.

> If the desertions were spontaneous, they must therefore have been due to sudden and unprecedented wave of anti-semitism in the Polish Army. This is not supported by the fact and events of the last three years. The official Polish attitude has been increasingly tolerant of the Jews and there has been no obvious outburst of cruelty in the day to day relations of Poles and Jews. If it seems unlikely that the desertions were spontaneous, it is reasonable to suppose that they were the result of an organized influence which chose the psychological moment for the desertions and the requisite element of publicity. There are in fact indications of such outside influence in the case of both Jews and Ukrainians. It may be significant that this situation has arisen during the present Soviet-Polish deadlock, and at a time when the New Zionist Organization in this country is particularly active.

The report goes on:

The critics have not proved or even sought to prove that anti-semitism is general. Yet by these judicious citations of isolated cases they have succeeded in creating an impression which they are content to leave distant from the truth. Impetuous and sensational exaggerations of the few available facts by the Press almost as a whole, has created a regrettable myth, and has subjected a credulous public to an invidious propaganda.

The report of the Foreign Office concludes with this final statement, which in current parlance, says it all!

It has been the unexpected one-sidedness of the British Press which has most discouraged the average (i.e., Polish) soldier. It is true to say that apart from official Polish announcements, which have naturally been considered biased, the amount of consideration from the purely Polish side of the question has been negligible.[6]

This was now the climate in the United Kingdom. The issue was not Polish boundaries, though many still believed that to be the case; the fundamental issue was the breakup of the Polish Government, of its A.K., and the extension of absolute Soviet hegemony over not just Poland, but all of Eastern Europe. But not many saw this until many years later. The third enemy was baring its anti-Polish teeth.

There were some, but rare, exceptions to this general anti-Polish tirade in the British press. The *Daily Telegraph* continued to be objective, and the *Illustrated London News* still remembered that the Poles were Allies and fighting on the same side. On February 15, 1944, it carried a piece, captioned "Poland's Militant Underground Movement Fights On." Four scenes were portrayed of life in Warsaw under occupation. One showed the typical German random roundup on a street, another a court handing a verdict on a German police officer guilty of crimes, and two showed the carrying out of such court decisions. It should be emphasized that the courts were only convened after the perpetrator of the crimes had been alerted that he would be tried and, if guilty, executed.

Poland's Government Tries Compromise

The Polish Prime Minister attempted to be as accommodating as possible, facing strong opposition to any form of appeasement, not only from the majority of Poles in the United Kingdom but also vehement opposition from the strongest and largest contingent of Poles outside of Poland, the Polish 2 Army Corps in Italy. His own Peasant Party in Poland was also strongly opposed to any territorial loss and this view reflected the Coalition of Parties in occupied Poland.

It is important to stress again that the Polish Government was in fact a coalition government, a government that reflected and also represented the views, feelings, and concerns of its citizens. The majority of the Poles in the West were military. Therefore, there seemed to be a misperception, one that was fueled by the inimical British press, that the Polish Government was reactionary and authoritarian and dominated by the military. In fact the majority of the Polish soldiers in the 2 Corps were not career soldiers. The majority of the career elite were dead at places like Katyn or in German prisoner of war camps following the September Campaign. It was also a tragedy of fate that the overwhelming majority of the officers and men of the Polish military in the West, the famous 2 Corps, were from the Eastern Regions of Poland, the historical, *Kresy*, that were coveted by the Soviets.

But the Polish Government also represented the views of the Polish Underground, and at this stage, there was adamant opposition to the very idea that Poland, after having been brutalized, martyred, devastated, and plundered, should accede to any loss of its historic territory. The Polish Prime Minister's own Peasant Party in Poland would not allow him any such options. So in a way, that was not appreciated, or was conveniently ignored, the "recalcitrant" Polish Government was merely legitimately representing its coalition parties.

Mikolajczyk went so far as to accept the Curzon Line, urged on the Poles by the British, as a provisional demarcation between the Polish and Soviet administrations, pending a postwar settlement. This was a face-saving acceptance of the Soviet demands, which had British support and American *disinteressement*. The Soviets refused. It is clear in hindsight that any concession by the Poles in 1944 would have been met by further nonnegotiable ultimatums. The willingness to give the Soviets de facto sovereignty over Polish territory was in fact a Polish fig leaf to save a semblance of face. But if one accepted the Soviet viewpoint that the Polish Government in London did not represent any legitimate constitutional body, then the Soviet rejection of this offer is particularly striking. They were in fact more than aware that the London Poles represented fighting

Poland and that the Polish Home Army looked up to the Polish Government for guidance and leadership. This was an all-out effort to dominate, coerce, intimidate the vibrant Polish Underground. Were the London Polish Government to give up territory during the war, then the state of morale in the country would perhaps collapse and the people would begin to look for other options to save the remnants of the Polish sovereignty. In fact something like this happened in the tragic circumstances after Yalta and the failed Warsaw Uprising. These Polish offers were refused and a categorical demand made that only a complete and unconditional acceptance of the Soviet demand would be the basic condition of renewing formal diplomatic relations between the Poles and the Soviets. The Soviets made it clear that the Polish Government needed to get rid of the figures that represented the governinng faction prior to 1939, that is anybody in any way connected to the *sanacja*. The two individuals who in fact were the major banner holders of the continuity of the prewar constitutional philosophy and were adamant about allowing any foreign agency, Soviet or Western Allied, to infringe on Polish sovereignty were the President, His Excellency Wladyslaw Raczkiewicz, and the Commander-in-Chief, Sosnkowski.

As the Soviets advanced into Poland the conditions changed until the demand was made that all Polish Forces in the West be subordinated to the Lublin Committee, which was formed on July 22, 1944, coupled with an invitation for Mikolajczyk to join this group as one of three vice-prime ministers. The Soviets stated that while this was short of the Government they wished to see established on Polish lands, they would give this committee full responsibility for all civil administration in Polish territories west of the so-called Curzon Line.

The Polish Government now embarked on a final political endeavor to seek American support for its policies and took the step of promoting, in a very subtle way, the centralizing of all Polish-American groups to form the Polish-American Congress. The Polish Prime Minister, Mikolajczyk, also solicited an invitation from Roosevelt, which was finally extended and implemented on May 6, 1944. The goal of the new organization was to exert political pressure on Roosevelt since he was running for his unprecedented fourth term in November 1944.[7]

The visit by Mikolajczyk to Washington achieved nothing for the Polish cause, but possibly strengthened Roosevelts's chances for reelection by firming the overwhlemingly democratic vote of the Polish-Americans. But both Churchill and Roosevelt strongly encouraged Mikolajczyk to travel to Moscow and to attempt to resume diplomatic ties with the Soviets.

In this endeavour, Mikolajczyk was bitterly and strongly opposed by Sosnkowski, who began an active campaign in London as well as in Poland to discredit Mikolajczyk's efforts, painting them as appeasement and alluding to the infamous historic Targowica in late eighteenth-century Poland.

But the Prime Minister and Commander in Chief were in agreement on the futility of further military collaboration with the Soviets unless there was a political agreement. The tragic experiences of the Polish A.K. units, which had attempted to collaborate with the Soviets and were then disarmed, their officers arrested, and their soldiers forcibly enrolled in the Soviet-officered Polish communist army, were just more than could be tolerated. With each passing week, such a political settlement appeared further away.

On July 11, Sosnkowski flew to Italy to join the 2 Army Corps, where his views were widely shared and endorsed by a body of men who had been through the experience of the Soviet camps. This also placed Sosnkowski in the midst of the largest contingent of Poles in the West, and the largest Polish formation, consisting of two infantry divisions, one armored brigade, and a very large Artillery group of over ten field artillery regiments. The Polish 2 Army Corps was in the process of carrying out the Ancona maneuver, and the Allies had no other reserves; in other words, all knew that the Poles were essential. Sosnkowski was prepared to use this fact to stalemate any Mikolajczyk initiatives inimical to Polish interests.

It was in the middle of these accomplished facts, never criticized by the West, that Mikolajczyk made his decision to fly to Moscow, a trip urged on him both by Churchill and Roosevelt.

With fifty years' hindsight it is really impossible to know which potential policy was better. Mikolajczyk was guided by pragmatism; a surprisingly shrewd politician given his limited education, he was not the easy mark that Churchill must have originally assumed him to be. Mikolajczyk was pushed by strong British pressures and was a man of the Wielkopolska region, i.e., western lands that had little historic enmity to Russia. Sosnkowski was a Polish patriot and had a historic sense of the struggle, and was convinced that any seeming compromise and accommodation would lead to further demands. His sense was that the Poles should say No, since the ultimate consequences would be the same. Either the Soviets would be powerful and take Poland over, all of it, regardless of the political accommodations, or would be pressed back by the Western Allies and then it would be time to make political compromises.

Polish Special Duties Flight in Italy

In late 1943 the Polish flight consisting of six crews plus a small number of reserves was moved to southern Italy, in Allied liberated territory, and began to fly special missions to Poland and also to other occupied countries. This quickly became a bone of contention between the Royal Air Force authorities and the small but independent-minded unit, which was attempting to implement its own commander's orders. The Polish flight was equipped with three Liberators and three Halifaxes. In Italy the flight attempted unsuccessfully to function in an autonomous fashion. On the first four-plane expedition to Poland from their new Italian base, two of the Polish Liberators crashed, with the loss of six airmen, thus reducing the effectiveness of the flight by 33 percent.

In addition, the autonomy was constantly challenged and there was a constant source of friction between the Polish flight commander, insisting on his understanding of the orders from his Polish Headquarters in London, and the local R.A.F. command. There was annoyance at the Olympian heights of the British Air Ministry, when the Polish Commanding officer, Major Krol, flew to the United Kingdom on an unauthorized flight to report directly to Polish authorities the plight of his unit's situation. The Polish complaint was that the equipment situation was catastrophic and that the Polish flight was not receiving logistical help in the rotation of engines after a manadatory number of hours flown, etc. The British Air Ministry responded with considerable annoyance and did not refute the facts, but placed the blame on the local Polish flight commander, who failed to follow regular and proscribed R.A.F. policies. The Polish C-in-C was also requested to hold the Polish flight to R.A.F. policies and Air Marshall Slessor was ordered to ensure that the Poles abided by R.A.F. rules. Portal to Sosnkowski on January 28, 1944:

> Thank you for your letter No. 96/GNW/44 of the 24th January. I fully understand the difficulties with which the Polish Flight in Italy must be faced in an endeavouring to maintain their operational effi-

ciency, and I am sorry to hear from you that the numbers of aircraft in the Flight have been so seriously reduced. At the same time, I feel bound to point out that, owing possibly to a misunderstanding on the part of the Commander of the flight, who has not regarded his unit as being, for operational and administrative purposes, an integral part of the Special Duty Wing formed in Italy for the conduct of Special Operations, neither the Headquarters of the Mediterranean Allied Air Forces nor the Air Ministry have ben kept informed of the aircraft state in this Flight. It was only as a result of representations by S.O.E. to the Air Ministery, made, I understand on information received through S.O.E. channels, that we were informed that 2 of your Liberators had crashed and that urgent replacements were required.

My staff were informed by the Flight Commander when he recently visited this country, that in addition to the loss of the 2 Liberators, 2 of the Halifeaxes in his Flight were without engines. It transpired, however, that these engines were in fact being provided from M.A.A.F. resources and arrived at Naples on the 14th January. It thus appears that, as a result of the coincidence of normal unserviceability and unfortunate accidents, the strength of the Flight was reduced by about the 13/14th January to a strength of 2 serviceable aircraft.

It is, of course, possible that the remaining Halifax was also temporarily unserviceable, which would have reduced the strength to 1 serviceable aircraft at that particular time.

For Portal to argue with a straight face that senior Royal Air Force commanders were unaware of the loss of two Polish planes and of two crews is not merely unbelievable but preposterous. Portal acknowledges the importance that the Poles place on their flight, but also places the blame for the loss of two Polish planes on the Polish Major, in his message to Sosnkowski.

I must remark that the return of the Flight Commander of No. 1586 Flight to this country apparently to report to you upon matters about which the Air Ministry had not been informed, as they should have been, appears to have been a somewhat irregular proceeding. It is not clear, from my information, that he had been granted permission by the Officer Commanding No. 344 Wing to return, or that there was, from the point of view of the Royal Air Force, any service technical reason for the visit.

I have given instruction for the Flight Commander to be informed of the system of higher command of his flight, and for him to be instructed to conform to normal R.A.F. procedure both as regards reporting his aircraft strength and serviceability and also the operational control of his unit, and I should be grateful if you would arrange for confirmatory instructions to be sent. I would assure that if this procedure is followed, everything possible will be done for lack of provision of the agreed complement of aircraft.[8]

There is evidence that the Air Ministry sent a scathing message to M.A.A.F. but no evidence that the Polish C-in-C complied with Portal's request for a "confirmatory instructions" to be sent. In view of the fact that Krol continued in command and was one of a small handful of officers to be decorated with the Polish Virtuti Militari Gold Cross (Class IV) it does seem that he was complying with Polish policies at the risk of burning his bridges with the British.

But the above exchange illustrates that local Polish requests were being ignored. It is hard to imagine that the Royal Air Force Wing Commander had no idea that his Polish Flight was so short of planes. It was clearly a way of making the Poles toe the line. It also illustrates the generally negative attitudes of the British field commanders to all clandestine activities but in particular those that seemed to be outside of their control. The Cypher telegram, to M.A.A.F. from Air Ministry, Whitehall, January 26, 1944, Personal for Slessor from CAS, addressed London's unhappiness with the situation in Italy and went on to state:

I would be grateful if you would arrange for the Flight Commander to be disabused of his wrong ideas since without up-to-date information here we cannot hope to make up the strength of the Polish Flight should casualties occur such as those of the night of 5/6 January. (You will be well aware of the political implications involved.)

More important than the submission of returns however appear to be the operational control of the Flight. The Flight Commander Squadron Leader Krol recently arrived in this country in his remaining Liberator on the pretext that the aircraft was in need of overhaul whereas in fact it was due only for a routine inspection which should have been made at the parent airfield or at any rate within the Command.

The real reason for his visit appears to have been to enable the Flight Commander to report to Polish Headquarters in London on a) the low serviceability rate in his unit and b) the circumstances in which two Liberators were lost with their crews on the night of 5/6 January. As a result General Sosnkowski the Polish Commander in Chief has written personally to me about a) and Lord Selborne has written personally to S. of S. about b).

The matter of replacement aircraft was already in hand but the

second question of Lord Selborne's letter, appears to merit full investigation and although I suspect that the independent attitude of
the Polish Flight Commander may have a bearing on the accident I
cannot advise S. o S. how to reply until an enquiry has been held.

It is a pity that you must have to be bothered with these matters
when your hands must be very full but I must ask you to look into
the question of the control of S.D. Squadrons with particular reference to No. 1586 Flight and ensure that we are not again exposed to
criticism of R.A.F. Operational or Administrative arrangements either by the Minister of Economic Warfare or the Polish High Command. Finally, you should make it absolutely plain to the Polish
Flight Commander that his flight is just as much under your command as are all the other R.A.F. units in the Mediterranean. For all
operational and administrative purposes, he is under your orders
and must deal with nobody but yourself acting through the Commanding Officer of No. 334 S.D. Wing. on all questions other than
the reception arrangements in Poland and details of loads to be carried which are dealt with in London between S.O.E. and Polish general Staff. Please confirm that Squadron Leader Krol fully under-
stands the position.[9]

Line officers do not appreciate political interventions. This message speaks a thousand words. It addresses the frustration of Portal
in dealing with Lord Selborne and with the Poles, and clearly
commiserates with the local R.A.F. commanders in Italy, in having
to deal with such political issues. The Polish cause could not have
been well served by such a message. But that is only part of the
problem.

It has often been commented that Poles have a ethnocentric pre-
occupation with conspiracy theories, inevitably directed at them
and to their disadvantage. But the British had a very elegant manner of always having an alibi for their failures. The R.A.F. Bomber
Command is unable or unwilling to commit planes for Poland and
seeks to impeach the integrity of the Polish clandestine organization, an integrity that was a model for all and that was to be followed by the Germans when they considered their Werewolf organization under Allied occupation. Portal "suspects" that it is the
independent attitude of the Polish flight commander that may be
responsible for the two crashed Liberators. Apparently the fact that
the Polish Flight, which was to have six four-engined planes on establishment is down to merely one (!) seems to be a set of circumstances beyond the knowledge or control of any senior R.A.F.
Command.

Later in the war other Polish traits will be alluded to as causes for British incapacity, failure, or helplessness at the hands of their more powerful Allies, the Americans and the Soviets.

The Poles were not completely satisfied and continued to press their demands for the flight (i.e., six four-engined planes) to be developed into a full squadron of twelve aircraft. This was argued on the merits of the need for that many planes to deliver the requisite supplies to Poland, and also by concern that a loss of one crew and the mechanical impairment of another would leave the Polish effort short as happened in January 1944 when the two Polish crews that were lost curtailed the establishment of the flight by 33 percent. This added weight to Polish arguments. Understandably, the fact that the Poles had to be supplied by the R.A.F. logistical tail but were less than completely receptive to being involved in other special duties must have grated. But it needs to be remembered that the special duties missions enjoyed little sympathy with any of the R.A.F. senior officers, who viewed all such missions, whether flown by R.A.F. or other crews, as a waste of resources and a distraction from other more important combat flights.

In February 1944 Slessor reported his views of the problem of special duties under his command:

> It assumes that the Poles will allow their Halifaxes to be used in the MAAE pool for operations in the Balkans on some nights when operations in Poland are impossible. This is essential and I suggest you put it squarely to the Polish authorities on the following lines. I will do my utmost to see that the effort outlined in para 4 is achieved and will help out on favorable nights with aircraft provided the Poles put their aircraft into MAAE pool. They have not a dog's chance of doing this planned effort without our assistance in view of the weather conditions, and if they do not agree to pooling their aircraft I shall leave them to stew in their own juice and they will be lucky if they get their planned effort.[10]

British Policy Continues to Support the Polish Cause

Meanwhile in the United Kingdom there continued to be tension within British ranks. The Poles certainly had a great friend and ally in Lord Selborne, the Minister of Economic Warfare; and the Air Ministry predictably downplayed the military advantages of special duties flights, particularly at a time when the bomber offensive appeared to be bringing the long-desired results. It is the British

Prime Minister's position that is both interesting and at least somewhat perplexing given his other acts and speeches. A case in point
is illustrated in the minutes of the Defence Committee section of
Special Operations in Poland and Czechoslovakia on February 3,
1944:

> Minister of Economic Warfare agreed with the opinion expressed
> by the Chiefs of Staff in their report that the control of special opera-
> tions in both countries (i.e., Poland and Czechoslovakia) should re-
> main with S.O.E. in London, subject to the direction of the Chiefs of
> Staff. As regards Poland the position was as follows. Assistance to
> the Poles had to be provided from the Mediterranean. The German
> night fighter strength made S.O.E. operations over Poland based in
> this country impracticable. On the other hand, the Polish Govern-
> ment was established in London. Relations with the Poles involved
> many difficult political problems which had to be settled here. In the
> circumstances it would be inconvenient for the control of S.O.E. op-
> erations over theat country to be centred in the Mediterranean thea-
> tre. As regards Czechoslovakia, Lord Selborne said that after the as-
> sassination of Heidrich the Germans had conducted a terrible
> campaign of repression and slaughter which had the effect of
> stamping out the Secret Army in that country. S.O.E. had made sev-
> eral attempts to encourage the reorganization of resistance, but had
> met with no success and had received little support or encourage-
> ment from the Czechoslovak Government in this country.
>
> Apart from the matters specifically included in the agenda, the
> Minister wished to raise a few other questions regarding the Polish
> Resistance Movement. A recent report by the Joint Intelligence Sub-
> Committee had criticised the degree of autonomy allowed the Polish
> authorities in the use of cyphers and in expenditure of money. He
> reminded the Committee that in 1940, under the authority of the
> Prime Minister, a credit had been opened for the Polish Government,
> for the purpose of fostering resistance in Poland, of L600,000, a year.
> Up to date a total of only L400,000 had been spent. The Poles had re-
> cently asked for money to be released from this credit and he had
> agreed; but in view of the criticism levelled by the Joint Intelligence
> Sub-Committee, he had thought it desirable to seek confirmation
> from the Committee.
>
> The Secretary of State for Foreign Affairs stated that he would
> have liked His Majesty's Government to have had the same control
> over the Poles as they possessed over our other Allies. He felt, how-
> ever, that this was not a happy moment to make change, and sug-
> gested that the existing arrangements should for the time being, be
> allowed to continue.

The Minister of Economic Warfare next asked the Committee to give directions for an increase in the assistance to be given to the resistance movement in Poland. At present only 6 aircraft had been allocated for S.O.E. work over Poland and lately only 2 of these were serviceable.

He was satisfied that the Polish Resistance was most vigorous and efficient. The Poles were expert in resistance, and in this respect compared favourably with the people of any other countries occupied by Germany. The Poles themselves claimed that they were containing large German forces. He had heard a figure mentioned of half million men. He urged the Committee to authorise the allocation of 17 aircraft for S.O.E. work over Poland.

The Chief of Air Staff said he felt confident that an increase of supplies to Poland could be achieved were the pool of aircraft for S.O.E. operations in the Mediterranean not restricted as to operations they were permitted to carry out. This pool of 32 aircraft was now available for operations over the Balkans only. If the pool were "unfrozen" he believed that it would pay great dividend. Weather conditions would at some periods make operations possible in some areas when they were impossible in others.

The Secretary of State for Foreign Affairs stated that the number of aircraft allotted for S.O.E. work over Jugoslavia, Greece and Poland was only 38. It seemed a very small allocation in view of the importance at this stage of the war of encouraging the patriot forces in those countries to resist the enemy and to contain his forces.

The Chief of the Air Staff said our supreme task in the air was to sustain the battle which was being waged by Bomber Command, and which might prove decisive if we did not allow ourselves to be drawn away by less essential calls on our resources. If our Bomber crews felt at this time, when the German defence was increasing its efficiency, that they were not receiving support, their morale was bound to suffer. The large scale bombing of the distant parts of Germany was only possible in the months of February, March, and April, which were the same months which were alone suitable for operations over Poland.

The Prime Minister said that he considered it a matter of high public importance that greater assistance should be given by the Air Staff to resistance movements in occupied Europe, even at some small expense to other responsibilities of the Royal Air Force. Treble the present allocation of aircraft to Poland should be accorded. A diversion of 12 aircraft from the bomber effort over Germany was a small price to pay. There was danger in rigid adherence to overriding priorities. Priorities should only be considered in relation to the assignment to which they referred. An extra 12 aircraft for Poland at this stage might make a considerable difference. Now that the Russians were advancing onto Poland it was in our interest that Poland should be strong and well supported. Were she weak and overrun by the advancing Soviet armies, the result might hold great dangers in the future for the English speaking peoples.[11]

This comment by Churchill not mentioned in his Nobel Prize for Literature–winning memoirs was made at a highly secret meeting of the highest members of his war cabinet subcommittee. It was not a propaganda speech delivered to encourage the Poles or, as a British officer said at the time of Yalta, to "jolly them along." It illustrates at least two points, firstly that British policy to Poland was not at this stage of the war completely disinterested and secondly, that the Poles who had intimate dealings with the British must have been subtly encouraged to proceed with their own Polish long-term plans.

In Italy the Poles had little choice but to participate in a team effort. In fact from a purely logical view the British position was well justified and well argued. Weather conditions varied and at times it made sense for crews to fly to a local target such as North Italy or the very close Balkans. Such missions also allowed the crews a respite from the hazardous and exhausting flights of well over twelve hours to Poland.

But the Polish effort to help their R.A.F. and Royal South African crews to other drop zones were not reciprocated. It was not a question of lack of goodwill or of courage, it was just that the Poles had a different perception of the flight to Poland. The flights to Poland were difficult and while Allied (British and South African) crews assisted, their results were uniformly less successful. For the Polish crews a flight to Poland was a crusade. Table 1 illustrates the actual breakdown of the flights to Poland by Polish and other crews; and the role of the Polish crews in carrying out assistance to other targets.

Final Polish Air Staff Plans on Behalf of the A.K.

In April 1944, the Poles and the British signed a new Air Agreement, which corrected many of the deficiencies of the prior 1940 agreement and which also changed the Polish Air Force Inspectorate to the Polish Air Force Command. This allowed the Poles to form their own staffs.[12]

The terse rejoinder to the A.K. must have been thought inade-

TABLE 1   Breakdown of the Flights by Polish and Allied Crews to
Poland and Other Targets

Year	Polish Crews to Poland	Polish Crews to Other Targets	Allied Crews to Poland
1941	2	0	2
1942	21	93	16
1943	61	130	168
1944	339	604	133
1945	0	95	0
Total	423	922	319

quate and on May 12, 1944, the new Polish Air Force Commanding
Officer, Major General Mateusz Izycki, cabled the last air-related
message to the A.K. This memorandum on the crucial question of
air support to the A.K. is essentially an outline of the obvious but
does offer a number of new options. In a more realistic and highly
imaginative manner, the report urged that more Polish crews, particularly pilots, but also ground support crews, should be trained
on British captured German planes, so that when such planes fell
into Polish hands in Poland, pilots and ground crews would be
familiar with their flying and maintenance characteristics. (There
was such a secret squadron in the United Kingdom, and some Polish pilots were given an opportunity to pass through the base, including Colonel Bialy, but the unit was obviously highly secret and
the number of planes and trainees limited.) The report also identified a number of pre-1939 Polish air bases and newly developed
German ones on Polish territory that were to be considered as possible Polish air bases. Further A.K. reports were requested and the
A.K. was urged to form and train ground units for their capture
and defense. The bases identified were: Bielany, Bielice, Borowina,
Piastow, Klikawa for fighter squadrons, and had the estimated
ability to land 220 planes each day.

The hindsight reaction to this report is that in circumstances
analogous to November 11, 1918, the Polish Air Force could be
moved to Poland, but that for any meaningful air support of the
Uprising, Allied intervention was an absolute imperative. Since it
was unrealistic to give the A.K. air support by moving the units to
Poland, the memorandum proposed that tactical air support be
provided from bases in the West. The plan analyzed air transport

needs of moving both the Polish Para Brigade and daily tonnage required to support the Polish air units in Poland. The Polish Air Group, which at this point did not yet exist except in a planning stage, but which was to consist of 13 squadrons, would have required 168,784 tons of gasoline and oil; 54,630 tons of munitions plus food; and reserve material. To ensure such a logistical support would have required 339 two-engined transport planes of the DC Dakota type. Since air support to the Home Army had to be coordinated, the importance of improving communications was stressed.

But British support was a sine qua non of any Polish endeavor. This scrupulously honest assessment also speculated that an Allied Composite Group, which could consist of 24 fighter and fighter/ bomber squadrons and in which Poles would participate, might be strong enough to give local air support based from Polish captured and controlled airfields. This would still have required significant air support by Allied units operating from Western bases. Izycki went on to stress that the Poles had not received any such Allied commitment. Izycki reiterated that for the necessary and appropriate number of combat squadrons to be moved to Poland and supplied from Western bases would require an air transport of a size that the Allies did not possess, and that the British lacked actual experience in such operations. Because of all these points the support of the Uprising by the Polish or Allied/Polish Air Groups was unrealistic even if a political agreement was reached. The telegram concluded that the London-based staffs had forwarded and would continue to cable numerous instructions and technical specifications to Poland, particularly technical specs of German communication systems and German aircraft, but warned that there were only limited possibilities for training on captured German planes in the United Kingdom. In turn Izycki requested details of airfields in Poland, the specific targets for eventual bombing from Western bases. For this purpose a questionnaire was developed and cabled regarding details of airfields, with particular emphasis on the number, direction and length of runways, local impediments, guard activities, night flying capability, bunkers, hangars, etc.[13]

There were no further plans or developments prior to the Warsaw Uprising of August 1, 1944, but during the spring of 1944 there were three successful landings in Poland. This was the typical technique for inserting and picking up agents in the German occupied countries of Western Europe and was also practiced by the Soviets in their support of their communist agents in Eastern Poland. But there were two major problems for this to be accomplished between the West and Poland. The long distance required a long-range plane, and that in turn meant a heavy, at least two-engined aircraft. To land a such a big plane on the primitive fields accessible to the control and protection of the Polish Home Army was difficult. But on the night of April 15/16, 1944, a R.A.F. two-engined Dakota, piloted by Flight Lieutenant E. Harrod with Captain B. Korpowski as second pilot of the 334 Special Duty Wing, made the first successful flight. Five Poles were picked up, including General Stanislaw Tatar, who was one of the senior members of the VI Section of the Polish General Staff. About a month later this was repeated and one of the Poles flown to Poland was General Tadeusz Kossakowski (*Krystynek*), who had commanded the Polish Engineering Forces in the United Kingdom and was being inserted to organize the Polish clandestine armaments production. A number of individual were flown out, including Col. Roman Rudkowski, who had been parachuted to Poland in January 1943 as an emissary of the Polish Air Force Staff to the Polish Underground Army. The third and, it turned out to be, the final operation was the most important and most dramatic. On the night of July 25/26, 1944, a Dakota from the same wing, flown by a New Zealander with a Pole as navigator, picked up the parts of a German V rocket and also two important people, namely the British emissary to Poland, Jozef Retinger, and Mr. Tomasz Arciszewski, leader of the Polish Socialist Party, later to be the Polish Prime Minister. These three flights were code named *Mosty*, or Bridges. But by the time the Poles and the Allies had the techniques, the Soviets were in physical control of at least half of prewar Poland.[14]

The War Against the Germans
Continues Unabated

The Polish Air and Naval Forces continued their fight and in the late winter months of 1943, the Polish 2 Army Corps, under the command of Lt. General Wladyslaw Anders, entered operations in Italy. From now on the Poles, in addition to their own famous *syrena* (the Warsaw Mermaid), also wore the cross of the crusaders, the insignia of the British Eight Army.

The Polish Navy continued to take part in all the naval operations. These operations were continuous and were thus described by the First Lord of the Admiralty, Alexander, when he opened the exhibition dedicated to the Polish Navy and Merchant Marine in the spring of 1944 in London:

> Whenever in the course of naval operations in this present world conflict at sea a great concourse of ships is gathered together, there is almost always to be seen one or more Polish ensigns, worn either by Polish warships or by vessels of the Polish Mercantile Marine, or by both.
>
> In view of its small size, the number of operations in which the Polish Navy has taken part is almost incredible, especially bearing in mind that some of them are continuous. Amongst these operations are Narvik, Dunkirk, Lofoten Islands, Tobruk, Dieppe, attacks on shipping in the Channel, Sicily, Italy, Oran and patrols notably in the Mediterranean, and convoy escorting. The recent work of the Polish ships in the Mediterranean has been especially brilliant.[15]

The stirring words, which attest to the actual facts better than anything the could be written, and which most Poles would say, were well deserved, were in fact directed at a different audience. This was an attempt by the British Government to both bolster the Poles and to show the Soviets that the British still regarded the Polish Government in London as the constitutional and legitimate authority representing the Polish State. Such was no longer the position of the Roosevelt Government. While the Polish ambassador in Washington continued to function and be accorded all pertinent diplomatic privileges, there was no successor following the resignation of the highly respected and pro-Polish U.S. ambassador, Mr. Biddle, in late 1943.[16]

The Polish Government failed to read the tea leaves from this resignation and the prolonged delay in appointing a replacement. It continued until late in 1944 to work through its agencies in the United States to attempt to influence the political process on behalf of the cause of Poland, by arguing that the issues transcended mere Polish interests, that in fact the cause of Poland was the question of the Principles of the Atlantic Charter.

The Mission of the Parachute Brigade Is Changed

The Polish Parachute Brigade grew in numbers and by early 1944 had a total of 266 officers and 2,300 other ranks. However, it was still significantly under strength since there were only a total of 420 riflemen in each of the three parachute battalions. Even so,

British interest in that unit began to appear. On March 11, 1944, General Grasset, representing the European section of SHAEF (Supreme Headquarters Allied Expeditionary Force) in a formal letter to the Polish High Command, wished to ascertain whether the Polish High Command would amend existing agreements and release the Polish Parachute Brigade for combat action in Northwest Europe. The letter from a high British officer left open the possibility of British support for such combat operations as were planned by the Poles.

> Field Marshal Sir Alan Brooke fully realizes that in accordance with the existing agreement the Polish Parachute Brigade is unreservedly at your disposal for operations in Poland, and is excluded from any operations that are to be undertaken by the Allied Forces. Since this agreement was made the general outlook and requirements of the War have changed and we are now faced with the probability of the most formidable operations of War of alltimes and one will require the employment of the maximum effort and resources at the disposal of the Allies. In this operation we must not fail.
>
> It was for this reason that the Chief of the Imperial General Staff instructed me to enquire whether you would agree to altering the present agreement concerning the Polish Parachute Brigade and place it at the disposal of the Supreme Allied Commander for operations in Western Europe. Sir Alan Brooke is fully aware of the importance that you and your Government attach to keeping this Brigade intact and available for your own requirements in Poland at a later date. Should you agree to the Brigade taking part in operations in Western Europe, casualties will undoubtedly occur.
>
> On the other hand the prestige and battle experience of the Brigade would be greatly enhanced. It is because the Polish Parachute Brigade is composed of such fine fighting material that the Chief of the Imperial General Staff hopes that it may be available for the critical operations to come.[17]

Grasset's comments are interesting if analyzed. It acknowledges prior agreements but also admits by default the shortages of British forces, which makes a small brigade, as was the Polish Para unit, worth entering into such a set of negotiations. It encourages those in the Polish Government who still looked to a positive and British-sponsored outcome to the struggle with the Soviets. It is also a trifle amusing for a senior British general to be so concerned about Polish "prestige." But possibly the cynicism is not justified. It may be that the British Government hoped that an active land participation by Polish forces would revert the mass media anti-Polish attitude.

Furthermore in the letter Grasset suggested that the British would welcome the Polish Brigade for one major operation in Northwest Europe and that if losses went over 25 percent the unit would be withdrawn forthwith. The letter also stated: "When an opportunity arises for employing this Brigade in Poland, it will be placed at the disposal of the Polish Commander-in-Chief. It is not possible at this stage to give a definite guarantee on the subject of aircraft for the transport of the Brigade to Poland."

The Poles responded outlining both their concerns and their reservations. The Polish position was that there were inadequate reserves (the fourth battalion of the Brigade had been cannibalized); reiterated their long-standing goal that the Brigade was to reinforce the Polish uprising in Poland; and made the following conditions: that the Brigade would be used as a Polish Airborne Brigade-group, only in one major operation or a number of minor ones, and that if casualties exceeded 15 percent would be withdrawn. Finally the two most pressing and probably unrealistic conditions:

> The Brigade will be immediately withdrawn from action and placed at the disposal of the Polish C.-in-C. as soon as the possibility or at least probability of its use in Poland will arise. The Polish side will be competent to choose the right moment.
>
> Field Marshal Sir Alan Brooke to give assurances of providing the means of transporting the Brigade by air/aircraft, gliders, flying personnel and also fighter escort for the protection of the Brigade's transportation and that of its supplies/ when the Polish Government and the Polish Commander-in-Chief will decided to use the Brigade in Poland.

The memorandum concluded by stating: "I understand that as long as the new agreement is not reached the prinicpals contained in the letter of the C.I.G.S. No. 0175/329/MOI of the 13 June, 1943 are still in force."

On May 21, 1944, Grasset responded to the Polish communiqué. It is fair to say that the original British letter requested Polish acquiescence to the British proposal and made no mention of asking for Polish conditions.

> General Sir Bernard Montgomery does not feel able to accept this Brigade under the conditions mentioned in your above letter. Gen-

eral Montgomery fully realises the shortage of Polish reserves in the United Kingdom and the difficulty which will arise in the replacement of casualties. He also realises the importance which you and your Government attach to this Brigade. But General Montgomery considers that if the Brigade is to be placed under his command he must be given a free hand to employ it in any manner that operations may demand. I am instructed to inform you that the British Chiefs of Staff, whilst unable to give any guarantee regarding the provision of aircraft to transport the Brigade to Poland, or about replacements of equipment, will do their best in the light of the circumstances existing at the time, to meet the requirements of the Polish Authorities in these respects.

I feel sure you will appreciate the position of the British Chiefs of Staff and recognize their inability to commit themselves specifically at this stage of the war.

The Chief of the Imperial General Staff and General Sir Bernard Montgomery both fully understand your wishes regarding the employment of the Polish Parachute Brigade. They consider that this Brigade being composed as it is of such fine fighting material, if available, might make a valuable contribution to the war at some stage in the operations.[18]

Finally the Polish Government was consulted and in turn the Polish Underground Leadership. The political pros and cons of acceding or refusing British requests were considered as well as the merits of having a combat-seasoned unit for possible use in Poland. Between March and May 1944 a whole set of meetings occurred, and memoranda were exchanged between the British and Polish High Commands on this issue.[19]

The final consensus was that political issues were vital, that British goodwill needed to be considered, and that it might be better to have a smaller but more experienced unit. This was a real dilemma, placing the Poles between the Scylla and Charybidis of losing British support in the future and possibly losing the Brigade now.[20] There is no reason to dispute the British intentions, which were sufficiently flexible and big enough to allow the proverbial truck to drive through. There was no way the Poles could move the Brigade to Poland without major British logistical and political support. The British did not guarantee such cooperation, yet it did not require much foresight to know that if the British were refused, there would be no assistance in the future. Clearly, to also use another phrase currently in American language, "the moral obligation of people in responsibility is to be optimistic." The Polish General

Staff had no alternative choice but to plan the best-case scenario and to develop contingency plans and resources accordingly.

It may not be fair to the British to assume that the acerbic and petty remarks of the petit bourgeois Montgomery represent either majority view or the views of the governing men. But Montgomery's admiring biographer Nigel Hamilton attributes to him the following remark about difficulties with the final strength of the Polish Armored Division, which like all Polish Forces in the middle of that year was struggling with reaching established strength.

> We have got difficult problems ahead, and to employ the forces of those Allies circumscribed by various restrictions is militarily unsound, and appears to me politically unwise. Some of those countries who did very little to help us fight the enemy, e.g. France, now appear to be laying down conditions because they see the end in sight. I consider that nations that have been under the heel of Germany must do as we tell them until the war is over and Germany defeated. They will probably have to do as we tell them even after that. I would rather not have them at all.[21]

This view should be contrasted with the more pragmatic, less doctrinaire, and politically more sophisticated attitudes of Churchill, who minuted to General Hollis on June 23, 1944:

> I consider that the Polish Parachute Brigade should not be lightly cast away. It may have a value in Poland itself far out of proportion to its actual military power. I trust these views may be conveyed to Generals Eisenhower and Montgomery before the brigade is definitely established in France.[22]

It is again a hint that the British Government, and certainly Churchill, looked at all options to save some form of a free Polish state from the rapacious Soviets. Was the reason for the Polish Brigade being spared a part in the French operations due to Churchill? Was there even a British level discussion to dissolve the unit and thus to reinforce the badly understrength Armored Division that landed in France in July? Was there a major shift after the Warsaw Uprising or was the British need for troops so desperate in the Arnhem operations?

The Polish Independent Parachute Brigade was placed unconditionally in the o. de b. of the Allied Airborne Army on June 6, 1944. Grasset wrote a letter of appreciation as did Sir Alan Brooke and even Eisenwhower. The Polish Parachute Brigade H.Q. received a cordial telegram, "'Delighted you have joined us, will visit you as soon as I can get away. Keep me informed of your difficulties.' Originator HQ Airtroops."[23]

The Brigade began a grueling and accelerated period of training.

Churchill as always took a personal interest in all matters military. He was very invested in the Polish Forces, particularly the Polish First Armored, which he had visited with Sikorski in the winter months of 1940/41 when Polish units, however small, were all the Allies the British had outside of their Commonwealth Forces. The following message illustrates Churchill's interest in the division, his concern about the Polish future, and finally a tacit recognition of the desperate shortages of men in the British Army. On May 21, 1944, Churchill wrote to the CIGS;

> Why are we told that the 1st Polish Armoured Division cannot function because there are not sufficient rear administrative units available to maintain it? Surely a reasonable effort at adjustment could be made to enable this fine division to strengthen our already too slender forces on the Continent.

A week later on May 28, 1944, Churchill followed this point by commenting the following: "Please do not on any account let the Polish Division be kept out of the battle-front. Not only is it a magnificent fighting force, but its exploits will help to keep alive the soul of Poland, on which much turns in the future."[24]

The two different philosophies illustrate the growing ambiguity in the British attitudes to the Poles and the inevitable perplexity that must have arisen in Polish Governing circles.

Polish 2 Army Corps in Italy

The reward of the Polish units of the Home Army, who collaborated with the Soviets in the fight for Wilno and Lwow, was to be surrounded by their short-lived allies, to be disarmed, and to have their officers arrested. The men were given the option of sharing their officer's fate or enrolling in the communist-sponsored so-called Polish Army.[25] But in the West the Poles, through their sacrifice on the field, were able to note certain successes.

The summer of 1944 was full of exciting and also momentous events for the Western Allies.

The Polish 2 Army Corps opened up the road to Rome by capturing the strongly defended Monte Cairo and Santa Angelo. But the symbolic crown was the Monastery of Monte Cassino, and the Polish Commander, General Wladyslaw Anders, cabled his C-in-C the traditional old-age Polish military message of victory: "God gave us a Victory. The Polish Flag was placed on the ruins of the monastery at 10.30 of May 18th."[26]

The pro-Polish British press, and even at this late stage there were such papers, as the *Daily Telegraph* and *Illustrated London News*, carried the picture of the Polish flag flown side by side with the Union Jack.[27] This military success was in reality more of a political success and was accomplished by the loss of over eight hundred dead and many thousand wounded. The Poles had won their "prestige." The Polish Corps, which entered operations without any reserves, was indeed hard pressed. But by the middle of June, the Poles had regrouped and entered operations on the Adriatic Coast.

General Anders, who received the Military Order of the Bath from General Alexander for the victory, now to all intentions operated independently with the orders of capturing the port of Ancona.

Moving up the Via Adriatica #16 the Poles reached the Chienti River and were halted after a relatively bloodless advance. The first attempt to cross the river was repulsed, and it was obvious that the Germans were going to make a stand. After the second infantry division and all artillery were deployed, the Germans abandoned the position. The Poles in turn continued to advance and were held at the Mussone River. The Third Carpathian Infantry Division, supported by the Warsaw Armored Brigade, forded the river under heavy fire. The Battle of Ancona was now initiated by the Fifth Kresowa Division, while the Carpathians held the right flanking the Via Adriatica. Utilizing radio deceptions, which suggested that the attack would in fact come on the west of the Corps, up the Via Adriatica, the Poles regrouped their units and attacked inland up the Monte Della Crescia on July 17. The Polish maneuver was fully successful, the attack inland as a flanking left hook worked, and the city and port were encircled. The port of Ancona was very important to the Allies, for logistical purposes and the inadequate Italian roads running across the mountains from west to east. The port of Naples was able to supply the armies fighting on the western side of the Italian peninsula but only with marked difficulty the eastern side. But it was also vital that the port be captured intact. The Polish plan worked, the port was in fact captured in excellent condition, and three thousand German prisoners taken.

The significance of the battle of Ancona was that due to the unique physical circumstances of the narrow coastal plain, the operation was totally carried out by Polish troops, and supported by the Polish 318 City of Gdansk, Fighter-Reconnaissance Squadron.[28]

Invasion of Normandy

The Invasion of German-occupied Normandy, code named *Overlord,* was carried out by Allied Forces on June 6, 1944, under the overall command of general Dwight Eisenhower. The naval part of the operation was code named *Neptune.*[29]

The Poles did not participate in the first wave that stormed the beaches. But all the Polish air squadrons based in the United Kingdom took part. The Poles flew as many as four missions a day to give their land troops air support. But while all the Polish squadrons took part in the air battle over Normandy only two Polish wings were specifically dedicated to the 2nd Tactical Air Force.

A Polish senior officer, Colonel Gabszewicz, was given command of the 18th Fighter Group, which consisted of three wings and a total of nine fighter squadrons, five Polish (302, 306, 308, 315, and 317), two R.A.F., one Belgian, and one Royal New Zealand Air Force. These two Polish wings had an actual establishment of 230 officers, 618 noncommissioned officers, and 1,525 airmen, which represented close to 30 percent of the whole strength of the Polish Air Force in mid-1944. The third Polish wing, consisting of 303, 316, and 307, stayed as part of the Royal Air Force's new command—Air Defence of Great Britain—but also flew operations on behalf of the invading forces from bases in south England.

On June 6, 1944—D-Day—the 18th Fighter Group flew four missions each and the whole group scored thirty victories, becoming the top Group in TAF. By June 11, the squadrons were operating out of field bases in Normandy.

On July 9, one of the Polish wings returned back to the United Kingdom to reinforce the defenses against the attack of the German flying bombs.

The German flying bomb (V-I) offensive surprised the British public and also startled it. Coming at a time of victories, when many assumed the war would be over by the end of the year, the new horror seemed unfair and unthinkable. The British threw all their energeis into combating this new horror weapon. The launchers were bombed, batteries of antiaircraft artillery placed in South England, and fast fighter squadrons placed on standing patrols to intercept over the sea. The speed of the flying bombs did not allow for the standard radar interception and fighter squadron scramble. The Polish squadrons that took part in this operation scored a total of 190 successes, which was 10 percent of the total number shot down. Again the friendly *Illustrated London News* carried a sympathetic story, on August 5, 1944, captioned: "Exit Two Robots. Polish Fighter Pilots in Action over the Channel." It showed one of the Polish-flown Mustangs tipping the wing of the flying bomb to send it out of control into the sea.

Neptune

All but one (*Garland*) of the Polish surface warships also took part in the invasion. The Polish medium cruiser *Dragon* was part of Task Force D and gave the Canadians artillery support while the two small destroyers, *Slazak* and *Krakowiak,* were deployed on the eastern wing of British landings near Ouistreham to cover Allied minesweepers and landing craft. But it was the two fleet destroyers, the *Blyskawica* and *Piorun,* that were involved in the most dramatic sea battle of the Neptune operations. Both Polish warships were part of the Tenth Destroyer Flotilla, which consisted of two divisions, 19th and the 20th, of which *Blyskawica* was the leader. In the famous night encounter off Ushant the Allied navies totally put to rest the German naval effort to interdict the Allied landings. The Germans made strenuous efforts to attack Allied shipping by their fast E-boats out of Cherbourg. But a shortage of torpedoes for their craft and the inability to move torpedoes by land from the main depot in Brest led to an attempt to move them by sea. This fact only became known after the war.

On June 7, 1944, air reconnaissance identified four German destroyers in Brest. On June 8 they were gone and the assumption was made (correctly) that they were sailing in harm's way, to inderdict Allied ships. The German ships were part of the 8th German destroyer flotilla under the command of von Bechtolsheim and consisted of three *Narvik* class destroyers and one *Elblag* class. The Allied Flotilla destroyers were divided into two divisions: 19th—HMS *Tartar* (flotilla leader, Captain B. Jones), HMS *Ashanti,* HMS *Huron,* and HMCS *Haida*. 20th—ORP *Blyskawica*, ORP *Piorun*, HMS *Javelin*, and HMS *Eskimo*.

In weather described as overcast with intermittent rain, light southwesterly wind, calm sea, and visibility of one to three miles, the Allied Force sailed south from Plymouth. At midnight the Allied warships were about fifty miles from the shores of Brittany. The distance between the divisions was 4,000 yards. At 01.16 hours of June 9, HMS *Tartar* got a radar bearing on the Germans at a range of ten nautical miles. The direction was also given as 251 degrees. The position when contact was established was 49.03N & 04.11W. Very shortly the other Allied warships also established radar contact. All crews were at their full alert and with heightened nerves, since it was common knowledge that the German practice was to initiate a torpedo attack at a distance of less than 9,000 meters. The Allies had a new radio intercept system called *headache*, which picked up internal telephone transmissions from enemy ships. At 01.28 HMS *Eskimo* reported that enemy destroyers had fired torpedoes. At the same time Allied warships opened artillery fire on the enemy ships. The Allies used illuminating shells. *Blyskawica* achieved covering fire on the lead ship in her second salvo and managed to get in 12 salvoes altogether with the result that the lead *Narvik* was on fire. But the German warships with their 150mm outgunned the Allied warships equipped with their 120mm guns. There is some dispute whether *Blyskawica* changed course because she was heavily engaged or as a result of the German torpedo attack. It is likely that the reason for turning away from the enemy was due to both reasons. Normally one would turn into the torpedoes to comb them but being also straddled by enemy shells it would make sense to turn away.

While *Blyskawica* lost contact with the enemy, the *Piorun* following did not. HMS *Tartar*, in the best tradition of the Royal Navy, turned to the enemy and received punishing fire. A number of British officers and other rank were killed and *Tartar* was in bad straits but saved by *Ashanti*, which carried out a torpedo attack on the lead *Narvik*. Hit by the British torpedo, and carrying an extra supply of torpedoes for its E-Boats, the German flagship exploded.

Tartar at this point withdrew, while the battle was now carried on by the Canadians. *Piorun*, which had not turned with *Blyskawica*, continued its artillery fire and found itself between the two divisions of Allied warships.

It should be remembered that the action was taking place at night, and took about ten minutes to complete. At this point decisions were made as in a fighter plane, on impulse, without thinking, and certainly not on the basis of a planned strategy. *Blyskawica* rejoined the Canadians after coming perilously close to being attacked by them. This was only prevented by the Pole lighting up his ship. Since *Piorun* was missing from the ranks of the 20th division, there was short-lived fear that the explosion (i.e., of the German destroyer) was due to the *Piorun* being hit.

The Allied warships now embarked on the search for the remaining German warships. *Blyskawica* was now leading the Allied contingent and at 04.49 at a bearing of 195 the enemy was sighted and attacked. The Germans now sought the protection of their own land-based artillery but Allied superiority was overwhelming, and another German destroyer was beached and exploded.

One of the ironic things was that the search and chase for the Germans was confounded by an Allied minefield, QZX.1330, which had been placed to prevent and hinder Germans from coming to interdict Allied convoys. The Allied ships were forced to sail around it while the Germans, oblivious to their danger, sailed the direct way and two escaped.

At 05.37 the action was called off. The Allied warships had sailed close to the German occupied shores of France looking for the two damaged German destroyers. But to no avail. However, the German action *Torpeden* was a fiasco.

The Allied command issued the following report:

> This action, one of the very few which had been fought between large and modern destroyers at night during this war, effected the destruction of half the enemy's force and inflicted damage on at least one of the two who escaped. It was thus a not inconsiderable success and a useful contribution to the safety of our convoys.[30]

After expending all its ammunition, the Polish cruiser *Dragon* returned to Plymouth to replenish supplies. On sailing back to the coast of Normandy to continue its artillery support of Allied troops, it was hit by a German one-man submarine and suffered extensive damage. A number of Polish sailors were also killed in the ensuing explosion and fire. The cruiser had to be beached and the British admiralty urged the Poles to allow the ship to become part of the breakwater. As a recompense the Polish took over a sister ship H.M.S. *Danae* and renamed it O.R.P. *Conrad*.

The *Pierwsza Pancerna* Enters Battle

In July 1944 the Polish Armored Division landed in Normandy as part of the Canadian First Army. Except for the Parachute Brigade and two training divisions, the Seventh Infantry in Egypt and the Fourth Infantry in Scotland, all other Polish Army, Air, and Naval Forces were now fully committed to the Allied cause.

The action of the Polish Armored, the *Pierwsza Pancerna*, deserves a short description. The Poles were assigned to the Canadian First Army, whose orders were to attack south from the bitterly contested area of Caen towards Falaise and to join up with the Americans, whose exhilarating performance after breaking out near St. Lo led to the fanning out of American divisions, virtually unopposed in the regions of south Normandy and northern Brittany. The plan was to sweep around the Germans and surround them. This Allied plan was facilitated by the Germans when they decided to counterattack into the flank of the Americans fanning out south of Mortain.

The Poles were centered near Bayeux with the Canadian II Corps, which was a cosmopolitan formation consisting of the famous 51st Highland Division of the British Army and the 2nd and 3rd Canadian Infantry and 4th Canadian Armored. This was a powerful Corps and operations started on August 8, 1944, directed at capturing Falaise. The Germans were the famous Panzergruppe Western consisting of two SS Corps. The Germans were still without equals in defensive fighting and the Allied attack quickly bogged down. Neither the Poles nor the Canadians advanced a mile but both divisions suffered heavy causalities. The operation originally planned to take two days, in fact took eleven. The Canadian infantry now entered the fight attempting to break out of the tightly held German positions and took heavy losses without any advantage.

On August 12, the Canadian II Corps regrouped and the orders were that in view of the German inability to break the American flank, the enemy units are slowly pulling out west and the opportunity for a decisive battle may be lost. The Poles again attacked south towards Trun. This time the operation proceeded better and the river Dives was crossed. On August 17 the Canadian Corps commander brought the personal order of Montgomery that Chamboise was to be captured that night. The Poles were now divided into two independent acting brigades, eastern and western. While the Poles were making slow but bloody progress, the neighboring Canadian divisions were held by the Germans. The battle was becoming like a battlefield of the eighteenth century, with units operating independently and no formal line between friend and foe. During the hours of August 19, the eastern units captured and dug in on Mont Ormel. The famous *Maczuga* (club) was named after the clublike appearance of the height contours on the map. The eastern wing captured Chamboise and linked up with the American II battalion of the U.S. Army's 395 Regiment, 90th Division. But this link was very tenuous. Now the Poles were isolated from their supply base and Allied divisions, but in fact the Polish units themselves were parceled out holding on to the various towns and hilltops that they had captured and subjected to progressively more violent German counterattacks from the east and of the retreating Germans from the west. At this point an attempt was made to supply the Poles by airdrops. The Germans had now managed to throw back the American units and there was no contact even with the Yanks who had been able to route some supplies to the Poles. The artillery fire was intense and the crisis day was August 21. The Canadian 4th Armored finally reached the Poles, bringing badly needed supplies of ammunition, gasoline, food and allowing the thousands of wounded to be evacuated.

The Poles captured 150 German officers (including the German 84th Corps commander Elfeldt) and 5,550 other rank. Polish losses were 135 officers and 2,129 other rank killed and wounded. The hilltop of Mont Ormel—Maczuga—is a beautiful site with a moving monument to the Poles. The German general, who was captured, when he became aware that his victors were Poles, is supposed to have said, "we, Germans, made a big mistake, we should have had the Poles as our Allies, not as our enemies."[31]

8

The Warsaw Uprising Fails, Only Allied Loyalty Remains, August 1944–May 1945

Warsaw Uprising

On July 20 there was an assassination attempt on Hitler, and the Soviets broke through German defenses on the Bug and raced for Warsaw. At the same time, the Soviets began to broadcast appeals to the citizens of Warsaw to rise up and throw off the German chains. In this unpredictable military situation, General Bor-Komorowski, G.O.C. of the A.K., cabled London on July 25, 1944, stating that he wished to be empowered to order an uprising at the best moment. "We are ready to fight for Warsaw at any moment. I will report the date and hour of the beginning of the fight."

But on July 26, 1944, independently the Polish Government without the authorization of the Polish C-in-C who was in Italy, sent off a telegram to the A.K. stating: "At a session of the Government of the Republic, it was unanimously decided to empower you to proclaim the insurrection at a moment which you will decide as most opportune. If possible, let us know beforehand."

In Italy, Sosnkowski became concerned about the situation and cabled the A.K. through London:

> In the face of Soviet political pressures and known actions, a heroic uprising would be an act lacking in political value—and it could require unnecessary sacrifices. If the aim of the uprising is the occupation of part of Polish territory, it must be taken into account that in this case it will be necessary to defend Poland's sovereignty on recaptured territory, against whatever power questions this sovereignty. Remember, to put this into its proper perspective, that a he-

189

roic uprising and cooperation mean nothing in the face of Soviet lack
of goodwill.

Sosnkowski enjoyed the rather uncomplimentary opinion of a
Polish Hamlet. One of the most brilliant and analytical minds in the
Pilsudski circle, he was also a very loyal follower of the Marshal
and spent time with Pilsudski in the German Magdeburg prison in
1917–1918. But when Pilsudski staged his coup, Sosnkowski pre-
varicated between his loyalty and affection to the Marshal and his
loyalty to the Constitutional Government. There are many opinions
that the order cited above is one more example of prevarication. But
that seems unfair. Sosnkowski could not issue an order forbidding
that the Poles rise up against the Germans. That would have been
militarily stupid and politically suicidal. Neither could Sosnkowski
issue an outright order for the Uprising. He did what any prudent
C-in-C has to do, namely outline the parameters of operations and
in this case gave a major warning of the political consequences.

That General Bor and his comrades reached a decision to fight
seems inevitable given the close to five years of German occupation
and bestiality.

The Soviet-controlled (so-called Polish) communist army of General Berling was fighting alongside the Soviets and supposedly
helping to liberate Polish territory. For the Poles to refuse to fight
was a terrible political and public relations defeat, one which would
never be easily explained to one's own countrymen, let alone allies.
To sit passively while the miniscule but vociferous communist
groups liberated Warsaw and imposed their own authority was just
not possible. Without direction there was also every reason that the
populace would go to the streets. In August 1944 there were no
choices. If Smigly-Rydz in early 1939 really said, "with or without
ammunition, fight we must and fight we shall," then August 1944
was the time when these words were prophetically true. Having
embarked on a military defiance of its enemies, it was in 1944 that
the Poles had to prove their resolve and did so heroically!

The issues were not merely political, as to who would get the
credit for a liberation of Warsaw, though that was a vital point for
the future of the country. The issue was as much the fact that a
small struggling uprising would destroy the city while the possibility that a well coordinated uprising would save the historic city and
its population as well as ensure that the Soviets would need to deal
with the constitutional leaders of the country. It was accepted, and
probably correctly, that the kind of tragic arrests perpetrated on the

Polish units in Lwow and Wilno would not be repeated in Warsaw, to which even Soviet greed and expansionism made no claim.

On August 1, 1994, the Polish Underground and the population of the City of Warsaw rose up against the Germans.[1]

The tragedy of Warsaw was that even the most suspicious and skeptical of Soviet intentions, and those most pessimistic of British support, could not imagine and certainly could never have predicted the unholy alliance of the machiavellian Stalin, the rage of Hitler, coupled with British impotence and Roosevelt's disinterest.[2]

The tragedy of Warsaw struck the men of the Polish Parachute Brigade Group especially hard, because only a few months earlier they had received a flag, smuggled out of Poland, embroidered by the women of Warsaw. It was a symbolic expression of the destination of the unit and of the expectation of the citizens of Warsaw that help would come to them from the West.

For the British the Warsaw Uprising was at best a symbolic question. From a practical point of view it had no consequence for their political or military ends. For the Polish Government and the Polish military, it represented one last attempt to place a free Polish leadership in Poland and to restore sovereignty before the yoke of Nazi tyranny was replaced by communist imperialism. This indeed was the last and final campaign of the war.

Aid to Warsaw

The Polish Government and military staff undertook every effort to help Warsaw. The military assistance was directed at efforts to supply the Warsaw insurgents by air and by endeavors to have the Polish Parachute Brigade Group, or part of it, dropped to assist them.

On August 12, 1944, the Polish Commander-in-Chief (General K. Sosnkowski) initiated this exchange with a letter to Sir Alan Brooke.[3]

> The question of employing part of the Polish Paratroop Brigade in the Battle of Warsaw has not yet been decided upon. The date of the participation of this brigade in the fighting in France is approaching. Therefore, I would be much obliged to you if you would give instructions for one battalion to be diverted from operational duties in France and designated for use in Poland.

Sir Alan Brooke replied the same day:

I would like to assure you of the sympathy of all of us here in the difficulties with which you are faced in seeking to support the Polish soldiers now fighting so bravely in Warsaw.

I think you will have been told already from the War cabinet that the British Chiefs of Staff have lost no opportunity of impressing upon the authorities in the Mediterranean the importance of sending help to Warsaw at the earliest possible moment. A flight of British and Polish aircraft was arranged to take place last night, but most unfortunately the weather prevented it. The intention now is that it should take place tonight, and I hope very much that it will be as successful as the flights of Polish aircraft during the past few nights.

As General Ismay informed General Kukiel in a letter of August 2nd, we had regretfully to decide against sending part of the Polish Parachute Brigade to Warsaw. It is not possible for us to find the necessary transport aircraft to fly in a unit and maintain it in the Warsaw area. Large numbers of transport aircraft would be required for this purpose and those could not be spared at this critical stage of the campaign in the West.

I would like to assure you that we are doing all that is humanly possible.[4]

On the 13th the Polish Commander-in-Chief responded:

As regards the Polish Parachute Brigade, this unit as formed in accordance with British-Polish understanding, with the aim that their main task would be to give support to the rising in Poland, when the need should occur. It would, therefore, not be easy to explain to these parachutists that they must fight on another front at the time when their brothers are giving their lives in the barricades of Warsaw. I am afraid that a crisis in morale may occur in the ranks of the brigade which could deprive the unit of its fighting value. I fear that acts of desperation may ensue. You, as a soldier, will understand and appreciate my fears.

In the light of the above, I will ask you kindly to reconsider the question of using the brigade for assistance to Warsaw. I suggest the use of one battalion of the unit, or at least one company duly reinforced with heavy weapons. This, I think, would be the minimum capable of dissipating to a certain extent the disquieting adverse atmosphere now prevailing amongs the rank and file of the brigade, which its commander has quite recently reported to me.

I urge, therefore, that in consideration of this situation, as well as in the interests of my suffering country, you would assist the Polish soldier to resolve the anxieties which are besetting him today, and aid me in contriving an honorable way to solve an extremely complicated problem. Would you also find it possible to take into account, while considering your decision, the evidence of good will shown by the Polish Government and myself in having altered the initial arrangmenets regarding the employment of the brigade and placing it at the disposal of the Supreme Allied Commander.

Last night's flights to Poland, so far as I am informed, were carried out by 11 crews. Of these, I understand only 5 had the task of dropping supplies to Warsaw.

I am sure you will realise the insufficiency of such scale. It is essential that these flights continue. The speediest possible reinforcements of the Polish crews in Italy by sending there the whole of 300 Squadron is, in my view, the only way to meet the existing bitter necessities.[5]

The Poles were appealing to the gentleman's honor. At the same time on August 13, the Polish Parachute Brigade went on a twenty-four-hour fast to protest the lack of help to Warsaw.

The British reply of August 15 was one more polite but negative letter. General K. Sosnkowski (the Polish Commander-in-Chief) then wrote a long, impassioned, and bitter letter on August 20, which outlined the issues. Sosnkowski wrote that all interventions on the part of the Poles (and he enumerated them one by one, including the Polish Minister of National Defense, the Polish Chief of Staff, and the various members of the Polish Government, had produced "no tangible results." Sosnkowski outlined the Polish postulates, a continuous supply of arms and ammunition to besieged Warsaw, a temporary diversion of Polish crews from 300 Squadron to the Polish flight, the dispatch of the Polish Parachute Brigade or at least part of it to Warsaw, the bombing of specific targets in or near Warsaw and the conferment of combatant status on the soldiers of the Home Army.

Sosnkowski concluded his letter with a reminder to the British of their obligations to Poland under the provisions of the Polish-United Kingdom Treaty of Mutual Assistance signed in late August, 1939.

> The rising of the Polish Underground Army in Warsaw, as an integral part of the Polish Armed Forces fighting side by side with the Allies, is an operation of a military character, directed against the German aggressor and falls clearly under Art. I of the Agreement of Mutual Assistance between the United Kingdom and Poland, signed on 25th August 1939. The two contracting parties are bound, by the provisions of this Article, to afford, one to the other, all the support

and assistance in their power. The armed struggle of the Polish Forces, developed since the fall of France and cooperating with Great Britain on land, sea, and in the air, continuously since September 1939, is based primarily on this Alliance.

Sosnkowski then pointed out the fact that the Poles had lost 1,770 air crew, or 60 percent of their air personnel, in the Allied bomber offensive and had never hesitated in pursuing the common cause. He finished with this admonition.

> The eventual second fall of Warsaw now, in the fifth year of the war, if due to a lack of necessary assistance, would, as I have already mentioned in the previous correspondence, adversely affect not only public opinion in Poland, but also the feelings of all Poles abroad; undoubtedly it will not remain without echo throughout the world, and in Europe in particular.[6]

In this last comment, Sosnkowski was deluding himself or was naive, since the world before, then, and since has been singularly impervious to moral issues.

As the Home Army was fighting for its life, and as the city and its civilian population was being systematically destroyed by the Germans, the British with complete insensitivity requested that the Poles implement their Monika/Bardsea plans by parachuting a small group of officers to northeast France (near Lille), to prepare the ground for a drop by all or part of the Polish Parachute Brigade. This was to be an action on behalf of the French Resistance. On August 22, 1944, the Chief of Staff of the Polish H.Q., General Tadeusz Kopanski, recommended to the Ministry of National Defence that this be categorically refused since the Brigade was placed as part of the Allied Airborne Army operations, not for small guerrilla operations. However, the Polish C-in-C had no objections to the use of the previously trained and organized Grenadier Company that had specially been designated for action with the Polish Underground in France.

The uprising in Warsaw caught the Polish special duties flight based in Italy near Brindisi unprepared and at the end of a long spring and early summer season of very active operations. The official establishment of the flight was a mere six crews, but in fact there were ten full crews but only six air-worthy planes, three Liberators and three used-up Halifaxes. The main problem was that having carried out a considerable number of flights to northern Italy and Jugoslavia and thirty-seven flights to Poland, a number of Polish crews had reached that airman's nirvana—a completion of a tour of operational duty—and by regulations, to say nothing of common sense, leave. The Poles had signaled their chief of Sixth Section (responsible for coordinating airdrops to Poland) that their establishment would be down to: ten crews on July 3; six crews by August 1, and four by the end of August.

On August 1, even before the flight was aware of the Warsaw Uprising, the flight was depleted when a plane was shot down on a mission to Hungary. Thus on the first day of the Uprising, the Poles had only five crews. The new Polish crews that reached the flight were directly from training and had no combat experience and no experience of flying either the Halifax or the Liberator, hence there were more delays as the crews were retrained.

The Polish flight (1586) was so commonly referred to by Poles by the name of its old derivative, 301 squadron, that many just assumed that it had the same potential for effectiveness as would a twelve-plane unit. Both Polish and local R.A.F. authorities quickly agreed that the Polish flight needed to be beefed up and that Polish crews completing training on four-engined planes and destined for the Polish 300 Lancaster Squadron would be seconded to Italy, and that all Polish crews flying in the Air Transport Command would also be moved to reinforce the Polish capability.

The following is based on a number of historic accounts and the reports of the R.A.F. Command in the Mediterranean Theater of Operations.[7]

It also needs to be emphasized that by prior agreements, when weather conditions precluded flights to Poland, the Poles flew special duties operations to other countries. On August 4, the British ordered that all flights to Warsaw be stopped due to losses. But the C.O. of the flight, Major Arciuszkiewicz, got four crews to volunteer for Warsaw. All returned safely, though one Halifax crashed on landing. Bad weather prevented flights to Warsaw until August 8, when three Polish crews made it to Warsaw. Slessor telegrammed on August 9 to CAS

> Three Poles went to Warsaw last night and dropped supplies on the city. A good many nightfighters were seen and flak experienced at Warsaw, but they got away with it. A gallant show. They will send five more tonight. They are pressing me to send 148 Squadron also. But I intend to adhere to my original decision and not to send any British Halifaxes till last quarter of moon, night of the 11th or

12th of August. A few aircraft on a show like this will sometimes get away with it. Larger numbers will not. Latest effort was a personal signal Sosnkowski to Wilson (which latter has ignored) asking him to order me to continue flights and implying that I am ignorant of the military and moral implications. He probably imagnies last night's flights were due to his intervention with Wilson. I gather Sosnkowski has got the sack but I hope further political intervention by Poles in London may be discouraged as much as possible. I am sure it is just as much a nuisance to you as to me.[8]

Slessor must have been aware of the great efforts by the British to get rid Sosnkowski, who represented a moral force that haunted the British conscience. It is unclear whether the rumors of British pressure on the Polish President to dismiss Sosnkwoski were that rife among the British, or whether Slessor became aware that Racz-kiewicz had replaced Sosnkowski with Arciszewski as his Presidential successor.

This move actually strengthened Sosnkowski's role as C-in-C since the Polish Underground parties and the Polish Prime Minister urged a separation of the two roles. But the die was cast and now British efforts would be directed as much at the Polish general as at aiding the Poles.

Between August 11 and 18 due to favorable weather conditions the Poles carried out operations each night. To reflect on the stress and wear, each Warsaw flight was an endurance test of nearly eleven hours, in unpressurized planes over enemy-held territory. After one day's break another eight nights of consecutive flights were carried out. The R.A.F. squadron also attempted to aid the insurgents of Warsaw as did the Royal South African Air Force. A short list of the initial flights is included here:

8/9 August	3 Polish aircraft. supplies dropped and all returned.
9/10 August	4 Polish aircraft. ditto.
10/11/12 August	no operations. adverse weather.
12/13 August	11 aircraft (mixed British and Polish). 6 successful enthusiastically received by defenders of Warsaw.
13/14 August	26 aircraft. successful drops from 8 aircraft.
14/15 August	aircraft (also mixed) 7 crews lost. 11 drops executed.

On August 15 Air Marshal Slessor reported in his summary that planes from all of his units had the following results:

Twelve successes, six failures, eight missing. In all cases the target was Warsaw. There were no other operations to Poland. Last nights operations to Warsaw. 26 dispatched. 11 successful. 8 missing including 6 Liberators of 205 Group. One of the 148 Squadron and one Pole. A great deal of flak experienced and night fighters seen. Am going Bari to-day to see Elliott but the two squadrons of 205 Group have lost 25% of their strength in two nights and it is obvious we cannot go on at this rate of loss which fully justifies my misgivings about the whole operation.

I drafted a reply to Polish President which I understand has gone home as chain 42 and 43 to Deuputy PM (comment not yet received) and Foreign Secretary, but am told that my last sentence was omitted which was to the effect that: I must warn you that we cannot maintain these arduous operations indefinitly on a large scale.

In view of last night's experience something to that effect must be included. Colonel Kent is away so I cannot consult him. Will signal you further later in the day. Are the Russians doing anything at all? We have now lost 16 heavy bombers and crews trying to help Warsaw which I imagine is about one for every ton of supplies that has reached the Underground Army.[9]

On August 16 Slessor cabled CAS:

1. Result of operations to Warsaw night 15/15. Nine aircraft despatched to three dropping points in reserve outside Warsaw. Five successful. All returned safely. To-night sixteen are detailed to four dropping zones in same area. Field reports two crews missing night 14/15 baled out and are safe one with Poles and one with Russians.

2. Eaker has heard from Walsh in Moscow that frantic six scheduled for to-day from UK has been cancelled by Russians apparently on grounds that they did not agree with target. I wonder if target was supply Warsaw.

3. You know we are continuing to extend full assistance to Russians in their activities to Jugoslavia. Ten Dakota loads of medical personnel and stores are due to arrive from Russia to-night. We are also helping them shuttle operation with B 25s which I feel would be much better employed supplying Warsaw. Difficult to resist conviction that Russian failure to supply Warsaw is deliberate policy.[10]

On August 17 Slessor cabled:

Eighteen aircraft dispatched, eight successful, six missing including four Liberators of 205 Group and two Poles of 1586. This is a second occasion in three nights in which about 30% of the force despatched has failed to return and our losses in 13 night operations to
Poland this month have amounted to 21 lost, three destroyed on
landing owing to flak damage, and many damaged out of 113 despatched. I cannot possibly go on at this rate and have instructed Elliott to stop operations to Poland. You will note that this rate of loss
was not on Warsaw itself but on woods outside, of which value to
the underground can only be rated as better than nothing. The fact
must be faced that unless supplies can be sent by say from the UK or
by the Russians, the Underground Army is beyond our help. The
Prime Minister has been informed, and I understand has accepted
the position but this should not be taken from me as he is signalling
London himself today.[11]

Kalinowski writes that in August the Poles carried out ninety-
seven flights of which eighty were to Warsaw, three to other drop
zones in Poland, and fourteen to northern Italy. Eight Polish crews
were lost, seven on missions to Warsaw.[12]

On September 2 Evill cabled Slessor from London stating that the
British were being "pressured" by Polish authorities to take action
and that to alleviate the shortage of aircraft nine Halifax had been
dispatched and eight more would be withdrawn from Squadron
161. The cable concludes that, "We must rely on you however as
soon as moon and other conditions permit to try further operations
and possibly higher dropping. If these prove successful and you are
satisfied that this is a reasonable operation we hope you will again
employ British crews."[13]

The British had now developed a barometric parachute opener
that allowed airdrops from a higher, and thus safer, ceiling but
which alleviated the wide dispersal of airdrops. The parachutes
were aimed, in some was like old-fashioned bombing runs, and
only opened at a low altitude, optimizing the reception by the intended recipients.

Slessor stopped all flights to Warsaw but under heavy pressure
from the Polish Government agreed that Polish crews could volunteer for what the British considered to be near suicidal missions. Only
a third of the supplies actually fell into the hands of the Poles. On top
of that the British were bedeviled by a shortage of suitable planes and
the offer of the nine Halifaxes was not well received as Slessor considered them completely unsuitable for such long operations.

On September 8, Slessor cabled Air Ministry at Whitehall. He objected to the Halifax fitted with Merlin 20s as unsuitable. He also advised London that all his Halifax planes were due for a major inspection and were deemed dangerous to fly. He also advised London that the Halifax situation in squadron 148 and flight 1586 (Polish) was serious and then went on to say:

> Understand from Eaker that Spaatz and Eisenhower are prepared to release U.S. Liberator special duty group to this theater if we can use it. The difficulty and delay in shipping out ground echelons is such that Eaker and I do not think this desirable at this stage of the war. But I suggest this U.S. Group should take over such commitments as may remain at Tempsford, and that you should send out S.D. Halifax II and IIA with experienced crews to build up 148 and 1586. We could take and make good use of 16 at once.

Slessor then recommended that if the war was prolonged beyond the winter, Stirlings would need to be brought into service with Special Duty Squadrons.[14]

In return Slessor was reassured that the Halifax planes being dispatched to Italy had plenty of hours of operation left, and was advised that Tempsford was being equipped with Sterlings (not a happy time for the Tempsford squadron, which dreaded flying these planes) and that the Italian theater would just have to accept and do the best they could. In retrospect it not absolutely clear whether Slessor was in fact convinced that the Halifax planes being sent to him were dangerous and unsuitable or whether he was to some extent protecting his units, including the Polish flight, from what he perceived to be complete operational folly and near suicide. There has to be some suspicion of that because Slessor reacts in a very angry and undignified manner to a cable dated September 19 from London, which stated that Rayski, "has suggested that the Americans be asked to transfer up to twelve Liberators from Fifteenth Air Force to 1586 Flight. As operations to Warsaw area are purely supply dropping these aircraft may be suitable without modification and would tide over present period."

Slessor responded immediately on September 20:

> 1. Your AX 449 19 Sept. Do not agree Rayski's suggestion and am not clear who made it to you. I cannot understand this Warsaw business. Should have thought even a Pole might be capable of hoisting (?) in that it does not make sense to send aircraft from Ice-

land to drop supplies in Mayfair when the Russians, who now appear to be cooperating, have their forward troops in Southwark and aerodromes in Middlesex.

2. Fortunately the weather is limiting the extent to which we are able to expend effort and aircrews lives on this folly. But should like to be clear that I continue to exact maximum effort including division of Heavies from Strategic bombing on supply to Warsaw in present conditions in the face of our experience of the very high casualty rate involved.[15]

Slessor was reacting to the one and only American shuttle expedition, which took place on September 18, after many discussions and negotiations with the Soviets. That day 107 Flying Fortresses under the command of Col. Carl Truesdell flew over Warsaw and successfully delivered 388 containers of supplies. The Americans flew on to a Soviet landing base and after a number of days returned through Italian bases to the United Kingdom. As a result of this, the Soviets canceled all such future shuttle flights, including bombing missions of Germany, alleging that they needed those bases for their own air operations.

In September the Polish Flight only managed forty-two operations. Seventeen were to Warsaw, all the others to other countries. Eight crews were lost. The last flight to Warsaw was made on the night of September 20/21. During the totality of the Warsaw Uprising the Polish flight lost seventeen crews. Only two Polish crews survived the Uprising. It can be stated categorically that the only reason why the casualty rate among Polish (and also Royal Air Force) crews was not higher was quite simply due to the shortage of suitable and airworthy aircraft. Whether this was due to the actual shortage of suitably engined planes, as the British averred, or whether this problem, which was also confirmed by Polish air experts, was magnified to prevent unnecessary loss of life will probably never be known.

On September 15, the Commander-in-Chief, General K. Sosnkowski, gave the Polish Unit the honor of being called the "Defenders of Warsaw."

That may have just about been his last order, because on September 25 the Polish President, under heavy pressure from the British and from the Polish Prime Minister, accepted Sosnkowski's resignation.[16]

Another Pole, who also attempted to succor the Warsaw Uprising, even though he wore a different uniform and owed loyalty to a different cause, Berling, the titular head of the First Polish Communist Army, was also dismissed from his post by the Soviets.

Polish Parachute Brigade in Action

While Warsaw was fighting, the Polish Parachute Brigade, originally destined for operations in Poland, took part in the tragic fiasco of the Arnhem drop.[17]

Between June 1944 and September 1944, the Polish Parachute Brigade Group was placed on alert on a number of occasions, and drops were planned for the vicinity of Paris, then canceled; and again for Belgium, to be canceled again. One of the diaries has the following poignant comment:

> During the first days of August 1944 the whole brigade took part in brigade strength parachute drop and also participated in other maneuvers to hone the unit prior to action. It was obvious to all that the brigade would see combat in a short time. We all considered and argued amongst ourselves as to where and when that drop would take place. The wish of us all was that we would go to Warsaw. The heart and minds of all us soldiers, particularly those of the Parachute Brigade, were consumed by Warsaw's tragedy; everybody wanted to help. The pivilege of fighting in the ranks of its defenders was our most heartfelt desire.

However, the plans for Market Garden were not canceled. The brigade, consisting of just over 2,000 officers and men, was assigned 114 planes and 45 Horsa gliders. The Brigade consisted of three paratroop battalions and supporting services. The fourth battalion had been disolved due to manpower shortages in order to bring the three other battalions up to relative strength. Even so each battalion only had 565 officers and men, about 60 short of the establishment.

The British plans for the Polish Brigade can only be characterized as militarily absurd, but it is possible that the intent was not military but primarily political. It was, after all, in the middle of the Warsaw Uprising, and there was pressure to have at the very least a small, symbolic part of the Brigade parachuted into Warsaw or more reasonably into its environs. Using the whole Brigade and making its importance so vital to Allied success was the best argument for not considering the Polish request.

The whole glider component of the Polish Parachute Brigade Group, carrying all the Polish antitank batteries as well as some component groups of the Polish Brigade Headquarters, particularly Polish liaison officers and signals, was to be flown on the second and third day of the operation and to land north of the Rhine, within the perimeter already held by the British First Airborne Division. Thus by British staff planning the Polish Parachute Brigade was being deprived of its antitank artillery and was also deprived of its small howitzers, which were sent by the sea train and never took part in the operations.

The orders for the rest of the Polish Parachute Brigade Group, consisting exclusively of riflemen and engineers, were to drop and capture the south end of the Arnhem bridge, whose north end was to be held by the British Parachute Brigade of the First Airborne Division, the famous Red Devils. (This enduring appellation came from the color of their beret, which in a strange way is the color of the current Polish airborne troops but was not at the time of the Second World War.) This drop was planned for the third day of operation. The Poles were then to march over the bridge to reinforce the British perimeter instead of anchoring the south connection until the arrival of the 30th Corps. This was another absurdity. Why air-drop infantry south of a bridge merely to have them march over it? The Polish Brigade Group was being dropped, bereft of its field howitzers and even without any supporting antitank artillery, on the south bank end of the river on the third day of an operation when one could easily speculate that German alertness and response would be immediate. Malaszkiewicz describes the sense of dismay and impending disaster which greeted these orders in the Polish Brigade.[18]

The first Pole to land on the ground was pod-porucznik Albin Krzyski, seconded to the British 21 Independent Parachute Company, whose task was to mark the fields for the major parachute drop and glider landing.

The first Polish glider component consisting of ten gliders which took off from Manston landed on the British-held perimeter without loss on the second day of the operation, i.e., namely September 18. This glider component carried seven antitank guns (6 pounders), but with only two artillery men each. The rest of the artillery personnel were to be parachuted in following days. The guns went straight into action near Oosterbeek close to the now famous Hartenstein Hotel.

On September 19 the second Polish glider component, consisting of thirty-five gliders carrying eight antitank guns (this being the full brigade complement of antitank artillery) and part of the headquarters of the brigade and of the three infantry battalions, took off and was caught in the air by German fighters. It landed in an area that was only minimally protected on one side by British troops. Five of the guns were lost and casualties among the troops heavy. Brigadier Urquhart, the British commander, in his intelligence summary writes, "Glider elements of Polish Para Bde landed on LZ'L' but was very heavily opposed from ground and air and suffered severe casualties."

Those that survived the landing were dispersed to support the defense perimeter of the British Airborne Division around the now famous and historic Hartenstein. The baptism by fire had begun.

Bad weather prevented the body of the Polish Brigade from taking off. Things began to go wrong for the Allies. Bad weather, which delayed the departure of the rest of the Polish Parachute Brigade, also interfered with supply drops to the British Airborne Division and did not allow for Allied air support. The adverse weather and the now near legendary ability of German units to counterattack allowed the enemy to keep control of the south end of the Arnhem bridge. This led to a change of orders for the Poles. The new task was to land south of the river, but closer to Driel, and to capture the ferry. The British were unaware that the previous day the ferry had floated down river after damage to its moorings. But bad weather again aborted part of the mission.

On September 21 the Polish paratroopers boarded their planes for takeoff at 14.00 hours. On the previous day the start was canceled at 15.00 hours due to bad weather. Sosabowski was described then by one of his staff officers, Lt. Dyrda, as pensive. Sosabowski was very pessimistic about the whole British plan and was not the only one to view Browning's behavior as cavalier.[19] After a telephone conversation with General Brereton, C.O. of the Allied Airborne Army, Sosabowski was assured that the ferry was already in British hands.

At 16.35 the American planes carrying the Poles reached the projected landing zone, and the Poles landed on a field lightly held by German infantry, not by the British as was the intelligence summary. The brigade suffered moderate casualties and proceeded to dig in. The Germans attempted to make sense of this operation and came to the logical but erroneous conclusion that this was an Allied attempt to capture the south end of bridge and a small German force consisting of regular Wermacht infantry, airmen, sailors, and Dutch SS *Sperverrband Harzer* was marched to confront the Poles.

The landing zone was a flat field traversed by drainage ditches, which made movement difficult but gave the Germans a good field of fire. The Poles put up smoke grenades. After landing, General Sosabowski realized that most of his First and part of his Third Battalion were missing. (These were on the 41 planes recalled due to bad weather.) On that first day on the landing zone, General Sosabowski had fewer than 1,000 men under his command with no artillery or antitank guns and separated from the rest of the British Army.

The Poles were unable to establish radio contact with the British Airborne. Also their patrols found no Germans and no ferry in Driel. At 23.00 hours the Polish liaison officer with the H.Q. of the Airborne, Lt. Zwolenski, swam the river and gave Sosabowski a summary of the near tragic situation faced by the British. Zwolenski then swam back to alert the British that the Poles would try to ford the river. Also that day the forward elements of the 30 Corps (5th Battalion of the Duke of Cornwall's light Infantry, part of the 43 Wessex Division, reached the Poles. The British helped the Poles beat back sporadic German attacks, but had no fording equipment.)

The Polish engineers, with great initiative, scrounged among the downed planes and pulled out some of the round aircraft rescue dinghies. These were utilized, in addition to some wood rafts quickly constructed on September 22, to cross the river. All these preparations were made while under continuous harassing fire of German artillery and mortars. When the Poles attempted to cross the river they were met with a hail of mortar and machine gun fire, which only allowed one company (8th Company, Third Battalion) to make it across the river. The circular shape of the dinghies and makeshift rafts made from doors, etc., as well as the fast current of the river made ferrying extremely difficult. The ferrying went on till all the dinghies were sunk.

On September 23, the commanding officer of the First Battalion of the Polish Parachute Brigade, still in England, was able to centralize his unit and the remnants of the Third Battalion, whose flight had also been aborted, on one airfield and the six hundred or so strong unit was dropped by parachute within the perimeter of the American 82nd Airborne Division. They were then trucked up to join the Polish Brigade.

During the night of September 23 another attempt was made by the Polish troops to aid their colleagues on the north side of the river. The British (30th Corps) were now able to provide some larger dinghies, and about 260 Polish paratroopers of the Third Battalion (the 7th and rest of 8th Company) and the parachute component of the antitank batteries (i.e., only men without guns) were ferried across. The ferrying again went on till all the large rubber rafts were sunk. The British intelligence reports comment that Polish troops "thickened up all units on the northeast of the perimeter." These new additions never joined up with the original Polish troops of the Third Battalion. Urquhart wrote on 23 September, 1147 hours, "1st Airlanding Bde. reports that South Co. 1 Border reinforced by Poles have repelled attacks but Polish casualties 50% of force."

On September 24, the First and remnants of the Third battalion arrived to report to Sosabowski having been transported by American trucks. It is one of the enigmas of this whole operation, that trucks with Polish paratroopers were able to get through to the Poles, but major Allied units and river fording equipment just seemed to be stuck somewhere in the rear echelons.

The British leadership was now in a crisis. Marshal Montgomery, in his role as the commander of the Twenty-First Army Group and from his Olympian heights, passed the buck to General Dempsey, the G.O.C of the British 2nd Army. Horrocks, who was the G.O.C. of the 30th Corps, is on record as wishing to press forward and make a major river crossing. The British still had the 52nd Lowland Division in reserve that was trained and adopted for air movement. Dempsey was more pessimistic and conservative. Each side had a slightly different account of the staff conference and of the tragic events of the night. This began the historic phase of blaming the lower levels. Montgomery dissociated himself from the fiasco, while Brereton claimed a success. Browning took no responsibility but felt that Sosabowski had failed him.

The British made one last attempt to ford the river, but it is unclear from the literature whether it was a feint to distract German attention from the evacuation of the First Airborne or a test to determine German defenses.

The Dorsets were badly mauled; and those that crossed the river never did join the British Airborne Division, whose own perimeter had shrunk and contracted away from the river.

The war diaries of the Third Battalion Polish Parachute Brigade, which did ford the river, comment on the bitter nature of the fighting and the fact that the unit covered part of the British retreat when evacuation was ordered on September 25. The losses of the battalion were four officers and twelve other ranks killed and five officers and forty-five other ranks missing. Of seventy-eight men of the Polish antitank unit, only twelve made it south of the river.

The best critic of the campaign, Australian reporter Chester Wilmot, in his study analyzed many of the problems of *Operation Market Garden* and described it as "strategically superbly conceived and tactically badly carried out."[20]

On September 27, the First Sea Train of the Brigade joined up with the Parachute unit; and on September 29, the Second Sea Train, including all the pack artillery, disembarked at Arromanches in Normandy hundreds of miles away.

The Polish Parachute Brigade Group was regrouped and ordered to protect bridges near the Dutch town of Neerloon. The effective strength at that point was 1,283 officers and other ranks. On October 7, it left Holland. It also left many Dutch friends. But the controversy over the fiasco was about to begin. Major figures never make mistakes, so a scapegoat had to be found. The worst thing that a subordinate can do is to question orders and to be proved right. Sosabowski's independent attitude, and the fact that he had resisted strongly all British blandishments to have his brigade be part of the British 1st Airborne Division and most importantly that all his original warnings were proved correct made him the obvious target.

On arrival in the United Kingdom, Sosabowski received orders from Airborne Corps that his brigade was placed under the command of Urquhart, the G.O.C. of the 1st Airborne. Sosabowski immediately contacted his superior—the chief of staff, General Tadeusz Kopanski—and alerted him to this continuing effort to renege on the original agreements. Kopanski intervened in a diplomatic fashion, accepting the situation only in respect of training aspects.

Very shortly after that the British made it clear that they could not work with Sosabowski and insisted on his transfer from the command of the unit that he had created and commanded in battle. But the Polish Parachute Brigade remained as an independent formation reporting directly to the Polish Chief of Staff. With Sosnkowski's resignation the duties of this office fell on Kopanski.

Sosabowski's staff officer wrote many years later that Sosabowski was ascerbic in his dealings with the British but protested strongly at the decision to withdraw the British Airborne from north of river. Sosabowski urged strongly that the Allies had enough punch to mount a major river assault and continue the offensive. Sosabowski was astounded to hear that the British Army did not have any river crossing equipment.[21]

The name of this small strategically placed Dutch town on the northern branch of the Rhine River Estuary is forever linked with the Battle Honors of the Polish Army from World War Two. It joined other exotic places where the Polish army fought: Narvik, Tobruk, Monte Cassino, Ancona, Falaise, Bologna. But all the other were major Polish victories fought by significant bodies of men under Polish command. At Narvik, the Podhalanska Brigade of well close to six thousand men helped capture the strategic port of Narvik. At Tobruk, the nearly five-thousand-man Carpathian Brigade fought off the famed German Afrika Korps for many months, earning renown and proud epithet, with other allied troops, particularly the Australians, as the "Rats of Tobruk." Monte Cassino, Ancona, and the final battle of Bologna marked the march of the nearly sixty-thousand-man Polish 2 Army Corps, which, in the words of DeGaulle, "lavished its bravery in the service of its hopes." At Falaise the Polish First Armored, seventeen thousand strong, contributed by its glorious stand on the Maczuga Hill to the destruction of the German Army Group Center. The Germans suffered their worst defeat, a quarter of a million of their soldiers were dead, another quarter captured. Eleven of the twelve armored divisions were destroyed, and only twenty one of the forty-eight infantry divisions were still in the German o. de b. Why did Arnhem enter this hallowed pantheon of battle honors, a disastrous military operation, flawed from day one, poorly executed and, in the case of the Poles, fought by scattered units of no more than company size? At the height of the battle the Polish G.O.C., Major General Stanislaw Sosabowski, had a mere thousand men under his command, bereft of any artillery. The only answer to this question is that a stand by a small group of men, whether at Thermopylae, Rorke's Drift, or at Westerplatte, seems to excite a greater admiration than victorious battles. But there is another reason why it has entered Polish military tradition and symbolism, and that has to do with the fact that the Polish Brigade, small as it was, misused as it was, was in fact the only major parachute unit of the Allied armies outside of the British and Americans. Even the Canadians did not have a major airborne unit. Whether it was wise for the Poles to go to such effort to recruit and train such a force is really beside the issue.

October 2, Warsaw Capitulated

The most bitter tragedy for the Polish forces fighting in the West was to realize that their Western friends and Allies were at best impotent or at worst indifferent about the events in Warsaw. The Soviets had placed all kinds of obstacles on shuttle runs for the dropping of supplies from the West and suspended their own operations until January 1945. Even at this late stage in the war the two competing ideologies of communism and nazism, locked in a death struggle, still cooperated to put an end to Polish hopes and aspirations for true freedom and sovereignty as they had in September 1939.

The five-year battle for Warsaw had been lost, not just on the bloody streets, in the damp and dark cellars and sewers of Warsaw, but in the printing presses of papers published in London, New York, and many other cities of Britain and the United States. The more liberal the paper, the more vehemently it took an anti-Polish and pro-Soviet stance. The Poles lost their last campaign, the Warsaw Uprising not merely because the distance was so long, but because the Western Allies lacked the will to enforce their military prowess and keep their original treaty of August 1939. In that sense Sosnkowski was right; the British had reneged once again. Churchill confirmed that view in his comment about the Warsaw Uprising:

> I should have liked to say, "We are sending our aeroplanes to land in your territory, after delivering supplies to Warsaw. If you not treat them properly all convoys will be stopped from this moment by us." But the reader of these pages in after years must realise that everyone always has to keep in mind the fortunes of millions of men fighting in a world-wide struggle, and that terrible and even humiliating submissions must at times be made to the general aim.[22]

Everything that happened after the Warsaw Uprising was a nightmare and tragedy for the Poles, both in the West and also in Poland. Churchill eventually prevailed on Mikolajczyk to espouse a humiliating accommodation to the Soviets and their puppets of the Lublin Committee. He was given a vote of no confidence by the Polish Government and resigned his office. In his capacity as leader of the Polish Peasant Party, Mikolajczyk was invited to join the Lublin Committee in the very humiliating role of vice-prime minister. The Polish President appointed Mr. Tomasz Arciszewski, leader of the Polish Socialist Party who had been extracted from Poland in one of the three successful *most* operations, to the post of Prime Minister.

Churchill wrote to Stalin:

> A change of Prime Ministers does not affect the formal relations between States. The desire of His Majesty's Government for reconstitution of a strong and independent Poland, friendly to Russia, remains unalterable. We have practical matters to handle with the Polish Government, and more especially the control of the considerable Polish Armed Forces, over 80,000 excellent fighting men, under our operational command. These are now making an appreciable contribution to the United Nations' war effort in Italy, Holland, and elsewhere. Our attitude to any new Polish Government must therefore be correct, though it will certainly be cold.[23]

Churchill accurately reflected the ongoing Polish military effort at the side of the Allies. The events of the last two months of 1944 and the last four months of the war in 1945 were bittersweet for the Poles. Victories for the Allied side were punctuated by Polish feats of arms and tragic irreparable political defeats.

Polish Naval Units continued to take part in actions, and the most notable were the actions of the *Garland* in the Dodecanese and of the two fleet destroyers, *Blyskawica* and *Piorun*, in patrols off the south French coast.

The Polish Armored Division started its famous race north on September 1, 1944, the fifth anniversary of the beginning of the war. The Poles covered 470 kilometers in ten days, captured forty officers and 3,447 soldiers, took its first breath on September 10, in Yepres. The Poles captured Abbevile, Ghent, Breda, helped liberate Antwerp fighting through the river- and canal-dotted countryside of Belgium and Holland. This became tough fighting as the Allies had to cross innumerable rivers and canals. The engineers of the division were the unsung heroes.

The Polish Tactical wing scored its greatest one-day success on New Years Day at Ghent. The Polish wings returning back to base attacked and destroyed eighteen German planes that were participating in the final German offensive that has passed into history as the Battle of the Bulge.

December 1944 was the date for the final death throes of the Polish effort. The British informed the Polish Government, through the Polish ambassador in London, that henceforth all Polish radio dispatches to territories occupied by the Soviets, albeit the British used the word "control," were to cease; while such dispatches to the "adherents" of the Polish Government in German-occupied Poland were to be cleared by the British authorities. The Polish Government had repeatedly requested the British to send a British military mission to Poland, akin to their missions to Jugoslavia, Greece, and of course France. Churchill asked Stalin's permission, which was of course refused, but finally in the summer Churchill personally briefed Col. Hudson, who finally with a small group of gallant Englishmen, were parachuted to the southwest corner of Poland on December 26/27, 1944. They landed in a small corner of prewar Poland (that was about to be occupied by the Soviets) and met with General Okulicki.

The British mission code named *Freston*, in the words of one of the British participants, Major Solly-Flood, was to report fully and to keep reporting on all that was seen, to distinguish what was seen from hearsay, to be observers in combat operations but not to undertake any initiatives in such areas, and to hold out no hope of increased supply or help to the Poles and particularly to discourage any possible thought of anti-Soviet military activity. Solly-Flood wrote in his moving piece *Pilgrimage to Poland*, that:

> We went to Poland because the Poles wanted, in the face of tendentious accusations of the Russian loud-speaker, impartial official witness of their heroic struggle against Nazi tyranny, and because there were fortunately in the United Kingdom some high-placed persons who did not in the end dissent from this Polish view point. We went too late to be of any public service, and were to see but the death-throe; but this does not detract from the personal experience.[24]

Captured eventually by the Soviets, the British were held incommunicado until after the Yalta Conference, which was the next diplomatic and final blow to Polish hopes.

On December 28, 1944, the Polish crews of the 301 Defenders of Warsaw, which had now been enlarged into a full twelve-plane unit, flew their last mission to Poland.

On January 19, 1945, the Polish President dissolved the Polish Home Army.

Yalta

On February 28, 1945, Mr. Petherick moved that:

> . . . remembering that Great Britain took up arms in a war of which the immediate cause was the defense of Poland against German aggression and in which the overriding motive was the prevention of the domination by a strong nation of its weaker neighbours, regrets the decision to transfer to another power the territory of an ally contrary to Article 2 of the Atlantic Charger and furthermore regrets the failure to ensure to those nations which have been liberated from German oppression the full right to choose their own governmnet free from the influence of any power.

After a very prolonged debate, 25 members of the House of Commons voted for this motion and 396 voted against. It is probably fair to say that the degree of sympathy for the Polish cause was much greater than the mere 25 individuals but the opposition was not merely strong but once again vitriolic.[25]

The British were very concerned how the Polish Military would react to the Yalta communiqué, which occurred in February 1945. All Polish warships were conveniently in dock for major overhaul.[26] But there were Polish troops in the front line and of course the Polish air units. This concern about the Poles was particularly followed by the Air Ministry, which did a comprehensive assessment of the Polish situation. The following are some of the excerpts.

> The Poles in the Air Force, in common with most Poles outside Poland, are bewildered and uncertain about the future, but this has not yet had any effect on the morale or fighting value of the Polish Squadrons. February 17, 1945.

In a meeting with Major General Izycki, the Air Ministry representative (signature illegible, but I doubt he was a physician) wrote,

> Speaking quite unofficially and without full consideration, it seemed that they were and would remain until the end of the war with Germany, and indispensable part of the forces operating from Britain, France and the Low Countries against Germany. In any event, one of the greatest assets of the Polish Nation in its present tragic situation was the glorious renown won by its armed forces, and I feel confident that they would continue to maintain and enhance that reputation until Germany was defeated.

A summary conclusion is that, "The Polish Air Force Headquarters and the Squadrons at present remain loyal to the R.A.F. organisation within which they serve."

One of the interesting points is the concern about the British press: "The Press in articles or cartoons, so often depicts the London Poles as inept or as trouble makers. Whereas this form of publicity has increased, the one-time publicity given to the achievements of the fighting forces, especially the P.A.R. has decreased."[27]

A number of other interesting comments may be cited. Macmillan wrote in his diaries at that time of his concern regarding the Polish 2nd Army Corps fighting bitterly in Italy: "At the worst they will disintegrate into a rabble of refugees. At the best they will keep enough together to hold a sector of line without attacks or counterattacks. I do not think they could now be used offensively." The Poles went on to arguably their greatest victory of their Italian campaign, the capture of Bologna. Macmillan then wrote: "I have underestimated the marvelous dignity and devotion of Anders and his comrades. They fought with distinction in the front of attack in the last battles of April. They had lost their country but had kept their honour."[28]

The Polish 2 Corps was about to fight its last and perhaps second most difficult and bloody battle, the battle for Bologna. One of the Polish war correspondents, Swiecicki, wrote it up "Seven Rivers to Bologna."[29] The Poles had to fight their way through very determined and well-prepared German defenses and ford seven rivers. This was a battle fought by the infantry and by the engineers. The Poles had grown in numbers from their earlier battles in Ancona. Each of the two infantry divisions now had a third infantry brigade. But the most impressive part of the Corps was its artillery, which was deployed under the command of the commandant of artillery of the Corps, General Roman Odzierzynski. Artillery was the queen of the battlefield and the Poles had a superb artillery group that consisted of 15 field regiments amounting to 323 artillery pieces. The artillery group now had its own air spotting and artillery control flight. During this battle the Poles were aided by the Allied air forces and in particular by the Polish City of Gdansk squadron. (This units had actually grown to an establishment closer to that of a wing, having over thirty pilots). The fierceness of the battle can be gauged by the fact that the Poles used 3,128 tons of artillery ammunition and casualties amounted to 17 officers and 214 other rank killed and 1,228 wounded, which included 88 officers. This high percentage of killed officers (8 percent) speaks to two things: the nature of the fighting, predominantly infantry; and the traditional Polish expectation that officers led their men and did not just command.[30] This battle of the Corps was fought under the command of General Zygmunt Bohusz-Szyszko since Anders was in London having assumed the temporary duties of Commander-in-Chief. He was to return shortly after the Yalta announcement in complete disgust with the British.

In England the Polish Parachute Brigade began intensive training with new personnel in December. On May 8, 1945, the Brigade embarked by ship for Ostend to assist in the capture of the German-held part of Dunkirk. The news of the German capitulation led to new orders. The Brigade was moved to Germany, where it rejoined its old neighbor from Scotland, the First Polish Armored Division (which had enjoyed greater martial glory and success), and assumed occupation duties as part of the British Army of the Rhine through 1946, when demobilization was implemented.

There was one more Polish infantry division (the 4th Infantry) training in the United Kingdom. It was part of the Polish First Corps and composed of many Poles liberated in France and those who had been interned in Switzerland and were now able to escape. This division of close to twenty thousand officers and men was completed by a training armored brigade. As the war was coming to an end, the Poles had been able to muster a formidable modern and superbly equipped and trained army. There were hopes that this army would be allowed, if not encouraged, to move across the European continent to Poland. But fate was not to be that kind to Polish hopes.

There has to be some speculation that had Mr. Churchill's Conservative Party been given a governing majority in the elections of July 25, 1945, the Polish situation may have had some different results. Churchill continued to be an advocate of the Polish cause, even though with each passing month of the war, the role of the United Kingdom diminished in importance compared to the growing industrial, military, and economic might of the United States.

Churchill's concern is well-documented in what may have been one of his last letters to Roosevelt of March 3, 1945, when he wrote, "At Yalta we agreed to take the Russian view of the frontier line, Poland has lost her frontier. Is she now to lose her freedom?"[31]

In March 1945 the Soviets invited the Polish Underground leadership to a meeting at Pruszkow, near Warsaw, arrested them and flew them to Moscow and placed them on trial for anti-Soviet activities. The fourth and last C-in-C of the Polish Underground, Major General Okulicki, died in a Soviet prison.[32] The arrest of Allied leaders in their own country elicited little negative comment from a press or leadership vociferously given to mouthing platitudes of freedom of speech and due process.

On the last day of the war, the Polish Armored Division now under the command of General Klemens Rudnicki, since Maczek had been seconded to Scotland to take over the Polish First Corps from Boruta-Spiechowicz, crowned their success with the capture of Wilhelmshaven, with its booty. Were the Poles fighting in the sixteenth century, each soldier would have been a rich man indeed. The following were taken prisoner: two admirals, one general, 1,900 officers, and 32,000 soldiers and sailors. Three cruisers (*Prinz Eugen, Nurnberg,* and *Koln*) eighteen U-Boats, 205 smaller warships, and well over two hundred artillery pieces and food for 50,000 men for three months.

The most welcome was the liberation at Niederlangen and Oberlangen of many hundreds of Polish women soldiers who were taken prisoner of war at the demise of the Warsaw Uprising.

In May 1945 the Polish First Armored Division hosted the crew of the Polish cruiser O.R.P. *Conrad* and the victor of Monte Cassino, Ancona—General Anders.

During the first months of 1945 the Polish Air Force carried out patrols, escorting of bombing missions, and interdictions of German transport. Bad weather in January and February affected operations, but in March the Poles carried out 2,585 missions. On April 9 the 309 squadron fought a battle with the new German jets, ME-272, and shot down three of them, while 306 managed to shoot down one of the jets. These were the last air victories of the Polish Air Force.[33] The last symbolic strike at Hitler was carried out on April 25, by 225 heavy bombers that bombed Hitler's lair—Bertchtesgaden. The Polish 300 heavy bomber squadron took part in this last operation, achieving the record of having flown more combat missions than any other Allied squadron, British or American.[34]

The Allied bombing expedition was escorted by a number of fighter units, including four Polish squadrons, the 303, 306, 309, and 315. This was the longest flight of the single-engined Polish fighter units and lasted six hours.

Conclusion

When the achievements are objectively analyzed the only verdict can be that the Poles came close to achieving their goals. It was a damned close thing. But luck had also run out.

A major, highly confidential, and efficient system of radio communications was implemented and a Polish-controlled system of courier developed. The amount of material actually transferred to Poland was also quite impressive. During the war years, between 1941 and 1944, Section VI of the Polish General Staff arranged for 485 drop missions, of which 240 were by Polish, 138 by R.A.F. and South African, and 107 by American crews. Six hundred tons of material were dropped; and thirty-four million dollars, one and half million gold sovereigns, and in addition German- and Polish-occupation money transmitted to the Polish Home Army. The lion's share of this money was for military purposes, the balance for various political, propaganda, and charitable goals.

The Poles may be quite correct in blaming the British for insufficient support of the Polish special duties air component. There were more than sufficient Polish crews competent to fly four-engined planes. Had the British released those crews from other activities such as the Ferry Command and 300 Bomber Squadron, and dispatched the number of planes advocated by Lord Selborne, then a different story could have been told. In late December 1944 the Poles achieved a full squadron complement. Had such been the case for the whole of 1944, one can safely assume that the tonnage dropped to Poland would have been at least double that achieved by the Poles and the less than enthusiastic British crews flying to Poland.

But would it have made any difference? Had the Poles been able to even send a small symbolic group from the Parachute Brigade, would it have made any difference? Had many years before, Sikorski acceded to the loss of Lwow and survived the storm of Polish protest, would it have made any difference? People often compare the fate of Poland to that of Finland, and of course with disparaging remarks directed at the Poles. But Poland lies in the main area of possible Soviet expansion. Finland is sideshow.

The actualization of a Polish parachute training center was a highly desirable success, but the efforts to expand the cadre unit to a full brigade group a gross misjudgment of reality. The blame can only be attached to the Polish General Staff, which failed to heed the very obvious British warnings that air transport was not available for such a major unit. In fact Paszkiewicz was right in 1943 when he cautioned the Poles against expanding the cadre unit to a full brigade and urged that it stay a cadre unit.

Had there been a possibility of a drop of a company-sized unit in Poland, then the symbolic value would have been as significant as the dropping of a whole brigade. In retrospect the cadre training base should have trained some small company-sized units available for special commando-type missions and a large number of *cichociemny* officers (in fact well over two thousand volunteered for such service) trained to lead locally recruited groups increased and dropped to Poland.

It made little sense to train a rifle-carrying paratrooper so that he could be parachuted to Poland when there were thousands of eager young men able to carry a rifle and familiar with the surroundings. It was a different situation for the senior officer material and specialists.

The Polish Government can probably be correctly criticized for not placing more effort into the air force, particularly the single-engined fighter, ground support squadrons. But not all the men available to the Poles were suitable for service in such a specialized and highly technical service. Finally, was there any need for the Polish Navy to commission large destroyers let alone a cruiser? In this situation we have one of the strange paradoxes of the Polish Military in Exile. The Polish Navy started off the war by having a considerable pool of young trainees in the West due to the fortunate fact that the training ship *Iskra* was on a summer cruise off Africa. The Poles also had a small number of fleet destroyers at the beginning of the war in British waters and brought to the Allied side well-trained and cohesive ship complements. It made sense to keep them as it did to keep the submarine crews. But more effort in the direction of the small and less glamorous ships, such as minesweepers and certainly motor-torpedo-gunboats, would have been important were the Poles to return to the Baltic.

There is a tendency to see the Polish-British situation in rather radical black and white. Many denigrate the Poles for their unrealistic, romantic view of world politics; and many a Pole is convinced that the British practiced duplicity and exploited the Polish resolve to fight. First, the administrative effort that went into the creation of the Underground Army and its support is anything but romantic.

Hard work, effort, and that factor too often scorned, bravery, contributed to the Polish success. That the Poles failed had as much to do with the long distance and the problem of Polish-Soviet and Western Allied–Soviet relations as any factor. That the Poles continued to try to implement their policies surely cannot be held against them. But even though the British more often than not honestly stated their inability or possibly unwillingness to assist the Poles in their very ambitious endeavors, it should be remembered that there were often hints of indirect support.

The political realities were bitter, but there was one more unnecessary insult which the Polish forces had to experience. This is best summarized by a letter published in the *Daily Telegraph*, June 5, 1946, and signed by ten members of the British Parliament:

> Sir—Polish dead lay in hundreds on Monte Cassino in 1944. The Poles fought at Tobruk, Falaise and Arnhem. Units of the Polish Navy took part in most of the major actions at sea from September 1939 to VE Day; Polish fighter pilots shot down 772 German planes between July 1940 and VE Day. The Polish Underground Army was the biggest and best organized in any of the occupied countries.
>
> The Polish Army and Navy who fought under British command have not been invited to take part in the Victory March on Saturday, June 8. Insult has been added to injury by asking the Polish Provisional Government, a non-elected Government to whom the men in the Polish armed forces outside Poland owe no allegiance, to send a contingent "representative of the Polish Fighting Services."
>
> In view of the above it is not surprising that the Polish Air Force, which was to have been represented by one officer and 25 men, has refused an invitation to take part in the march.
>
> Ethiopians will be there; Mexicans will be there; the Fiji Medical Corps, the Labuan Police, and the Seychelles Pioneer Corps will be there—and rightly too. But the Poles will not be there.
>
> Have we lost not only our sense of perspective, but our sense of gratitude as well? We fear so.

This is a succinct comment and a fine tribute to a five-year history of British-Polish military collaboration. There were still ten British Members of Parliament who were willing to depart from what was then the politically correct view.

While the official British position ignored the Poles as if they had never been around, two of the Services went out of their way to show a gesture of courtesy and collegial warmth. The Royal Navy in its official parade in Plymouth invited Polish participation and the Royal Air Force appointed a special historical committee to publish the story of the Polish Air Force in the United Kingdom, aptly named in the circumstances, *Destiny Can Wait;* and in a ceremony that only the British are capable of putting on unveiled the Polish Air Force memorial at Northolt. Every year, in September, Polish air force veterans and British Air Ministry and, subsequently, Defence Ministry representatives attended to pay tribute to the heroes and Allies of the war, which bring to mind the words of the immortal bard, "but we shall be remembered; We few, we happy few, we band of brothers."

In the official Royal Air Force history the tribute to the Polish Air. Force was also generous and warm,

> All these allied contingents gave something unique; and if we mention especially the Polish airmen, it is not only that their contribution was the greatest in size—with fourteen squadrons and some fifteen thousand men, including their own ground staff, besides many pilots in the British squadrons—and that their fighting record in all Home Commands and Europe and the Mediterranean was unsurpassed, but also that victory brought them no reward only further exile from home and loved ones they had fought so long and bravely to regain.[35]

Lord Ismay wrote after the war:

> It is easy, and perhaps natural, to blame President Roosevelt and, in a lesser degree, Mr. Churchill for not having taken a tougher line with Marshal Stalin. Nobody can deny that the failure to secure freedom and independence for Poland had brought shame on the Western democracies. At the same time, those who now aspire to prescribe what ought to have been done, must in fairness bear in mind the circumstances of those days. For over three years, public opinion in America and Britain had been led to believe that Russia was a brave and faithful ally who had done the lion's share of the fighting, and endured untold suffering.[36]

Lord Ismay accurately reflected the issue. Probably being British, he was not as sensitive to the issues that I have confronted, namely that the third enemy was the most implacable and the most difficult for the Poles to confront. Willen did a splendid review[37] in the postwar period of the unthinking and pro-Soviet attitudes which enjoyed great United States governmental support, particularly from the United States Information Service. Therefore the Americans as well as the British Government have to assume considerable burden of guilt and responsibility for the fact that the vicious four-year mass media anti-Polish propaganda was never challenged and was allowed to play such an insidious role in the final outcome of not just Polish but even British fortunes. This mass media propaganda never ceased. For the last eight months of the war, the Poles fought only to preserve their honor; and the greatest defeat that they suffered was in fact the impeachment of their honor by their enemies, and the complete silence of their past friends.

No Pole in 1945 expected the British to go to war against the Soviets on behalf of Poland. Many were convinced that sooner or later there would be a war by the West against Soviet imperialism and expansion. They were certainly partially right, the communist coup in Prague, the civil war in Greece, and the Berlin blockade with the resulting formation of the North Atlantic Treaty Organization were in line with such predictions. Many thought and believed that a firm line with the Soviets would have forced them to back down, and at least expected the British to allow Polish troops on Polish ships escorted by Polish warships to sail to the Polish coastline and to disembark. The Allied fears of a civil war were justified but a civil war was fought anyway for many years.[38]

The majority only wanted the British to say: "We are truly sorry!"

The immediate postwar years saw a number of publications that in their title addressed the tragedy of defeat. Ciechanowski wrote his memoirs, *Defeat in Victory;* Anders, *Without the Last Chapter;* and the official Polish Air Force history was titled, *Destiny Can Wait.* In 1992 the veterans of the Polish Air Force and their cherished standard were received with full military ceremony at Pilsudski Square by President Walesa and welcomed home. In May 1944, on the fiftieth anniversary of the storming of Monte Cassino President Walesa, who attended the ceremonies, addressed the grave of the hero, General Anders, and assured him and his buried soldiers that the last chapter had been written. But it is still far from clear that Ciechanowski's provocative title can be undone.

Notes

Notes to Chapter 1

1. Wandycz, *The Lands of Partitioned Poland, 1795–1918*. Kukiel, *Czartoryski and European Unity, 1770–1861*. Kukiel, *Dzieje Polski Porozbiorowe, 1795–1921*. Davies, *God's Playground. A History of Poland. The Cambridge History of Poland*. Zamoyski, *The Polish Way*.

2. The Congress of Vienna condemned Poland to well over a hundred years of cultural and political subjugation as well as economic exploitation by the three partitioning countries. The Versailles Treaty gave international sanction to Poland's freedom, already grasped by the *Polska Organizacia Wojskowa*. In 1990 at a meeting of the American Military Institute held in Arlington, Virginia, a prominent British military historian argued that the Congress of Vienna was a paradigm for international success, since it gave Europe a hundred years of peace and was not vindictive towards France, while the Treaty of Versailles was to be condemned since it placed great trial and tribulation on a defeated enemy—Germany!

3. Less than six months after the first fully free presidential elections held in Poland, the *New York Times* (4/29/1991) reported that in a public opinion poll held in Poland, the Polish Army took precedence over the Roman Catholic Church as the most trusted institution in Poland.

4. Recently this fabled trilogy has seen a new and excellent translation by W.S. Kuniczak, thanks to the efforts of the Copernicus Society of America, and published by Hippocrene Books, N.Y. Kuniczak himself authored a trilogy on the experiences of the Poles in the Second World War; namely: *The Thousand Hour Day* (takes place in Poland in September 1939), *The March* (the tragic story of Poles deported to the Soviet Gulags in 1940); and *Valedictory* (the strongly fictionalized history of Polish airmen in the United Kingdom).

5. D'Abernon, *The Eighteenth Most Decisive Battle of the World*, Warsaw, 1920. There is a general impression in the West that the Polish-Russian war was a mere boundary skirmish. The Polish losses suggest that the war was bloody and bitterly contested. The number of killed and wounded was substantial and broken down by officers and noncommissioned officers was 2,059 and 45,542 respectively. There were nearly 51,000 missing and

well over a 100,000 wounded. Also, Zamoyski, *The Battle for the Marshlands.*
Davies, *White Eagle. Red Star.*

6. Rothschild, *Pilsudski's Coup D'Etat.*

7. Newman, *March 1939: The British Guarantee to Poland.* "The value of
Poland lay not in the capacity of her army to launch an offensive against
Germany, which was virtually non-existent, but in her capacity to absorb
German divisions. Above all she must not be allowed to supplement them
[! author's exclamation] by subordinating her foreign policy to Hitler, or to
allow them free reign in the west by maintaining an attitude of benevolent
neutrality," p. 156. Later, "It seems reasonable to argue that in choosing
the path that they did in March 1939, the British Government took upon
themselves a certain measure of responsibility for the conflict that ensued.
They were fully aware of the probable consequences of their decision. The
guarantee reduced the likelihood of a settlement between Germany and
Poland and increased the probability of a clash between them. It is hardly
acceptable to argue that Beck would have been intrasigent anyway, even
admitting that his attitude towards Hitler's hitherto rather polite initiatives
had been firm all along. For we simply cannot predict how Polish policy
would have evolved without the guarantee," p. 220. It is fair to say that
Polish public opinion would never have stood for a any policy that might
have been historically analogous to the first and second partitions, and
that the Polish Armed Forces would have fought in the most unfavorable
circumstances, yet had Hitler been a diplomat some form of modus
vivendi might have been arrived regarding the status and Polish rights in
Danzig. It was the Polish Army that precluded the British from such an
acceptance of events. See Newman, "Since the Chiefs of Staff advised that
'it was better to fight with Poland as an ally than without her' . . . we ought
to take steps to ensure that Poland did resist German aggression," p. 194.
This argument can be moderately criticized. The seminal point that Britain
wished to preclude the Polish Armed Forces from enhancing German
military might can be stipulated to, but an argument can also be made that
the final British step was only arrived at on August 23—German-Soviet
treaty—when it became clear that the Soviet Union would not aid Poland
nor fight Germany. This is the only logical explanation for what otherwise
has always been assumed to be a long series of British and French inepti-
tudes. But the sophistry of the British Prime Minister, Foreign Office, and
Treasury was finally confronted by the British Parliament's and society's
realization that the German menace had to be confronted, and that the
time was September 1939.

8. Kozlowski, *Wojsko Polskie 1936–1939,* pp. 74–108. The pages cited discuss the administrative structure of the Armed Forces.

9. *Konstytucia Rzeczypospolitej Polskiej.* Reprinted by the Joseph Pilsudski
Institute of America, N.Y., 1944. Enacted in 1935. This constitution was in
force in 1939 and was the basic constitutional foundation for the Polish
Government's legality in exile and for the role of the Commander-in-Chief.

Article 2. (1) The President is the Head of the Republic. (2) He is responsible before the God and History for the fate of the Country. (3) He is responsible for the welfare of the Country and its defenses and standing in the concert of nations. (4) His is the total and undivided leadership of the State. Also, Jedruch, *Constitutions, Elections and Legislatures of Poland, 1493–1977. A Guide to their History.*

10. *The Memoirs of General Lord Ismay.* Lord Ismay finished his career by becoming the first Secretary General of the North Atlantic Treaty Organization in 1952.

11. Kozlowski, *Wojsko Polskie 1936–1939,* pp. 74–108. This is one of the seminal studies on the pre-1939 Polish Armed Forces, though tainted by the prevalent socialist view of history held in Poland at the time the monograph was published. The pages cited discuss the administrative structure of the Armed Forces. A number of publications deal with Poland's pre-1939 endeavors to modernize. Krzyzanowski, *Wydatki Wojskowe Polski w Latach 1918–1939.* Kozlowski, op. cit., pp. 24–73. *Polskie Sily Zbrojne w Drugiej Wojnie Swiatowej,* Vol. 1, Part One. Stachiewicz, *Przygotowania Wojenne w Polsce, 1935–1939.* (General W. Stachiewicz was Poland's Chief of Staff, and these posthumous memoirs were edited by his son.) Wiatr, Jozef "W Sprawie Polskiego potencialu gospdarczego przed 1939 rokiem," *Bellona,* 2, pp. 25–30, 1953, and "Przyczynki do historii materialowych przygotowan obrony Polski w latach 1921–1939." *Bellona,* 3, pp. 235–256, 1959. (General Wiatr was Chief of the First Section of the Polish General Staff, i.e., Quartermaster general.)

12. Many opponents of Pilsudski have alleged that he lacked technological sophistication and was militarily at best uninformed and at worst a self-proclaimed illiterate prophet. The following translation of Pilsudski's comments on the Polish Navy in the early 1920s does not allow for such superficial criticism. It is probably true to say that Pilsudski did mix his metaphors, and his literary style even in Polish was laborious, while after translation, very baroque. Kozlowski, ed., *Jozef Pilsudski w opinii politykow i wojskowych,* MON, 1985. "If in our strange climate of megalomania, expressed in words which lack substance, if in our amusing mania for planning which projects an elephant out of a mouse or at the very least a panther or tiger, we have some flowers in our army, then our unhappy navy leads the field in these great statements. For when ideas have no boundaries, where should one seek them if not in the oceans. In my opinion this is the worst problem of the navy, which is the most difficult to integrate into a comprehensive system of the nation's defence. The state lacks the means and ability to manifest its might by the creation of navy which would be able to fight on the oceans. Naval power grows much slower than land forces since many countries have taken centuries to create a country with a modest budget and citizenry so land bound as the Poles any thought of a fast build up of a naval fleet and of enlarging its purpose beyond that of a humble but vital role of defence of the small shoreline, is out of the ques-

tion. In all my operational concepts I never go beyond the vital and achievable goal of controlling the sea lanes in the Gulf of Danzig. I also do not wish to abjure the need for the use of the navy and its reserves, growing every year, to fight on land. Therefore, I seek to find an answer in an amphibian role rather than in that of a whale. We do have an amphibian in the riverine flotilla based in Pripec. I don't know enough about that force. Even here I fear that the operational doctrine is to fight on water,—heaven forbid on land. This reminds me of our cavalry which can only plan to fight on horseback, and considers it ignominous to get off a horse. I would think that fighting on the water of rivers where the banks can be reached by carbine, let alone machine gun fire from the other side, is at best useless. I would therefore seek utilizing the rivers as mode of transport rather than a place for fighting. Writing these words I do not wish to make our navy subservient to the organized command structure nor influence its budget. But I do wish to ensure that the issues be discussed by the inspectors of the Army so that by year's end I will have a memorandum for a decision. I specially urge that thought be given to motor boats which will be important for the defence of the coastline as well as for work on the rivers. The growth of such a service and the ability to maneuver such boats and for landing men with carbines and machine guns coupled with the ability to camouflage such boats to have the potential for swift transport of small bodies of men, is essential for the defence of the coast and for operations on the rivers, which will facilitate the capture or defence of isolated positions until the arrival of our own infantry, or the arrival of major naval units." I believe that these words were nearly prophetic, since a flotilla of small motor-torpedo-gunboats would have been priceless in September 1939, and such small warships could have either supplied or evacuated the Polish garrison of Westerplatte.

13. Wandycz, *France and her Eastern European Allies, 1919–1925.*

14. Korbel, *Poland between East and West: Soviet and German diplomacy toward Poland, 1919–1933.* von Riekhoff, *German-Polish Relations 1918–1933.*

15. Beck, *Final Report.* Hitler in his April 1, 1939, speech revoked the German-British Naval tonnage limitation treaty signed in London in 1935. On April 28, 1939, he revoked the Polish-German Declaration of Nonaggression of 1934 stating that "This agreement contained one single exception which was in practice conceded to Poland. It was laid down that the pacts of mutual assistance already entered into by Poland—this applied to the pact with France—should not be affected by this agreement." Hitler proceeded to argue that the British initiatives guaranteeing Poland's sovereignty infringed on this declaration.

Notes to Chapter 2

1. Cynk, *Polish Airccraft, 1893–1939.* Kwiatkowski, *Pisma o Rzeczy-pospolitej Morskiej.*

2. Chocianowicz, ed., *W 50 Lecie Powstania Wyzszej Szkoly Wojennej w Warzsawie.*

3. Kutz, C.R. "Pilsudski and the Russian Bear" in Chapter 8, *War on Wheels. The Evolution of an Idea.*

4. *Wojna Obronna Polski, 1939. Wybor Zrodel*, pp. 33–44. This encyclopedic work is a compilation of over 557 selected archival documents from the pre-1939 and the September Campaign.

5. Nalecz, *Polska Organizacia Wojskowa, 1914–1918.* Mierzwinski, *Generalowie II Rzeczypospolitej.* Kryska-Karski and Zurakowski, *Generalowie Polski Niepodleglej.*

6. Kopanski, *Wspomnienia Wojenne, 1939–1946.* (General Kopanski was a senior staff officer in the operational section of the Polish General Staff in 1939, and finished the war as Chief of Staff of the Polish Armed Forces in Exile.)

7. Litynski, Stanislaw, "Udzial Wyzszej Szkoly Wojennej przed rokiem 1939 w ksztaltowaniu Polskiej doktryny wojennej," *Bellona*, 1. pp. 30–38, 1955.

8. Hart, *History of the Second World War*, writes "moreover, Poland's leaders still pinned their trust to the value of a large mass of horsed cavalry and cherished a pathetic belief in the possibility of carrying out a cavalry charge." A number of other authors such as Young, *World War, 1939–1935:* "the Poles were fighting by the rules of 1918"; Montgomery, *A History of Warfare:* "handled them in the 1916–1918 manner." Citino, *The Evolution of Blitzkrieg tactics. Germany Defends itself against Poland, 1918–1933*, writes that the German military attaché in Poland in 1930 reported that: "the horse is seen as a means of transport but not of battle." He added that attacks are not made from the saddle "troopers assiduously dismounted and fought on foot." The following facts may also place the Polish situation in a perspective. Many other armies in 1939 had horsed cavalry, see Piekalkiewicz, *The Cavalry of World War Two.* The German Army depended on horses for its transport and most of its artillery right up to 1944 was horse-drawn. In 1939 during the invasion of Poland, the thirty-nine German infantry divisions had 197,000 horses requiring 135 rail cars of fodder per day. Over two and a half million horses served in the German Army throughout the war. See Cooper, *The German Army, 1933–1939.* For a commentary on the times and military attitudes prevalent at that time, see Dixon, *On the Psychology of Military Incompetence*, pp. 116–117. Dixon discusses that in the mid-1930s the British War Office opposed the expansion of the Tank Corps (forerunner of the British Armored Corps) and that on the same day as Hitler announced the expansion of his peacetime army to 36 divisions in defiance of the Versailles Treaty, the British increased their allowance for horse forage from 44,000 pounds to 400,000 pounds and allotted two horses to each cavalry officer while each Royal Tank Corps officer was to have one!

9. Lukasiewicz, ed., *Poland in the Brit. Parliament.* Roos, *A History of Modern Poland.* Wandycz, *France and Her Eastern European Allies.*

10. A number of publications deal with Poland's pre-1939 endeavors to modernize. Krzyzanowski, *Wydatki Wojskowe Polski w Latach 1918–1939.* Kozlowski, op. cit., pp. 24–73. *Polskie Sily Zbrojne w Drugiej Wojnie Swiatowej,* Vol. 1. Part One. Stachiewicz, *Przygotowania Wojenne w Polsce, 1935– 1939.* Wiatr, Jozef, "W Sprawie Polskiego potencialu gospdarczego przed 1939 rokiem," *Bellona,* 2. pp. 25–30, 1953, and "Przyczynki do historii materialowych przygotowan obrony Polski w latach 1921–1939," *Bellona,* 3, pp. 235–256, 1959. (General Wiatr was Chief of the First Section of the Polish general Staff, i.e., Quartermaster general.)

11. Skibinski, *Ulanska Mlodosc, 1917–1939.* Also Zaleski, *W Warszawskiej Brygadzie Pancerno-Motorowej, 1939.* The British were also going through a major reassessment of their motorization efforts, see Winton, *To Change an Army. General Sir John Burnett-Stuart and the British Armored Doctrine, 1927– 1938.*

12. Krzyzanowski, *Wydatki Wojskowe Polski w latach, 1918–1939.*

13. Grove, *World War Tanks.* Szubanski, *Polska Bron Pancerna w 1939 roku.*

14. Bartel, Chojnacki, Krolikiewicz, Kurowski, *Z Historii Polskiego Lotnictwa Wojskowego, 1818–1939,* Chapter II, by Adam Kurowski, pp. 47–77.

15. Report of General J. Zajac to the Inspector General regarding the lack of fighter defenses, dated November 28, 1938, cited in *Wojna Obronna Polski 1939. Wybor Zrodel,* pp. 174–189. Also see Hastings, *Bomber Command: They Myths and Reality of the Strategic Bombing Offensive, 1939–1945.* This succinct analysis of the R.A.F. bomber offensive in which 55,573 aircrew (British, Canadian, Australian, New Zealand, and Polish) were lost also has some interesting comments on British prewar aviation budgets and doctrine. It comments that for the first three years of the war a typical British bomber crew was quite unlikely to find its primary or even secondary target. This reality was the underlying reason for R.A.F.'s leaflet offensive during the early months of the war. Hastings also confirms that till December 1937 R.A.F. policy was for a strong bomber component of 1,422 bombers as against a mere 532 fighter in July 1941. Britain was unable to meet such costs and trimmed its bomber plans while increasing its fighter strength. Predictably in Britain as in Poland proponents of the bomber force criticized the British Minister Inskip. In hindsight the successful outcome of the Battle of Britain was decided by this change of policy, p. 46. Also, see Rick, "Confronting Complacency: The R.A.F. Girds for War, 1933–1939," *Air Power History,* 1994; 41:23–29.

16. The very successful P.Z.L.-11 series of gull winged planes, which equipped all (but three) Polish fighter squadrons in 1939 had been introduced into service in 1935. The engine plants were Polish built under license from Bristol (Mercury V or VI). The horsepower of these engines varied between 595 and 630. The Polish aircraft manufacturer (*Polskie Zaklady Lotnicze*), continued its run of the gull winged plane for export. The various P.Z.L.-24s, which were exported to Greece, Turkey, and Bulgaria,

had a French Gnome-Rhone engine of 950 horsepower. This version of the series was armed with four Colt-Browning machine guns or two 20mm Oerlikon cannon. Able to take two 50 kilogram bombs, the pilot's seat was armor-protected and the windshield was bulletproofed. This plane was about fifty kilometers per hour faster than the fighters in Polish squadrons. However, the French were unwilling to sell Poland a license for this power plant and the Poles reluctant to depart from their policy of ensuring that all Polish-built planes also had Polish-manufactured engines. Furthermore, the aviation authorities had decided that the future of fighter aircraft lay in low-wing monoplanes with retractable undercarriage. The plane that came closest to being introduced into service was the P.Z.L.-50 *Jastrzab*. It was a low-winged monoplane (similar in appearance to the American Seversky fighter planes of the period) and was to be powered by a Polish-built Bristol Mercury VIII producing 840 horsepower. A second follow up variant that was already in planning stage was to be armored, stressed for dive bombing, and to be powered by a completely Polish-designed *Waran* engine of 1200 horsepower. Except for the retractable undercarriage, which the British firm Dowty procrastinated for five months in delivery the first set of retractable undercarriages so that the it was all Polish-built. The first test flight occurred in February 1939. The tests showed the plane to be underpowered (worth remembering that the P.Z.L.-24 engine delivered 950 horsepower as compared to 840 for *Jastrzab*), and the original order for three hundred craft was cancelled! Since this resulted in a surplus of Bristol Mercury engines built for the *Jastrzab*, the authorities decided to use them for an improved series of the P.Z.L.-11 to be named P.Z.L.-11g— *Kogut*. This plane would have entered service early in 1940. In 1941, the export version of this Polish fighter, the P.Z.L.-24 fought successfully in Greek colors against the Italian Air Force. It would have served Polish interests well had the Polish aviation possessed four hundred of these planes, a number well within the capability of the Polish industry and air personnel. On the other hand, the *Los* was a great technical achievement for the Polish industry. For a superb history of the development of the Polish two-engined bomber see Cynk, *Samolot Bombowy PZL-P.37 Los.*

17. The Polish Air Staff considered a number of American fighter planes; these were Brewster, Curtiss, Grumman, and Seversky. The most advanced negotiations were with Curtiss, since the French by purchasing this plane gave it a stamp of approval. The negotiating agent was a firm of Ulen Company, and the price was eight million dollars for 143 planes. Allegedly the American middleman offered this sale on a loan with 3 percent interest. On July 21, 1939, the Polish Military attaché in Washington was advised that the deal was off due to the lack of hard currency. LOT. A. I. 2/16. Negotiations also took place in the United Kingdom. On June 16, 1939, the Polish Air Attaché cabled Warsaw, requesting that four experienced pilots be sent to the UK and on July 1, 1939, communicated his satisfaction that the British would sell a hundred Fairey-Battles; but that the

British were reluctant to sell their modern fighter planes albeit had agreed to the sale of fourteen Hurricanes. The British posture was explained by the Polish attaché, Col. Bogdan Kwiecinski as due to the small British credits for Polish rearmament and the Royal Air Force's needs. Polish Institute LOT. A.I. 2/15.

18. Historical Commission of the Polish General Staff, *Polskie Sily Zbrojne*, Vol. I, Kampania Wrzesniowa, Part 1, pp. 87–106.

19. There is archival evidence that on August 8, 1939, the Polish aviation authorities prepared to receive a French bomber and a crew of French experts to plan for future shuttle bombing missions. P.I. Lot A.I. 2/11.

20. Kozaczuk, translated and edited by Wladyslaw Kasparek, *Enigma*. Lewin, *Ultra Goes to War*.

21. Cieplewicz and Zgornik, *Przygotowania Niemieckie do agresji na Polske w 1939 roku w swietle Sprawozdan odzialu II sztabu glownego Wojska Polskiego*. Dokumenty.

22. Bekker, *Luftwaffe War Diaries*, writes: "despite all assertions to the contrary, Polish air force was not destroyed on the ground in the first two days. The Bomber Brigade in particular continued to make determined attacks on the German forces up to September 16th." Bekker omits to point out that the date of 16th was a function of the Soviet invasion in the early hours of September 17, which threatened the Polish air bases and forced the remaining Polish planes to fly to Romania where they were interned. Bekker also cites the figures of the Luftwaffe Quartermaster General for October 5, 1939, which states that 285 German planes were destroyed in the Polish Campaign and a further 279 damaged beyond repair.

23. Polish Naval archives in the Polish Institute: MAR A v51/1. B-1028, B-1029, B-1031, B-1033, B-1039, B-1104, B-1045. Also the following British P.R.O. files: ADM 199/1187, /1178, /1180, /1854, /1807. Polish Institute in London and also on the published Study, *Polskie Sily Zbrojne Tom I, Kampania Wrzesniowa, Marynarka Wojenna i Obrona Polskiego Wybrzeza*.

24. *Documents Concerning German-Polish relations and outbreak of hostilities between Great Britain and Germany on September 3, 1939*. "In the event of any action which clearly threatened the Polish independence, and which the Polish Government accordingly considered it vital to resist with their national forces, His Majesty's Government would feel themselves bound at once to lend the Polish Government all support in their power," p. 36. The full text of the Polish–United Kingdom Treaty of Mutual Assistance is given in Appendix 1.

25. There are only two English language histories of the Campaign: Kennedy, *The German Campaign in Poland, 1939*. Zaloga and Madej, *The Polish Campaign, 1939*, who write: "The Polish Army fought before the blitzkrieg had ever been demonstrated. It should not be forgotten that the Polish Army fought for nearly five weeks against the full weight of the Wehrmacht and later the Red Army, even though it was substantially outnumbered. In contrast, the British, French, Belgian and Dutch armies,

which outnumbered the Wehrmacht in men, tanks and aircraft, and which did not suffer from a precarious strategic encirclement as Poland did, held out for only a few weeks more. The myth of the "eighteen-day war" is not borne out by German casualty figures. The German Army Group South, which bore 75% of the German casualties in Poland, lost more men killed in the final half of the war than in the first two weeks." Kennedy wrote: "Two hundred and seventeen tanks were destroyed during the period between September 1 and 30. The casualty figures and losses in material for the period of combat showed that the campaign was more than an exercise with live ammunition. Rundstedt supported this view on operations in Poland in one of his rare commentaries following World War Two. The bulk of the German Armed Forces had to be committed to overcome the Poles, and expenditure in ammunition, gasoline, and material was such as to preclude concurrent German operations on a similar scale in the west or elsewhere. The opportunity for a successful Allied attack against the Westwall had passed by the time the Polish Campaign ended. Hitler and his generals were well aware of the risk they had taken in throwing almost all their resources into the gamble for a quick victory in the east." The official German Standing Orders dated January 2, 1940, lists the last battle of the German invasion of Poland as the battle of Kock-Adamow between October 2 and 7, 1939. The Polish submarine O.R.P. *Orzel* in a symbolic manner carried out patrolling in the Baltic till October 10, 1939. For literature on the military events of the September Campaign, which is overwhelmingly Polish language, see Neugebauer, *The Defense of Poland, September 1939.* The Polish language literature is prolific and deals with general issues, detailed military analysis, and also has complete monographs on the major field armies. But pride of place in this compilation has to go to the London-based Polish Institute, which has published a five-volume history of the campaign over a number of years. This monumental work still being written was initiated by the Polish General Staff's Historical Commission, on December 10, 1946, by an executive order signed by Lt. General Stanislaw Kopanski, the last Chief of Staff. This mandate was carried on by the Polish Institute in London, which is the primary repository of all wartime Polish military archives. *Polskie Sily Zbrojne w Drugiej Wojnie Swiatowej. Vol. I. Kampania Wrzesniowa.* 1954, 1959, 1986 respectively, while the section dealing exclusively with the navy was published in 1962. Bauer and Polak, *Armia Poznan w Wojnie Obronnej, 1939.* Godlewski, *Bitwa nad Bzura.* Ciechanowski, *Armia Pomorze.* Kutrzeba, *Bitwa nad Bzura.* Kirchmayer, *Kampania Wrzesniowa.* Dalecki, *Armia Karpaty.* Jurga and Korbowski, *Armia Modlin.* Pindel, *Obrona Narodowa, 1937–1939.* Wroblewski, *Armia Lodz, 1939.* Wroblewski, *Armia Prusy, 1939.* Porwit, *Komentarze do Polskich Dzialan Obronnych, 1939.* Rzepniewski, *Wojna Powietrzna w Polsce, 1939.* Rzepniewski, *Ibrona Wybrzeza w 1939 roku.* Los, *Artyleria Polska, 1914–1939.* For a selection of personal memoirs, see Cieplewicz and Kozlowski, eds., *Wrzesien 1939. W relaciach i wspomnieniach.*

Wojna Obronna Polski, 1939. This is a compilation of over 557 selected archival documents from the pre-1939 and the wartime period.

26. Taylor and Munson, *Military Air Power.*

27. Liszewski, *Wijna Polsko-Sowiecka, 1939.*

28. Polish Institute—LOT A. I 3/1e. This is a personal narration of Stanislaw Riess, written in November, 1939 for the Polish general Staff in Paris. It is captioned: "Report from the Flight Bucharest-Warsaw-Kowno." This narrative describes the deatils of the flight over the Carpathians, in difficult weather conditions and landing in a race track in no man's land, between Polish defensive and German positions. 35. Bekker, op. cit.

29. Bekker, op. cit.

30. In a postwar report, Major Jan Lesniak, head of the German Division of the Polish Military Intelligence (Section II of the General Staff or popularly called *dwojka*) wrote that a large amount of information regarding German movements, particularly after September 7th was provided by the aviation service. Suchcitz, ed., *Kampania Wrzesniowa 1939 roku*, p. 22.

31. Final report of the Polish Navy submitted to the Polish General Staff in 1945 and archived in the Polish Institute under MAR A v51/1. P.R.O. ADM 171/9971. 53557. There are two reports in the British Public Record Office on the escape of the Orzel, one of seven types pages is captioned ISHMAEL, by "Naval Eye Witness"; and the second, much shorter is captioned: The *Orzel.* The following extract is from the longer document but the shorter one has some interesting information and the salient point are in square brackets when pertinent. The author has always been assumed to be Captain S.W.Roskill, R.N. also the author of the official history of the Royal Navy in WW II.

32. Churchill, *The Second World War: The Gathering Storm.*

33. See also Churchill, *The Gathering Storm*, p. 722. Churchill as First Lord to Director of Naval Intelligence on September 6, 1939: "What is the position on the west coast of Ireland? Are there any signs of succoring U-boats in Irish creeks and rivers?"

Notes to Chapter 3

1. Wiatr, J. "Decyzia Naczelnego Wodza przejscia granicy rumunskiej dnia 17go wrzesnia 1939 roku," *Bellona*, No. I and II, 1961.

2. Sword, editor, *Sikorski: Soldier and Statesman.* Kukiel, *General Sikorski. Zolnierz i Maz Stanu Polski Walczacej.* Korpalska, *Wladyslaw Eugeniusz Sikorski. Biografia Polityczna.* Terlecki, *General Sikorski,* and *General Ostatniej Legendy. Rzecz o Generale Wladyslawie Sikorskim.*

3. Polish language historical literature is quite profuse in discussing the internal political dynamics of the change of Presidency which occurred after Moscicki's internment and decision to pass his constitutional prerogatives to Wladyslaw Raczkiewicz in Paris. By and large foreign historians have been oblivious to the nuances of the internal political crisis which

undoubtedly had some French input. The best history of this constitutional crisis is in Pobog-Malinowski, *Najnowsza Historia Polityczna Polski, 1864–1945*, Vol. 3 *(1939–1945)*, pp. 63–82. See also, Duraczynski, *Rzad Polski na Uchodzstwie, 1939–1945*, pp. 37–51.

4. Article 13 and 24 of the 1935 Constitution provided that when the country was at war or occupied and an election was impossible, the President could appoint a successor.

5. Jedrzejewicz, ed., *Memoirs of the Polish Ambassador to Paris.*

6. Bor-Komorowski, *The Secret Army.* Garlinski, *Poland, S.O.E. and the Allies.* Karski, *Story of a Secret State.* Korbonski, *Fighting Warsaw,* and Korbonski, *The Polish Underground State. A Guide to the Underground, 1939–1945*, Polskie Sily Zbrojne w Drugiej Wojnie Swiatowej*, Vol. III. *Armia Krajowa.* The most comprehensive published account of the Polish Home Army, *Armia Krajowa,* is Czarnocka, ed., *Armia Krajowa w Dokumentach, 1939–1945.*

7. For a very comprehensive study of the recruitment, organization, and evacuation of Poles from internment, see *Polskie Sily Zbrojne* Vol. II, Kampanie na Obczyznie, Part 1. Wronski, *Poza Krajem—Za Ojczyzne.* Kukiel, *Six Years of Struggle for Independence.*

8. Merrick, *Flights of the Forgotten. Special Duties in World War Two,* p. 16.

9. P.R.O. ADM 199/1393 80530.

10. Howard, *The Mediterranean Strategy in the Second World War.* Woodward, *British Foreign Policy in the Second World War.* For an excellent discussion of Polish wartime, see Meiklejohn Terry, *Poland's Place in Europe.* Wandycz, *Czecho-Slovak-Polish Confederation and the Great Powers, 1940–1943.*

11. Estreicher, *The Jagiellonian University,* writes that on November 6, 1939, 183 professors were arrested by the Germans, the University shut, and the University converted into a Institut fur Deutsche Ostarbeit. The fate of Poland's oldest university (founded in 1364) was also the fate of every other Polish University. See also Garlinski, *Poland in the Second World War,* p. 31.

12. Kopanski, *Wspomnienia Wojenne, 1939–1946.* General Kopanski, prior to the war, occupied a number of high positions in artillery and during the September Campaign was Chief of Section III (Operations) of the Polish Staff. Promoted to the rank of Major General in 1940, he distinguished himself by his command of the Polish Carpathian Brigade in the siege of Tobruk and then in the battle of El Gazala. His impeccable military record and bearing brought him to London to assume the post of Chief of Staff of the Polish General Staff in 1943. Decorated with many high Polish decorations, he was also awarded the British Order of the Bath—Military Division. He stayed in the United Kingdom after the war.

13. Mitkiewicz, *Z generalem Sikorskim na Obczyznie.* Batowski, Henryk, "O Udzial Polski w Miedzysojuszniczym Komitecie Wojskowym w Londynie, 1939–1940," *Wojskowy Przeglad Historyczny* 1971: 259–270. Also, see also Churchill, *The Gathering Storm,* p. 505. However, Churchill refers to

Sikorski as the "Head of the Provisional Polish Government." It has to be assumed that this phrase was not a mistake but an attempt in 1948 to obfuscate issues and cast doubt on the validity and constitutionality of the Polish Government.

14. Woodward, *British Foreign Policy in the Second World War*. For specific aspects of the British policy, see Medlicott, *The Economic Blockade*. Given the fact that during this time the Soviet Union was collaborating with Germany, and at least economically an ally, the British plans were futile.

15. See Appendixes 2, 4, and 5 for the full text of the Polish-French Military agreements.

16. "Dwa memorialy sztabowe na temat Zwiazku Sowieckiego z polowy 1940 roku." *Bellona*, Nr. 1. 36–40, 1960.

17. *Destiny Can Wait*, pp. 370–382, and Kalinowski, *Lotnictwo Polskie w Wielkiej Brytanii, 1940–1945*, pp. 13–17.

18. For the full text of the Polish-British Naval Agreement, see Appendix 3.

19. Sopocko, *Orzel's Patrol. The Story of the Polish Submarine*.

20. Taylor, *The March of Conquest. The German Victories in Western Europe*. Harvey, *Scandinavian Misadventure: The Campaign in Norway, 1940*.

21. Dec, *Narvik. Falaise*.

22. Krol, *Polskie Skrzydla nad Francia*, and *Walczylem pod Niebem Francji*.

23. Taylor, *The March of Conquest. The German Victories in Western Europe*.

24. Blum, *2 Dywizia Strzelcow Pieszych w Szwajcarii. Poczatki Internowania, 1940–1941*.

25. *Polskie Sily Zbrojne, Tom II. Na Obczyznie.* (Part One dealing with the Polish Forces in Exile between September 1939 and July 1941).

26. Krol, op. cit.

27. Kukiel, *General Sikorski, Zolnierz i Maz Stanu, Polski Walczacej*.

28. Raczynski, *In Allied London*.

29. Roskill, *The War at Sea, 1939–1945*, Vol. 1, Her Majesty's Stationery Office, London 1954, p. 239, cites the figures for the evacuation from Brittany and South France, called *Operations Aerial and Cycle*. A total of 191,870 men were evacuated to the United Kingdom. Of this number, the lion's share were the British: 144,171; Polish: 24,352; French: 18,246; Czech: 4,938; Belgian: 163.

30. Kopanski, *Wspomnienia Wojenne, 1939–1945*.

31. The Polish Government boarded the Royal Navy Cruiser HMS *Arethuse* in the Girondin estuary on June 17 at 200.00 hours. On June 18 and again on June 19, the British warship was bombed. On June 20 at 11.05 it weighed anchor. P.R.O. ADM 53/111412. At the same two other momentous events were occurring. Major and still-classified exchange of views through Sweden, by Rab Butler representing Lord Halifax, and Germany regarding a negotiated peace. Costello, *Ten Days to Destiny. The Secret Story of the Hess Peace Initiative and British Efforts to Strike a Deal with Hitler*. Sikor-

ski was also flying back and forth between London and France, negotiating the evacuation of the Polish Forces in France to the United Kingdom. It was around this time that the episode, called the Litauer memorandum, took place. Kukiel also writes that before boarding the Royal Navy Cruiser, one of the Polish ministers said to the President, that after arriving in the United Kingdom a change in the premiership would be inevitable. Kukiel, *Sikorski*, op. cit.

Notes to Chapter 4

1. See Appendix 6 for a text of the Polish-British Land Forces Agreement.

2. Raczynski, *In Allied London*, p. 58. Also, Cienciala, Anna, "The Question of the Polish-Soviet Frontier in 1939–1940: The Litauer Memorandum and Sikorski's Proposals for Re-establishing Polish-Soviet Relations," *Polish Review*, 33: 295–323, 1988. "Dwa memorialy sztabowe na temat Zwiazku Sowieckiego z polowy 1940 r." *Bellona*, 1960, pp. 36–46.

3. Tucholski, Jerzy, "W sprawie oddzialu lacznikowego Komendanta Glownego AK przy Naczelnym Wodzu na Emigracji," *Wojskowy Przeglad Historyczny*, Nr. 4, 1983, pp. 209–228.

4. Pobog-Malinowski, *Najnowsza Historia Polityczna Polski, 1864–1945*, Vol. III, 1939–1945, pp. 150–162, and Duraczynski, *Rzad Polski na Uchodzstwie, 1939–1945*, pp. 74–79. Also, Westerby and Low, *The Polish Gold*.

5. On December 10, 1939, Marshal Edward Smigly-Rydz escaped from his internment to Hungary and attempted to establish contact with the Polish Underground Army. Sikorski became alarmed and, since the Marshal successfully disappeared, wrote on January 16, 1941 to the British Foreign Secretary, Eden, that: "It is indispensable that Marshal Smigly-Rydz should have no possibility of direct contact with the Polish Army. It would be advisable for the Marshal, accompanied by his closest attendants to reside until the end of the war in one of the British Colonies." Polish Institute Archives A XII. 1/12. On February 25, 1941, Sikorski sent a long telegram to the G.O.C. of the Polish Home Army ordering that Smigly-Rydz was not be allowed to partake in any military activities and be given assistance in crossing into a neutral country, presumably back to Hungary. This telegram was again repeated in much the same form on September 27, 1941. But the Marshal only arrived in Poland on October 26, 1941, under the name of Adam Zawisza. His efforts to contact the Polish Underground Army leadership were turned down at the express orders of Sikorski. The Marshal died on December 2, 1941, from a heart attack. He was buried in the cemetery of Powazki. I visited the grave in 1973. It was a simple grave with no indication that it contained a Polish Marshal and victor of the Battle of Niemen in 1920.

6. The Poles received a full-page photo in the June 1941 weekly *The Il-*

lustrated London News, with a complimentary caption: "Poland's Navy in the Vanguard: The *Piorun* finds the *Bismarck."* The official report of the Commander-in-Chief Home Fleet thus acknowledged the part played by the *Piorun.* "The *Bismarck* was sighted by the *Piorun,* on the port wing at 22.38 hours, just after the last shadowing plane left to return to the Ark Royal. Destroyers were ordered to take up stat shadowing; at 22.42 hours the enemy opened a heavy fire on *Piorun,* who made a spirited reply before turning away under smoke cover. The Commanding Officer of the *Piorun* had not worked with the Fourth Destroyer Flotilla before and therefore decided to wait until the last to deliver his attack as he did not wish to interfere with the flotilla and was not conversant with their methods. He had drawn *Bismarck's* fire for an hour during the period dusk hoping that this would assist the other destroyers to get in their attack but after dark he retired to a distance of some 6 to 8 nautical miles to wait for them to finish. He had not succeeded in regaining touch when at 05.00 hours he was ordered by the Captain (D) Fourth Destroyer Flotilla, to proceed to Plymouth to fuel if not in contact with the enemy. The Captain (D) was concerned lest a valuable ship and a fine crew be lost without need. The *Piorun* continued to search until 06.00 hours and left an hour later." P.R.O. ADM 199/1187. It should be emphasized that in those early days of the war, even fleet destroyers like the *Piorun* did not carry radar. For an excellent account of the sea battle and chase, see Greenfell, *The Bismarck Episode.*

7. *Polskie Sily Zbrojne, Vol. II. Na Obczyznie,* op. cit. Also for details of Polish warships during the Second World War, see Piaskowski, *Okrety Rzeczpospolitej Polskiej, 1920–1946,* and *Kroniki Poskiej Marynarki Wojennej 1918–1946.*

8. *Destiny Can Wait: The History of the Polish Air Force in Great Britain.* Kalinowksi, *Lotnictwo Polskie w Wielkiej Brytanii.* Winston Churchill wrote in his *Finest Hour,* Vol. II of his major history, *The Second World War,* that he made two conditions of the French were they to seek an armistice with the Germans in June 1940: that the French Fleet not fall into German hands and that the 400 Luftwaffe prisoners of war be turned over to the British. This illustrates the importance that Churchill attached to fighter pilots. The 140 Polish pilots who fought in the Battle of Britain were a major addition to the Fighter Command, p. 161. Also Mason, *Battles of Britain,* gives a comprehensive list of all the participants of the greatest and most decisive air battle to date. Three thousand eighty names are listed, giving rank, nationality, squadron assignments, and substantiated victories. The following figures can be calculated on this basis: 303 Kosciuszko Squadron had 117 victories; 501 R.A.F. came in second, with 87; and 603 R.A.F. and 41 R.A.F. tied for third place, with 69. This outstanding performance continued. Deighton and Hastings, *Battle of Britain,* p. 178, wrote: "The Poles were the most numerous" (i.e., of non-British pilots, author's comment), "and also made the greatest contribution. They deeply resented the canard that their air force had been wiped out in the finest hours of the German

invasion in September 1939, for some of them had flown and fought until the bitter end. They were much more highly-trained than most British pilots of the period although they had no experience of high performance monoplanes, and they were remarkable marksmen. In a Fighter Command gunnery the contest early in 1941, three Polish squadrons took the first three places with scores of 808, 432 and 193. The best British squadron came fourth, with 150. This helps explain how the Poles achieved such remarkable results in the Battle of Britain."

9. The Poles had a number of major intelligence networks in France, Switzerland, and North Africa. These archives are part of the British closed archives. But enough has been written to suggest that the *Jerzy* network was the only allied group until SOS until Donovan came on the scene in 1943. Also the Poles had a major clandestine system in Northeast France built around the prewar Polish migration.

10. Foot, *SOE: The Special Operations Executive*, p. 195.

11. Ibid., p. 109. The actual quote from "The Arms and Techniques of the Resistance, 1941–1944," by Pierre Lorain adapted by David Kahn, is as follows: "The Polish series was certainly one of the most brilliantly designed in the domain of clandestine transmissions. The high quality of finishing afforded the smallest details reveals both the German school, of which the Poles had been students, and the natural desire of the weak to assert themselves in the face of British secret services and to prove that the Poles were capable of supplying the best, most technologically advanced sets. Between 1941 and 1944, about ten models were manufactured in substantial quantities. It was not until 1943 that the British specialists produced sets of equal and perhaps superior quality."

12. Eckert, *Eksperymnent. Polscy Oficerowie w Afryce Zachodniej w latach, 1941–1943.* Also see Churchill, *The Grand Alliance*, p. 686, London edition only. "About four hundred Polish officers were sent as proposed to the West African Division, and served with high credit."

13. Balfour, *The Armoured Train. Its development and usage.*

14. Ciesielski, S., "Rekrutacia do Polskich Sil Zbrojnych w Kanadzie 1940-1942," *Wojskowy Przeglad historyczny*, 24 (1979), 80–101.

15. For a history of the Polish-American volunteers in 1917, see *Czyn Zbrojny Wychodztwa Polskiego w Ameryce.* For the Second W.W. political work of the Polonia, see Jedrzejewicz, *Polonia Amerykanska w Polityce Polskiej. Historia Komitetu Narodowego Amerykanow Polskiego Pochodzenia.*

16. Kopanski, *Wspomnienia Wojenne, 1939–1946.*

17. Only the Polish Medical School in Edinburgh has been recognized by a cited paper. Rostowski, J., "Polish School of Medicine, University of Edinburgh, 1941–1945," *British Medical Journal*, pp. 1394–1351, 1966.

18. P.R.O. AIR 8/295 80530.

19. Terry, *Poland's Place in Europe.* Also Wandycz, *Czechoslovak-Polish Confederation and the Great Powers.*

20. Sosabowski, *Freely I Served.* Also *Najkrotsza Droga.* For a very com-

prehensive list of all the names of the officers and men of the Brigade, see Lorys, *1st Polish Independent Parachute Brigade Group. List of Participants.*

21. Gilbert, *Winston Churchill,* Vol. VI. *Finest Hour, 1939–1941,* p. 667.

22. Foot, *SOE: The Special Operations Executive,* p. 30.

23. On September 15, 1938, near Luck, Poland, a small group of trained paratroopers executed an exercise, in which they carried out a successful simulated diversionary attack on enemy forces. This was repeated two days later and led to the formation of a special Parachute Training Center at Bydgoszcz. One of the officers who trained the volunteers was Lt. Jerzy Gorski. Later in the war, in March 1943, promoted to Captain, Gorski was parachuted to Poland to be attached to the Home Army's Aviation Staff.

24. Jackson, *The Secret Squadrons. Special Duty Units of the R.A.F. and USAAF in the Second World War.* The first R.A.F. unit operating on behalf of SOE was Flight 419/1419 formed on August 21, 1940, at North Weald, and equipped with two (!) Lysanders. In October of that year two Whitleys were added and flight renamed 1419. This flight became the nucleus of No. 138 formed on August 25, 1941, and eventually based at Tempsford. Equipped initially with Whitleys, it then had Halifaxes and due to short-age and problems with plane equipped with Stirlings in September 1944. No. 161 was formed at Newmarket on February 15, 1941, from personnel drawn from the King's Flight and some crews seconded from 138. It also was equipped with Whitleys, Halifaxes, and finally Stirlings. The squad-ron for a period also had the one-engined Lysander for pick-ups in France. Thus during the whole of the war, R.A.F. only had two home-based long-range special duty squadrons. There were also a number in the Mediterra-nean and Asian areas.

25. P.R.O. AIR 19/818 80530, and in general *Destiny Can Wait: The His-tory of the Polish Air Force in Great Britain,* pp. 214–228. Kalinowski, op. cit., pp. 249–281. Kalinowski was a combat flyer in the Second World War, a lecturer at the Polish War College in the United Kingdom, and a very dis-tinguished air historian, with numerous Polish and English language arti-cles to his credit. His book is based primarily on the unpublished official report of the Polish Air Force Commission, after the conclusion of hostili-ties, to the Polish Air Force Commander, Major General Mateusz Izycki. This is as close as we will ever get to an official published Polish history of the Polish Air Force in W.W. II.

26. PIL. LOT AV II/1a.

27. The Polish Air Force in the United Kingdom at this point consisted of four (two-engined) bomber squadrons, eight (single-engined) fighter squadrons and one army cooperation squadron assigned to the Polish First Army Corps in Scotland and equipped with the out-of-date Lysanders. See *Destiny Can Wait,* and Kalinowski, op. cit.

28. See Appendix 5.

29. Pimlott, ed., *The Second World War Diaries of Hugh Dalton,* p. 142. Also three Polish senior rank officers had by then been awarded the British

Order of the Bath—Military Division: Major General Stanislaw Ujejski, the Inspector of the Polish Air Force on January 1, 1941; Vice Admiral Jerzy Swirski, Commanding Officer, Polish Navy on January 1, 1941; and Lt. General Marian Kukiel, G.O.C. Polish First Corps based in Scotland on December 2, 1941. These awards recognized the achievements of the Services they commanded.

30. *The Unrelenting Struggle. War Speeches by the Right Hon. Winston S. Churchill, C.H., M.P.* This speech is frequently aired on American television but never in its entirety for obvious reasons, and always begins with the phrase: "Every week his firing parties are busy in a dozen lands. Monday he shoots Dutchmen; Tuesday Norwegians; Wednesday, French or Belgians stand against the wall; Thursday it is the Czechs who must suffer. And now there are the Serbs and the Greeks to fill his repulsive bill of executions." It always finishes at this part so there is never any mention of the Polish suffering and certainly never any allusion to the fact that this whole speech was meant for the Poles.

Notes to Chapter 5

1. Churchill, *The Grand Alliance,* p. 378.

2. Ibid., p. 391.

3. Kurzman, *The Bravest Battle,* wrote that following the formation of the Jewish secret military there ensued negotiations between the Polish Home Army and the Jewish group regarding their allegiance to the Polish Government. The Poles were clearly concerned about the proclivity of the Jewish groups to the communist cause. Kurzman writes: "Mordechai finally authorized Arie to tell the Home Army with diplomatic ambivalence, since we are citizens of Poland, the decisions of the Polish government binding upon us." The Polish Home Army was both aware of the ambivalence and highly mistrustful of any left-leaning group. See Schatz, *The Generation. The Rise and Fall of the Jewish Communists in Poland.*

4. Docs. Vol. 1, 392–393, and *Poland in the British Parliament,* Vol. 1, pp. 469–480. Also Duraczynski, *Uklad Sikorski-Majski.*

5. Ibid., pp. 108–146.

6. For the actual text of the Polish-Soviet Military agreement signed on August 14, 1941, in Moscow, see Appendix 7.

7. Docs. Vol. 1, p. 156 and p. 165.

8. Anders, *An Army in Exile.*

9. Joseph E. Davies, author of *Mission to Moscow,* once again became ambassador to Moscow and wrote as follows in a well-publicized article in *Life* (March 29, 1943). "The Soviet Government is not a predatory power like Germany and Japan's"; while the editors of *Life* compared Lavrentii P. Beria's N.K.V.D. to the United States F.B.I. The editors furthermore compared the Soviet Union favorably with American democracy; "like the USA the USSR is a huge melting pot, only in a different way. It contains

175 nationalities speaking 150 languages and dialects. They don't mix as much as our ethnic groups do; yet the system by which all these people are held together runs parallel to ours in that it is a federation." Mr. Davies, on the other hand, in his interview also posited that, "It would be natural for them to demand what any other people would, under similar circumstances. First they would naturally want that back which had previously been taken away from them by force after the last war." This from the ambassador of the country that signed the Atlantic Charter, which stated in its first two principles: "*countries seek no aggrandizement, territorial or other; and second, they desire to see no territorial change that does not accord with the freely expressed wishes of the peoples concerned.*" Also, Perlmutter, *FDR and Stalin*, p. 69 and pp. 102–108.

10. P.R.O. WO 216/19 38026. This memorandum further suggests India as the best place for their concentration and rehabilitation from the "harsh treatment they received before the Polish-Russian Pact." Shortly thereafter the Chief of the Imperial Staff expressed an opinion that the Poles be moved to Persia. "I should like to stress the importance which I attach, for military reasons, to the evacuation of as many Poles as possible. We want 10,000 in this country, 2,000 in the Middle East to bring up to strength the Polish Forces now in existence. The successful withdrawal of the remainder—I believe that something like 150,000 are involved—would be a great contribution of good fighting men to our cause."

11. *Destiny Can Wait*, pp. 28–29.

12. Ibid., pp. 171–258. Also see Kot, *Conversations with the Kremlin and Dispatches from Russia*. Mr. Kot was Polish ambassador to the Soviet Union.

13. *Docs. Vol. 1*, p. 374. The Polish embassy delivered a protest to the effect that the Polish Government could not accept the Soviets deciding who was a Polish citizen and therefore able to carry a Polish passport and to be able to join the Polish forces (dated June 24, 1942).

14. One of the most moving historical records are the films of the soldiers of the Polish Army in the USSR in the winter of 1941/42. See *As Crosses are Measure of Freedom*, Contal International Ltd., produced by the Documentary and Feature Film Studios in Warsaw, 1989.

15. Zaron, *Kierunek Wschodni w strategii wojskowo-politycznej gen. Wladyslawa Sikorskiego, 1940–1943*.

16. Churchill, *Their Finest Hour*, p. 598, and also *The Grand Alliance*, pp. 111–155. Also for the account of the code breaking that finally won the Battle of the Atlantic in 1943, see Kahn, *Seizing the Enigma. The Race to Break the German U-Boat Codes, 1939–1943*.

17. Churchill, *The Hinge of Fate*, p. 279, and Hastings, *Bomber Offensive. The Myths and Reality of the Strategic Bombing Offensive, 1939–1945*.

18. P.R.O. AIR 8/295 80530.

19. A total of 1,244 Polish air crews were lost in the bomber offensive. The shortage of crews was never undone and one of the Bomber Squadrons. Kalinowski, *Lotnictwo Polskie w Wielkiej Brytanii*.

20. P.R.O. AIR 19/818 80530, also Kalinowski, op. cit.

21. Ibid.

22. P.R.O. AIR 19/815 80530. Dalton's diaries throw little light on this subject.

23. Churchill, *Hinge of Fate*, p. 499.

24. *Docs. Vol. 1*, pp. 301–309.

25. *P.S.Z. na ob.* part 2, pp. 127–135.

26. PIL. A. XII. 1/129.

27. Sikorski quoted in, *Documents on Polish Soviet Relations 1939–1945*, pp. 344–347.

28. Regulski to Klimecki quoted in *Documents on Polish Soviet Relations 1939–1943*, p. 373.

29. *P.S.Z. na ob.* part 2, p. 283, and *Docs. Vol. 2*, p. 344.

30. Churchill, *Hinge of Fate*, p. 269.

31. Anders, *Army in Exile*.

32. Churchill, *Hinge of Fate*, p. 496.

33. Englert and Barbarski *General Anders*.

34. Churchill, *Hinge of Fate*, p. 919.

35. Patton, *War as I Knew It*.

36. PIL.A. V. 20/31 18.

37 P.R.O. WO 193/42 80751.

38. Ibid.

39. PIL. AV 20/31/ 18.4.

40. Chlebowski, *Wachlarz*. Also see *PSZ* Vol. III, *AK*, pp. 482–498.

41. Iranek-Osmecki, *The Unseen and Silent*, and Bystrzycki, *Znak Cichociemnych*. Of this group, exactly one hundred were killed in operations, or after capture tortured and executed. A number committed suicide after capture. In this group of Polish heroes there was one Polish woman, Elziebeta Zawacka, who made the clandestine journey from Poland to the West through the Balkans, France and Gibraltar, and was returned by parachute on 9/9/1943.

42. Tucholski, *Wojskowy Przeglad Historyczny*, op. cit., pp. 209–228.

43. Foot, *S.O.E.: The Special Operations Executive*, p. 131.

44. PIL. LOT AV II/1b.

45. P.R.O. AIR 19/815 80530.

46. P.R.O. ADM 199/1393 80530.

47. Ibid.

48. P.R.O. AIR 19/815 80530.

49. *Destiny Can Wait*, p. 142.

50. Franks, *The Greatest Air Battle*; Kalinowski, *Lotnictwo Polskie w Wielkiej*.

51. Each nationality and epoch had its heroes, but this group of Poles, parachuted back to their country, were certainly brave men. There were 578 such silent and unseen heroes, *Cichociemni*. But in this group of brave Poles, Lt. Col. Roman Rutkowski deserves mention. In 1940 he became the

C.O. of 301 Polish Bomber Squadron with which he completed thirty operational missions. Transferred to staff work and delegated to head the Polish section of the Special Duties operations of the R.A.F. squadron, he flew the first mission to Poland as an observer on a plane commanded by Major Krol, and later he was parachuted to Poland. He was picked up on May 29, 1944, by a R.A.F. Dakota in a *Most* operation, and again parachuted to Poland on October 18, 1944. Arrested by the Communists after the war, he survived and after release moved to Britain where he died. He was awarded the gold (class IV) Order of the Virtuti Militari.

52. PIL LOT AV II/1b.

53. Ibid.

54. Laquer, *The Terrible Secret.* Also, see Nowak, *Courier from Warsaw.*

55. P.R.O. WO 193/33 80751.

56. Bartosik, *Wierny Okret*; Pawlowicz, *O.R.P. Garland: In Convoy to Russia*; Romanowski, *Torpeda w Celu*; Domiczek *Opowiadania Marynarskie*; Rudzki, *Polskie Okrety Podwodne, 1926–1969*; Pertek, *Wielkie Dni Malej Floty*; and *Druga Mala Flota.* British P.R.O. ADM 199/1187, ADM 199/1178, ADM 199/1180, ADM 199/1854, ADM 199/807. PIL B-1028, B-1029, B-1031, B-1033, B-1039, B-1104, B-1045, MAR. AV. 51/1. *PSZ na Ob.* Vol. 1 and Vol. 2.

57. Pertek, *Druga Mala Flota*, and Mozdzenski, L. "Wklad Polskiej Marynarki handlowej do wysilku Sojuszniczego w II Wojnie Swiatowej," *Bellona*, 1954.

Notes to Chapter 6

1. Churchill, *Hinge of Fate*, p. 760, also see J.K. Zawodny, *Death in the Forest.*

2. Karski, *The Great Powers and Poland. 1919–1945. From Versailles to Yalta*, Jedrzejewicz, *Poland in the British Parliament, 1939–1945*, Umiastowski, *Poland, Russia and Great Britain, 1941–1945.*

3. In 1990 while a guest of the Polish Naval Association in at their annual meeting, I met a veteran who had been a Soviet prisoner during his late teens. Released by the provisions of the Sikorski-Maiski Treaty, he then volunteered for the Polish Naval Forces and left in the first evacuation from the Soviet Union. He then served aboard Polish destroyers throughout the war, undergoing all the rigors of the Battle of the Atlantic. We had a long chat while traveling by train from Henley's Polish Fawley Court back to London. The only thing that brought tears to his eyes and the admission that he would rather be dead than re-experience his brutal treatment by the mindless, primitive, and bestial agents of the Soviets.

4. James, *Victor Cazalet. A Portrait.*

5. This cemetery also contains the bodies of nearly four hundred Polish airmen, who died in plane accidents, or whose battle-damaged craft failed them over Britain. In 1947, the President of Poland, His Excellency Wla-

dyslaw Raczkiewicz, was also interred with his soldiers. The British had to be entreated before they most reluctantly allowed a Polish Para detachment to have arms as the last guard of honor. In 1993, the body of General Wladyslaw Sikorski was exhumed and moved to the Royal Crypts in the Cathedral on Wawel Hill, Cracow.

6. This magnificent speech is not included in Churchill's Nobel Prize–winning history of the Second World. I found it in a sketch form in the British archives (FO 371/7683) and also in the final form as reproduced above in the pro-Polish conservative paper *Daily Telegraph*, London, July 15, 1943.

7. Leitgeber, *W Kwaterze Prasowej. Dziennik z lat Wojny*, pp. 222–248. The background to the anti-Polish attack in the House of Commons was the announcement on May 1, 1943, by the Polish consulate in line with established practice: "The Consul General of the Polish Government in London calls for the enlistment of all Polish citizens residing in Great Britain, born in the years 1902–1925 inclusive, who have not yet come forth. They are to register between May 10 and May 28. Individuals in the above mentioned group who do not enlist will be considered as avoiding service and will be treated according to precepts of Polish Law." Since the majority of Polish citizens residing in the United Kingdom who were reluctant to serve in the Polish Armed Forces were in fact Jews, a storm broke out over this announcement, which was consistent with all Polish-British agreements, was consistent with established consular practices of all countries, and was in the spirit of the Allied effort to carry on the war. Now Mr. Shinwell, Mr. Driberg, Mr. Silverman, etc., all expressed concern about the dire threats against those who would rather not serve in the Polish Forces but were willing to serve in the British Army. Mr. Silverman sought immunity from Polish Law for those who were Polish citizens, avoided service in the Polish Forces but were willing to serve in the British Army which in fact did not wish to accept them for active service, only in the noncombatant Pioneer Corps. Mr. Law (the undersecretary of State for Foreign Affairs) stated that the Polish Government (and all the other Allied governments) did not posses the legal power to enforce such a call up; and that the British Government did not have the powers to alter Polish Law in Poland. Jedrzejewski, *Poland in the British Parliament*, Vol. II, pp. 202–228.

8. P.R.O. AIR 2/9234.

9. P.R.O. FO 371/7863 and Jozef Zaranski, "Zagadka katastrofy Gibraltarskiej po 15 latach," *Bellona* 1958, 274–283.

10. Colonel Leon Mitkiewicz (Polish representative to the Combined Chiefs of Staff in Washington), writes in his memoirs *Z Generalem Sikorskim na Obczyznie*, pp. 239, 240, and 259 that, as early as April, 1942, Sikorski seriously considered throwing the Polish cause to the side of Stalin. Mitkiewicz, himself reminisces that Pilsudski was contemptuous of other Polish diplomats that they failed to seriously parlay Polish alliance for Polish gain.

11. Churchill, *Closing the Ring*, p. 653.

12. Menachem Begin in his *White Nights,* writes that he only enrolled in the Polish Army after it was obvious that the units were being evacuated, and excused his earlier avoidance of military service either in the Polish or Soviet Armies, as due to Polish anti-Semitism. Hirschler and Eckman in their biography of Begin, *From Freedom Fighter to Statesman,* make a point that Begin did not desert but was released (true), but that "most other Jewish refugees from Poland who had come to Palestine with the Anders Army shed their uniforms almost immediately after their arrival without the formality of an official discharge." Silver in *Begin, The Haunted Prophet.*

13. *P.S.Z. na Ob.* Part 2, p. 114.

14. Ibid, pp. 345–387, also Bieganski, *Dzialanie 2 Korpusu we Wloszech.*

15. National Archives Washington CCS 334 218.

16. Ibid., and PIL.KOL 3/3/8 17. National Archives CCS 334 218, Leon Mitkiewicz, *W Najwyzszym Sztabie Zachodnich Aliantow,* pp. 285–288, also, P.R.O. WO 193/41. 80751.

17. National Archives Washington CCS 334 218, Leon Mitkiewicz, *W Najwyzszym Sztabie Zachodnich Aliantow,* pp. 285–288, also, P.R.O. WO 193/41. 80751.

18. Ibid.

19. Mitkiewicz, op. cit. Wedemeyer in his *Wedemeyer Reports* makes no mention of either this discussion or even of ever dealing with the Polish issues.

20. PIL. LOT AV II/1b.

21. P.R.O. WO 193/42 80751.

22. Ibid.

23. Ibid.

24. Ibid.

25. P.R.O.AIR 19/815 80530.

26. Ibid.

27. PIL. LOT AV II/1a.

28. PIL LOT A VII/1b. Also, see Kalinowski, op. cit., p. 264.

29. Polish authorities, with great cooperation from the British Air Ministry, worked hard to develop many of the vital supporting services. This short listing is merely to point out the variety of effort. Seventy-six officers and 751 other rank were assigned to communications. Many had been trained in radar techniques but were assigned primarily to the radar needs of the Polish Coastal Command and night fighter squadrons. Thirty officers and 640 other rank were armorers; while twenty-six officers and 124 other rank were in meteorological services. All Polish combat units had photo sections.

30. Duraczynski, *Rzad Polski na Uchodzstwie, 1939–1945,* pp. 291–328, Karski, op. cit., pp. 473–484, Jedrzejewicz, op. cit., pp. 311–407.

31. Major General Stanislaw Kopanski became the Polish Chief of Staff following the death of Major General Klimecki who died with Sikorski in the plane accident off Gibraltar on July 4, 1943.

32. PIL. LOT AV II/ 1a.

33. Ibid.

34. Ibid.

35. Ibid., Lt. Col. Jan Bialy was C.O. of 2nd Bomber Wing in September, 1939, while in 1940 in the United Kingdom he was C.O.of the Polish 304 bomber Squadron. After a number of years in staff liaison work, he flew at the age of forty-six as a pilot with the Polish Coastal Command Squadron. He then volunteered for service in Poland and spent time at the British secret squadron that had captured German planes. He undertook a short familiarization course. I knew Col. Bialy and corresponded with him and have also seen his official report in the Polish Institute. I am personally convinced that he would have given a perfectly accurate account of the capabilities of the Polish Air Force in the West to the staff of the Home Army. However, according to his account the most senior officer he was able to see in the situation of conspiracy prevailing in Poland was Col. Adam Kurowski, the Home Army's Air C.O. During a visit to Warsaw in 1973 I met Col. Kurowski and attempted to discuss the situation but was politely turned off. During the communist days, being a senior member of the staff of the Home Army was not a plus for a citizen of Poland. One fears that the success of the Polish crews and their undoubted renown may have obfuscated the actual potential for independent action. See next footnote.

36. Szoldraska, *Lotnictwo Podziemia czyli dzieje Wydzialu Lotniczego Komeny Glownej Armii Krajowej*, describes many details of the functioning of the different subsections; but has no comment or any information or discussion on the bleak possibility of moving any Polish air units to Poland.

37. Shores, *2nd Tactical Air Force*. The Second Tactical Air Force consisted of two Fighter Groups (83rd and 84th) and one Bomber Group.

38. P.R.O. AIR 37/90 96925.

39. Ibid.

40. The shortage of men in the British Army is well illustrated by the fact that in September 1944, Montgomery was asked to asked to provide: Army HQ for Mountbatten in Burma, two divs for Burma, give up his only existing airborne div-52nd, provide a Corps HQ for Burma and was forced to disband the 50th. Hamilton, *Final Years of the Field Marshal, 1944–1974*, p. 102. The only Polish Armored Division in the United Kingdom represented about 20 percent of all major armor units under British command.

41. PIL LOT AV II/1a.

Notes to Chapter 7

1. Nowak, *Courier from Warsaw*, p. 388.

2. Jedrzejewicz, *Poland in the British Parliament*, Vol. II, pp. 286–407.

3. Feingold, *The Politics of Rescue. The Roosevelt Administration and the*

Holocaust, 1938–1945. Wyman, *The Abandonment of the Jews. America and the Holocaust, 1941–1945.* Churchill on April 7, 1943, stating the policy of the British Government regarding quotas to Palestine (this is not the full citation but the final section): "As the secretary of State for the Colonies announced on 3rd February, His Majesty's Government are prepared, provided the necessary transport is available, to continue to admit into Palestine Jewish children with a proportion of accompanying adults, up to the limits of immigration permissable for the five year period ending 31st March, 1944, that is up to approximately 29,000 children." *War Speeches by the Right Hon. Winston Churchill.*

4. P.R.O. WO 371/139484 118894.

5. P.R.O. FO 371/39481. These files of the British P.R.O. also contain a letter to the British Foreign Office, dated February 7, 1944 on a telling letterhead: "Committee for a Jewish Army of Stateless, Refugee and Palestinian Jews" (85 New Cavendish Street).

6. P.R.O. FO 371/139484 118894 and for details of the debate see Jedrzejewicz, *Poland in the British Parliament,* Vol. II, pp. 422–494.

7. Pienkos, *For Your Freedom through Ours.* President Roosevelt avoided meeting with the President of the Polish American Congress until October, 1944, Pulaski Day, when he hosted a delegation of the Polish Americans and was photographed in front of a large map of Poland in its 1939 boundaries. Roosevelt also promised that he would faithfully adhere to the Atlantic Charter and the four freedoms and not allow any harm to Poland. This was just about a year after he had expressed a complete *disinteressement* in Tehran regarding Polish boundaries. As a result of the meeting the Polish American Congress endorsed Roosevelt. Also, Lukas, *The Strange Allies.* In the studies of the recently declassified archives from the Soviet Union, the following is interesting. Solomon Bloom, Chairman of the United States House of Delegates Committee on Foreign Affairs, communicated the following to Andrei Gromyko on July 2, 1943: the Committee is not interested in either Polish or Baltic territorial questions. See Perlmutter, *FDR and Stalin,* p. 251. The chronological juxtaposition of the failed trip by Sikorski to the United States, and Mr. Bloom's professed *disinteressment* in the Polish issues, needs to be further confronted by the British aide de memoir in the Foreign Office based on their intercepts of trans-Atlantic telegrams. On July 18, 1944, "Considerable Jewish circles in America, mostly Zionist but apparently including some of the Orthodox as well, are agitating that all the property in Poland which before the war belonged to Jews should be regarded as belonging to the Jewish community. This would not presumably apply to property the pre-war owners of which are still alive but after the appalling massacres beginning with the destruction of the Warsaw ghetto in 1942 there must be a great deal of former Jewish property to which no one will be able to put in valid claim as next of kin. The American Jews are clearly out to keep all this his property in Jewish hands. There is, I should say, no chance whatsoever that the Polish Gov-

ernment would agree to this suggestion, the result of which would certainly be to build up state within a state in Poland" (*FO 371/39524/10*). This
archival detail, which only became available many years after the war,
confirms some of the rumors surrounding Sikorski's trip to the United
States, that international support was conditioned on such a property
transaction.

8. P.R.O. AIR 19/816 80530.

9. Ibid.

10. P.R.O. AIR 19/815 80530.

11. P.R.O. AIR 19/815 80530, and for British government attitude, Harriman and Abel, *Special Envoy to Churchill and Stalin, 1941–1946*. In May
1944, Harriman noted that there was a sharp swing in British opinion and
quotes Beaverbrook as saying, "everyone in the British Government except
himself (i.e., Beaverbrook) was anti-Russian now."

12. Polish-British Air Agreement of April 1944, see Appendix 8.

13 PIL LOT AV II/1a.

14. *Mosty* is a Polish word for bridges and the three successful pick-up
operations were in fact to be bridges to Poland. Major General Tadeusz
Kossakowski had been the G.O.C. of the Polish Military Engineers in the
First Polish Corps in Scotland in 1940–43 and was responsible for the con-
struction of anti-invasion defenses on the east shore. He was the most
senior Polish officer expedited to Poland, being senior to Major General
Leopold Okulicki, who was parachuted and assumed the mantle of the
G.O.C. Home Army after Bor-Komorowski was taken prisoner of war at
the end of the Warsaw Uprising. Kossakowski was one of the thirteen
Polish generals and admirals who were awarded the prestigious British
Order of the Bath, Military Division. This award undoubtedly also was for
the accomplishments of the Polish engineers who developed the Polish
Land Mine detector, without which the Battle of El Alamein in 1943 may
not have been won, or would have exacted more British lives. The actual
work was done by the Polish Signal Training Section in Dundee headed by
Lt. Jozef Kosacki (a graduate of the Warsaw Polytechnic and Polish Signal
School near Zegrze) and Sergeant Andrzej Garbos.

15. Remarks of the First Lord, quoted in Jordan and Janta, *Seafaring Poland*.

16. Ciechanowski, *Defeat in Victory*, pp. 272–273. Anthony J. Biddle, a sin-
cere friend of Poland, had been the U.S ambassador to the Polish Government before and through the war years until December 1943. His resignation
was (in retrospect) seen by the Poles as discouragement with American policies. Tony Biddle, as he was know to the Poles, left diplomatic service and
entered the military. See Cannistraro, Wynot Jr., and Kovaleff, *Poland and the
Coming of the Second World War. The Diplomatic Papers of A.J. Drexel Biddle Jr.,
United States Ambassador to Poland, 1937–1939*. Also, see Nowak, op. cit., p.
246. There was no replacement for Biddle until September 1994, when Bliss
Lane was appointed but never dispatched to London. This was clearly a

cheap and dishonest move by the Roosevelt administration to buy Polish votes but not to become engaged in the Polish question. There are many histories of the diplomatic posture of the Western Allies to the problems of Poland. But the most objective and most damning is the actual correspondence of the two chief architects of that policy from the period in which they made it. Kimball, ed., *Churchill and Roosevelt. The Complete Correspondence.* The two volumes to consult are the last two: *Alliance Forged* and *Alliance Declining.* Also for an excellent succint review, Nadeau, *Stalin, Churchill and Roosevelt Divide Europe.* Particularly chapter 10, "The Agony of Poland." Also see Karski, *The Great Powers and Poland, 1919–1945;* Polonsky, *The Great Powers and the Polish Question;* Rozek, *Allied Wartime Diplomacy;* Umiastowski, *Poland, Russia and Great Britain.*

17. PIL. A. V. 20/31 18.

18. PIL. AXII/32/72.

19. PIL. A.V. 20/31 18.

20. PIL. PRM - K 102/70 f.

21. Hamilton, *Master of the Battlefield, Monty's War Years, 1940–1944,* p. 558. On March 13, 1944, Montgomery visited the units of the First Polish Armored Division as well as of the Polish Parachute Brigade. He seemed very impressed with the soldiers and kept making remarks such as "these paratroopers are first rate soldiers—they will kill everyone." Montgomery was behaving as if he was visiting some primitive colonial troops. Sosabowski replied "only the enemy." Montgomery, unlike most educated English, had not lost the primitive attribute of the bully which is the hallmark of the English schoolboy and of the English educational system. Also see PIL. A XII 23/772.

22. Churchill, *Triumph and Tragedy,* p. 592. English edition only.

23. PIL A XII 23/72.

24. Churchill, *Closing the Ring,* p. 711.

25. Wegierski, *W Lwowskiej Armii Krajowej.*

26. This priceless relic hangs in the Polish Institute and General Sikorski Museum in London. See Denfeld, *World War Two Museums and Relics of Europe,* p. 154. The Polish Museum and the Sikorski Museum in London is also the repository of all the regimental flags of the Polish Regiments that were formed in the West during the war. In addition there are a considerable number of pre-1939 regimental flags, which were carried out by their their troops into exile. There are however two very unique flags in the museum those of the Polish Air Force and of the Polish Parachute Brigade. Both were embroidered by Polish women in German-occupied Poland. The Air Force flag was created in Wilno and smuggled out through Polish intelligence operatives to Berlin and hence by the good offices of the Japanese military attaché to Tokyo, then to the free world. The women of Warsaw embroidered the flag for their Polish boys of the parachute Brigade from a cardinal's coat and subsequently it was flown out of Poland by one of the three successful *most* operations. The flag was accompanied by this

poignant and, in the historical context, heart-wrenching letter, which is difficult to translate into idiomatic English, but the following highlights illustrate the spirit behind the gift—Loved Ones, We send you a flag which will accompany you to victory. The flag is a missive to all of you from your loved ones. The parchment is a cardinal's coat, treasured by his ancestors for many generations; the ink is silk, silver and gold thread, purchased by universal contributions. . . . Your Mothers and Fathers want you to know that you are their pride and love, your families wish you to know that you are their hope and example, your wives and loved ones miss you. This letter finishes with one of those Polish words which defies an easy idiomatic translation, *tesknota.* Another word which eventually affected the majority of the Poles is *tulacz,* which also has no synonym in English (but can be translated as a wandering exile), a society which has been spared that fate. See *PSZ na Ob. II.* pp. 345–390. Bieganski, *Dzialania 2 Korpusu we Wloszech,* pp. 159–250.

27. Churchill ". . . The Poles triumphantly hoisted their red and white standard over the ruins of the monastery. They greatly distinguished themselves in this their first major engagement in Italy. Later, under their thrustful General Anders, himself a survivor from Russian imprisonment, they were to win many laurels during the long advance to the river Po." *Closing the Ring,* p. 600.

28. Bieganski, *Dzialania 2 Korpusu we Wloszech,* pp. 289—376. Bieganski, *Ankona.* The history of the 318 Squadron is well told by Nycz, *W Powietrznym Zwiadzie.*

29. The invasion of German-occupied Normandy, code named *Overlord,* was carried out by Allied Forces on June 6, 1944, under the overall command of general Dwight Eisenhower. The naval part of the operation was code named *Neptune.* See Ambrose, *D-Day: June 6, 1944, The Climactic Battle of World War II.* Ryan, *The Longest Day.* According to all statistics, Polish, British, or American, this Polish division represented 20 percent of all armored units under British Command. See Eisenhower, *Crusade in Europe,* p. 513. Listing is: Guards, 7th, 11th, 29th British Armored Divisions and the Polish First Armored. Two Canadian Armored Divisions completed the roster of the Twenty-First Army Group under the command of General Montgomery.

30. There are a number of versions of this night battle. Some are clearly embellishments, some are the result of a natural proclivity to give a most favorable account of one's actions. The account given here is based on the common denominators of the various personal narratives and logs of warships. But primarily it is based on the official Royal Navy accounts in P.R.O. ADM 199/1644. For details of this naval battle see Roskill, *The War at Sea, 1939–1945,* Vol. 3, pp. 56–57.

31. Keegan, *Six Armies in Normandy.* Maczek, *Od Podwody do Czolga.* Skibinski, *Pierwsza Pancerna.* Copp and Vogel, *Maple Leaf Route: Falaise.* The Poles were part of the Canadian Army.

Notes to Chapter 8

1. Zawodny, *Nothing but Honor. The Story of the Warsaw Uprising, 1944.* Ciechanowski, *The Warsaw Rising of 1944.* Churchill. *Triumph and Tragedy,* p. 141.

2. Kimball, op. cit., Vol. III, pp. 259–365. Roosevelt responded on September 5, 1994, to Churchill's entreaty for a unified and strong stand against Stalin's policy of refusing landing rights to Allied planes on Soviet bases: "I am informed by my Office of Military Intelligence that the fighting Poles have departed from Warsaw and that the Germans are now in full control. The problem of relief for the Poles of Warsaw has therefore unfortunately been solved by delay and by German action." This blatantly dishonest statement is a matter of historic record and a moral indictment.

3. P.R.O. WO 216/98 3802.

4. Ibid.

5. Ibid.

6. Ibid.

7. P.R.O. AIR 8/1170 15969. Official report of the Polish Air Force Historical Commission, chaired by Col. Olgierd Tuskiewicz, to the A.O.C Polish Air Force, Major General Mateusz Izycki, dated 1947. This is in my personal possession. Kalinowski, *Lotnictwo Polskie w Wielkiej Brytanni, 1940–1945,* pp. 266–279. *Destiny Can Wait,* pp. 218–228. Jackson, *The Secret Squadrons,* pp. 129–135. Merrick, op. cit., pp. 208–230. Orpen, *Airlift to Warsaw.* Orpen, a South African air historian, wrote in his introduction, "During the writing of *Eagles Victorious. A history of the Royal South African Air Force in WWII,* I first realized the extraordinary nature of the Warsaw airlift of 1944, which I have since regarded as the most shining example of selfless courage in all my experience and research." For the United States attempts to aid the Uprising, see, Thomas A. Julian, "The Role of the United States Army Air Forces in the Warsaw Uprising, Aug.–Sept. 1994," *Air Power History* 1995; 42: 22–35.

8. P.R.O. AIR 8/1170 15969.

9. P.R.O. AIR 8/1170 15969.

10. Ibid.

11. Ibid.

12. Kalinowski, op. cit., p. 270.

13. P.R.O. AIR 8/1170 15969.

14. Ibid.

15. Ibid. Also, Major General L. Rayski was discriminated against by Sikorski and was not allowed to join the Polish Air Force but flew as a ferry pilot for the British. After Sosnkowski succeeded Sikorski, Rayski was brought back to full service and became the senior Polish Air Force officer in Italy. He loved to fly and brought the commanding officer of the 317 Polish reconnaissance Squadron in Italy to despair since he would use his seniority to demand to fly combat missions on Spitfires. He also per-

sonally flew as a second pilot a number of operations to Warsaw. The proposal by Rayski was reasonable and the invective against Poles by Slessor, who was a man of tact and sincerity, can only be explained by Slessor's own despair at seeing his crews decimated on such a lost campaign. The word "hoisting" is also marked by a question mark in the cable. Whatever, it was, it was meant to be uncomplimentary and can only be explained by the Air Marshal's feelings of frustration. Air Marshal Slessor after the war was a good friend of the Polish Air Force Association in the United Kingdom.

16. Kazimierz Sosnkowski, *Materialy Historyczne*, pp. 198–203. On September 4, Sosnkowski's order #19 was published in the Polish daily in the United Kingdom, *Dziennik Polski*. This controversial order was a direct challenge to the British and alleged that they had consistently broken their mutual aid treaty with Poland. The British foreign secretary, Mr. Eden, personally requested an audience with the Polish President and presented the British ultimatum that His Majesty's Government could no longer deal with Sosnkowski. Sosnkowski stated that while for many years the Poles were criticized for not shedding sufficient blood in the underground, now that they were fighting hard and engaging as many as eight German divisions, the Allies could not, or as Sosnkowski argued, would not help. General Sosnkowski traveled to Canada as a private person in December 1944, and found himself in virtual internment. He was denied visas to the United States and forbidden from coming back to the United Kingdom. This state of affairs lasted till 1949. One of the less-known episodes in the long tradition of human rights and free speech enjoyed and guaranteed by two Anglo-Saxon countries.

17. The history of the participation of the Polish Parachute Brigade in Operation Market Garden is drawn from the following sources: (1) primary archival, (2) secondary from the memoirs of combatants, and finally from the numerous (3) published books. (1) P.R.O. WO 171/3933784, Polish Inst. London. A.V. 20/31/26; A.V. 20/31/32; A.V.20/31//34; A.V. 20/31/36, A.V. 20/31/38, A.V. 20/31 /40, A.V. 20/31/42. (2) Urquhart, *Arnhem*, Sosabowski, *Freely I Served*; Cholewczynski, *Poles Apart*; Malaszqiewicz, R. (who was the chief of staff of the Polish Para Brigade at Arnhem) "Bitwa pod Arnhem i udzial w niej 1 Polskiej Samodzielnej Brygady Spadochronowej," *Wojskowy Przeglad Historyczny* (1957) Part 1 in No. I, pp. 57–88 and Part II in No. 2, pp. 32–67. (3) a number of books about Arnhem, the most popular being, Ryan, *A Bridge Too Far*; Piekalkiewicz, *Arnhem 1944*; Powell, *The Devil's Birthday. The Bridges to Arnhem*; Wilmot, *The Struggle for Europe*; Swiecicki, *With the Red Devils at Arnhem*; Middlebrook, *Arnhem, 1944*.

18. Malaszkiewicz, op. cit.

19. Badsey, *Arnhem, 1944*, p. 35, describes the special uniform that Browning fashioned for himself.

20. Wilmot, op. cit.

21. Jerzy Dyrda, "Przyczyny Niepowodzenia pod Arnhem," *Wojskowy Przeglad historyczny* (1984) Nr. 4, pp. 112–125.

22. Winston Churchill, *Triumph and Tragedy*, p. 141.

23. *Documents on Polish-Soviet Relations*, p. 485–486.

24. Solly-Flood, Peter, "Pilgrimage to Poland," *Blackwood's Magazine*, May 1951, Vol. 269.

25. Jedrzejewicz, *Poland in the British Parliament*, pp. 334–594.

26. Wronski, *Wspomnienia Plyna jak Okrety*, pp. 185–186. Wronski was an outstanding Polish naval officer and naval artillery expert. In February 1945 his command, the escort destroyer O.R.P. *Slazak*, went for a refit in London. He was invited by Admiral Dunbar-Nasmith for lunch. Before lunch the British Admiral asked Wronski, as a naval officer and gentleman, whether Lwow was a Polish city. Wronski replied that Lwow had never been part of Russia, not even during the hundred-year-old partitions, and that in Lwow there were three Catholic cathedrals of the Latin, Uniate, and Armenian rite testifying to Polish tolerance. Furthermore in Lwow was located the third oldest Polish University (Jana Kazimierza from the seventeenth century), one of Poland's two major Polytechnics and the magnificent Ossolineum library. The British admiral, after listening in silence, said, "I am sorry." General Maczek had a different experience, when invited to lunch. But his host had all the sensitivity of the bully. Field Marshal Montgomery, after enquiring about Maczek's background and being told that Maczek was a native of Lwow, responded that he now looked forward to Maczek being a Russian general. Maczek riposted that he wished Montgomery a commission in the American Army. The lunch came to a quick finish. Maczek, *Od Podwody do czolga*, p. 219.

27. P.R.O. AIR 19/420 80530.

28. Macmillan, *The Blast of War*, pp 572–573.

29. Swiecicki, *Seven Rivers to Bologna*.

30. Bieganski, *Bolonia 1945*. Madeja, *The Polish 2nd Corps in the Italian Campaign*.

31. Kimball, *Churchill and Roosevelt*, p. 565.

32. Major General Leopold Okulicki was the final of the four G.O.C. of the Home Army. There was a tragic symmetry in the fate of the four men who led the Polish clandestine organization. Lt. Gen. Michael Karasiewicz-Tokarzewski was captured by the Russians in early 1940 and was released by the Soviets in 1941 as part of the short-lived Polish-Soviet collaboration. He served with great distinction in the Polish 2 Army Corps in Italy and was one of the thirteen Poles awarded the highly esteemed British Military Order of the Bath. His successor, Major Gen. Stefan Rowecki (Grot), presided over the greatest growth of the Home Army but was captured by the Germans in 1943 and executed. He was succeeded by Lt. Gen. Tadeusz Bor-Komorowski, who was appointed the Polish Commander-in-Chief in September 1944, and became a German prisoner of war after Warsaw's surrender. Bor-Komorowski was liberated by the Americans and for a

brief period assumed his titular duties. Okulicki was the fourth G.O.C. and accepted a Soviet invitation for a meeting with their military command. Flown to Moscow he was accused of anti-Soviet activities and sentenced to ten years in a Soviet prison. He allegedly died shortly after. His only son died in battle as an officer of the Polish 2 Army Corps. For biographies of Polish Generals, see Kryska-Karski and Zurakowski, *Generalowie Polski Niepodleglej*. I formation regarding British decorations comes from a personal communication to author by the Secretary of the Central Chancery of the Orders of Knighthood. But even that was not quite the end of the fight. As the Polish Underground Army was dissolved, the Poles formed a new, highly secret organization—Nie—under the command of Major General August Emil Fieldorf, one of the *Cichociemny*.

33. Kalinowski, *Lotnictwo Polskie w Wielkiej Brytanii, 1940–1945*, p. 243.

34. Ibid., and also Middlebrook and Everitt, *The Bomber Command War Diaries. An operational Reference book, 1939–1945.*

35. Saunders, *Royal Air Force, Vol. III, The Fight is Won.*

36. Hastings, *Lionel Lord Ismay, The Memoirs of General Lord Ismay*. Also see Dalton's comment to Polish Socialist leaders in August 1944: "I speak to them frankly and tell them that unless they make friends with the Russians, who are great favourites in this country, there will be nobody left to back the Poles over here except a 'few Roman Catholic priests.'" Pimlott, *The Second World War Diary of Hugh Dalton*, p. 781. West, *Spymaster. The Betrayal of MI5*, writes that Burgess directed the BBC during many years of that period; and finally that George Orwell's *Animal Farm*, a biting criticism of Communist Society, was banned by the British Ministry of Information. The British ambassador to Poland, Sir Owen O'Malley, many years after the war, wrote these words in an otherwise most restrained memoir: "They (i.e., the Poles) were not indeed surprised at the naivete of American Public opinion and they know that the mind of the illustrious President was near the end of its tether. Also they could understand that British public opinion needed tactful handling, having been misled for many years into willfully thinking that Stalin & Co. though a bit rough in their methods, were not bad fellows at bottom and would yield to and eventually reciprocate patience, tolerance and amity. But they could hardly believe that the British Government—usually sceptical of the professions of foreigners—were equally ingenuous; and they were mystified and disconcerted by seeing British Ministers not only expansively courting Stalin at Tehran and Yalta but propagating through every channel those very illusions about Russian policy which in turn constrained the British Cabinet to pretend that the dangers of yielding to Russian pretensions were negligible. Confidence in Russian intentions being unwarranted by any known facts why was it, the Poles asked themselves, that it was stimulated by all Government departments, nearly all newspapers, the BBC, the Army Bureau of Current Affairs, the Army Education Department, the Political Warfare Executive, and every other organ of publicity susceptible to offi-

cial influence? Why indeed? Why was it that in all these establishments were to be found individuals with curious foreign names or person who had changed their names, or were mixed of blood or of multiple allegiance, self-appointed saviours of society, bitter little Messiahs, do-gooders, cranky professors, recognizable fellow travellers and numberless camp-followers, from among the frustrated and ambitious intellectual proletariat—all burrowing like wood-beetles, corrupting the oaken heart of England?" O'Malley, *The Phantom Caravan*, p. 231. In 1945 Sir Owen was moved to Lisbon, a grade III post, while his prior position was grade II. Sir Owen asked why he was being downgraded and the answer given, "I had been right too often and too soon," p. 234. Churchill, *The Tide of Victory*, p. 122, cites his own memo to the Minister of Information of August 23, 1944, "is there any stop on the publicity for the facts about the agony of Warsaw, which seem, from the papers, to have been practically suppressed? It is not for us to cast reproaches on the Soviet Government, but surely the facts should be allowed to speak for themselves? There is no need to mention the strange and sinister behaviour of the Russians, but is there any reason why the consequences of such behaviour should not be made public?"

37. Willen, "Who Collaborated with Russia?" in Divine, ed., *Causes and Consequences of World War Two*.

38. Kersten, *The Establishment of Communist Rule in Poland, 1943–1948*. Woodward, *British Foreign Policy in the Second World War*, Chapter XXXV, "Great Britain and the Russo-Polish relations from the German attack on Russia to the end of 1943." With notes on the Curzon Line. Chapter XXXIX, "Great Britain and Russo-Polish relations, January–August 1944." Chapter XL, "Great Britain and Russo-Polish relations, September 1944–February 1945." Chapter XLV, "Great Britain and Russo-Polish relations, February 1945–July 1945." Out of forty-six chapters on British foreign policy in WWII, four are devoted to Polish issues.

Appendixes

Appendixes

Appendix 1
Polish-British Treaty of Mutual Security

Agreement between the Government of the United Kingdom and
the Polish Government regarding mutual assistance.
(With protocols)
London, August 25, 1939.

The Government of the United Kingdom of Great Britain and Northern
Ireland and the Polish Government:

Desiring to place on a permanent basis the collaboration between their
respective countries resulting from the assurances of mutual assistance of a
defensive character which they have already exchanged:

Have resolved to conclude an Agreement for that purpose and have
agreed on the following provisions:

Article 1.

Should one of the Contracting Parties become engaged in hostilities with a
European Power in consequence of aggression by the latter against that
Contracting Power, the other Contracting Power will at once give the
Contracting Power engaged in hostilities all the support and assistance in
its power.

Article 2.

i.   The provisions of Article 1. will also apply in the event of any action
by a European Power which clearly threatened directly or indirectly, the
independence of one of the Contracting Powers, and was of such a nature
that the Party in question considered it vital to resist with its armed forces.
ii.   Should one of the Contracting Powers become engaged in hostilities
with a European Power in consequence of action by that Power which
threatened the independence or neutrality of another European State in
such a way as to constitute a clear menace to the security of that Contracting Party, the Provisions of Article 1. will apply, without prejudice, however, to the right of the other European State concerned.

Article 3.

Should a European Power attempt to undermine the independence of one
of the Contracting Powers by a process of economic penetration or in any
other way, the Contracting Powers will support each other in resistance to
such attempts. Should the European Power concerned thereupon embark
on hostilities against one of the Contracting Parties, the provisions of Article 1. will apply.

Article 4.

The methods of applying the undertakings of mutual assistance provided for by the present Agreement are established between competent naval, military and air authorities of the Contracting Parties.

Article 5.

Without prejudice to the foregoing undertakings of the Contracting Parties to give each other mutual support and assistance immediately on the outbreak of hostilities, they will exchange complete and speedy information concerning any development which might threaten their independence and, in particular, concerning any development which threatened to call the said undertakings into operations.

Article 6.

i   The Contracting Parties will communicate to each other the terms of any undertaking of assistance against aggression which they have already given or may in future give to other States.

ii   Should either of the Contracting Parties intend to give such an undertaking after the coming into force of the present Agreement, the other Contracting Party shall, in order to ensure the proper function of the Agreement, be informed thereof.

iii   Any new undertaking which the Contracting Parties may enter into in future shall neither limit their obligations under the present Agreement nor indirectly create new obligations between the Contracting Party not participating in these undertakings and the third State concerned.

Article 7.

Should the Contracting Parties be engaged in hostilities in consequence of the application of the present Agreement, they will not conclude an armistice or treaty of peace except by mutual agreement.

Article 8.

i   The present Agreement shall remain in force for a period five years,

ii   Unless denounced six months before the expiry of this period it shall continue in force, each Contracting Party having the Right to denounce it at any time by giving six months notice to that effect.

iii   The present Agreement shall come into force on signature.

Halifax
Raczynski

Protocol

The Polish Government and the Government of the United Kingdom and Northern Ireland are agreed upon the following interpretation of the Agreement of Mutual Assistance signed this day as alone authentic and binding:

1. (a) By the expression of "a European Power" employed in the Agreement is to be understood Germany.

(b) In the event of action within the meaning of Article 1 or 2 of the Agreement by a European Power other than Germany, the Contracting Parties will consult together on the measures to be taken in common.

2. (a) The two Governments will from time to time determine the hypothetical cases of action by Germany coming within the ambit of Article 2 of the Agreement.

(b) Until such time as the two Governments have agreed to modify the following provisions of this paragraph, they will consider: that the case contemplated by paragraph (1) of Article 2 of the Agreement is that of the Free City of Danzig; and that the cases contemplated by paragraph (2) of Article 2 are Belgium, Holland, Lithuania.

(c) Latvia and Estonia shall be regarded by the two Governments as included in the list of countries contemplated by paragraph (2) of Article 2 from the moment that an undertaking of mutual assistance between the United Kingdom and a third State covering those two countries enters into force.

(d) As regards Roumania, the Government of the United Kingdom refers to the guarantee which it had given to that country; and the Polish Government refers to the reciprocal undertakings of the Roumano-Polish alliance which Poland has never regarded as incompatible with her traditional friendship for Hungary.

3. The Undertakings mentioned in Article 6 of the Agreement, should they be entered into by one of the Contracting Parties with a third State, would of necessity be so framed that their execution should at no time prejudice either the sovereignty or territorial inviolability of the other Contracting Party.

4. The present protocol constitutes an integral part of the Agreement signed this day, the scope of which it does not exceed.

Halifax

Raczynski

One of the original English language copies of this Treaty is in the Polish Institute and General Sikorski Museum, London. A. II. 76/1. and A.II. 76/2. Both are graced with the respective family seals of the signers.

Appendix 2
First Polish-French Military Agreement

The first agreement between the Poles and the French was signed by the Polish ambassador in Paris (Lukasiewicz) and the French Prime Minister (Daladier) as early as September 9, 1939, and formalized the formation of a Polish infantry division in France.

I

Une division polonaise faisant partie de l'armée polonaise commandée par des officiers polonais sera formée en France.

II

La division se recrute parmi les citoyens polonais résident en France:
1) par appel des classes,
2) par appel des officiers, sous-officiers et hommes de réserve,
3) par engagement volontaire.

III

Les classes et les réserves à appeler seront determinées par l'Ambassadeur de Pologne a Paris.

IV

L'appel des classes et des réserves, ainsi que la faculté de s'engager volontairement seront étendus aux citoyens polonais de deux catégories susmentionnées venant en France des pays tiers.

V

Le Gouvernement français aura de droit de maintenir dans leurs emplois les citoyens polonais appelés sous les drapeaux suivant la procedure applicable aux citoyens français de la catégorie correspondante.

A titre d'exception, les citoyens polonais employés dans les mines et les industries metallurgiques appelés sous le drapeaux pourront être maintenus dans leur emploi par la requsition collective ou individuelle pendant trois mois au plus; passé ce delai la procedure visée à l'alinea 1 du present accord leur sera appliquée.

There were four other articles, which defined the responsibility for the costs, etc., of the Polish mobilization.

Appendix 3
Polish–United Kingdom Naval Agreement

Agreement concluded between the Governments of the Polish Republic and the United Kingdom concerning the formation of a detachment of the Polish Navy in Great Britain.

The Government of the Polish Republic and the Government of the United Kingdom and Northern Ireland desiring to make provisions for the cooperation of certain units of the Polish Naval forces with those of the United Kingdom, have agreed as follows:

Article 1.

A detachment of the Polish Navy shall be attached to the British Navy for the duration of the hostilities and so long as may be mutually agreed.

Article 2.

The units or groups of the Polish Naval Detachment under the Polish flag and under the command of Polish officers and manned by Polish crews, shall cooperate with the British Fleet and shall constitute a part of the Allied Naval Forces.

Article 3

The Polish Naval Detachment shall include the following units:
a) vessels which are already attached to the British Navy,
b) other vessels which it may be possible to incorporate in the Polish Naval Detachment during the period of hostilities.

Article 4.

The personnel of the Polish Naval Detachment to be recruited shall be Polish nationals of the following categories:
a)   men now on service in units operating as well those detached to supervise the units under construction,
b)   officers and men of the Naval Reserve who are available on the territory of Allied Powers and in neutral countries and who will be called up for active service on the strength of the mobilization decree issued by the President of the Polish Republic.
c)   officers and men of the Polish Mercantile Marine who do not belong to the Naval Reserve, but who may be called up for active service in the Navy in case of increased demand.
d)   skilled men who may volunteer to serve in the Navy in case of increased demand.

Article 5.

For the purpose of:

a) concentrating personnel of the categories mentioned in Article 4 (b), (c), (d),

b) the formation of reserves for the units operating,

c) training in special branches which may require strengthening, a suitable naval depot will be established at a place allotted by the British authorities, which shall be under the command of Polish officers and staffed by Polish petty-officers and instructors.

Article 6.

Any costs incurred by the British naval authorities n connection with the operation of this agreement shall, on demand, be reimbursed by the Polish Government to the Government of the United Kingdom.

Article 7.

The ways and means of enlarging the Polish Naval Detachment as well as recruiting, concentrating and supplementing personnel, the organization of command, training of officers and men, etc., shall be dealt with by separate agreements between the contracting governments.

In faith whereof the undersigned, duly authorized thereto by their respective Governments have signed present agreement.

Raczynski
Cadogan.

Appendix 4
Polish-French Agreement
Regarding the Land Forces

But the agreement of September 9, 1939, no longer sufficed to cover all the issues, which confronted the Polish and French military administration. On January 4, 1940, the French and Polish Prime Ministers, Daladier and Sikorski, signed the following accord militaire.

Le Gouvernement polonais et le Gouvernement français. Se réferant aux accords franco-polonais de 1921 at de 1925 ainsi qu'au Protocole du 4 Septembre 1939. Desireux de collaborer en vue de la reconstitution de l'Armée polonaise. Sont convenus des dispositions suivantes:

Article I

L'Armée polonaise avec son Haut Commandement sera reconstitutée sur le térritoire français.

Article II

L'Armée polonaise sera soumise aux Autorités Suprêmes polonaises.
Jusqu'à la cessation des hostilités, l'Armée polonaise sera placée, en tant qu'Armée d'Etat allié, sous les ordres du Général Commandant en Chef de l'Armée Française, Commandant en Chef des forces terrestres.

Article III

L'Armée polonaise se recrutera parmi les ressortissants polonais, dans les catégories suivantes:
1. Militaires venant de Pologne,
2. Militaires de classes de réserve convoqué sous les drapeaux sur le térritoire français ou ailleurs,
3. Recrues appelées sous les drapeaux sur le territoire français ou ailleurs en vertu de la conscription,
4. Engagée volontaires.
Le Gouvernement français aura le droit de maintenir dans leurs emplois les citoyens polonais mobilisables dans les mêmes conditions que les citoyens français de la catégorie correspondânte et non-obstant les dispositions de l'Article 8 du décret du 15 Mai 1939.
Les dispositions de la Loi du 11 Juillet 1938 sur l'organisation de la Nation en temps de guerre, et notamment celles prévues par l'article 14 de

cette Loi, sont applicables aux citoyens polonais dans les mêmes conditions qu'aux citoyens français.

Les cadres de l'Armée polonaise pourront être, sur la demande du Haut Commandement Polonais, completés ou renforcés par les militaires français detachés à cette fin.

Des éléments destinés à entrer dans la composition de l'Armée polonaise pourront être formés sur le territoire d'autres pays.

Article IV

L'Armée polonaise sera composée des Etats-Majors et Unités suivantes:
1.   Haut Commandement,
2.   Eléments à constituer au première urgence:
a)   des divisions en nombre correspondant aux effectifs, b) des centres de perfectionnement d'officier d'Etat-Major et de toutes armes, et des écoles d'élèves-officiers et d'élèves sous-officiers,
c)   des forces aériennes dont l'organisation fait l'objet de deux accords, l'un entre le Gouvernement polonais et le Gouvernement français, l'autre entre le Gouvernement polonais et le Gouvernement britannique,
3.   Eléments à constituer en seconde urgence:
a)   des unités légeres mécaniques,
b)   des unités de D.C.A.,
c)   des Etats-Majors, éléments et services de groupes d'opérations.
4.   Des unités blindées, constituées en première ou en seconde urgence, suivant les disponibilités en materiel.
5.   Une Marine de Guerre dont l'organisation fait l'objet d'un accord entre le Gouvernement polonais at le Gouvernement britannique.

Article V

Les Autorités militaires françaises mettront à la disposition du Haut Commandement polonais les camps nécessaires à l'instruction de l'Armée polonaise.

Article VI

Les militaires polonais seront justiciables des tribunaux militaires polonais dont la competence et le fonctionnement seront déterminés dans un Protocole qui sera annexé aux présent accord.

The agreement was also accompanied by a Polish text and had seven more articles, dealing with issues of salaries, welfare for widows and orphans, the obligation of the Polish Government to repay the French for the costs incurred and finally the annulment of the original agreement of September 9, regarding the formation of one infantry division.

Appendix 5
Polish-French and Polish–United Kingdom Air Agreements

The Agreement pertaining to the Polish Air Force followed much discussion between the Polish, French and United Kingdom delegates. The Polish military authorities, undoubtedly correctly, considered the nine thousand cadre of the Polish Military Aviation to be a dowry worth its weight in gold for the allied cause. The Polish personnel interned in Romania, spontaneously proposed that the Poles go to Britain to recreate that branch of the service alongside the Royal Air Force. The Poles were more familiar with and more impressed by British technical equipment and the prestige of the Royal Air Force (as well as of the Royal Navy) exceeded the French counterparts.

The British expressed a willingness to accept the Polish flyers as individuals but not to form national units. Sikorski did not agree to this and the initiative seemed dead, until October 25, 1939, when a staff conference was held in Paris. The Poles were represented by Lt. General J. Zajac (Inspector of the Polish Air Force), Air Vice-Marshal Evill, and General Romatet, of the French Armee de l'Air.

The Polish side opined that there would be at least seven hundred trained pilots, nearly two hundred navigators, and mechanics, armorers, etc., to a number of well over five thousand. The Poles argued that they would like to see Polish squadrons formed in both France and Britain. The allied representatives in principle accepted the Polish postulates, and the British agreed to accept about two thousand Poles to form two light bomber squadrons, equipped with the old one engined Battle. The first group of Poles left France for Britain as early as December 3, 1939, for Eastchurch. But the British insisted on one provision which was to be a bone of contention and misunderstanding, namely: that all Polish officers be enrolled and commissioned in the Royal Air Force Volunteer Reserve and given a functional rank, commensurate with duties, not past Polish rank; and that as commissioned officers in the Royal Air Force Volunteer Reserve, the Poles would take an oath of allegiance to His Majesty the King.

This agreement, reached in unseemly haste in December 1939, was flawed and the Polish authorities spent considerable time and effort trying to undo it, while exposing a large number of senior officers unwittingly to the humiliation and distress of their new status as semi-mercenaries of the

King. This unfortunate situation was only partially remedied in August 1940, when as a result of the mass evacuation of Polish land and air personnel, the British had to give way from their rigid stance.

The Government of the Polish Republic and the Government of the United Kingdom of Great Britain and Northern Ireland, reaffirming their determination to prosecute the war to a successful conclusion,

Recognizing the importance in their common interest of maintaining the armed forces of Poland,

Desiring to establish the principles on which those forces, under the Supreme Command of the Polish Commander-in-Chief, shall be organized for co-operation with the Allied Armed Forces, and recalling the Agreement and Protocol signed in London on the 18th November 1939, providing for the co-operation of certain units of the Polish naval Forces with those of the United Kingdom, have agreed as follows:

Article 1.

The Polish Armed Forces (comprising Land, Sea and Air Forces) shall be organised and employed under British command, in its character as the Allied High Command, as the Armed Forces of the Republic of Poland allied with the United Kingdom.

Article 2.

Units of the Polish Air Force referred to in Article 1 shall be organised to operate with the Royal Air Force. The organisation of the Polish Air Force in the United Kingdom shall be extended, in accordance with the provisions of Appendix I of the present agreement, so as to utilise such Polish Air Force personnel now in the United Kingdom as maybe necessary for the execution of those provisions.

Article 3.

The Government of the United Kingdom shall afford their assistance in the reconstitution of the Polish Land Forces, in accordance with the conditions laid down in Appendix II of the present agreement.

Article 4.

Any costs incurred by or on behalf of any Departmemt of the Government of the United Kingdom in connection with the application of the present agreement shall be refunded out of the credit granted by His Majesty's Government to the Polish Government to finance the cost of maintaining the Polish military effort.

In witness whereof the undersigned, duly authorised thereto by their respective Governments, have signed the present agreement and have affixed their seals.

Done in London, in duplicate, in the English language the fifth day of

August, 1940. A Polish text shall be agreed upon between the Contracting Governments, and both texts shall then be equally authentic.

Appendix I (Relating to the Polish Air Force)

Article 1.
Constitution

1.   The Polish Air Force will be reorganised from those officers and men of the Polish Air Force arriving in British territory who are selected for service by a joint board or boards composed of Polish and British representatives. The personnel selected will be required to pass a medical examination according to the normal Royal Air Force standard. This will be carried out by an Anglo-Polish medical commission.

2.   Four bomber squadrons, two fighter squadrons and one army co-operation squadron will be formed as soon as possible, with about 200 per cent. reserves of flying personnel and about 50 per cent. reserves of other personnel. Three or more additional squadrons with the same reserves will be formed as facilities become available.

3.   (i) All the trained personnel of the Polish Air Force who are not required for the squadrons now forming will be utilised as soon as possible individually, or in groups in appropriate units or establishments of the Royal Air Force, or in the British aircraft industry until it becomes possible to absorb them in Polish Air Force units. It is understood that Polish flying personnel not required for the squadrons now forming and for the reserves of about 200 per cent. allotted to these squadrons will be employed for operational service in units other than those of the Polish Air Force only during the present critical period and with the specific consent of the Polish Commander-in-chief. If so employed, they will operate only from bases in the territory of the United Kingdom.

(ii) All possible assistance will be given by the Royal Air Force in the expansion of the Polish Air Force and in forming further reserves for the squadrons of the Polish Air Force. Partly trained personnel, in particular pilots, will be given every opportunity to complete their training in the appropriate Royal Air Force establishments. Until training facilities are available, they will be retained with the Polish Air Force and will be given employment on ground defence duties or other work in connection with the Polish Air Force units.

(iii) Untrained personnel who are not required for service with the Royal Air Force will be at the disposal of the Polish authorities for employment with the Polish Army or otherwise.

(iv) Arrangements will be made as soon as circumstances permit to train more pilots for service with the Polish Air Force.

4. An Inspectorate of the Polish Air Force will be formed whose duty it will be to inspect the units of the Polish Air Force. The Inspectorate will communicate with the British Air Ministry on all matters relating to the work of these units. The Inspectorate will also maintain liaison, if necessary through special liaison officers, with the Headquarters of Royal Air Force Commands in which Polish Air Force units are placed. The channel of communication between the Inspectorate and formations of the Royal Air Force will be the Directorate of Allied Air Co-operation in the Air Ministry.

Article 2. Employment.

1.   With regard to duties, rights and amenities, Polish Air Force personnel will be treated on the same footing as Royal Air Force personnel.

2.   The units of the Polish Air Force will be used in the same manner as the units of the Royal Air Force, but when circumstances permit, the units of the Polish Air Force will operate together. One Polish Army Co-operation Squadron when formed will be attached to the Polish Army while operating under British Command in its character as the Allied High Command, and will be entirely under the operational control of the Commander of the appropriate Polish military formation, subject to the normal flying regulations and restrictions laid down by the Royal Air Force. Other squadrons of the Polish Air Force may be used in support of the Polish Army when necessary.

Article 3. Organisation.

1.   Except as provided in Article 2 for the employment of a Polish Army Co-operation Squadron, operational control of the Polish Air Force units will rest entirely with the Royal Air Force Command to which they are attached.

2.   The stations at which units of the Polish Air Force are based will be commanded by British officers. Where a station is used solely or primarily for the accommodation of units of the Polish Air Force there will be a Polish commanding officer who will co-operate with the British Station Commander, the latter being senior. Circumstances may arise in connection with the employment of Polish Army Co-operation Squadrons which may require variations in the application of the present paragraph.

3.   Polish Air Force units will be provided with equipment of a similar kind and on the same scales as the corresponding units of the Royal Air Force.

4.   The supply, maintenance and training of all units of the Polish Air

Force serving with the Royal Air Force will be organised through the normal Royal Air Force channels.

5. The numbers and gradings of the officers and men to be authorised for units of the Polish Air Force serving with the Royal Air Force will be those which would be allowed in accordance with normal Royal Air Force practice, and Royal Air Force regulations as to the qualifications of the personnel will be applied. In special circumstances Royal Air Force practice may be varied where it is in the interests of effective co-operation that this should be done. Where it is necessary for administrative convenience, certain posts may be duplicated to enable British as well as Polish personnel to be borne against them. Where it is found that suitable Polish personnel are not available to fill posts in the establishments of the Polish Air Force units, British personnel may be appointed to fill them.

6. All promotions within the approved establishment of the Polish Air Force units serving with the Royal Air Force will be made on the authority of the Commander-in-Chief of the Polish Forces.
   (i) Recommendations for the promotion of officers will be forwarded to him through the normal Royal Air Force channels and will be subject to the concurrence of the appropriate Royal Air Force authorities.
   (ii) Responsibility for the promotion of airmen will belong, in the first instance, to the holder of the post to which the responsibility would normally attach under Royal Air Force regulations. If such post is held by a Polish Officer, the promotion will be effected forthwith. If it is held by a British Officer, the recommendation for promotion will be forwarded to the Commander-in-Chief of the Polish Forces or to an officer nominated by him, in order that effect may be given to it without delay.

Article 4. Discipline.

1. Personnel of the Polish Air Force serving with the Royal Air Force, whether in Polish units or individually, will be subject to Royal Air Force discipline and to Royal Air Force law, as if they were commissioned or enlisted in the Royal Air Force, so long as they are serving with the Royal Air Force. They will be subject also to Polish Military Law, but where the terms of Polish Military Law and British Air Force Law differ, the latter will prevail.

2. Where a military court is constituted for the trial of an officer or airman of the Polish Air Force serving with the Royal Air Force, it will consist of an equal number of British and Polish officers as judges, with, in addition, a British officer as president of the court.

3. Officers and airmen of the Polish Air Force serving with the Royal Air Force will, however, be liable to be tried and punished in accordance with

the laws for the time being in force of the United Kingdom or of any territory outside the United Kingdom under the authority of His Majesty's Government in the United Kingdom for offences committed by them against such laws.

Article 5. Pay and Allowances.

A detailed scale of pay and allowances for officers and men of the Polish Air Force serving with the Royal Air Force will be drawn up and agreed as soon as possible. So far as possible the rates will be based on those in force in the Royal Air Force, after allowance has been made for taxation to which British personnel are liable.

Article 6. Miscellaneous.

1.   The personnel of the Polish Air Force serving with the Royal Air Force will take an oath of allegiance to the Polish Republic.

2.   The uniform of the Royal Air Force will be adopted as the uniform of the Polish Air Force with such distinctive Polish symbols or other badges as the Polish authorities desire. On grounds of security, rank-badges of the Royal Air Force pattern will be worn and will correspond to the posts held under Royal Air Force establishment.

3.   Aircraft used by the Polish Air Force while serving with the Royal Air Force will bear British military markings with a distinctive Polish marking on the fuselage.

4.   The Polish Air Force ensign will be flown with the Royal Air Force ensign at all Royal Air Force stations at which units of the Polish Air Force are based.

Article 7.

Any difficulties arising out of the preceding articles, and any matters not covered by them will be settled, so far as possible, by direct discussion between the appropriate Polish and British authorities [PIL LOT A V 1/16].

Polish-French Air Agreements

Accord
relatif aux Forces Aériennes Polonaise.

Le Gouvernement polonais et le Gouvernement français, en vue de compléter l'accord en date du 4 Janvier 1940 relatif à la reconstitution de l'Armée polonaise en France par un accord particulier concernant la création des Forces Aériennes Polonaises sur le territoire français, sont convenus des disposition suivantes:

Article I

Des Forces Aériennes Polonaises faisant partie de l'Armée Polonaise seront formées sur le territoire français. Elles seront constituées avec du personnel polonais et encandrées par des officiers polonais. Au fur et à mesure de leur formation elles seront organisées en unités conformément aux textes organiques régiseant de l'Air française.

Les unités aériennes polonaises seront employées par le Haut Commandement français dans les mêmes conditions que les Forces Aériennes Françaises tout en conservant leur caractère de Forces Aériennes Alliées. Les unités aériennes polonaises seront engagées autant que possible dans le secteur ou seront groupées les unités de l'Armée Polonaise du terre.

Article II

Le Haut Commandement de l'Armée Polonaise aura le droit d'inspecter le personnel des unités aériennes polonaises.

Article III

Le personnel navigant, technique et auxiliaire des unités aériennes polonaises sera recruté:
a)   parmi le personnel de l'aviation polonaise venant de Pologne,
b)   parmi les Polonais appelés sous les drapeaux ou engagés volontaires quel que soit leur lieu de résidence.

Article IV

L'article VIII de l'accord relatif à la reconstitution de l'Armée Polonaise, est complété par les dispositions suivantes:

Les brevets spéciaux exigés pour l'exercice de conditions du personnel navigant et spécialistes de l'Armée de l'Air polonaise seront assimilés aux brevets français du même nature. Leurs titulaires bénéficieront des avantages attachés à ces brevets dans les conditions fixées par la réglementation française en vigueur.

Article V

Les modalités d'application du présent accord seront réglées par un accord complémentaire qui sera conclu entre le Ministre de l'Air français et le Ministre des Affaires Militaires Polonais.

Article VI

Le présent accord entrera en vigueur à la même date que l'accord sur la reconstitution de l'Armée polonaise.

As the main document it consisted of two texts, one in Polish and the other in French, both signed by Daladier and Sikorski. Paris. January 4, 1940.

Protocole
Relatif À l'Organisation de la Justice Militaire
Polonaise en France.
(Annexe aux accords militaires Franco-Polonais signés le 4 janvier, 1940)

Article I

Les tribunaux militaires polonais ont en territoire français compétence pour connaître de toutes infractions commises par des personnes qui font partie de l'Armée polonaise à un titre quelconque à l'exception de celles auxquelles la loi française reconnaît la nationalité française, même si elles sont co-auteurs ou complices.

Ces tribunaux rendent la justice au nom de la République de Pologne et appliquant la législation polonaise.

Article II

Les peines que prononcent les tribunaux polonais sont subies dans des conditions qui seront établies d'accord avec les autorités françaises compétentes.

Les frais qui pourront être nécessités par la détention préventive et l'exécution des peines, sont avancés par le Gouvernement français à charge du Gouvernement polonais.

Article III

1.—Dans les établissements militaires situés dans leurs zones de stationnement, les autorités militaires polonaises pourront exercer tous les pouvoirs de police judiciaire. En dehors de ces établissements, elles devront solliciter le concours des autorités françaises.

2.—En dehors des dites zones, tous actes de police judiciaire nécessaires à la constation ou à la répression des crimes et délits seront effectués par les autorités françaises, soit d'office, soit sur la demande des autorités polonaises qualifiées.

Article IV

Si une infraction de droit commun commise par une personne justiciable des tribunaux militaires polonais est prévue par la législation française. tandis que la législation polonaise ne la prévoit pas, les tribunaux militaires polonais en connaîtronte en appliquant la législation française.

Article V

Le présent protocole n'est pas applicable à l'action civile en réparation du préjudice causé par un crime ou un délit commis par une personne justiciable des tribunaux militaires polonais.

Article VI

Les autorités militaires françaises pourront demander aux autorités polonaises de saisir les Tribunaux militaires polonais d'infractions relevant de leur compétence.

Les Tribunaux français connaîtront des infractions commises par les militaires de l'Armée polonaise lorsque ceux-ci auront cessé d'appartenir à la dite armée avant que les autorités militaires polonaises aient engagé contre eux des poursuites en raison des faits incriminés.

Article VII

Les parquets et les greffes des Tribunaux Militaires polonais peuvent être composés en tout ou en partie de Français mis à la disposition des autorités polonaises sur leur demande.

Article VIII

La date de l'entrée en fonctions de chaque tribunal militaire polonais sera notifiée par les autorités polonaises au Gouvernement francais.

Article IX

Toutes les modalités de l'application du présent protocole seront réglées par la voie d'entente directe entre les Administrations compétentes des deux pays.

Article X

Le présent protocole fait partie intégrante de l'accord sur la reconstitution de l'Armée polonaise, signé à Paris, à la date de ce jour.

Article XI

À la date de l'expiration de l'accord mentionné ci-dessus, les deux Gouvernements se concerteront pour régler le sort des instances en cours, ainsi que celui des individus détenus en France dans les établissements pénitentiares.

Paris, le 4 Janvier, 1940.
Signé: Sikorski and E. Daladier.

Appendix 6
Polish-British Land Forces Agreement

Article 1.

1.   Polish Land Forces will be organised out of the Polish troops now in the territory of the United Kingdom and the Polish troops now in the Middle East.

2.   The following articles refer to these Land Forces and their composition will be as follows:—

(i) The necessary Headquarters Staffs and a certain number of formations (possible motorised) together with the necessary ancillary services.

(ii) The number of these formations will depend on the Polish possibilities, especially as to personnel.

Article 2.

The Polish Land Forces will be completed by the following means:—

(i) A mobilisation of Polish citizens living in the United Kingom.

(ii) The drafting of volunteers who may come from Poland, the British Commonwealth of Nations or other countries.

Article 3.

1.   The Polish Land Forces form the Army of the Sovereign Polish Republic.

2.   In principle all the units of the Polish Land Forces will be used so as to form one operational formation in any one theatre of operations under the Command of the Polish Commander in that theatre or of a Commander appointed by him. These forces will be under British Command, in its character as the Allied High Command, which may delegate the Command to a British Commander of appropriate rank. Nevertheless, in exceptional cases, Polish units or formations may be placed under different British Commanders provided that the consent of the Polish Commander is given in each case.

3.   Polish units and formations will be commanded by Polish Officers. Polish organisation, Polish regimental colours and all distinctions of rank and badges of the Polish Army will be retained.

Article 4.

The soldiers of the Polish Land Forces will take an oath of allegiance to the Polish Republic.

Article 5.

The Government of the United Kingdom agree to arm and equip the Polish Land Forces.

Article 6.

The British Military Authorities will detach a suitable number of officers and non-commissioned officers of the British Army as instructors to other Polish Land Forces for the period of their instruction and to facilitate the familiarising of the Polish cadres with British material. Officers of the Polish Staffs and of the various Services of the Polish Land Forces will be attached by the British Military Authorities to units of the British Army for short periods of training.

Article 7.

1. All officers and other ranks of the Polish Land Forces will be subject to Polish military law and disciplinary ruling, and they will be tried by Polish Military Courts.
2. They will, however, be liable to be tried and punished in accordance with the laws for the time being in force of the United Kingdom or of any territory outside the United Kingdom under the authority of His Majesty's Government in the United Kingdom for offences committed by them against such laws.
3. A separate agreement will define the method of application of the present article.

Article 8.

At least one field hospital will be organised on the territory of the United Kingdom for wounded and sick Polish personnel. Accommodation will also be provided in stationary hospitals. These medical installations will be manned by Polish Staffs and Polish personnel.

Article 9.

Officers and other ranks of the Polish Land Forces will be remunerated in accordance with a separate agreement to be negotiated between the two Governments.

PROTOCOL.

The Government of the United Kingdom shall lend to the Polish Government such assistance as is in their power, with a view to the negotiation of an agreement between the Polish Government and the Government of Canada concerning the establishment in Canada of a recruiting and organising base for the Polish Armed Forces. The method of negotiation of such an agreement will be a matter for settlement between the Polish and Canadian Governments, but if the United Kingdom Government are invited by those Governments to assist in the negotiations, they will be happy to do so.

Done in London in duplicate the fifth day of August, 1940, in the English language. A Polish text shall subsequently be agreed upon between the Contracting Governments, and both texts shall then be equally authentic.

Winston S. Churchill
Halifax.
Wladyslaw Sikorski
August Zalesky.

(This was accompanied by a letter from Winston S. Churchill to his excellency, General Wladyslaw Sikorski, G.B.E. on August 5, 1940)

Your Excellency,

With reference to Article 4 of Appendix I and Article 7 of Appendix II to the agreement which we have signed to-day concerning the organisation and employment of the Polish Forces, I have the honour to inform your Excellency that his Majesty's Government in the United Kingdom intend to invite Parliament to pass as soon as possible the necessary legislation to empower the competent Polish authorities and courts to exercise the jurisdiction over the Polish air and land forces for which provision is made respectively in the above mentioned articles, and to authorise the British civil and military authorities concerned to extend the necessary measures of assistance to the Polish authorities to enforce that jurisdiction. You will appreciate that until these powers have been obtained from Parliament, it will not constitutionally be possible for the provisions in question concerning the jurisdiction of the Polish authorities and courts to be enforced by the authorities of the United Kingdom. I can, however, assure your Excellency that His Majesty's Government will do their utmost to regularise the position as soon as possible.

I have the honour to be,
With the highest consideration
Your Excellency's obedient Servant,
Winston S. Churchill.

[PIL LOT A V 1/16]

Appendix 7
Polish-Soviet Military Agreement

1.   The Military Agreement derives naturally from the political agreement of July 30, 1941.

2.   A Polish Army will be organized in the shortest possible time on the territory of the USSR, whereof:
a)   it will form part of the armed forces of the Sovereign Republic of Poland,
b)   the soldier of the army will take an oath of allegiance to the Republic of Poland,
c)   it will be destined with the Armed Forces of the USSR and other allied States for the common fight against Germany,
d)   after the end of the war, it will return to Poland,
e)   during the entire period of common operations, it will be subordinated operationally to the High Command of the USSR.
In respect of organization and personnel it will remain under the authority of the Commander-in-Chief of the Polish Armed Forces, who will coordinate the orders and regulations concerning organization and personnel with the High Command of the USSR through the Commander of the Polish Army on the territory of the USSR.

3.   The Commander of the Polish Army on the territory of the USSR will be appointed by the C-in-C of the Polish Armed Forces; the candidate for this appointment to be approved by the Government of the USSR.
4.   The Polish Army on the territory of the USSR will consist of units of land forces only. Their strength and number will depend on the manpower, equipment and supplies available.
5.   Conscripts and volunteers, having previously served in the Polish Air Force and Navy, will be sent to Great Britain to complement the establishments of the respective Polish Services already existing there.
6.   The formation of Polish Units will be carried out in localities indicated by the High Command of the USSR. Officers and other ranks will be called from among Polish citizens on the territory of the USSR by conscription and voluntary enlistment. Draft boards will be established with the participation of the USSR authorities in localities indicated by them.
7.   Polish units will be moved out to the front only after they are fully ready for action. In principle they will operate in groups not smaller than divisions and will be used in accordance with operational plans of the High Command of the USSR.

8. All soldiers of the Polish Army on the territory of the USSR will be subject to Polish military laws and decrees. Polish military courts will be established in the units for dealing with military offences and crimes against the establishment, the safety, the routine or the discipline of the Polish Army.

For crimes against the State, soldiers of the Polish Army on the territory of the USSR will be answerable to the military courts of the USSR.

9. The organization and war equipment of the Polish units will as far as possible correspond to the standards established for the Polish Army in Great Britain. The colours and insignia of the various services and military ranks will correspond exactly to those established for the Polish Army in Great Britain.

10. The pay, rations, maintenance and other material problems will be in accordance with regulations of the USSR.

11. The sick and wounded soldiers of the Polish Army will receive treatment in hospitals and sanatoria on an equal basis with soldiers of the USSR and be entitled to pensions and allowances.

12. Armament, equipment, uniforms, motor transport, etc., will be provided as far as possible by

a) the Government of the USSR from their own resource,

b) the Polish Government from supplies granted on the basis of the Lend-Lease Act. (approved on March 11, 1941)

   In this case the Government of the USSR will extend all possible transportation facilities.

13. Expenditures connected with the organization, equipment and maintenance of the Polish Army on the territory of the USSR will be met from credits provided by the Government of the USSR, to be refunded by the Polish Government after the end of the war. This problem will be dealt with in a separate financial agreement.

14. Liaison will be established by

a) a Polish Military Mission attached to the High Command of the USSR,

b) a Soviet Military Mission attached to the Polish High Command in London.

15. All matters and details not covered by this agreement will be settled directly between the High Command of the Polish Army on the territory of the USSR and the corresponding authorities of the USSR.

16. This agreement is made in two copies, in the Polish and Russian languages, both texts are equally valid.

Plenipotentiary of the Polish
High Command.
Major—General
Szyszko-Bohusz

Plenipotentiary of
the USSR. General

A. Vassilevsky.

Appendix 8
Revised Polish-British Air Force Agreement

Protocol

The Government of the Polish Republic and the Government of the United Kingdom of Great Britain and Northern Ireland,

Desiring to make fresh provision for the organisation and employment of the Polish Air Force in association with the Royal Air Force, as well as for the exercise of jurisdiction over members of the Polish Air Force in the United Kingdom or in any territory outside the United Kingdom which is under the authority of the Government of the United Kingdom,

Have decided to conclude a Protocol for the purpose of amending as required the provisions of the Agreement concluded between the two Governments in London on the 5th August, 1940, respecting the Polish Land and Air Forces, and of the Protocol concluded between the two Governments in London on the 22nd November, 1940, concerning jurisdiction over the Polish Armed Forces, and have agreed as follows:

Article 1

From the date of the signature of this Protocol the provisions of Article 2 of the aforesaid Agreement of the 5th August, 1940, and the provisions of Appendix I to that Agreement to which the same Article 2 relates, shall cease to have effect, and personnel of the Polish Air Force shall be organised and employed in accordance with the conditions laid down in the Annex to this Protocol.

Article 2

(i) From the date of signature of this Protocol the provisions of Article 2 of the aforesaid Protocol of the 22nd November, 1940, shall cease to have effect, and the reference in Article 1 of the aforesaid Protocol to Article 2 thereof shall be read as a reference to this Article.

(ii) From the date of signature of this Protocol jurisdiction over members of the Polish Air Force shall be exercised in accordance with the remaining Articles of the Protocol of the 22nd November, 1940, except in so far as is specifically provided to the contrary in Article 6 of the Annex to the present Protocol.

In witness thereof the undersigned, duly authorised for this purpose by their respective Governments, have signed the present Agreement and have affixed thereto their seals.

Done in London, in duplicate, the 6th day of April, 1944.

Edward Raczynski
Alexander Cadogan

ANNEX

Article 1
Constitution of the Polish Air Force

1. The Polish Air Force in the United Kingdom, which constitutes a part of the sovereign Polish Armed Forces, shall be composed of—
i)   The General Headquarters of the Polish Air Force.
ii) Appropriate staffs of their cadres.
iii) Operational units of various types.
iv) Non-operational units and services of various types or their cadres— in particular, Training, Maintenance and Signals units.
v)   Trained reserves of personnel for the above-mentioned General Headquarters, Staffs, and other units.

2. In addition to the establishments already authorised or subsequently amended by mutual agreement, the Polish Air Force shall possess, where practicable, all the other institutions and organisational elements required for the future development of a modern Air Force in accordance with establishments to be agreed between the Air Ministry of the United Kingdom (hereinafter referred to as the Air Ministry) and the General Headquarters of the Polish Air Force.

3. The existing number and types of squadrons shall only be changed as a result of direct discussions between the appropriate Polish and British authorities.

4. An establishment shall be worked out in each Royal Air Force Command to be spread through Command, Group and Station Headquarters to ensure the provision of training facilities for Polish Staff officers in each branch of the Staff and their appropriate employment.

5. (i) At the head of the Polish Air Force shall be an Air Officer Commanding-in-Chief, appointed by the Polish Commander-in-Chief of the Polish Armed Forces.

(ii) The Air Officer Commanding-in-Chief of the Polish Air Force shall have at his disposal a Staff called the General Headquarters of the Polish Air Force.

(iii) The Air Officer Commanding-in-Chief of the Polish Air Force shall possess the power of a Commanding Officer, but in the operational sphere the powers of the appropriate British Air Officers Commanding-in-Chief shall be safeguarded in accordance with Article 2 of this Appendix.

The General Headquarters of the Polish Air Force shall communicate with the Air Ministry and with the Headquarters of the Royal Air Force Commands through the Directorate of Allied Co-operation and Foreign Liaison of the Air Ministry.

Article 2
Command of the Polish Air Force

The following principles shall be accepted to secure the Command of the Polish Air Force:—

i)   The operational control of units of the Polish Air Force shall remain vested in the Air Officer Commanding-in-Chief of the Royal Air Force Command concerned.

ii) (a) Where a station is used solely or primarily for the accommodation of units of the Polish Air Force, there shall be a British Station Commander. At such Stations a Polish Commanding Officer shall also be appointed in the same rank but subordinate to the British Commanding Officer. Consideration shall be given by Air Officers Commanding-in-Chief to the possibility of Polish officers taking over command of Stations used solely or primarily for the accommodation of units of the Polish Air Force.

(b) At Stations other than those specified in sub-paragraph (ii) (a) of this Article, where Polish units or comparable bodies specifically organised for Polish personnel are accommodated, a Polish Commanding Officer shall be appointed.

(c) For detachments of Polish personnel, other than those specified in sub-paragraphs (ii) (a) and (b) of this Article, a Senior Polish Officer may be appointed by agreement with the Air Ministry.

(d) The British Station Commander shall exercise his command over Polish Air Force units or personnel exclusively through the Polish Commanding Officer or the Senior Polish Officer. The Polish Commanding Officer or the Senior Polish Officer shall be responsible to the British Station Commander for all the matters relating to Polish units or personnel at a given Station.

(e) The Polish Commanding Officer or Senior Polish Officer on a Royal Air Force Station shall be entitled to communicate directly with his superior Polish authorities.

Article 3
Organisation and Employment

1. With regard to duties, rights and amenities, personnel of the Polish Air Force shall be treated on the same footing as personnel of the Royal Air Force, if not otherwise provided by this Appendix.

2. Units of the Polish Air Force shall be used in the same manner as units of the Royal Air Force, but when circumstances permit, units of the Polish Air Force shall operate together.

3. The Polish Air Force shall conform to the organisation at Royal Air Force Stations as laid down by the Royal Air Force Air Officers Commanding-in-Chief. A deviation from this principle may be admissible by mutual agreement.

4. The Polish Air Force shall continue to make use of certain Royal Air Force Organisations in so far as this may be necessary in order to avoid duplication and ensure administrative economy.

5. Squadrons and units of the Polish Air Force shall be commanded exclusively by Polish officers and shall be subordinated to the Royal Air

Force for operational duties. Royal Air Force control over operational and non-operational units shall be exercised through the Polish Commanding Officer or Senior Polish Officer at the Station.

6. Units of the Polish Air Force shall be provided with equipment of a similar kind and on the same scales as the corresponding units of the Royal Air Force.

7. The supply, maintenance and training of all units of the Polish Air Force shall be organised through the normal channels of the Royal Air Force.

8. In special cases where it is necessary for administrative convenience, certain posts may be duplicated to enable British as well as Polish personnel to be borne against them. Where it is found that suitable Polish personnel are not available to fill posts in the establishments of units of the Polish Air Force, British personnel may be appointed to fill them and Polish personnel may similarly be appointed to fill posts in the establishments of units of the Royal Air Force.

Article 4
Training

1. Subject to the Agreement of the British Air Ministry Polish Flying and Ground Personnel and Instructors shall be trained in numbers considered necessary by the Air Officer Commanding-in-Chief, Polish Air Force, to fill the establishment requirements of the squadrons, organisational units and reserves specified in paragraphs 2 and 3 of Article 1 of this Appendix.

2. Conditions, methods and syllabi of training, duties and rights of Polish personnel in training shall normally be based upon Royal Air Force regulations.

3. Personnel for the Polish Air Force shall normally be trained in Polish Training Schools. When this is not possible, they shall be trained in groups or singly in Royal Air Force Training Schools.

4. Where these are not provided under British regulations, the General Headquarters of the Polish Air Force shall be entitled, subject to the agreement of the Air Ministry, to organise such special Schools and Courses as are obligatory under Polish regulations and are considered necessary for the future development of the Polish Air Force.

Article 5
Personnel

Within the limits of the agreed establishments the General Headquarters of the Polish Air Force shall be responsible for the posting, commissioning and promotion of the personnel of the Polish Air Force and other related matters, provided that—

i)   the machinery for actually effecting the above shall remain as at present;

ii) The General Headquarters of the Polish Air Force shall conform generally to Royal Air Force procedure and regulations;

iii) The posting by the General Headquarters of the Polish Air Force of officers above the rank of Flight Lieutenant shall be subject to prior consultation with the Royal Air Force Command concerned, or with the Air Ministry, as may be necessary;

iv) Polish Air Force personnel shall remain subject to the same conditions as regards operational tours, and tours of duty overseas, as personnel of the Royal Air Force. In special circumstances, exceptions to this principle may be permitted, but they shall be subject to consultation between the Air Ministry and the General Headquarters of the Polish Air Force.

v) Personnel accepted for service in the Polish Air Force shall be required to pass a medical examination according to the normal standards of the Royal Air Force. This examination shall be carried out by an Anglo-Polish Medical Board.

Article 6
Discipline

1. In accordance with Article 2 of the present Protocol, of which this Annex forms a part, members of the Polish Air Force shall, except as provided in Paragraph 2 of this Article, be subject to the jurisdiction of the Polish Military courts and authorities, applying Polish Military Law, under the conditions laid down in the Protocol of the 22nd November, 1940, consigning jurisdiction over the Polish Air Force as amended by the aforesaid Article 2.

2. For practical reasons, individuals and small detachments of Polish Air Force personnel serving within units of the Royal Air Force and not under the immediate command of a Polish Commanding Officer or a Senior Polish Officer shall continue to be subject to Royal Air Force Law in so far as breaches of discipline are concerned which can be dealt with summarily under Royal Air Force law until such time as they are formed into Polish units or comparable bodies specifically established for Polish personnel, or until a Polish Commanding Officer or a Senior Polish Officer is appointed to command them by agreement with the Air Ministry. Personnel of the Polish Air Force alleged to have committed offences against discipline which cannot be dealt with summarily under Royal Air Force law, shall be handed over to the competent Polish authorities for disposal. The Air Ministry and the General Headquarters of the Polish Air Force shall agree upon the particular Polish detachments to which this exceptional arrangement shall from time to time apply.

3. In order to avoid any risk of confusion and misunderstanding at Stations where units or personnel of the Polish Air Force are serving, the General Headquarters of the Polish Air Force shall arrange for the necessary instructions to be issued to all personnel of the Polish Air Force who are serving at Royal Air Force Stations to comply strictly with all flying regulations, station orders and similar regulations for the safety and security of the Stations.

4. Officers of the Royal Air Force commanding Stations at which units or personnel of the Polish Air Force are serving shall have the power, if necessary, to order the arrest of members of the Polish Air Force for any breaches of discipline on the Station and to retain them in custody until they have been disposed of summarily or until they can be handed over to the appropriate Polish authorities for disciplinary action under the Polish Military Law.

Article 7
Pay and Allowances

1. So far as possible the rates of pay and allowances for officers and men of the Polish Air Force shall be based upon those in force in the Royal Air Force, after allowance has been made for taxation to which personnel of the Royal Air Force are liable.

2. Except as may hereafter be agreed between the Air Ministry and the General Headquarters of the Polish Air Force, the existing rates shall continue in force, as shall also the arrangements under which such pay and allowances are issued through Air Ministry channels.

Article 8
Formation of Ancillary Sections

1. It is agreed in principle that ancillary sections shall be formed as soon as sufficient Polish personnel become available.

2. In order to allow Polish officers to gain general experience in all branches of modern aviation, the Air Ministry shall endeavor, when opportunity occurs, to introduce individual Poles into Air Ministry departments and branches and into ancillary sections, including those concerned with civil aviation and the supply and maintenance of aircraft.

Article 9
Miscellaneous

1. The uniform of the Polish Air Force shall be Royal Air Force blue with such distinctive Polish symbols or other badges as the Polish authorities desire. The rank badges of the Royal Air Force pattern shall be worn and shall correspond to the posts held under Royal Air Force establishment.

2. Aircraft used by the Polish Air Force while serving with the Royal Air Force shall bear British Military markings with a distinctive Polish marking on the fuselage.

3. The Polish Air Force ensign shall be flown with the Royal Air Force ensign at all Royal Air Force Stations at which there is a Polish Commanding Officer.

4. At Royal Air Force Stations where a Polish Commanding Officer has been appointed, the internal organisation of squadrons and units shall be governed in so far as possible by Polish rules and regulations.

Article 10

1. The provisions of this Annex apply equally to personnel, units and other organisational groups of the Polish Air Force serving outside the United Kingdom as a result of mutual agreement between the British and Polish authorities.

2. Any difficulties arising out of the preceding articles, and any matters not covered by them shall be settled so far as possible by direct discussions between the appropriate Polish and British authorities.

Appendix 9
O. de B. of the Polish Armed Forces in September 1939

Field Army	Divisions	Brigades
Karpaty K. Fabrycy	11, 24, 38	two mountain
Krakow A. Szylling	6, 7, 21, 23 45, 55	*Krakowska* Cavalry
Lodz J. Rommel	2, 10, 28, 30, 44	*Kresowa & Wolynska* Cavalry
Poznan T. Kutrzeba	14, 17, 25, 26	*Wielko-Polska & Podol- ska* Cavalry
Pomorze W. Bortnowski	4, 5, 9, 15 16, 27	*Pomorska* Cavalry
Modlin E. Przedrzymirski	8, 20	*Nowogrodzka & Ma- zowiecka* Cavalry
Operational Command *Narew* (Strategic Reserve)	18, 33, 35	*Podlaska & Suwalska* Cavalry
Coast Defence J. Unrug		Two Marine Brigades

The Commander-in-Chief, Marshal Edward Smigly-Rydz, had the following forces under his potential command as the strategic pivot.

Prusy S. Dab-Biernacki	3, 12, 13, 19, 29, 39, 46	*Wilenska* Cavalry
Operational Group *Wyszkow* Kowalski	1st Legionary & 41	

The following significant units were initially under the command of the C.-in-C.

The Bomber Brigade	86 bombers
(C.O. Col. W. Heller)	
The Fighter Brigade	54 fighters
(C.O. Colonel S. Pawlikowski)	
The 10th Motorized Cavalry Brigade	
(C.O. S. Maczek)	
The Warsaw Motorized Brigade	
(C.O. Col. S. Rowecki)	
Three independent Tank Regiments	

On September 1, 1939 the Polish Army fielded seven field armies and two operational commands plus the independent Coastal Defence Force. (see table in appendix). The foundation of the army were the 471 infantry battalions, of which most were organically part of the thirty nine infantry divisions with some free standing battalions assigned to fortifications and cavalry brigades. Each infantry battalion consisted of one thousand officers and men, with a company of heavy machine guns, a battery of anti-tank guns (the Bofors 37mm).

The regular thirty infantry divisions (numbered one to thirty) were augmented by nine reserve divisions (numbered from 31 on), which were formed from the mobilized battalions of the *Korpus Ochrony Pogranicza* (Frontier Defense Corps) and*Obronna Narodowa* (National Guard). There were eleven cavalry brigades assigned to the seven army groups. The cavalry brigades were named after the regions where they were garrisoned in peacetime.

The table shows the assignment of the major units to the various field armies. The most striking aspect is the relative large number of field armies and operational commands and reserves which were all under the direct command of Marshal Smigly-Rydz. This had the result of each field army being relatively weak. Each field army had numerous supporting services which need not be detailed but which should be mentioned in general such as supply columns, hospitals, military engineers, military police. But what should be mentioned specifically is that each field army had an aviation component. This was usually one fighter wing, and a number of reconnaissance and liaison squadrons.

In turn each infantry division consisted of three infantry regiments, of three battalions each and had an organic component of a field regiment of artillery, reconnaissance (usually horsed), engineers, and anti-aircraft artillery. A Polish infantry division fully mobilized represented a strength of about eighteen thousand officers and men. The Polish infantry regiments were all standardized and had a strength of 91 officers, 3,212 other ranks, and fielded 90 light machine guns, 36 heavy machine guns, 27 light and 6 heavy mortars, 9 anti-tank guns, 2 howitzers.

The cavalry brigades were of three different strengths. Some had four, others three cavalry regiments. A number also had organic infantry battalions. It had been the intention of the staffs to motorize these infantry units but in 1939 they were an awkward appendage since they lacked the mobility of the horsed troopers. The fire power of a four regiment cavalry brigade was at best equivalent to that of an infantry regiment, but the much maligned horsed brigade had considerably more mobility.

A special word has to be said about Poland's *Lotnictwo Wojskowe* in September 1939. The actual strength of the Service on September 1, 1939, was nine bomber squadrons organized into the Bomber Brigade directly under the command of the C.-in-C., and a five fighter squadron Fighter Brigade whose task was the defense of Warsaw. In addition ten fighter, seven tactical and eleven army co-operation squadrons were assigned to field army commands. Total combat aircraft—433. Total personnel was 16,000 officers and men, of whom 1181 were pilots, 497 navigators, and 219 air gunners. The anti-aircraft artillery was composed of territorial units and of batteries assigned to armies. This totalled nearly three hundred modern Polish built Bofors 40mm, a hundred outdated French 75mm and forty-four modern, Polish designed and built 75mm guns. The defenses were augmented by 95 companies of heavy anti-aircraft machine guns. Polish industry was just in the process of developing a 20mm heavy machine gun which would have had A.A. and anti-armor capability.

Appendix 10
O. de B. of the Polish Armed Forces in May 1945

Supreme Commander .... The President of the Polish Republic, His Excellency, Wladyslaw Raczkiewicz
Commander-in-Chief .... Lt. General Tadeusz Bor-Komorowski
Prime Minister.............................. Tomasz Arciszewski
Minister of Defence .... Lt. General Marian Kukiel
 Military Headquarters, Rubens, London
 Chief of Staff .... Major General Tadeusz Kopanski
 Chief of Air Force...................... Major General Mateusz Izycki
 Chief of Navy .... Vice Admiral Jerzy Swirski
 Directly under Headquarters:

> Liaison with Combined Chiefs of Staff, Washington, D.C.
> Liaison with SHAEF
> Liaison with British Ministries
> Liaison with Royal Air Force Commands, e.g., Fighter
> Polish War College Polish Military Technical Institute
> Polish Officer and Non-commissioned Officer Schools
> Provost Marshal's Office
> Two military hospitals
> Field Headquarters in Gask, Scotland
> Section VI for liaison with Home Army

The following is the o. de b. of the Polish Ground Forces.

First Corps (G.O.C. Lt. General Stanislaw Maczek)
 The following units were based in Germany as part of the British Army of the Rhine. First Armored Division
  10th Armored Cavalry Brigade 1st Armored Regiment
   2nd Armored Regiment
   24th Ulan Regiment
   10th Dragoons (motorized infantry) 3rd Rifle
  Brigade Podhalanski Rifle Battalion
   8th Rifle Battalion
   9th Rifle Battalion

10th Armored Strzelcow Konnych Regiment
Divisional Artillery The following units of the 1st
Corps were based in the United Kingdom:

First Polish Corps Headquarters
    1st Szwolezer Armored—Corps reconnaissance
    4th Grenadier Division
        Grenadier Brigade (old 1st Rifle)
           three battalions
    2nd Rifle Brigade
        three battalions
    8th Infantry Brigade
        24th Slaski
        25th Pomorski
        26th Poznanski
    9th Ulan (Malopolski) Regiment, divisional reconnaissance
    Heavy machine gun battalion
    Five Artillery Regiments

16th Armored Brigade
    3rd Armored Regiment
    5th Armored Regiment
    14th Jazlowiecki Regiment
    16th Dragoons

Administratively part of the First Corps, but based in Germany in close proximity to the First Armored Division, and also part of the British Army of the Rhine.

    Independent Parachute Brigade
        Three parachute battalions
        Artillery Engineers
------------------------------------.

2 Polish Army Corps (G.O.C Lt. General Wladyslaw Anders) Italy
    3rd Carpathian Infantry Division
        consisting of three infantry brigades each of three battalions
        12 Lubelski Regiment (reconnaissance)
        Three artillery regiments
    5th Kresowa Infantry Division Wilenska Infantry
        Brigade Lwowska Infantry Brigade Wolynska
        Infantry Brigade each of three infantry battalions
        15th Wielkopolski Regiment (reconnaissance)
        Three artillery regiments
    2nd Warszawska Armored Division 2nd Armored Brigade
        1st Krechowiecki Ulans
        4th Armored Regiment

6th Lwow Armored Regiment
2nd Dragoons
7th Pomorska Infantry Brigade each of three infantry battalions
14th Wielkopolska Armored Brigade.
   3rd Slask Ulans.
   10th Hussar
   15th Poznanski Ulans

Corps level organic services.
   Artillery Group, consisting of eleven field regiments
   Engineers
   Provost Marshal
   Medical Services— four field hospitals
   3rd Carpathian Ulans. Corps Reconnaissance.
   Headquarters Battalion
   Artillery Spotting flight—665 flight.
7th Training/Cadre Infantry Division.

Naval Units

List of warships that served under the Polish Flag during the Second World War. This list does not include the numerous smaller ships, such as torpedo boats, minesweepers, trawlers, submarine chasers, motor torpedo gunboats and other auxiliary and training ships.

Wicher, Burza	Destroyers. French built, similar to the *Simoun* Class, 1929. *Wicher* sunk by enemy air action in September 1939, off Hel Peninsula. *Burza* on active combat to April 1944, then training ship. After WW II, *Burza* became a museum ship in Gdynia.
Rys, Zbik, Wilk	Submarines built in France,–1930. *Wilk* broke out to the United Kingdom in September 1939. Initially combat, subsequently training ship. *Zbik* and *Rys* sustained damage from enemy action while on patrol in Baltic and sought internment in neutral Sweden.
Gryf	French built minelayer and training ship. Ordered 1934, launched 1936, but commissioned in 1938. Damaged by enemy air action September 1939. Beached, guns removed for land defense, which are still on exhibit Military Museum in Warsaw.

Blysawica, Grom .... Polish designed and British built destroyers with many unique features.
Fast, 39 knots and equipped for mine-
laying. Commissioned 1938. *Grom*
sunk off Narvik, May 1940. *Blysawica*
on combat duties throughout war.
Two further destroyers of this class
were to be built in Polish Naval Yards
and named *Orkan* and *Huragan*.

Orzel, Sep .... Dutch built and designed ocean going
submarines. Commissioned just be-
fore the war, 1939. *Sep* sustained damage and was interned in Sweden.
Orzel broke out to the United Kingdom and lost on patrol, May 1940.

Ouragan (ex-French Ouragan) .... French destroyer of the *Simoun* Class.
Details as for *Burza*. After the capitu-
lation of France taken over by Royal
Navy and August 1940 transferred to
the Polish Navy. Returned to the Free
French on April 1941.

Garland (ex-HMS Garland) .... British *G* Class destroyer transferred
to the Polish Navy in May 1940. Built
1934, Returned to the Royal Navy
after World War II. Then transferred
to the Royal Dutch Navy as *Marnix*.

Piorun (ex-HMS Nerissa) .... British *Javelin* Class destroyer built
1939, transferred to the Polish Navy in
September 1940. Returned to the
Royal Navy after World War II and
renamed *Noble*.

Krakowiak (ex-HMS Silverton) .... British built *Hunt* Class destroyer es-
Kujawiak (ex-HMS Oakley) .... corts. Transferred to the Polish Navy
Slazak (ex-HMS Bedale) .... in April 1940 and April 1942.
Launched, 1939–1940. *Kujawiak* sunk
by enemy mine June 1942 and re-
placed by *Slazak*. Both returned to the
Royal Navy after World War II and
served under original names.

Sokol (ex-HMS Urchin) .... British built, 1939 and 1941 *Dzik* re-
Dzik (ex-HMS P-52) .... spectively. *U* Type submarines trans-
ferred to the Polish Navy in January
1941 and October 1942 respectively.
After the war both returned to the
Royal Navy.

Jastrzab (ex-USS S-25)....................... United States built submarine of the *S* Class, transferred to the Polish Navy on November 1941. Lost due to unfortunate accident on 2/5/1942 by depth charging initiated by HMS Seagull.

Orkan (ex-HMS Myrmidon)............... British built *Milne* Class destroyer launched March 1942 and transferred to the Polish Navy in November 1942. Hit by an acoustical mine fired by U-378 on 8/X/1943 with loss of 178 crew.

Dragon (ex-HMS Dragon).................. British light cruisers built 1916–1918
Conrad (ex-HMS Danae) .... *Dragon* transferred to the Polish Navy in January 1943. Poles intended to name it *Lwow* but the British objected and for a time there was a question whether the transfer would take place. *Dragon* was lost due to enemy small submarine during the invasion of Normandy. *Conrad* given as replacement in October 1944. *Conrad* returned to Royal in 1946.

For details of the Polish Warships, see, Piaskowski, *Okrety Rzeczpospolitej Polskiej, 1920–1946*, and *Jane's Fighting Ships* The Following English language descriptions haveot Polish warships have been published. These are superb articles with detailed diagrams; Kolesnik, Eugene, "Thunder and Lightning. The Polish Destroyers Blyskawica and Grom," *Warships*, London, 1980 Twardowski, Marek, "The Jaskolka Class Minesweepers," *Warships*, London, 1980. Budzbon, Przemyslaw, "Wicher and Burza. Big Ships of a Small Navy," *Warships*, London, 1980, and "Pride of Poland. The Orzel Class Submarines," *Warships*, London, 1987.

Polish Air Force Squadrons

300 Land of *Mazowsze*........... Heavy Bomber—Lancasters I
301 Land of *Pomorze*.............. Special Duties—Warwick III
304 Land of *Slask* .... Coastal Command—Wellingtons XIV
305 Land of *Wielkopolska*....... Light Bomber—Mosquito VI Fighter and fighter reconnaissance
302 *Poznanski*......................... Spitfire XVI
303 *Kosciuszko*....................... Mustang IV
306 *Torunski*........................... Mustang III
308 *Krakowski*......................... Spitfire XVI
309 Land of *Czerwiensk*......... Mustang III
315 *Deblinski*........................... Mustang III

316 *Warszawski* .... Mustang III
317 *Wilenski* .... Spitfire XVI
318 City of *Gdansk* .... Spitfire IX
307 *Lwowski* .... Mosquito XXX

All of these squadrons with the exception of the 318 City of Gdansk were based either in the United Kingdom or Northwest Europe. These units were either part of the Polish wing (131) assigned to the 2nd Tactical Airforce, or 133 assigned to the old defunct Fighter Command, renamed the Air Defence of Great Britain. The squadrons rotated between very active operational and being placed in reserve. 318 Squadron was based in Italy and flew ground support, reconnaissance and artillery plotting flights on behalf of the Polish 2 Corps.

For a detailed description of all the planes that equiped Polish squadrons during the war see, the specific brochures of the Profile Publications. These are numbered:

11—Handley page Halifax B III, VI and VII;
19—Consolidated Liberator B-24J;
24—Hawker Hurricane IIC;
34—Fairey Battle
41—Supermarine Sptifire Series I and II;
52—DeHavilland Mosquito, Marks 1-4;
65—Avro Lancaster I;
75—P.Z.L.-11;
100—North American Mustang P-51B and 51C;
104—P.Z.L.-23 Karas;
111—Hawker Hurricane!;
117—Boulton Paul Defiant;
125—Vickers Wellington I and II;
137—Bristol BeaufighterI and II;
147—Morane-Saulnier 406;
159—Westland Lysander;
166—Supermarine Sptitfire V;
285—P.Z.L.-37 Los.

Total manpower in May 1945
Ground Forces　　　171,220
Air Force　　　　　19,400
Navy　　　　　　　3,840
TOTAL　　　　　　194,460

Appendix 11
Losses Suffered by
the Polish Armed Forces in Exile

Formation or Service	Killed	Wounded
Brigade in Norway, 1940	97	189
Polish Divisions and Armored Brigade, France 1940	1,330	4,670
Carpathian Brigade, North Africa, 1940–1942	156	467
2 Army Corps, Italy, 1944–1945	2,301	8,543
Parachute Brigade, 1944	211	346
Commando Units, 1944	6	27
Air Force, 1940–1945	1,803	1,348
Navy, 1939–1945	404	191
Cichociemni, 1941–1944	100	
TOTAL	7,708	10,605

Appendix 12
Military Debt to the British

Due to the British decision to rescind the recognition of the Polish Government based in London on July 5, 1945, and to grant it to the Communist Regime, it was to the later that the British presented the account for all expenditures for the civilian and military aspects of the Polish Government and its employees and military personnel.

The total sum was:

Armament and Equipment	£75 million;
Pay and allowances for the military	£47 million;
Civilian and diplomatic missions	£32 million.

The British agreed that the sum of £75 would be wiped out but that the Poles would be expected to pay the £79 for salaries. The Polish communists objected and stated that the Soviets did not expect repayment for the military and that they would not pay those expenses, but would consider the civilian debt as reasonable.

It is not exactly clear how much of that amount was in fact ever paid to the British. The various trade and financial negotiations that occurred in the postwar years would require a chartered accountant to figure this out. But it is unlikely that even much of the civilian debt was ever paid back to the British. The Polish Gold went back to Poland and its fate is unknown.

Appendix 13
Women in Military Service

On February 12, 1940, in Paris, the Polish Ministry of Military Affairs issued instructions regarding the formation and conditions of service for a women's auxiliary service. The women were part of the auxiliary service of the Polish red cross.

In reality little was done in the first years of the war, though a number of Polish women served with heroism alongside their men colleagues in the French Campaign and in Norway.

In the United Kingdom, the number of women grew but the actual service was still confined to cultural and medical duties. There were a number of Polish women, who were civilian pilots before the war, and were seconded to the British Air Transport Auxiliary (ATA) including Marshal Pilsudski's daughter.

The release of many thousands of Polish women from the Soviet camps in late 1941 not merely allowed but mandated some form of military organization for the released prisoners. These women were unrolled in the Polish Forces under a little known pre-1939 regulation for universal service of all citizens. (April 9, 1938)

The numbers of women in the auxiliary service reached nearly two thousand during the evacuation from the Soviet Union to Persia.

In 1942 after Polish troops were moved to Palestine, further instructions regarding uniforms, ranks were introduced. Officer ranks for women were created and by October 1943, the number of Polish women in service in the Middle East alone had reached 3,141.

The women soldiers drove trucks, worked in kitchens, functioned in communications, and were the mainstay of the medical corps.

In 1942 the Polish Ministry of Defence in London formed the Polish Women's Military Auxiliary and based the training and duties on the British counterparts. Women were thus assigned to the Polish Navy, Polish Air Force and the lion's share to the Polish land forces.

On July 1, 1945, there were 6,700 Polish women in uniform serving with the Polish Forces in the west.

This short summary is based on a chapter by Maria Mackowska in *Wysilek Zbrojny w II Wojnie Swiatowej*.

Appendix 13
Women in Military Service

Chronological Table of Significant Events

1772	First Partition of Poland and Lithuania.
1788–1792	The four year session of the *four year Sejm,* famous for its progressive legislation.
1791	3rd of May Constitution.
1793	Second Partition of Poland and Lithuania.
1794	Kosciuszko calls for an Uprising against the Russians, and in his manifesto proclaims a new social policy for the Polish Kingdom.
1795	Defeat of Kosciuszko Uprising by combined Prussian and Russian Armies. Third and final partition. King deported to Petersburg and forced to abdicate.

1797–1802	Various Polish units fight in the West as Polish Legions, the most famous being the legion commanded by General Dabrowski.
1807–1813	Duchy of Warsaw.
1830–1831	November Uprising.
1863–1864	January Uprising.
1867	Galicia (Polish lands under Austrian rule) receives autonomy.

21 Feb 1914	Pilsudski addresses an international audience in Paris and outlines his political plan. Galicia (Austrian Poland) will be the crucible of Polish political and military effort; Germany an ally in the war to destroy Russia and then the Poles will aid the Western Allies to defeat Germany.
4 Aug 1914	The commander of a cadre rifle company of the Polish Rifle Association, a semi-military organization created in the Austrian part of Poland, orders his eight-man cavalry patrol to cross into the Russian-occupied part of Poland. The man was Pilsudski; the cavalry patrol—Belina's lancers.
6 Aug 1914	The cadre company of the Polish Rifle company (better known historically as Pilsudski's Legions) marched out of Oleander, near Krakow, to the front against the Russians. Pilsudski fabricates the myth of a Polish clandestine government in Russian-occupied Warsaw, to which he now pledges allegiance.

9 July 1917	Germans demand that the Polish Legions take an oath of allegiance and loyalty to their German and Austrian Allies. Pilsudski and the officers and men of the first brigade refuse and are arrested. Pilsudski and Sosnkowski are transported to Magdeburg. The Command of the Legions and the second legion Brigade take the oath. Among those who accept the pragmatics of the dilemma are: Sikorski, Kukiel, Zymierski, and Zagorski. Anticipating such an event, Pilsudski has, independently of the Legions, created a clandestine underground organization—*Polska Organizacia Wojskowa*, or *POW*—and gives Smigly-Rydz the command.
22 Jan 1917	Wilson calls for an Independent Poland. Later this becomes his thirteenth point.
4 June 1917	France decrees the organization of an autonomous Polish Army composed of volunteers from France and the USA, and from Poles conscripted into service by the Germans and Austrians and taken prisoner of war by Western coalition forces.
20 Sept 1917	France formally recognizes the Dmowski Committee as representing Polish interests.
3 Mar 1918	Treaty of Brest-Litovsk. Russia leaves the Allied anti-German coalition. The First postulate of Pilsudski's political program is met.
3 June 1918	Declaration of Versailles—The question of a united and independent Polish state, with free access to the sea, constitutes one of the conditions for a just and durable peace and rule of rights in Europe.

---

11 Dec 1918	Poland regains Independence after more than a century of partitions. Pilsudski and Sosnkowski released from German prison arrive in Warsaw. The German-appointed Regency Council appoints Pilsudski Head of State and resigns.
3 May 1920	Outbreak of the Polish-Soviet war.
18 Aug 1920	Battle of Warsaw won.
18 Oct 1920	Conclusion of hostilities.
19–21 Feb 1921	Polish-French political and military agreement signed in Paris by Pilsudski and Sosnkowski. Poland agrees to a standing army of thirty infantry divisions to aid France in event of war with Germany, while France agrees to keep the sea lanes open in event of war with the Soviet Union. This treaty was the keystone of Polish foreign policy and was in force in 1939.

3 Mar 1921	Polish-Romanian treaty of mutual assistance in event of danger from the East.
18 Mar 1921	The Treaty of Riga between Poland and the Soviet finalizes the Polish-Soviet boundary and leads to restoration of normal relations.
16 Apr 1922	Rapallo—a German-Soviet Treaty of collaboration. Poland viewed this as aimed at her interests.
11 Jan 1923	Belgian and French troops occupy the Ruhr. Britain and the USA dissociate themselves from this act. Marshal Foch visits Warsaw.
26 Apr 1925	The Polish Prime Minister, General Sikorski, visits Paris and signs a protocol to the 1921 Polish-French Treaty. It provided for significant financial aid to the modernizing of the Polish Armed Forces and for major French capital investment in such industrial projects as the construction of the port of Gdynia. Unfortunately the French signatory—Herriot—was opposed to this by the new French foreign minister, Briand, and in his utterances and behavior minimized and discounted the French obligations to Poland.
16 Oct 1925	Locarno Pact. Signatories were Germany and Western coalition partners. Germany agreed never to seek a revision of her western boundaries.
12 May 1926	Pilsudski's coup d'état
25 July 1932	Polish-Soviet Nonaggression Treaty signed in Moscow.
30 Jan 1933	Hitler becomes Chancellor of Germany.
26 Jan 1934	Polish-German *Declaration* of Nonaggression signed in Berlin.
23 Apr 1935	New Constitution enacted, which gave the President considerable authority and power. Frequently referred to as Pilsudski's constitution.
11 May 1935	Pilsudski dies. His last political testament to Beck, the foreign minister. Present relations with Germany, though unpopular, have to be preserved as long as possible, the alliance with France preserved at all costs, and Britain drawn into it.
7 Mar 1936	Germans march into the Rhineland. Openly break the Versailles Treaty obligation.
October 1936	Belgium declares its neutrality.
1936	KSUS reactivated.
6 Sept 1936	Marshal Edward Smigly-Rydz visits France and negotiates an agreement for the modernization of the Polish Armed Forces, known as the Rambouillet agreement.
15 Mar 1939	German troops enter Prague.

31 Mar 1939	The United Kingdom guarantees Polish sovereignty.
28 Apr 1939	Germany breaks off the Polish-German declaration of nonaggression and also the German-British treaty on warship tonnage limitation.
23 Aug 1939	Molotov-Ribbentrop Pact.
25 Aug 1939	Polish–United Kingdom Treaty of Mutual Aid.
25 Aug 1939	Polish Aviation Service placed on secret mobilization.
1 Sept 1939	Germany invades Poland.
3 Mar 1939	The United Kingdom and France honor their treaty obligations and declare war on Germany.
17 Sept 1939	The Soviet Union implements the secret protocol of the Molotov-Ribbentrop pact and invades Poland.
18 Sept 1939	The Polish Government crosses the Romanian boundary and is interned.
27 Sept 1939	Warsaw receives orders to capitulate, carried by a plane from Romania.
30 Sept 1939	Raczkiewicz appointed to the Presidency.
1 Oct 1939	Hel capitulates.
4 Oct 1939	General Kleeberg capitulates at Kock.
14 Oct 1939	O.R.P. *Orzel* sails into a British port.
18 Nov 1939	Polish–United Kingdom Naval Agreement signed in London. The Commanding Officer of the Polish Navy, Rear Admiral Jerzy Swirski, moves his headquarters from Paris to London.
4 Jan 1940	Polish-French Military Agreement.
8 May 1940 to 8 June 1940	The Podhalanska Brigade participates in Allied operations at Narvik.
5 June 1940	The Chief of Staff of the Polish Army, Col. Aleksander Kedzior, resigns in protest over Sikorski's agreement to dispatch the Polish Grenadier Division without its antitank guns and not as part of a Polish Corps to the front line. Replaced by Col. Tadeusz Klimecki.
17 June 1940	France seeks an armistice through its Madrid embassy.
18 June 1940	Polish troops begin to evacuate to the United Kingdom and North Africa.
22 June 1940	France capitulates.
25 June 1940	Poles complete their evacuation from France. British and Polish ships (*Batory*, *Sobieski*) transport over twenty thousand military personnel to Britain.
5 Aug 1940	Polish–United Kingdom Military Agreement.
31 Aug 1940	Polish 303 (*Kosciuszko*) squadron enters operations in the Battle of Britain.
3 Apr 1941	Sikorski embarks on his first trip to the United States.

21 June 1941	Germany attacks the Soviet Union.
30 Aug 1941	Sikorski and Maiski sign an agreement establishing diplomatic relations and the Soviet Union agrees to allow a Polish army to be formed on Soviet soil.
9 Sept 1941	The Atlantic Charter is signed by President Franklin D. Roosevelt and Prime Minister Winston S. Churchill.
7/8 Nov 1941	First Polish flight from the U.K. to Poland. The Halifax was piloted by Captain Krol and dropped three Poles, including the famous Lt. Jan Piwnik (Ponury). Lt. Col. Roman Rudkowski was aboard on behalf of the Polish VI Section to acquaint himself with the actual practicalities of the long flight. Due to head winds, the Halifax could not get back to the United Kingdom and crashed in Sweden. All were smuggled back to the United Kingdom.
7 Dec 1941	Pearl Harbor.
30 Dec 1941	Sikorski visits the Soviet Union and inspects Polish troops.
15 Feb 1942	Singapore falls to the Japanese. Churchill describes this as the greatest defeat ever suffered by British Armies.
18 Mar 1942	Anders's first meeting with Stalin.
20 Mar 1942	Sikorski's second visit to the USA.
1 Apr 1942	Sikorski hosts a major military and strategic planning conference of all his senior generals.
21 June 1942	Tobruk captured by the Germans.
1 July 1942	Poland is officially included by the United States as a recipient of the Lend Lease Act of March 11, 1941.
4 July 1942	All Polish troops evacuated from the Soviet Union to the Middle East.
19 Aug 1942	Allied Landings in Dieppe.
October 1942	British defeat the Germans at El Alamein. First British land victory of the Second World War over the Germans.
29 Nov 1942	Sikorski's third visit to the USA.
13 Apr 1943	Berlin radio announces the discovery at Katyn of the bodies of over four thousand missing Polish officers captured by the Soviets in 1939.
25 Apr 1943	After the Polish Government requests that the Red Cross investigate the cause and date of death of the Polish officers, the Soviet Union breaks diplomatic relations with the Polish Government in London.
24 May 1943 to 4 July 1943	Sikorski visits Polish troops in the Middle East and on his way back is killed in a plane accident at Gibraltar.
8 Sept 1943	Italy surrenders.

November 1943	Teheran Conference.
31 Jan 1944	The first elements of the 2 Polish Army Corps arrive in Italy.

4 Apr 1994	Jozef Retinger (Salamander), Churchill's personal representative, is parachuted to Poland and is extracted by the third *Most* operation on 7/25/44.
15/16 Apr 1944	First successful *Most* operation. A Dakota originating in Italy landed in Poland.
6 May 1944	Mikolajczyk flies to Washington for a ten-day visit, which includes three meetings with Roosevelt.
18 May 1944	Polish 2 Army Corps troops capture Monte Cassino.
6 June 1944	Allies land in Normandy. Polish naval and air units participate.
8 July 1994	President Raczkiewicz, reluctantly but bowing to the pressures of the Polish Government and of the Clandestine Polish Home Organization, strips General Sosnkowski of his status as the Presidential successor and appoints Tomasz Arciszewski, the leader of the Polish Socialist Party, to that position.
11 July 1944	Sosnkowski flies to Italy and while visiting the Polish 2 Army Corps urges the Polish President to hold firm against any accommodation with Moscow at Poland's territorial expense.
18 July 1944	Polish 2 Army Corps captures Ancona.
29 July 1944	The Polish First Armored Division enters combat in Normandy.
30 July 1994	Mikolajczyk flies to Moscow at Chrchill's strong urging and is confronted the next day by the Warsaw Uprising.
21 Aug 1944	The victorious conclusion of the Falaise gap.
1 Aug 1944	**Warsaw Uprising begins.**
13 Sept 1944	First Armored liberates Ghent.
18 Sept 1944	Polish Parachute Brigade participates in the Arnhem operation.
30 Sept 1944	General Kazimierz Sosnkowski is dismissed from his function as the Polish Commander-in-Chief. General Tadeusz Bor-Komorowski, the G.O.C. Polish Home Army, appointed to that now symbolic post.
2 Oct 1944	**Warsaw Capitulates.**
30 Oct 1944	First Armored Division liberates Breda.
7 Nov 1944	Polish Special Duty Flight 1586 enlarged to a full squadron and returns officially to its old numeration of Polish Squadron 301 and the Polish appellation of "Defenders of Warsaw."
15 Dec 1944	Mikolajczyk resigns as Prime Minister. Tomasz Arciszewski becomes the Prime Minister of the Polish Government.
21 Dec 1944	General Leopold Okulicki (Niedzwiadek) nominated as G.O.C. Home Army to succeed Bor-Komorowski in a German Prisoner of War camp.

23 Dec 1944	Polish Government advised, through the Polish ambassador in London, that henceforth all radio dispatches to Soviet-occupied territory are to cease, while all such communications with Polish clandestine organizations in German-occupied Poland are to be cleared with the British.
27 Dec 1944	Churchill's envoy to Poland, Hudson (*Freston* Mission), parachuted with five companions.
28 Dec 1944	Last flight to Poland by Squadron 301.
19 Jan 1945	Polish Underground Army dissolved by Presidential decree.
February 1945	Yalta Conference.
31 Mar 1945	Polish Underground leaders accept an invitation to meet with the Soviet representatives, are all arrested and flown to Moscow to be placed on trial. Public opinion in the West is delighted that none are given a death sentence. General Okulicki last G.O.C. of the Polish Army in Poland dies in Soviet hands of unknown cause.
21 Apr1945	Polish First Armored Division enters Wilhelmshaven.
21 Apr 1945	Polish 2 Army Corps enters Bologna.
8 May 1945	Victory Day in Europe.
5 July 1945	Allies rescind their recognition of the Polish Government in London.
1946	Polish Armed Forces in the West begin to be demobilized.
1945–1947	Civil War in Poland.
6 June 1947	President Wladyslaw Raczkiewicz dies in Ruthin, England. He is buried at the Polish Military cemetery, Newark.
1947–1951	Stalinist Repression in Poland.
1955	Poznan anti-Communist riots.
1978	Cardinal John Wojtylla of Cracow elected Pope.
1980	Solidarity Formed.
19 Dec 1990	First free elections in Poland. Walesa elected to the Presidency.
22 Dec 1990	President Ryszard Kaczorowski arrives in Warsaw, and is greeted as a Head of State. At the innaugural gives the Presidential Insignia of Office to Walesa. The 1935 Constitution has survived fifty years and is now subject to a democratic change.
3 Sept 1992	The Polish President and Commanding General, Glogawa, of the Polish Air Force, greet the remaining survivors of the Polish W.W.II. in Warsaw and Deblin. For those very few, Destiny had arrived.

Bibliography

All references which are marked with an asterisk (*) were published in the United Kingdom during the war and, though short on historical data and undoubtedly embellished, are a fascinating social commentary on the Polish situation in the United Kingdom.

Ambrose, Stephen E., *D-Day: June 6, 1944, The Climactic Battle of World War II*, NY, 1994.

Anders, Wladyslaw, *Bez Ostatniego Rozdialu* (Without the last Chapter), Newton, Wales, 1949.

———, *An Army in Exile*, London, 1949.

Baginski, Henryk, *Poland and the Baltic. The Problem of Poland's Access to the Sea*, London, 1942. *

———, *Poland's Freedom of the Sea*, Kirkcaldy, 1942. With a foreword by General Marian Kukiel. *

Baldwin, Hanson W., *The Crucial Years, 1939–1941*, NY 1976.

Baluk, Stefan, and Michalowski, Marian, *Poland at Arms, 1939–1945*, Warsaw, 1990.

Barbarski, Krzysztof, *Polish Armour, 1939–1945*, London, 1982.

Bardsey, Stephen, *Arnhem 1944. Operation Market Garden*, London, 1993.

Bartosik, Jozef, *Wierny Okret* (Faithful Ship), London, 1947.

Bauer, Piotr, and Polak, Boguslaw, *Armia Poznan w Wojnnie Obronnej, 1939* (The Poznan Army in the Defensive War, 1939), Poznan, 1983.

Beck, Jozef, *Final Report*, NY 1957.

Begin, Menachem, *White Nights. The Story of a Russian Prisoner*, NY, 1977.

Bekker, Cajus, *Luftwaffe War Diaries*, NY, 1969.

Bickers, Richard Townshend, *The Battle of Britain*, London, 1990.

Bieganski, Witold, ed. in chief, *Walki Formacji Polskich na Zachodzie, 1939–1945* (The Operations of the Polish Units in the West, 1939–1945), Warsaw, 1981.

———, *Zaczelo sie w Coetquidan* (It began in Coetquidan), Warsaw, 1977.

———, *Bolonia, 1945* (Bologne, 1945), Warsaw, 1986. This was the final battle of the 2 Polish Corps in Italy.

———, *Ankona* (Ancona), Warsaw, 1986.

Bieganski, Stanislaw, *Dzialania 2 Korpusu we Wloszech* (Operations of the 2 Corps in Italy), London, 1963.

Bieganski, Stanislaw and Szkuta, Aleksander, *Wysilek Zbrojny w II Wojnie Swiatowej* (Military Effort during the II World War), London, 1988.

Blum, Aleksander, *2 Dywizia Strzelcow Pieszych w Szwajcarii. Poczatki Internowania, 1940–1941* (The 2 Infantry Division in Switzerland. The beginnings of internment, 1940–1941), London, 1990.

Blumenson, Martin, *The Battle of the Generals*, NY, 1993.

Bond, Brian, *France and Belgium, 1939–1940*, U. of Delaware Press, 1975.

Bor-Komorowski, Tadeusz, *The Secret Army*, London, 1950.

Breitman, Richard, and Laquer, Walter, *Breaking the Silence*, NY, 1986.

Buchwald, Bernard Karol, *316. Warszawski Dywizjon Mysliwski* (316, The Warsaw Fighter Squadron), Warsaw, 1989.

Bystrzycki, Przemyslaw, *Znak Cichociemnych*, Warsaw, 1985.

Cambridge History of Poland, in two volumes. Original publication Cambridge U. Press, 1941, and reprinted NY, 1971.

Cannistraro, Philip V., Wynot, Edward D. Jr., and Kovaleff, Theodore P., *Poland and the Coming of the Second World War. The Diplomatic Papers of A.J. Drexel Biddle Jr., United States Ambassador to Poland, 1937–1939*, Ohio State Univ., 1976.

Cazalet, Victor A., *With Sikorski to Russia*, London, 1942.

Chlebowski, Cezary, *Wachlarz* (Fan, i.e., the code name of the Polish Underground Operation to disrupt German transport in support of the invasion of the Soviet Union), Warsaw, 1990.

Cieplewicz, Mieczyslaw, and Zgornik, Marian, *Przygotowania Niemieckie do agresji na Polske w 1939 roku w swietle sprawozdan odzialu II sztabu glownego Wojska Polskiego. Dokumenty* (German preparations for the attack on Poland in the light of documents of the Second Department of the General Staff of the Polish Army), Krakow, 1969.

Cieplewicz, Mieczyslaw, and Kozlowski, Eugeniusz, eds., *Wrzesien 1939. W Relaciach i Wspomnieniach* (September 1939 in personal memoirs and narrations), Warsaw, 1989.

———, *Obrona Warszawy 1939. We Wspomnieniach* (The Defense of Warsaw, 1939. Memoirs), Warsaw, 1984.

Chocianowicz, Waclaw, ed., *W 50-Lecie Powstania Wyzszej Szkoly Wojennej w Warszawie*, London, 1969.

Cholewczynski, George, *Poles Apart. The Polish Airborne at the Battle of Arnhem*, NY, 1993.

Churchill, Winston S., *The Unrelenting Struggle. War Speeches by the Right Hon. Winston S. Churchill*, London, 1942.

———, *The Second World War*, in Six volumes, *The Gathering Storm, Their Finest Hour, The Grand Alliance, The Hinge of Fate, Closing the Ring, Triumph and Tragedy*, published in Boston by Houghton Mifflin Company, 1948, 1949, 1950, 1950, 1951, and 1953, respectively. The London edition is different in some point, but the citations are to the American edition unless otherwise noted.

Ciechanowski, Jan, *Defeat in Victory*, London, 1947.

Ciechanowski, Jan M., *The Warsaw Rising of 1944*, Cambridge U. Press, 1974.

Ciechanowski, Konrad, *Armia Pomorze* (The Pomorze Army), Warsaw, 1982.

Cienciala, Anna M., and Titus Komarnicki, *From Versailles to Locarno*, U. of Kansas, 1984.

Cienciala, *Poland and the Western Powers, 1938–1939*, U. of Toronto, 1968.

Citino, Robert M., *The Evolution of Blitzkrieg Tactics. Germany Defends Itself against Poland, 1918–1933*, NY, 1987.

Cooper, Mathew, *The German Army, 1933–1945*, NY, 1978.

Copp, Terry and Vogel, Robert, *Maple Leaf Route: Falaise*, Ontario, 1983.

Cynk, Jerzy B., *Polish Aircraft, 1938–1939*, London, 1971.

———, *Samolot Bombowy, PZL-37, Los* (The PZL-37 Los Bomber Plane), Warsaw, 1990.

Cyprian, Tadeusz, *Komisja Stwierdzila, Londyn, 1942* (The Commission stated, London, 1942), Warsaw, 1960. This somewhat perplexing title refers to the work of the Judicial Commission appointed in June 1940 to investigate the responsibility for the defeat in September 1939. This Commission accomplished its work in London in 1942 and the conclusions were irrelevent given the defeat of the French and British Armies in France in 1940. But it was dug out by the Polish communist government and published as a fact rather than as a collection of bitter and acrimonious allegations made in France after the September Campaign.

Czarnocka, Halina, *Armia Krajowa w Dokumentach, 1939–1945*, in five volumes, London, 1970, 1973, 1976, 1977, 1981.

Czarnomska, F.B., *They Fight for Poland*, London, 1941. *

Czaykowski, Bogdan, and Sulik, Bogdan, *Polacy w Wielkiej Brytanii* (Poles in Great Britain), Paris, 1961. This is an excellent sociological study of the lives of the Polish military and their families who stayed in the U.K. after the war.

Czyn Zbrojny Wychodztwa Polskiego w Ameryce (Military Achievements of Poland's Immigrants to America), Chicago, 1957.

D'Abernon, Lord, *The Eighteenth Most Decisive Battle of the World, Warsaw*, London, 1931.

Dalecki, Ryszard, *Armia Karpaty* (The Karpaty Army), Warsaw, 1979.

Davies, Joseph E., *Mission to Moscow*, NY, 1941.

Davies, Norman, *God's Playground. A History of Poland*, Columbia U. Press, 1984.

———, *Heart of Europe. A Short History of Poland*, Clarendon Press, 1984.

———, *White Eagle—Red Star. The Polish-Soviet War 1919–1920*, London, 1972.

Dec, Wladyslaw, *Narvik, Falaise*, Warsaw, 1972.

Deighton, Len, and Hastings, Max, *Battle of Britain*, NY, 1990.

Denfeld, D., *World War Two Museums and Relics of Europe*, Manhattan, Kansas, 1980.

Derecki, Miroslaw, *Na Sciezkach Polskich Commandosow* (On the trail of the Polish Commandos), Lublin, 1980.

Destiny Can Wait. The Polish Air Force in the Second World War, London, 1949.

Dilks, David, ed., *The Diaries of Sir Alexander Cadogan*, London, 1971.

Divine, Robert A., ed., Causes and Consequences of World War Two, U. of Chicago Press, 1969, Paul, Willen, "Who Collaborated with Russia?"

Dixon, Norman, *On the Psychology of Military Incompetence*, NY, 1976.

Dmowski, Roman, *Polityka Polska i Odbudowa Panstwa* (Polish Politics and the Reconstruction of the State) Warsaw, 1989. Original Publication was 1925.

Documents on Polish-Soviet Relations 1939–1945, London, in two volumes, 1961 and 1967.

Domiczek, Andrzej, *Opowiadania Marynarskie* (A Sailor's Odyssey), London, 1945. *

Duraczynski, Eugeniusz, *Miedzy Londynem a Warszawa* (Between London and Warsaw) Warsaw, 1986.

_____, *Uklad Sikorski-Majski* (Sikorski-Maiski Agreement), Warsaw, 1990.

_____, *Rzad Polski na Uchodzstwie, 1939–1945* (The Polish Government in Exile, 1939–1945), Warsaw, 1993.

(Eden)—The Reckoning. The Memoirs of Anthony Eden, Earl of Avon, Boston, 1965.

Eisenhower, Dwight E., *Crusade in Europe*, NY, 1949.

Engel, David, *In the Shadow of Auschwitz. The Polish Government in Exile and the Jews, 1939–1942*, U. of North Carolina Press, 1987.

Englert, Juliusz, and Barbarski, Krzysztof, *General Anders*, London, 1989.

Englert, Juliusz, and Nowik, Grzegorz, *Pilsudski*, London, 1991.

Estreicher, Karol, *The Jagiellonian University*, Cracow, 1978.

_____, *Muzeum Uniwersytetu Jagiellonskiego* (The Museum of the Jagiellonian University), Cracow, 1980.

Feingold, Henry L., *The Politics of Rescue. The Roosevelt Administration and the Holocaust, 1938–1945*, Rutgers U. Press, 1970.

Feis, Herbert, *Between War and Peace. The Potsdam Conference*, Princeton U. Press, 1960.

Fiedler, Arkady, *Squadron 303*, London, 1942. This book saw two editions in London, two in New York, French and Portuguese translations, and three underground editions in occupied Poland. *

Filipow, Krzysztof, and Wawer, Zbigniew, *Passerby, Tell Poland . . .* , Warsaw, 1991. One of the few English language books on the Polish Armed Forces in the West, superbly illustrated.

Foot, M.R.D., *SOE. The Special Operations Executive, 1940–1946*, U. Publications of America, 1984.

Franks, Norman, *The Greatest Air Battle. Dieppe, 19th August, 1942*, London, 1992.

Garlinski, Jozef, *Poland in the Second World War*, London, 1985.

_____, *Poland, S.O.E. and the Allies*, London, 1969.

Gilbert, Martin, *Winston Churchill*, Boston, 1983.

_____, *The Second World War. A Complete History*. NY, 1989.

Glowacki, Ludwik, *Obrona Warszawy i Modlina, 1939* (The Defense of Warsaw and Modlin, 1939), Warsaw, 1985.

Godlewski, Jerzy, *Bitwa nad Bzura* (the Battle of Bzura), Warsaw, 1973.

Gorecki, J., *Stones for the Rampart*, London, 1945. * This was a translation of a booklet published by the Polish Underground in Warsaw in 1943 as *Kamienie na Szaniec*.

Greenfell, Russell, *The Bismarck Episode*, The MacMillan Company, NY, 1949.

Grove, Eric, *World War Tanks*, NY, 1976.

Hamilton, Nigel, *Master of the Battlefield. Monty's War Years, 1942–1944*, NY, 1983.

_____, *Monty. Final Years of the Field Marshal, 1944–1974*, NY, 1986.

Harriman, W. Averell, and Abel, Ellie, *Special Envoy to Churchill and Stalin, 1941–1946*, NY, 1975.

Hart, B.H. Liddell, *History of the Second World War*, NY, 1970.

Harvey, Harvey, *Scandinavian Misadventure; The Campaign in Norway, 1940*, NY, 1979.

Hastings, Max, *Bomber Command. The Myths and Reality of the Bombing Offensive, 1939–1945*, NY, 1979.

_____, *Overlord; D-Day and the Battle for Normandy*, NY, 1984.

Henderson, Neville, *Failure of a Mission. Berlin, 1937–1939*, NY, 1940.

Higham, Robin, *Air Power*, NY, 1972.

Hilberg, Raul, *Perpetrators, Victims, Bystanders. The Jewish Catastrophe, 1933–1945*, NY, 1989.

Hirshler, Gertrude, and Eckman, Lester S., *Menachem Begin. From Freedom Fighter to Statesman*, NY, 1989.

Howard, Michael, *The Mediterranean Strategy in the Second World War*, London, 1968.

Iranek-Osmecki, George, *The Unseen and Silent*, London, 1954.

(Ironside)—R. MacLeod and Denis Kelly, eds., *Time Unguarded. The Ironside Diaries, 1937–1940*, NY, 1962.

(Ismay)—*The Memoirs of General Lord Ismay*, NY, 1960.

Jackson, Robert, *The Secret Squadrons. Special Duty Units of the RAF and USAAF in the Second World War*, London, 1983.

James, Robert Rhodes, *Victor Cazalet. A Portrait*, London, 1976.

Jedruch, Jacek, *Constitutions, Elections and Legislatures of Poland, 1437–1977*, U. Press of America, 1982.

Jedrzejewicz, Waclaw, ed., *Poland in the British Parliament, 1939–1945*, NY, in three volumes published 1946, 1959, and 1962.

_____, Jozef Lipski, Diplomat in Berlin, 1933–1939, Columbia U., 1968.

_____, Julian Lukasiewicz, Diplomat in Paris, Columbia U. Press, 1970.

_____, Polonia Amerykanska w Polityce Polskiej. Historia Komitetu Narodowego Amerykanow Polskiego Pochodzenia (American Polonia in Poland's Politics). The History of National Committee of Americans of Polish Ancestry. NY, 1954.

_____, Pilsudski. A Life for Poland, NY, 1982.

Jordan, Peter, and Janta, Alexander, Seafaring Poland, London, 1944. *

Jordan, Peter, Aviation in Poland. A Brief Historical Outline, London, 1946. *

Jurga, Tadeusz, and Korbowski, Wladyslaw, Armia Modlin (the Modlin Army), Warsaw, 1987.

Jurga, Tadeusz, Obrona Polski, 1939 (The Defense of Poland, 1939), Warsaw, 1990.

Kacewicz, George, Great Britain, the Soviet Union and the Polish Government in Exile, 1939–1945, Hague, 1979.

Kahn, David, Seizing the Enigma. The Race to Break the German U-Boat Codes, Boston, 1991.

Kalinowski, Franciszek, Lotnictwo Polskie w Wielkiej Brytanii, 1940–1945 (The Polish Air Force in Great Britain, 1940–1945), Paris, 1969.

Karski, Jan, The Great Powers and Poland, 1919–1945. From Versailles to Yalta, U. Press of America, 1985.

Katelbach, Tadeusz, Rok Zlych Wrozb, 1943 (The Year of Bad Omens, 1943), Paris, 1959. Katelbach was a strong proponent of the Sanacja Party and thus both a supporter of Sosnkowski and a determined opponent of Mikolajczyk and his policy of appeasement towards the Soviets.

Keegan, John, Six Armies in Normandy, NY, 1982.

Kennedy, Robert M., The German Campaign in Poland, 1939, U.S. Government Printing Office, DC, 1956.

Kersten, Krystyna, The Establishment of Communist Rule in Poland, 1943–1948, U. of California Press, 1991.

Kimball, Warren F., ed., Churchill and Roosevelt. The Complete Correspondence, Princeton U. Press, 1984. In three volumes, "Alliance Emerging"; "Alliance Forged"; "Alliance Declining."

Kirchmayer, Jerzy, Kampania Wrzesniowa (The September Campaign), Warsaw, 1946.

Kleczkowski, Stefan, Poland's First Thousand, London, 1944. *

Kolinski, Izydor, Z Historii Polskiego Lotnictwa Wosjkowego, 1918–1939 (The History of Poland's Military Aviation, 1918–1939), Warsaw, 1978.

Komornicki, Stanislaw, Na Barykadach Warszawy (On the Barricades of Warsaw), Warsaw, 1981.

_____, ed., Wojsko Polskie. Barwa i Bron, 1939–1945 (Polish Armed Forces. Equipment and Insignia), Warsaw, 1990.

Kopanski, Stanislaw, Wspomniena Wojenne, 1939–1945 (Wartime Memoirs), London, 1961.

Korab-Zebryk, Roman, *Operacja Wilenska AK* (The Wilno Operation of the Home Army) Warsaw, 1985.

Korbel, Jozef, *Poland Between East and West: Soviet and German Diplomacy toward Poland, 1918–1933*, Princeton U. Press, 1963.

Korbonski, Stefan, *The Polish Underground State. A Guide to the Underground, 1939–1945*, East European Monographs, NY, 1978.

———, *Fighting Warsaw*, London, 1956.

Korpalska, Walentyna, *Wladyslaw Eugeniusz Sikorski, Biografia Polityczna* (General Eugeniusz Sikorski. A political Biography), Warsaw, 1981.

Kot, Stanislaw, *Conversations with the Kremlin*, Oxford U., 1963.

Kowalski, Wlodzimierz T., *Walka dyplomatyczna o miejsce Polski w Europie, 1939–1945* (Diplomatic war for Poland's place in Europe), Warsaw, 1979 (fifth edition).

Kozaczuk, Wladyslaw, *U Kregu Enigmy* (In the circle of the Enigma), Warsaw, 1979.

———, *Enigma* (Translated and edited by Kasparek, Wladyslaw), U. Publications of America, 1984.

Kozlowski, Eugeniusz, *Wojsko Polskie, 1936–1939* (The Polish Army), Warsaw, 1974.

———, *Jozef Pilsudski w Opinii Politykow i Wojskowych* (Joseph Pilsudski in the eyes of politicians and soldiers), Warsaw, 1985.

Kozlowski, Eugeniusz, chief editor, *Wojna Obronna Polski, 1939. Wybor Zrodel* (Poland's Defensive War, 1939. Selection of Archival Sources), Warsaw, 1968. This is a compilation of 557 original archival documents relating to the pre-1939 period and the September Campaign.

Kozlowski, Eugeniusz, chief editor, *Wojna Obronna Polski, 1939* (Poland's Defensive War, 1939), Warsaw, 1970.

Krol, Waclaw, *Polskie Skrzydla na Zachodnio-Europejskim Froncie* (Polish Wings in the Western European Operations), Warsaw, 1985.

———, *Polskie Dywiziony Lotnicze w Wielkiej Brytanii, 1940–1945* (Polish Squadrons in Great Britain, 1940–1945), Warsaw, 1976.

———, *Polskie Skrzydla na Zachodnio-Europejskim Froncie, Wrzesien 1944–Maj 1945* (Polish Wings in Operations over North-West Europe, September 1944–May 1945), Warsaw, 1985.

———, *Wielka Brytania, 1940* (Great Britain, 1940), Warsaw, 1990.

———, *Zarys Dzialan Polskiego Lotnictwa we Francji, 1940* (Outline of Polish Air Force Operations in France, 1940), Warsaw, 1988.

———, *Zarys Dzialan Polskiego Lotnictwa w Wielkiej Brytanii, 1940–1945* (Outline of Polish Air Force Operations in Great Britain, 1940–1945), Warsaw, 1981.

Kryska-Karski, Tadeusz, and Zurakowski, Stanislaw, *Generalowie Polski Niepodleglej* (Generals of Independent Poland), Warsaw, 1991.

Krzyzanowski, Kazimierz, *Wydatki Wojskowe Polski w Latach, 1918–1939* (Poland's Military Expenditures, 1918–1939), Warsaw, 1976.

Kukiel, Marian, *General Sikorski. Zolnierz i Maz Stanu Polski Walczacej* (General Sikorski. Soldier and Statesman of Fighting Poland), London, 1970.

———, *Czartoryski and European Unity, 1770–1861*, Princeton U. Press, 1955.

———, *Dzieje Polski Porozbiorowe, 1795–1921* (The History of Partitioned Poland, 1795–1921), London, 1961.

———, *Six Years of Struggle for Independence*, Newtown, Wales, 1947.

Kulakowski, Miroslaw, *Marynarka Wojenna Polski Odrzodzonej* (The Naval Service of Recreated Poland), Vol. 1, 1918–1939, Toronto, 1988.

Kurcz, F.S. (Wartime pseudonym of Skibinski, Franciszek), *The Black Brigade*, London, 1943.

Kurowski, Adam, *Lotnictwo Polskie w 1939 roku*, Warsaw, 1962.

Kurzman, Dan, *The Bravest Battle*, NY, 1976.

Kutrzeba, Tadeusz, *Bitwa nad Bzura* (The Battle of Bzura), Warsaw, 1957. (General Kutrzeba was G.O.C. of the combined Poznan and Pomorze Armies in the Polish counterattack at the river Bzura in September 1939.)

Kutz, C.R., *War on Wheels. The Evolution of an Idea*, Harrisburg, 1940.

Kwiatkowski, Eugeniusz, *Pisma o Rzerzyspospolitej Morskiej* (Essays on the Maritime Republic of Poland), Szczecin, 1985.

Lamb, Richard, *The Drift to War, 1922–1939*, NY, 1989.

Laquer, Walter, *The Terrible Secret. Suppression of the Truth about Hitler's Final Solution*, Boston, 1980. This is the best account of the efforts of the Polish Government in London to bring the murders of its citizens, Jewish as well as Polish, in occupied Poland to the attention of Western governments.

Leitgeber, Witold, *W Kwaterze Prasowej. Dziennik z Lat Wojny 1939–1945. Od Coetquidan do Rubensa*, London, 1972.

Lewin, Ronald, *Ultra Goes to War*, NY, 1979.

Liszewski, Karol, *Wojna Polsko-Sowiecka, 1939* (The Polish-Soviet War, 1939), London, 1986.

Los, Roman, *Artyleria Polska, 1914–1939* (Polish Artillery, 1914–1939), Warsaw, 1991.

Lukas, Richard C., *The Strange Allies. United States and Poland, 1941–1945*, U. of Tennessee, 1978.

———, *Forgotten Holocaust. The Poles under German Occupation*, U. of Kentucky, 1986.

McLaren, Anna, *Poland at Arms*, London, 1942. Interesting historical piece with a foreword by both Churchill and Sikorski. *

MacMillan, Harold, *The Blast of War*, NY, 1968.

Maczek, Stanislaw, *Od Podwody do Czolga* (From a Cart to a Tank), Edinburgh, 1961.

Madeja, Witold, *The Polish 2nd Corps and the Italian Campaign*, Allentown, PA, 1984.

Majdalany, Fred, *The Battle of Cassino*, Boston, 1957.

Marsh, L.G., *Polish Wings over Britain*, London, 1943. *

Mason, Francis K., *Battle over Britain*, London, 1969.

Merrick, K.A., *Flights of the Forgotten. Special Duties in World War Two*, NY, 1989.

Meysztowicz, Jan, *Saga Brygady Podhalanskiej* (The Saga of the Podhalanska Brigade), Warsaw, 1987.

Middleborook, Martin, *Arnhem, 1944*, Boulder, CO, 1994.

Middleborook, Martin, and Everitt, Chris, *The Bomber Command War Diaries. An operational Reference book, 1939–1945*, London, 1985.

Mieczkowski, Zbigniew, *Pomniki Pierwszej Dywizji Pancernej* (Monuments of the Polish Armoured Division), London, 1989.

Mierzwinski, Zbigniew, *Generalowie II Rzeczyspospolitej* (Generals of the II Polish Republic), Warsaw, 1990.

Mitkiewicz, Leon, *Z Generalem Sikorskim na Obczyznie* (With General Sikorski in Exile), Paris, 1968.

_____, *W Najwyzszym Sztabie Zachodnich Aliantow* (In the Highest Staff of the Western Allies), London, 1971.

Montgomery, Bernard L., *A History of Warfare*, NY, 1968.

Moulton, J.L., *Battle for Antwerp*, NY, 1978.

Murgrabia, Jerzy, *Symbole Wojskowe Polskich Sil Zbrojnych na Zachodzie, 1939–1946* (The Military Insignia of the Polish Armed Forces in the West, 1939–1946), Warsaw, 1990.

Murray, Michael, ed., *Poland's Progress*, London, 1944. *

Nadeau, Remi, *Stalin, Churchill and Roosevelt Divide Europe*, NY, 1990, particularly chapter 10, "The Agony of Poland."

Nagorski, Zygmunt, *Wojna w Londynie. Wspomnienia 1939–1945* (War in London. Reminiscences, 1939–1945), Paris, 1966.

Nalecz, Tomasz, *Polska Organizacia Wojskowa, 1914–1918* (The Polish Military Organization, 1914–1918), Warsaw, 1984.

Neugebauer, Norwid, M. *The Defense of Poland, September, 1939*, London, 1942. *

Newman, Simon, *March 1939: The British Guarantee to Poland*, Oxford U. Press, 1976.

Newman, Verne W., *The Cambridge Spies*, NY, 1991.

Nowak, Jan, *Courier from Warsaw*, Wayne State U. Press, 1982.

Nycz, Wladyslaw, *W Powietrznym Zwiadzie* (In Aerial Reconnaissance), Warsaw, 1982.

Offer, Dalia, *Escaping the Holocaust. Illegal Immigration to the Land of Israel, 1939–1945*, Oxford U. Press, 1990.

O'Malley, Sir Owen, *The Phantom Caravan*, London, 1954. (O'Malley was British ambassador to the Polish Government in London throughout most of the war.)

Orpen, Neil, *Airlift to Warsaw. The Rising of 1944*, U. of Oklahoma Press, 1984.

Patton, George, *War as I Knew It*, Boston, 1947.

Pawlak, Jerzy, and Nowakowski, Walerian, *Brygada Bombowa. Kurs Bojowy* (Bomber Brigade on Target), Warsaw, 1983.

Pawlak, Jerzy, *Brygada Poscigowa. Alarm* (Fighter Brigade. Alert), Warsaw, 1977.

Pawlowicz, Bohdan, *O.R.P. Garland: In Convoy to Russia*, London, 1943. *

Pease, Neal, *Poland, the United States and the Stabilization of Europe, 1919–1933*, Oxford U., 1986.

Perlmutter, Amos, *FDR and Stalin. A Not so Grand Alliance, 1943–1945*, U. of Missouri Press, 1993.

Pertek, Jerzy, *Wielkie Dni Malej Floty* (Great Days of a Small Fleet), Poznan, 1987.

———, *Druga Mala Flota* (The Second Small Fleet) Poznan, 1983. This second book is a history of the Polish Mercantile Marine in the Second World War.

Petrow, Richard, *Bitter Years: The Invasion and Occupation of Denmark and Norway. April 1940–May 1945*, NY, 1974.

Piaskowski, Stanislaw, *Okrety Rzeczpospolitej Polskiej, 1920–1946* (Warships of the Polish Republic, 1920–1946), Albany, NY, 1981.

Piekalkiewicz, Janusz, *Arnhem, 1944*, NY, 1976.

———, *Cassino. Anatomy of the Battle*, London, 1980.

———, *The Cavalry of World War Two*, London, 1979.

Pienkos, Donald, *For Your Freedom through Ours. Polish American Efforts on Poland's Behalf, 1863–1991*, East European Monographs, NY, 1991.

Pimlott, Ben, ed., *The Second World War Diaries of Hugh Dalton*, London, 1986.

Pindel, Kazimierz, *Obrona Narodowa, 1937–1939* (The National Guard, 1937–1939), Warsaw, 1979.

Pobog-Malinowski, Wladyslaw, *Najnowsza Historia Polityczna Polski, 1864–1945* (The modern political history of Poland, 1864–1945), in three volumes, London, 1950.

Polish Ministry of Information, London, *Polish Troops in Norway*, London, 1943. *

Polish White Book. Official Documents concerning Polish-German and Polish-Soviet Relations, 1933–1939, London, (date not given but undoubtedly between 1941–1944).

Polonsky, Anton, *Politics in Independent Poland, 1921–1939*, Clarendon Press, 1972.

———, *The Great Powers and the Polish Question, 1941–1945*, London, 1976.

Porwit, Marian, *Komentarze do Polskich Dzialan Obronnych, 1939* (Commentary to the Polish Defensive Operations, 1939), Warsaw, 1983.

Powell, Geoffrey, *The Devil's Birthday. The Bridges to Arnhem, 1944*, London, 1984.

Pragier, Adam, *Czas przeszly dokonany* (Past Definitive), London, 1966. Pragier was a very senior and distinguished member of the Polish Socialist Party, who had good connections with the British Labor Party.

Prazmowska, Anita, *Britain, Poland and the Eastern Front, 1939*, Cambridge U. Press, 1987.

Pruszynski, Ksawery, *Poland Fights Back*, London, 1941. *

Przygonski, Antoni, *Powstanie Warszawskie w Sierpniu, 1944r* (Warsaw Uprising of August 1944), Warsaw, 1988.

Raczynski, Edward, *In Allied London*, London, 1962. (Raczynski was Polish ambassador to the Court of St. James throughout the war.)

Riekhoff, Harald von, *German-Polish Relations 1918–1933*, Johns Hopkins, 1971.

Roberts, Geoffrey, *The Unholy Alliance. Stalin's Pact with Hitler*, Indiana U. Press, 1989.

Romanowski, Boleslaw, *Torpeda w Celu* (Torpedo on Target), Warsaw, 1981.

Roos, Hans, *A History of Modern Poland*, NY, 1966.

Roskill, Stephen W., *The War at Sea, 1939–1945*, Vol 3, Her Majesty's Stationery Office, London, 1960.

Rothschild, Joseph, *Pilsudski's Coup D'Etat*, Columbia U., 1966.

Rowecki, Stefan, *Wspomniena i Notatki Autobiograficzne, 1906–1939* (Autobiographical reminiscences, 1906–1939), Warsaw, 1988.

Rozek, Edward J., *Allied Wartime Diplomacy. A Pattern in Poland*, NY, 1958.

Rudnicki, Klemens, *Na Polskim Szlaku. Wspomnienia z lat 1939–1947* (The Polish path. Reminiscences from 1939–1947), Warsaw, 1990.

Rudzki, Czeslaw, *Polskie Okrety Podwodne, 1926–1969* (Polish Submarines, 1926–1969). Warsaw, 1985.

Ryan, Cornelius, *A Bridge too Far*, NY, 1974.

———, *The Longest Day*, NY, 1959.

Rzepniewski, Andrzej, *Wojna Powietrzna w Polsce, 1939* (The Air War over Poland in 1939), Warsaw, 1970.

———, *Obrona Wybrzeza w 1939 roku* (The Defense of the Seacoast in 1939), Warsaw, 1970.

Saunders, Hilary St. George, *Royal Air Force*, Vol. III, *The Fight is Won*, London, 1954.

Schatz, Jaff, *The Generation. The Rise and Fall of the Jewish Communists of Poland*, U. of California Press, 1991.

Shores, Christopher F., *2nd Tactical Air Force*, Reading, England, 1970.

Sikorski, Wladyslaw, *Modern Warfare*, NY, 1943.

Silver, Eric, *Begin, The Haunted Prophet*, NY, 1984.

Skibinski, Franciszek, *Ulanska Mlodosc, 1917–1939* (A Lancer's youth), Warsaw, 1989.

———, *Pierwsza Pancerna* (The First Armored), Warsaw, 1979.

Skrzypek, Andrzej, ed., *Wrzesien 1939r. W Relaciach Dyplomatow* (September 1939, in the narration of Diplomats), Warsaw, 1989.

Smith, E.D., *The Battles for Cassion*, NY, 1975.

Sopocko, Eryk, *Orzel's Patrol. The Story of the Polish Submarine*, London, 1942.

Sosabowski, Stanislaw, *Najkrotsza Droga* (The Shortest Way), London, 1957.

———, *Freely I Served*, Nashville, 1982.

Sosnkowski, Kazimierz, *Materialy Historyczne* (Historical Materials), London, 1966.

Stachiewicz, Waclaw, *Przygotowania Wojenne w Polsce, 1934–1939*, Tom 1, Paris, 1977.

———, *Rok 1939*, Tom II, Paris, 1979. (General W. Stachiewicz was Poland's Chief of Staff, and these posthumous memoirs were edited by his son.)

Stachiewicz, Piotr, *Starowka, 1944* (Old City of Warsaw, 1944), Warsaw, 1983.

Stafford, David, *Britain and European Resistance 1940–1945*, U. of Toronto Press, 1983.

Suchcitz, Andrzej, *Kampania Wrzesniowa 1939 roku. Sprawozdania Informacyjne Oddzialu II Sztabu Naczelnego Wodza* (September 1939 in the Light of Reports of the II Section of the General Staff), London 1986.

Swiecicki, Marek, *Seven Rivers to Bologna*, London, 1946. *

———, *With the Red Devils at Arnhem*, London, 1945. *

Sword, Keith, ed., *Sikorski: Soldier and Statesman*, London, 1990.

Szarota, Tomasz, *Stefan Rowecki, Grot.*, Warsaw, 1983.

Szoldraska, Halszka, *Lotnictwo Podziemia czyli dzieje Wydzialu Lotniczego Komendy Glownej Armii Krajowej* (The History of the Section of the Air Force of the Headquarters of the Underground Army), Warsaw, 1986.

Szubanski, Rajmund, *Polska Bron Pancerna w 1939 roku* (Polish Armored Forces in 1939), Warsaw, 1982.

Taylor, A.J.P., *The Origins of the Second World War*, NY, 1985.

Taylor, John W.R., and Munson, Kenneth, *Military Air Power*, London, 1975.

Taylor, Telford, *The March of Conquest. The German Victories in Western Europe, 1940*, NY, 1958.

Terej, Jerzy Janusz, *Na Rozstajach Drog. Ze studiow nad obliczem i modelem Armii Krajowej* (At Crossroads. A study on the face and structure of the Home Army), Cracow, 1978.

Terlecki, Olgierd, *General Ostatniej Legendy. Rzecz o Generale Wladyslawie Sikorskim* (The General of the Last Legend. The facts about General Wladyslaw Sikorski), Polonia Booksellers and Publishers Chicago, 1976.

———, *Pulkownik Beck* (Colonel Beck), Cracow, 1985.

Terry, Sarah Meiklejohn, *Poland's Place in Europe*, Princeton U., 1983.

Tolland, John, *The Last 100 Days*, NY, 1966.

Ulam, Adam B., *Expansion and Coexistence. The History of Soviet Foreign Policy 1917–1967*, NY, 1968.

Umiastowski, Roman, *Poland, Russia and Great Britain, 1941–1945*, London, 1946.

———, *Russia and the Polish Republic*, London, 1944.

Urquhart, R.E., *Arnhem*, NY, 1958.

Wandycz, Piotr S. *The United States and Poland*, Harvard U. Press, 1980.

———, *Lands of Partitioned Poland, 1795–1918*, U. of Washington, 1974.

———, *Soviet-Polish Relations, 1917–1921*, Harvard U. 1969.

———, *Czechoslovak-Polish Confederation and the Great Powers, 1940–1943*, Indiana U. 1956.

———, *France and Her Eastern European Allies, 1919–1925*, Minnessota U. 1961.

_____, *Twilight of French Eastern Alliance, 1926–1936*, Princeton U., 1988.

_____, *Polish Diplomacy. Aims and Achievements, 1919–1945*, London, 1988.

Warner, Geoffrey, *Iraq and Syria*, U. of Delaware Press, 1974.

Watt, Donald Cameron, *How War Came. The Immediate Origins of the Second World War, 1938–1939*, NY, 1989.

Wedemeyer, Robert, *Wedemeyer Reports!* NY, 1958.

Wegierski, Jerzy, *Lwowskiej Armii Krajowej* (In the Lwow Home Army), Warsaw, 1989.

Weigel, George, *The Final Revolution. The Resistance Church and the Collapse of Communism*, Oxford U. Press, NY, 1992.

Weinberg, Gerhard L., *The Foreign Policy of Hitler's Germany. Starting World War II, 1937–1939*, U. of Chicago, 1980.

_____, *A World at Arms. A Global History of World War II*, Cambridge U. Press, 1994.

West, William J., *The Betrayal of MI5*, NY, 1990.

Willmott, H.P., *The Great Crusade. A new complete history of the Second World War*, London, 1989.

Winton, Harold R., *To Change an Army*, U. Press of Kansas, 1988.

Witkowski, Henryk, *Kedyw* (Kedyw), Warsaw, 1984.

Woodward, Llewellyn, *British Foreign Policy in the Second World War*, London, 1962.

_____, *British Foreign Policy in the Second World War* (in three volumes), London, 1970, 1971, 1971.

Woytak, Richard A. *On the Border of War and Peace*, NY, 1979.

Wroblewski, Jan, *Armia Lodz, 1939* (The Lodz Army in 1939), Warsaw, 1975.

_____, *Armia Prusy, 1939* (The Prusy Army in 1939), Warsaw, 1986.

Wronski, Bohdan, *Poza Krajem—Za Ojczyzne* (In Exile—For the Country), Paris, 1975.

Wyman, David S., *The Abandonment of the Jews. America and the Holocaust, 1941–1945*, NY, 1984.

Wynn, Humphrey, and Young, Susan, *Prelude to Overlord*, Novato, CA, 1983.

Wynot, Edward D., *Polish Politics in Transition. The Camp of National Unity and the Struggle for Power, 1935–1939*, U. of Georgia, 1974.

Wysocki, Tadeusz A., *1. Polska Dywizja Pancerna, 1938–1947* (1 Polish Armored Division, 1938–1947), London, 1989.

Young, Peter, *World War, 1939–1945*, NY, 1966.

Zagorski, Waclaw, *Seventy Days. A Diary of the Warsaw Insurrection 1944*, London, 1957.

Zajac, Jozef, *Dwie Wojny* (Two Wars), London, 1964.

Zaleski, Waclaw, *W Warszawkiej Brygadzie Pancerno-Motorowej, 1939* (With the Warsaw Motorized Brigade, 1939), Warsaw, 1988.

Zaloga, Steve, and Madej, Victor, *The Polish Campaign, 1939*, NY, 1985.

Zaloga, Steve J., *The Polish Army 1939–1945*, London, 1982.

Zamorski, Kazimierz, *Dwa Tajne Biura 2 Korpusu* (Two Secret Sections of the 2 Corps), London, 1990.

Zamoyski, Adam, *The Polish Way. A Thousand Year History of the Poles and their Culture*, NY, 1988.

————, *The Battle for the Marchlands*, Columbia U. Press, 1981.

Zaron, Piotr, *Kierunek Wschodni w strategii wojskowo-politycznej gen. Wladyslawa Sikorskiego, 1940–1943*, Panstwowe Wydawnictwo Naukowe, Warsaw, 1988.

Zawodny, J.K., *Nothing but Honor. The Story of the Warsaw Uprising 1944*, Hoover Institution Press, 1978.

————, *Death in the Forest. The Story of the Katyn Forest Massacre*, U. of Notre Dame Press, 1962.

Zenczykowski, Tadeusz, *General Grot. U Kresu Walki* (General Grot in the Face of Battle), Warsaw, 1983.

Index